THE LAST
GREATEST
MAGICIAN

★ ★ ★

IN THE WORLD

THE LAST
GREATEST
MAGICIAN
IN THE WORLD

Howard Thurston versus Houdini & the Battles of the American Wizards

JIM STEINMEYER

JEREMY P. TARCHER ★ PENGUIN

a member of Penguin Group (USA) Inc.

New York

JEREMY P. TARCHER/PENGUIN
Published by the Penguin Group
Penguin Group (USA) Inc., 375 Hudson Street, New York, New York 10014, USA • Penguin Group (Canada),
90 Eglinton Avenue East, Suite 700, Toronto, Ontario M4P 2Y3, Canada (a division of Pearson
Penguin Canada Inc.) • Penguin Books Ltd, 80 Strand, London WC2R 0RL, England • Penguin Ireland,
25 St Stephen's Green, Dublin 2, Ireland (a division of Penguin Books Ltd) • Penguin Group (Australia),
250 Camberwell Road, Camberwell, Victoria 3124, Australia (a division of Pearson Australia Group Pty Ltd) •
Penguin Books India Pvt Ltd, 11 Community Centre, Panchsheel Park, New Delhi–110 017, India • Penguin Group (NZ),
67 Apollo Drive, Rosedale, North Shore 0632, New Zealand (a division of Pearson New Zealand Ltd) •
Penguin Books (South Africa) (Pty) Ltd, 24 Sturdee Avenue, Rosebank, Johannesburg 2196, South Africa

Penguin Books Ltd, Registered Offices: 80 Strand, London WC2R 0RL, England

Most Tarcher/Penguin books are available at special quantity discounts for bulk purchase for sales promotions,
premiums, fund-raising, and educational needs. Special books or book excerpts also can be created to fit specific needs.
For details, write Penguin Group (USA) Inc. Special Markets, 375 Hudson Street, New York, NY 10014.

Library of Congress Cataloging-in-Publication Data

Steinmeyer, Jim.
The last greatest magician in the world :
Howard Thurston versus Houdini & the battles of the American wizards / Jim Steinmeyer.
p.   cm.
ISBN 978-1-58542-845-8
1. Thurston, Howard, 1869–1936.   2. Houdini, Harry, 1874–1926.   3. Magicians—United States—Biography.
4. Magic—United States—History.   I. Title.
GV1545.T5S74   2011   2010035384
793.8092'2—dc22
[B]

Printed in the United States of America
1   3   5   7   9   10   8   6   4   2

BOOK DESIGN BY MEIGHAN CAVANAUGH

While the author has made every effort to provide accurate telephone numbers and Internet addresses
at the time of publication, neither the publisher nor the author assumes any responsibility for errors,
or for changes that occur after publication. Further, the publisher does not have any control over
and does not assume any responsibility for author or third-party websites or their content.

CONTENTS

INTRODUCTION

"I WOULDN'T DECEIVE YOU..."

 very work of art is a mystery. That's the difference between a crudely painted portrait—which is too honest and functional to intrigue us—and the *Mona Lisa*, which gives and conceals at the same time. The mystery provides a peculiar and distinctive thrill. We return to puzzle over the subject, her sanguine features, or the astonishing techniques used by the artist to so perfectly capture a brief moment of changing expression. We concoct stories to explain this layered puzzle. It initially attracts on an emotional level, and then continually challenges on an intellectual level.

Every performance is a magic show. The audience trusts the magician—depending on the performance, they might use the term *actor*, *comedian*, or *playwright*—who uses equal doses of deception and honesty to lure us through a transparent fantasy, and then engage us, bemuse us by the unexpected plausibility of it all, and ultimately delight us with a genuine surprise. If a magic show today seems old-fashioned or unnecessary, that's because so many of its essential elements have been purloined by other forms of entertainment. The wires, trapdoors, and artful exaggerations, which were once the specialty of magicians like Howard Thurston, the subject of this book, have been integrated into much of our storytelling.

I suppose this is a shame, for a good magic show, experienced in person, is uniquely, elementally entertaining. It encapsulates the experience of wonder and exploits our need for unadulterated fantasy. Modern audiences like to tell themselves that fashions have changed, or that unadorned marvels—magic for magic's sake—are out-of-date or unsophisticated. Yet audiences have developed a taste for songs that further a story (a Broadway musical), as well as songs that are presented for their own sake (a performer in concert).

It is the public's fickleness with their magicians that has left Howard Thurston all but forgotten today. His story is one of the most remarkable in show business. During his life, from 1869 to 1936, he successfully navigated the most dramatic changes in entertainment—from street performances to sideshows to wagon tours through America's western territories. He became one of the world's most renowned vaudeville stars, boldly performing an act with just a handful of playing cards, and then had the sense to leave vaudeville, expanding his show into an extravaganza with over forty tons of apparatus and costumes. His touring production was an American institution for nearly thirty years, and Thurston earned a brand name equal to Barnum, Ziegfeld, George M. Cohan, and Ringling Brothers.

Most remarkably, Howard Thurston was Houdini's chief rival during the first decades of the 1900s, and Thurston won. He won with a bigger show, a more successful reputation, and the title of America's greatest magician. Today Houdini may have earned legendary status for his daredevil feats. But Howard Thurston was the public's favorite. After generations of "greats," there's no question that Thurston was the last, greatest magician in the world. His ultimate struggle was with an economic depression and competition from Hollywood films, a very different kind of magic. That's when everything changed. After Hollywood, there was no longer any need for the great magicians of the past.

For anyone who has ever watched a magic show and dared to ask "How is it done?" I hope that I'm able to provide a few answers. In return, Howard Thurston presents an intriguing mystery to the reader: "Why was it done?"

INVARIABLY, at the start of the twenty-first century we perceive a magic show as old-fashioned because we imagine the common cliché of such a performance, evoking the dusty traditions of vaudeville, the bright footlights, and the rat-a-tat style of one indistinguishable performer after another. We might imagine these vaudeville magicians as they often appear in comic books, anonymous miracle workers flapping a cape and attempting to impress us by sheer force of their deceptions.

Of course, it was never really like this. By today's standards—television standards—vaudeville performers were given extravagant amounts of time onstage, between ten and twenty minutes for an individual act. They chatted to the audience and were highly valued for their personalities. If Thurston were to perform today, I can say with some experience that his show would be every bit as marvelous to a modern audience. We might recognize changes of fashion—the pace of Thurston's scripted patter, or the designs of his costumes or scenery—but there was nothing about the nature of his magic that would seem outdated or obsolete. The magic would still be miraculous because, like any talented magician, Thurston selected illusions that did not rely on the latest bits of technology, but on universal, fairy-tale themes: causing a person to float in the air, contacting the spirits, appearance, disappearance, destruction and restoration.

Most of all, Thurston's success depended upon his personality in front of his audience. These clues to a performer's manner are difficult to summon in any theatrical biography, and doubly so for a magician. Harlan Tarbell, a fellow magician and friend of Thurston's, wrote an influential course on magic, advising student magicians to remember that they must play "on a plane higher than the average person," with "a bit of supernatural power to do things ordinary folks cannot do." At the same time, a performer had to show deference and present himself as someone who could be trusted. "Audiences respect an artist who is sincere in his work. . . . He must make illusion seem like truth and must believe that the thing really happens."

Most magicians are remembered by their most sensational feats; my uncle used to tell me about watching Thurston at the Erlanger Theater in Chicago, describing the tremendous puff of smoke as an automobile, "loaded with pretty girls," instantly disappeared onstage. These accounts of Thurston's marvels imply a standoffish, grand character and ignore his appeal. In fact, there was no magic ever created without establishing a trust with an audience—without seducing them first. Howard Thurston was dependent upon charming his audience.

AL JOLSON, one of Thurston's contemporaries in the American theater, was famous for his dynamic and self-assured personality that seemed to wash over the footlights and overwhelm every member of the audience. Debatably, he may have been history's greatest entertainer, a powerful and daunting force of nature. Onstage he was always the great man. But his appeal was clearly tied to the human qualities behind his greatness, the soft cry in his voice that followed the booming solos. In Herbert Goldman's insightful biography of the singer, he described the death of Jolson's mother when the boy was just eight years old. Summoned to her bedside, Jolson opened the door to see her sitting up in bed, eyes wide, screaming with terror. The young boy tried to run to her, but the doctor pushed him from the room.

Years later, one of his most successful songs, "Mammy," Jolson interpolated his own finale, partly sung, and then, when his voice seemed to crack, partly spoken. He used it in every performance and it appears in recorded versions.

> *I'm a-coming, I hope I didn't make you wait!*
> *I'm a-coming. Oh God, I hope I'm not late. . . .*
> *Mammy, mammy!*
> *Don't you know me? I'm your little baby?*

No spectators were ever given the key to these phrases; nor did these words ever make sense within the context of the song's lyrics. But their meaning must have been sensed, on a deeply personal level, by thousands of audiences, and the emotion behind them gave a subconscious complexity to Jolson's performance.

There is similar evidence in accounts of Houdini. Most spectators remembered Houdini's self-confident performances; the brassy mannerisms complimented his daring escapes and his overenunciation seemed to formalize his performances. But more perceptive spectators realized the contradictions suggested by his appearance. Houdini was small and unimpressive onstage; he was intense rather than handsome, challenging rather than commanding. He gave every impression of the Everyman, a David about to encounter society's Goliaths: the police force, handcuffs, sealed tanks of water, straitjackets, and locksmiths.

His New York East Side mannerisms were always perceptible, just beneath the surface at each performance. Houdini's detractors—and there were many in the magic profession—sensed his pose and interpreted it as dishonesty or arrogance. But this was also a key to success: people sensed the conflict suggested by his performances, recognizing his overreaching as appealingly human. We root for the little man who tries hard.

Howard Thurston captivated audiences with a similar dichotomy. Immaculate, artistic, and possessing a self-assured grandeur onstage, which allowed him to preside over the sometimes funny, sometimes dramatic spectacle of the world's largest magic show, Thurston held his audiences in rapt attention. "My object is to mystify and entertain," he told his audience in a distinctive baritone, evoking his well-publicized training for the ministry. "I wouldn't deceive you for the world." Ultimately, this returns to the question of why Thurston sought to mystify many people, including business associates, fellow magicians, ex-wives, and a stepdaughter.

I actually feel that it was this simple phrase, uttered at every performance—"I wouldn't deceive you for the world"—that provided the momentary glimpse to the complexity of Thurston's performances and his appealing humanity. In retrospect, it was an astonishing promise for a magician, an appeal for legitimacy and acceptance. It was also the statement of a man who could believe and disbelieve simultaneously. We know that it echoed a desperate plea that had once been offered by a sad, dirty young street criminal who had reached his wit's end and realized that there was only one path left to him: honesty.

Then, once he was safe, once he had offered his promise and discovered the value of his word, he turned around and deceived them again.

The function of the magician has characteristics in common with those of the criminal, of the actor and of the priest . . . and he enjoys certain special advantages impossible for these professions. Unlike the criminal, he has nothing to fear from the police; unlike the actor, he can always have the stage to himself; unlike the priest, he need not trouble about questions of faith in connection with the mysteries at which he presides.

—Edmund Wilson

ONE

"A BIT OF FUN"

oudini pulled at his cardboard collar, tugged at his rumpled tweed suit, and slouched forward to avoid being seen. He felt trapped, completely, hopelessly trapped. He had always been comfortable standing in the rarefied atmosphere onstage, where each of his gestures was magnified and each expression examined by thousands of unseen eyes. On a stage, encircled by a warm halo of limelight, he had learned how to read the roars, whispers, and laughter from the mysterious darkness on the other side of the footlights. He could propel his voice across the void, emphasizing each word. But now he realized how uncomfortable he was sitting in a theater seat, anticipating a performance. Every squeal of a child seemed amplified; the laughter, catcalls, and murmurs of the arriving audience combined to form an uncomfortable buzz in his ears. As the orchestra stumbled into the pit with a clatter of bows and the squeak of chairs—finally, finally, the show was about to begin!—all Houdini could think about was how strange it was to be on the wrong side of the footlights, and how torturous it was waiting for someone else's magic show. He thumbed the program nervously—"Thurston, The Famous Magician." The oversized type, the grandiosity of the title rankled him.

In fact, Houdini had been scheming for years to become more than just a vaudeville escape artist, which is how he had earned his fame with the public.

He was tired of putting on a bathing suit to perform water escapes, or organizing his career around publicity stunts that left him dangling upside down from buildings and escaping from straitjackets. He wanted to be a real magician, with an impressive magic show full of sophisticated wonders. Houdini went about it with his typical bravura—finding an enemy and viewing the challenge as a battle. He had fixed Thurston in the crosshairs.

Standing behind the curtain, just out of sight of the audience, Howard Thurston heard the first notes of the ragtime overture. He instinctively began hopping up and down on the balls of his feet, then stopped to swing his arms. These little exercises, he found, allowed him to "get pep" for each performance. Then he stood closely behind the curtain, with his eyes closed. "Ladies and gentlemen, thank you for coming to my show tonight. I hope you enjoy it. Thank you. God bless you. God bless you," he murmured to himself, directing his thoughts to the nameless, faceless audience members who had just paid to see his marvels. The stage manager nodded to the magician. We're ready. Thurston adjusted his starched shirtfront and smoothed the front of his elegant black tailcoat. He looked immaculate, elegant, ministerial.

"He's here, Governor," said George White, peering along a crack at the edge of the curtain. Thurston stepped to the side of the curtain to look for himself. "That's him, isn't it?" Houdini was seated in the fifth row, on the aisle. Thurston had chosen the seat himself when he offered Houdini a complimentary pass. "Yes, that's him. Good old Harry," Thurston sighed.

Thurston was technically one of Houdini's old friends, a business associate, and a fellow member of the Society of American Magicians. He was also, in Houdini's eyes, an ever-present rival. They'd met in 1893 at the World's Columbian Exposition in Chicago, at the very first midway (literally, the "Midway Plaisance"). There, a nineteen-year-old Houdini had found work by donning dark makeup, dressing in a tattered white robe, and working as an "authentic Hindu" mystic, sitting cross-legged in front of the Algerian and Tunisian Village. His tour de force was apparently swallowing a packet of loose needles, then a long piece of thread. He regurgitated the thread, with all the needles neatly spaced along its length.

Howard Thurston, five years older, some four inches taller, wore a stylish felt hat and embroidered vest, twirled a cane, and worked as the "talker," standing in front of the Dahomey Village, a collection of "authentic African" attractions. When the crowds thinned out, Thurston used to pull a pack of cards from his pocket, performing a little magic, flourishing the cards from hand to hand, and changing one card into another by waving his hand over the face of the deck.

In Chicago, the two young men quickly found each other, and then found each other obnoxious. Thurston was bemused by Houdini's aggressive, boastful New York East Side personality. Houdini watched the card moves with disinterest. Yeah, he told his new acquaintance, he did all that stuff too, and better. No, the Hindu thing was just a temporary job; he actually had a sensational new act, an escape from a trunk, if only you could see it.

Houdini found Thurston's smooth, evangelical manner condescending. Actually, Thurston purred to his young compatriot, his work as a pitchman was just something to keep him busy. He had plans for a sensational new act, with brand-new card tricks. At the Columbian Exposition, the magicians were perfectly matched because they were both perfectly miserable—two young men teetering between the brink of success or failure, who could take no pride in anything they had done, but indulged in boasts of what they might accomplish someday . . . with the right show . . . with the right breaks.

Now, on December 6, 1920, at the Folly Theater in Brooklyn, they were both stars, and Houdini had agreed to watch Thurston's show once more. The timpani rolled, and the curtain was raised, showing a stage glowing with light and circled with pretty showgirls in bright silk dresses. The children seated around Houdini squealed and the audience burst into applause. Howard Thurston quickly stepped to the center of the stage, cupping the palm of one hand inside of the other hand and bowing slightly to the audience. And then he turned his eyes to Houdini's seat—a professional greeting that was brief and distinct—acknowledging his fellow magician with a nod.

ABOUT TWENTY MINUTES into the show—after a flurry of fishbowls and silk handkerchiefs, after Thurston had neatly plucked dozens of cards from the air at his fingertips, then hurled hundreds more into the audience, after finding a man inside an empty barrel and catching invisible pigeons in a long-handled net—his quick, colorful tricks reached a crescendo and Thurston stepped forward to introduce his feature illusion.

The music slowed and stopped. The stage was bathed in a mysterious blue light.

> Ladies and gentlemen, boys and girls . . . it was more than a decade ago, when I was performing in India, that I had the opportunity to study the methods of the Indian magicians, especially the wonderful effect in which a young lady is hypnotized and then suspended in mid air. Tonight, I shall place the young lady in mid air and pass a hoop over her form, from head to toe. That was the ritual that I witnessed . . . at the Temple of Love . . . in Allahabad . . . in India.

Orson Welles, who saw Thurston perform when he was a boy, always remembered the magician's beautiful, hypnotic intonations. "He was the master," according to Welles. "And I idolized him. He was the finest magician I've ever seen." Thurston's voice was a deep baritone with a slight nasal quality, which imparted a drone or hum, like the secondary notes of a musical instrument. He spoke without any of the usual tricks or affectations of actors, but a pure Midwest "accentless" accent; instead of the singsong modulation of orators, Thurston used delicate pauses to emphasize individual words or syllables.

> Just before we attempt this mystery, I would like to say to you in confidence, that I am playing the part of a magician, and it is my object to mystify you and entertain you. Whatever I may say or do on the stage this evening, please remember . . . I wouldn't . . . deceive you . . . for the world!

William Lindsay Gresham, the author of *Nightmare Alley* and a biographer of Houdini, first saw Thurston perform in 1916. "I had no preconceived notions as to what a magician should be like, but from the first moment when he began to speak, I knew. I knew I was seeing greatness, and I have never changed my opinion for all of the magicians I have ever seen. Thurston was the most magical. His voice was the most musical I ever heard. It rippled. It purled. It chanted, effortless, apparently artless, so profoundly moving that a word from him was misdirection enough."

Tonight, by special arrangement with the British government, we have brought with us from the Ancient Temple, Abdul. Abdul from Secundabad . . . Hitherow, Abdul, Hitherow!

Abdul, in an embroidered robe, white turban, and slippers with curled toes, hurried out from the wings, bowing to Thurston and kneeling obediently at one side. The curtain opened on a brightly lit stage draped with swags of Indian curtains. In the center of the stage was an upholstered sofa. The orchestra began a low, tinkling Oriental theme.

Allow me to introduce Fernanda, the Princess Karnac. Abdul . . . Fernanda, around you I cast a mystic spell.

Fernanda Myro portrayed the Indian princess, entering in a white and pink harem costume. She entered from the side, walking to the center of the stage, followed by two male assistants. Thurston held a crystal ball in front of Fernanda's eyes and paused, surveying her expression. After a moment, her long dark lashes fluttered closed. He snapped his fingers, and she fell backward, rigid as a board, into the hands of a waiting assistant. Two men supported her and placed her, horizontally, on the sofa. She was isolated in the center of the stage, some ten feet from the nearest scenery.

Abdul lowered his eyes and began praying in a quiet Hindi singsong, as Thurston continued.

Fernanda, Fernanda, I command you to rise. In the name of the Yogi and the wise men of the Orient, I command you to rise.

Gresham remembered the magical ritual that followed. "Thurston stands behind her. A rustle from the audience and he lays his finger to his lips. Silence, then soft chords . . . a wave of his hand and surely, the girl has moved. She moved as softly as a sigh, gently, lovely, light as thistle down, Fernanda floated in mid air, up and up, above the magician's head. When at last she came to rest with a spotlight centered on her face, the crowd was hushed with an almost religious awe."

> Safely, securely, rise. Rest, Fernanda. Nothing above, nothing below. Rest. There is the young lady, completely resting in mid air. And she could remain there for hours, for she is practically . . . dead . . . to the world.

The sofa was lifted and taken offstage. Another assistant appeared with a short stepladder as Thurston picked up a large metal hoop. He took two steps up the ladder, so that his shoulders were just above the level of the floating princess. The hoop was passed horizontally, from the lady's head to her feet, in one graceful swoop. Then Thurston paused, looking into the lady's face as he held the hoop, and repeated the motion—head to toe—once more, slowly, smoothly. He stepped from the stool and rolled the hoop along the stage so that it fell into the audience, allowing spectators to examine it.

The movement of the hoop tumbling into the auditorium and Thurston's steps forward invariably broke the spell, and the audience would start to applaud. But he immediately raised his hand, holding them in breathless anticipation.

> Rest, Fernanda, sleep, Fernanda, dream, Fernanda. Safely, securely. She floats in the air, just as she did at the Temple of Love. True in India, true here. This evening, I shall ask on stage a number of ladies and gentlemen, to witness a genuine miracle. Anyone may come. Those interested in the occult or the mysterious. Come right down the aisle and on the side of the stage. Come as quietly as you can. Come now, for in a few moments there will be so many coming that you can't come.

There was a clatter of seats in the audience as five, ten, fifteen spectators took advantage of his invitation and made their way down the aisle. Thurston's assistants and Abdul gathered the spectators into a crowd at one side of the stage as the magician turned his attention to his special guest on the aisle.

Would you like to come?

He stretched his hand toward the audience members at the side of the stage. Houdini smiled and shook his head. Now another delicate routine began, the dance of two professionals negotiating a performance.

You're welcome to come onto my stage.

Houdini shrugged, and remained in his seat. He was now aware that the eyes of the audience were on him. It was the third request that would solve the problem. Any good showman knows the rule of three; three repetitions to the climax, three steps to the trick, three beats to the joke.

Mr. Houdini, please honor me as my guest.

And Houdini rose from his seat, bouncing lightly up the steps and onto the stage. "You know, I am very modest," he wrote to a friend the next day—and of course, he was never modest. "I did not want [Thurston] to think that there was anything in his repertoire that baffled me, or that it was my intention to solve tricks. At the third request, however, I went up on the stage and became one of the committee of twenty to witness Princess Karnac at close range." Houdini took his place at the side of the group of spectators, aware that everyone in the audience would be watching him. But Thurston turned his attention back to the action on stage.

The surakabaja blessing is imparted by the high priests at the Temple of Love. Surakabaja means, among other things, that those who love shall be loved. That anyone touching the ring of the floating princess will be granted a wish. Abdul, hitherow!

"Surakabaja" was gobbledygook, a bit of slang that Thurston had picked up in India. But the word was intoned with such reverence that it had the feeling of a real spell. Abdul took his place in the center of the stage, prostrate, facing the floating princess. Meanwhile, Thurston selected a gentleman from the group on stage.

Sir, you are in love? Don't laugh. We're all in love, every one of us. I ask you to touch the ring of the floating princess. That the one you love, loves you in return. Abdul!

Abdul sat upright, chanting the word "Surakabaja, surakabaja," as Thurston placed a hand on the man's shoulder and led him beneath the floating lady, stopping in front of her so the man could reach his hand up to the lady's ring.

Surakabaja means that your wish will come true. True in India, true here.

The man was led to the auditorium steps, and he wandered back to his seat, gazing backward at the marvel and scratching his head.

Meanwhile, the group of spectators was slowly led across the front of the stage, from one side to the other, so that they could appreciate the vision of the floating lady. Houdini followed dutifully, now lost in the crowd.

Thurston found a young boy in the group, bringing him to the center of the stage.

And what's your name, son?

The boy responded: Albert.

Albert, I'll ask you to make a wish. A real wish. A solemn wish. Every good boy knows how to make a real wish. Don't you? For if you believe, your wish will come true.

He slowly walked the boy beneath the floating lady, and then lifted him straight up so that he could reach the princess's ring. Abdul began a series of chants, "Surakabaja, surakabaja." When Thurston lowered the boy to the stage again, his pumping legs immediately propelled him off the front steps, dashing back to his seat as if he'd seen a ghost. The audience giggled in approval. Then the applause started. A gasp, turning into a ripple of handclapping, rolling into a wave, to an ovation, to roars and cheers. As the assistants exited and the spectators were dismissed from the stage, Thurston reached over to Houdini, gripping him by the arm, so the two men were alone on stage with the floating princess.

> Ladies and Gentlemen, I want to tell you that my good friend, the magician and vaudeville star Harry Houdini, has honored me by coming to see my show tonight. There are only three human beings in the world who know the secret of this levitation. . . . Harry Kellar, Harry Houdini . . . and myself. And now, Houdini, will you please touch the princess's ring, and make a wish?

Harry Kellar was the American magician who had developed this incredible illusion, and then turned it over to Thurston more than decade earlier. The little speech delighted Houdini, a fairy-tale fantasy wrapped up in show business lore. And then, Thurston made a grand gesture toward the princess, indicating that Houdini could step back and take a look for himself, without any guiding hand. It was the ultimate compliment to a fellow performer, a very public, ostentatious show of trust. Thurston crossed his arms, and Houdini took his cue. Slowly turning away from the audience, he took several steps and reached up to touch the ring. As he did, he was able to examine the astonishing, secret apparatus from the perfect angle, an incredible assemblage of steel, brass, and fabric, neatly tucked into the space behind the lady's body.

Houdini turned, facing the audience again. He was grinning with giddy self-satisfaction but managed a stately bow to Thurston. He left the stage and returned to his seat. "He paid me a very pretty compliment," Houdini wrote the next day, "of being alone with the apparatus. Knowing exactly how it is done, it seems to me that I admire it even more than the public, who have not the slightest inkling of the mechanical problems."

Having completed his scene with Houdini, Thurston returned to the fairy tale that he'd arranged onstage. He stood to one side, undulating his hands in hypnotic gestures, and Fernanda slowly descended. The assistants entered with the sofa, placing it beneath her. Her body nestled into the cushions, suggesting that the illusion had been nothing more than a fantastic dream. Thurston's men lifted her to her feet; he snapped his fingers and her eyes opened again.

Now comes a miracle, a mystery not presented outside the Himalaya Mountains of India. Fernanda, do you give your willing consent?

She nodded her head.

Then prepare yourself for a flight into the astral world, and by the power of my right hand I command you to rest and sleep, rest and sleep.

Thurston raised his hand dramatically, and the lady fell backward into the arms of the two assistants, so her shoulders were supported, as two more assistants entered with a large silken sheet. This was draped over the lady. The assistants lifted her, horizontal, and then slowly removed their hands, stepping back so that the covered lady was once again floating over the stage.

Thurston stepped just behind Fernanda, waving his hands over her. As he took several careful steps forward, approaching the orchestra, the lady followed his gestures, hovering closer and closer to the audience. He turned on his heel, and the floating lady, just beneath his hands, turned with him.

Now Fernanda rose into the air, higher and higher. She drifted to the right side of the stage, and then to the left, finally describing a soft circular sweep, revolving in space so that the audience could see the floating lady from each angle. It seemed as if gravity had been suspended: no longer a person, but a flower petal turning pirouettes in a spring breeze.

I know the trend of your thoughts. Many of you are thinking that it is impossible for Fernanda to float in the air without any support. I beg you to remember you are attending a magic performance and that Fernanda is hypnotized. I'll prove it to you. Wake, wake Fernanda, and raise your right hand.

Still floating beneath the sheet, Fernanda raised her right hand, and then lowered it again.

In all our lives there are certain events that stand out that cannot be forgotten. I am going to show you something now . . . you will remember . . . as long . . . as you live! Behold a miracle. Abdul! Fernanda! Allah, Allah, Fernanda, Go!

Thurston reached up to grasp the lower edge of the sheet. He twitched it and it fell away, revealing that the lady had disappeared in mid air. Thurston tossed the sheet to his assistant and bowed a deep, solemn bow. It took the audience several seconds—a tense moment of stunned silence—until they came to their senses and remembered that they'd been watching a magic show. The crowded theater erupted in applause, and then cheers. In the fifth row, Houdini joined in the happy ovation.

HARRY HOUDINI HAD BEEN FLATTERED, flummoxed, and outmaneuvered by a master of the art. Just like when they were boys at the World's Fair, Thurston had proved a little more experienced and a little slicker, neatly sidestepping his competition and distracting him with pure theatricality.

It was a typical con game, first appealing to the pride or cupidity of the mark, and then offering a reward that makes the sucker complicit in the fraud. Of course Houdini wasn't one of just three men; he didn't even know how the levitation worked when Thurston coaxed him onto the stage and offered his wheedling praise. The quick glances as he stood in front of the princess might have been interesting, but it never showed Houdini the complicated machinery, concealed above and below the stage, that actually accomplished the illusion. Thurston knew that he had to satisfy Houdini's ego, not his curiosity.

More important, Houdini missed the fact that he'd just been publicly kneecapped. If he had ever been scheming to copy Thurston's Princess Karnac mystery, he now had been shown so much, so generously, that he would be forced to avoid the floating lady illusion in the future.

That night in December 1920, Houdini had seen the World's Greatest Magician.

WHO WAS HOWARD THURSTON? He was the hero of generations of American boys, like Orson Welles and William Lindsay Gresham, who sat spellbound in a theater, and pledged their lives to magic. Remembering Thurston's inspirations, many of them went on to make their own sort of magic. Thurston was a real innovator and a real adventurer. Every boy who studied the souvenir program knew that the great magician had been to India, and seen the photos that portrayed him in a pith helmet, studying the wonders of the Indian fakirs.

Thurston was an entrepreneur. Dale Carnegie used him as an example of business success through personal skills. "More than 60 million people had paid admission to his show," according to Carnegie. "He had the ability to put his personality across the footlights. He was a master showman. He knew human nature. Everything he did, every gesture, every intonation of his voice, every lifting of an eyebrow, had been carefully rehearsed in advance. But Thurston had a genuine interest in people."

Howard Thurston was also an entertainment commodity, as a popular brand name, through the early 1900s. He was the renowned wizard of the Roaring Twenties. According to Walter B. Gibson, the originator of *The Shadow* and a ghostwriter for Houdini as well as Thurston, "In their day, Howard Thurston was every bit as well known as Harry Houdini. In fact, Thurston was probably better known than Houdini." While Thurston toured with an elaborate magic show, Houdini had become famous as a vaudeville escape artist. But, according to Gibson, "every bit of Thurston's publicity was about getting you into the theater to see the show. And Houdini's publicity was about creating a legend. As each year passes, Houdini becomes more and more famous, and Thurston is forgotten."

"I wouldn't deceive you for the world," Thurston assured his audiences. It seems to be a ridiculous statement from a professional magician, but Thurston delivered the line with such warmth and sincerity that it became a sort of trademark for the great wizard. Of course, he did deceive them, for over forty years. He mystified children, and then their children and grandchildren. In fact, his most incredible illusion was not Princess Karnac, floating high above the stage, but the deception he never quite explained—the illusion of the con man and thief, the associate of petty criminals and the confidant of politicians and philanthropists. He fooled them all. Howard Thurston became the last, greatest magician in the world.

TWO

"CREATION"

illie Ryan gazed down at the floor, seemingly disinterested, arrogantly unrepentant, as William Round, the secretary of the New York Prison Association, shifted the papers in a do-si-do atop his desk. Round opened the file, gazed up at the boy, and then readjusted his glasses to look down at the handwritten report.

Ryan was wiry and dirty, dressed in a pretentious pair of riding boots that, Round suspected, must have been stolen. Although the boy wouldn't explain where he was from, or name his parents, his inquisitor noticed that his adolescent voice cracked with a deep, resonant baritone, without the usual Bowery slang. He wasn't a New Yorker. His small bundle of clothes and personal possessions gave no clues to his background, although he carried a scuffed, well-thumbed copy of a book diagramming the secrets of sleight of hand and stage magic, Professor Hoffmann's *Modern Magic*. Filled with diagrams on palming cards and concealing coins, the book provided further evidence of the boy's proclivity for cheating. Willie Ryan had clearly come to the metropolis looking for trouble. Now he found it.

Round shook his head as he scanned the paperwork. The boy was a sadly typical case. He had been living in flophouses in the Bowery, in lower Manhattan, circulating with a group of street toughs and thieves. This circle of criminals had dubbed him "The Nim Kid," short for nimble. Small and deft, he could be lifted and shoved through transoms, headfirst, for quick crimes. He had also become a skilled pickpocket, although Round realized that the boy was not quite as skilled as he'd thought he was. One day in 1886, he boldly boarded a Broadway horse-drawn car, picked an argument with the conductor, and was caught trying to pick the conductor's pocket. He was grabbed by a nearby policeman. The judge considered the boy's youth, his handsome, placid features, and the nature of his first offense. He told the judge he was sixteen. In fact, he was seventeen. Otherwise, Willie Ryan had been clever enough to keep quiet, allowing the judge to suspect the best, not the worst, about him. Ryan received a suspended sentence and was sent to Secretary Round at the Prison Association on Fifteenth Street.

William Marshall Fitts Round had been leading a one-man campaign to change the prison system in New York. The son of a Baptist minister, he had studied medicine at Harvard and had worked as a novelist and a newspaper reporter in Boston and New York City. He was critical of the system of short sentences that filled New York prisons and did nothing to rehabilitate prisoners. He publicly noted that in the months before election years, prisoners were discharged in order to give the appearance of efficiency to whatever political party was in power. "It is no longer a question whether severe punishment is a deterrent for crime," Round used to say in lectures. "It has no effect upon the criminal classes. It is an exploded idea." He pointed out that New York State was then spending over $5,000 a year to protect society from each of its criminals; the total was more than Great Britain spent annually to support her army. Drawing upon his Baptist upbringing, Round advocated a system "in harmony with the principles of the Gospel," treating prisoners with kindness, backed with severity in only the extreme cases. Above all else, he felt that prisoners needed honest labor that gave them a chance in the outside world. "If the inmates of our prisons are reduced to idleness, they will go insane."

Round knew that the New York courts had been glutted with young offenders like Willie Ryan. Many had scampered to the notorious Five Points area in the city, a crowded collection of bars, bordellos, and boardinghouses that served as a magnet for crime. But despite his tendency for Christian charity,

William Round had to carefully consider whether the Ryan case called for kindness or severity. He later wrote that the boy who stood before him that day "was the most bold and brazen young thief I ever knew, and I know hundreds and have seen thousands." He resolved to send Ryan to three weeks of honest effort at the House of Industry and Refuge for Discharged Convicts on Houston Street, and see the effect on him. At the House of Industry, Ryan would find honest work, making brushes and mats during the day. He had a simple cot at night, sharing a communal dormitory with the other workers around a potbellied stove.

Resigned to his punishment, Ryan spent the weeks sullenly, mechanically going about his work as if mentally crossing days off a calendar, asserting his prominence in the hierarchy of the dormitory with loud curses and roughhousing—the little boy who insists on being the bully. He did not seem to be one of Round's better examples, and with his workhouse duties coming to an end, he was aware that he was due for another evaluation. And then, one Sunday, January 16, 1887, Willie Ryan was corralled into attending the Broome Street Tabernacle. The church was an inner-city mission and a refuge for Bowery down-and-outs, run by a charismatic minister, John Dooly. That morning, William Round delivered a lecture, "There Is a Man in You." Round's sensible advice and Dooly's intense and imploring sermon inspired the boy, as if the very vibration of the words reached deep within Ryan's soul. More than likely, Ryan had never been forced to sit still for such honest advice or such stirring sentiment. Or perhaps he had just seen—in effect—another transom swinging open, through which he could maneuver a convenient, wriggling exit. When Reverend Dooly concluded his sermon, closing the Bible with a loud thud and asking if any listeners were ready, there and then, to pledge their lives and be born "under the blood of Christ," Willie Ryan, with tears in his eyes, slowly raised his hand.

In the final pages of *Modern Magic*, the manual on trickery that the boy had carried with him, the author advised, "Being perfect in the mechanical portion of the illusion, [the magician] must now devote himself to its dramatic element, which is by far the most important portion. The performer should always bear in mind that he fills the character of a person possessing supernatural powers, and should endeavor, in every word and gesture, to enter into the spirit of his part. As the true actor, playing Hamlet, will endeavor actually to be Hamlet for the time, [the magician] must learn to believe in himself." If Willie Ryan's transformation was nothing short of miraculous, "The perfection of conjuring lies in the *ars artem celandi*," according to the venerable expert in deception, Professor Hoffmann, "in sending away the spectators persuaded that sleight of hand has not been employed at all, and unable to suggest any solution of the wonders they have seen."

When he returned to William Round's office, Willie Ryan had replaced *Modern Magic* with the Bible. In the course of just days, he had scoured the pages, committing long passages to memory, and could bolster his conversations with trenchant quotations from the Lord. Round was suspicious, and questioned the boy intensely about his conversion, but as a regular churchgoer and the son of a preacher, he was in a good position to judge the boy's sincerity. Round confessed to being thunderstruck by the change. "There is no mistake to this," the secretary of the New York Prison Association wrote to a friend. "We have seen him every day since, and he has been an example to us all, in the consistency of his life, in the humility of his new character."

Standing before Round's desk, his head held high, the boy now spoke with shy deference but newfound pride. Determined to no longer be the bully or the criminal, he was unsure about his new role. He started by quietly admitting that his name wasn't Willie Ryan. It was actually Howard Thurston. Howard Franklin Thurston. Yes, he had a family, in Columbus, Ohio.

HOWARD FRANKLIN THURSTON was born on July 20, 1869, in Columbus, Ohio, the middle child of William and Margaret Thurston. His father, William Henry Thurston, served briefly as a private in the Third Ohio Regiment during the Civil War and then became a wheelwright and carriage maker. His mother, Margaret Cloude, was the daughter of an Ohio farmer. The couple had five children, daughter May (Myrtle) born in 1865, and then sons Charles, Howard, Harry, and William, the youngest, born in 1876.

This should have been a happy, successful, middle-class family, but William

Thurston's business suddenly collapsed in the financial panic of 1873. An amateur inventor, he was forced to tinker several ideas in desperation, which he then abandoned in boxes around the house. His inspirations included a curling iron, cigar-making machine, two-wheeled roller skate, and a fire escape. Each was a source of failure and frustration, the right idea at the wrong time, a near miss, of no interest to manufacturers. William had something of a nervous breakdown that left him unable to work or, it seems, direct the family finances. He often escaped to the corner saloon.

The boys were naturally fascinated by their father's inventions, even if his financial straits confused them. Nine-year-old Charles and seven-year-old Howard discovered a discarded box of beefsteak pounders in the attic, one of his father's failed products. It consisted of a round board with pointed projections and a wooden mallet with matching points. Two or three quick blows made even the cheapest cut of meat delectable—at least, that was the theory. Without telling their parents, the boys set out across the neighborhood, lugging the box. Reasoning that the people who ran the local bank must have money, they pushed their way in and demanded to see the president. When he heard they were Bill Thurston's boys, he seemed to take pity and quickly rewarded them with a silver dollar. Their success was tempered, that evening at the dinner table, when their father told them that the same bank president, that morning, had just foreclosed on their house.

Howard and Charles continued selling the pounders for pennies, or even better, trading them for bread or meat to support the family. One day Howard had his earnings, a princely eighty cents, converted to nickels. That night, he dug into his pocket, telling his mother that he'd found a nickel, and then another, and another, slowly piling silver coins on the table. This bit of showmanship resulted in one of Thurston's rare memories of laughter and joviality around the dinner table.

William Thurston liberally beat his sons, and was probably abusive to his wife. In a lightly fictionalized story written many years later, Howard recalled being beaten for hopping a train car and dropping $2 on the siding. He was beaten for riding, and then losing control of a horse that his father was using for a sales job. He was even beaten, inexplicably, when his younger brother broke a window. His mother interceded in these punishments, and Howard adored her. "Ma, I hate to see you cry. Has Pa been mean to you again?" he recalled asking her. "I like to sit in your lap. You know, Ma, when you die, I want to die, too."

When they were a little older, Charles and Howard found jobs as bellboys at the American House in Columbus. At twelve, Howard was working as a newsboy on the trains between Columbus and Akron, or the more prestigious business line from Columbus to Pittsburgh. One of Thurston's earliest memories of magic was, as a boy, when he saw a school performance of the Ink to Water Trick. The secret was then explained to the audience of children, and Thurston was fascinated by the deception.

It's not a surprise that Howard Thurston was looking for various means to escape his childhood—first opportunities to bring money to his family, and then escapades that allowed him to avoid his dreary Columbus home. It was around this time that he discovered the most delicious escape of all. It was customary for newsboys to work in pairs. On the trains, Howard was teamed up with a large, dull boy nicknamed Tugger who could be trusted for the heavy lifting. As a reward for a successful day, Howard and Tugger decided to treat themselves to their first magic show. Today the record of this event has been muddied by Thurston's many official accounts, interviews, and adjustments to the legend. It may have been at the old City Hall Theater in Columbus, or at an unnamed theater in Cincinnati, where the newsboys were working. Tugger was satisfied to see it once. Howard insisted on returning on the following two nights, spending his dimes lavishly on seats in the balcony and marveling at his first "Arabian Night's dream," as he later recalled it, where the "footlights were fairy lamps and the stage was peopled with wavering shapes, with fairies and elves, with witches and demons, for [all] I knew. Magic had gripped me in its spell, and its hold never has loosened." If the legend is right, Howard Thurston was twelve or thirteen years old, and he saw a performance by Herrmann the Great, a wildly popular American magician who had a sophisticated comic, devilish persona. Thurston recalled that the matinee was a "gift show," in which cheap novelty gifts were awarded to children in the audience. He patiently stood in line to obtain his wrapped bundle, which contained a brass collar button. Thurston treasured it as if he had received it from the master magician himself.

WITH A LITTLE extra money earned from selling newspapers, Thurston was drawn to the fairgrounds, then the races—he was just small enough to fantasize about being a jockey. Together with a friend, he found work as a stable boy and secured assurances that he could learn to ride. When the racing circuit left Columbus for Cincinnati, Howard left home without telling his parents. He knew that his decision would crush his mother. He pictured her standing by the window, waiting, sobbing. But he had come to fear his father's erratic behavior and violent discipline.

Once he joined the races, the stable duties were too hard and too humiliating. Instead, he found another newsboy partner in Cincinnati, a redheaded adventurer who introduced himself as Reddy Cadger. Cadger was a fearless and seemingly invincible companion, "the shiftiest youngster on his feet I have ever known," Thurston later recalled, "a wonder at jumping freights. I have seen him swing on passenger trains under circumstances that would make the most expert hobo think twice before risking his bones." They were both fourteen. Cadger taught him the finer points of "beating the rattlers," which suddenly made every midwestern city available for adventure, free of charge. They jumped "blind baggage," the space between the engine and baggage car, sometimes rode the cowcatcher, just beneath the sight of the engineer, or "hit the decks," clinging to the top of the passenger cars. The most dangerous procedure was to ride the "ticket," a long board under the car, where they could lie just above the track. Climbing beneath the train, the boys endured the roar of the rails and the squeal of the trucks; they were pelted with dust, pebbles, ashes, and cinders; they clung perilously to the boards until their knuckles became numb, because with a sudden lurch they could be thrown beneath the wheels. "Boring through the night on a teetering, racketing, plunging locomotive is very much what I imagine riding a cannon ball might be like," Thurston wrote.

The boys bounced from Chicago, to Cleveland, and then back to Cincinnati. Howard thought about returning home, feared that his father would confine him to a house of corrections, and instead followed Cadger to St. Louis for the summer. They effortlessly earned money by selling papers, slept with the hoboes, stole food when necessary, or took advantage of the big-city newsboy charities. Reddy bought a copy of *Modern Magic* for his friend, who carried it with him everywhere as the pages became dog-eared.

One night the two boys jumped "blind baggage" on a train out of Chicago, but the brakeman chased them off. They dashed back as the train lurched from the train yard. Thurston scrambled up to the second baggage car. He thought he saw Cadger swinging onto the "ticket" underneath, but he couldn't find him when the train reached Kansas City, Missouri. It was nearly a year later, in St. Louis, when Thurston heard from their friends that Reddy Cadger had been thrown to the tracks that night and killed.

He returned to the races, moving on to Iowa. In Oskaloosa, he was humiliated by a popular hazing ritual, "an old stable trick," inflicted by the wiseguys at the track. At eighty pounds, Thurston was told that he would have to lose some weight, so he was confined, up to his neck, inside a tall barrel of manure for a full day. When he was pulled out and scrubbed clean, he was too weak to stand, let alone sit upright on a horse. The trainer gave him twenty cents and told him to "beat it."

Thurston returned to the life of a tramp, riding freights and living in "hobo jungles" near rail yards. He scoured the newspapers to watch for the latest magicians and traveled to Louisville, Peoria, and Indianapolis just to see conjuring shows. He saw Herrmann again, studying his new tricks, as well as Harry Kellar, America's own homegrown wizard. Hoffmann's *Modern Magic* was the efficiently written textbook on magic that also whispered of impossible dreams; the chapters seamlessly transitioned from coin and card tricks to the costly, stage-sized marvels—appearing assistants, floating ladies—that were staples of Herrmann's performances. The boy carried a dirty deck of cards with him everywhere, practicing the palm, the pass, and the force: the rudiments of a secretive art.

As winter came, Thurston moved south, settling back in the fairgrounds

and longingly visiting the racetracks. In Denison, Texas, he met an old horserac-
ing friend and they decided to go into the program business—part salesmen,
part newsboys. They followed the racing circuit across the East Coast, buying
the program concession in each city and earning real money. Thurston bought
a gold watch, a new suit, and some magic equipment. He easily learned to
gamble, and naturally learned to cheat. His friends were amused by his magic
but valued his skills at palming or false shuffling—it only took one or two
good, fearless moves executed at the right moment to turn the fortunes of
a game.

Now fifteen years old and flush with money, Thurston circled back through
Ohio. He was safely too successful and too large to endure his father's threats.
His mother was delighted to watch his magic and told him that she had a dream
that he would one day be the world's greatest magician. Thurston remembered
the prediction with pride and some embarrassment, perhaps because he realized that he felt no such commitment to an honest life of hard work.

He left Ohio to return to the races, but he quickly returned to his worst
habits. Gradually his circle of friends had descended to a group of newsboys,
derelicts, and thieves. His skills at magic seemed a natural complement to their
world. He was taught to pick pockets in New York's Bowery and joined a gang.
The associates identified the victims, signaled to Thurston, and then jostled
the mark as Thurston worked his magic, dipping his fingers deftly into pockets
or purses, pinching watches and stealing wallets. It was the same type of misdirection and bold deception that he had been studying in *Modern Magic*. When
he was picked up in New York and turned over to William Round, he realized
that he had reached the very bottom. He had been lucky that he could still
make a good impression, and be scrubbed clean to impress as a handsome,
sincere young man. "My hard, early life had left no imprint on my features, and
actually I don't think it marked my personality very much," he later admitted.
"I always had a sort of inner conflict over right and wrong, especially when I
was working with the criminals." When William Round finally questioned
"Willie Ryan," asking if he were ready to behave and go to church, Thurston
broke down, realizing that his life had been helplessly out of his control, and
nodded his assent.

———

ROUND TESTED HIM with menial jobs around the office. One afternoon he gave Howard a $5 bill and a package for the American Express office, telling him to deliver the package and return with the change. Thurston returned quickly, offering the change plus an extra nickel, because he had only taken the street-car in one direction and walked for the rest of the journey. Round admitted that he had the boy followed, but now he was ready to offer his full trust. Thurston was made a janitor at the Prison Association building, and taken to the Rounds' personal church, the Berean Baptist Church. Howard had told them that his mother, Margaret, was a Baptist but, anxious to find some blame for all his problems, explained that his father was not a Christian. For the first time in months, he corresponded with his mother. Fearing the worst, Margaret Thurston was now pleased to hear that her son had found important friends in the city and been led to religion.

Through the Broome Street Tabernacle, Howard performed various missionary duties, preaching on street corners, quoting the Bible, and inviting other indigents back to the church. "He has lost no opportunity to lead his old comrades to Christ," Round reported. After a hard day on the streets, he arrived one night with a ticket for the Mission Home, entitling him to a cot and coffee in the morning. He trudged up to the large sleeping room, filled with hundreds of beds and a collection of outcasts and criminals. Thurston began to undress, but suddenly remembered his new ritual, a nightly prayer. He realized how these toughs would react to his show of piety—just weeks before, he had been one of them. But he reasoned that the experience was some sort of test of faith. He knelt down and audibly mumbled a long, sincere prayer. The room grew quiet. The men watched the boy at prayer, and then quietly went to their own beds. This public prayer made a lasting impression on Thurston and convinced him that he'd changed his life for the better—he remembered it as a demonstration of the marvelous, mysterious effect of faith.

If his conversion had been less than sincere, less an act of passion, it was becoming an act of logic: Thurston was sincerely humbled by his change of fortunes. "Possibly I would have soon tired of this, and looked for another fast train," he confessed years later, "but [then] I received a telegram that my mother had died." Margaret died on his eighteenth birthday, July 20, 1887. Howard was thrown into a deep depression. "His condition seemed to me such a forlorn one that I felt as if I would like to be a friend to him in some way," Round wrote to an associate. He suggested that Thurston be sent to Mount Hermon Academy, Dwight Moody's Christian school for boys in Northfield, Massachusetts.

Round was not a philanthropist and couldn't offer the funds to send Howard to school. But Round's mother-in-law, Ellen E. Thomas, had come to know the boy and offered to pay the $53 for each half-year term, board and tuition, for "three or four years."

On August 10, 1887, Thurston sent a letter filled with misspellings:

Dear Mrs. Thomas,

I hav thought a grate many times of wrighting to you but little did. I think my first letter would bear sutch sad news that is my mother is dead. She died on the 20th of July my birthday, but I did not hear about it until the 4th of August. It was a very hard trial but then I know that it is all for the best for it says in the Bible that All Things work together for the best for them that love God. Then I know that she is in a far better home than this wourld could afford her and so it doesn't worry me mutch for I know that I shall see her soon, where we shall never part. There is nothing on earth that I care about living for now but to sirve God and do his work whitch I hope he will give me power to do so. I think God has got some thing for me to do on this earth for he has worked so mysteriously since my conversion he has provided a way for me to go to school where I may learn to do his work so far and I will trust him in the future. . . .

I remain sincerely yours,
Howard Thurston

"He needs the school," Round admitted. "This letter is a vast improvement on those previously written. . . . He is not advanced in studies, but has been studying hard all summer. He is about as far along as boys of ten or twelve normally are." In the application, Round confessed that the boy "lacked push," and now had a certain shyness that seemed to put him at a disadvantage.

Mount Hermon rejected Thurston's admission, complaining that the information on his parents and background was unclear. Round responded with a letter-writing campaign, forwarding messages from ministers attesting to Thurston's miraculous conversion and strength of character. When he heard that the school was already filled for the next term, he wrote directly to Reverend Dwight Moody. "Can't we send him to live in the village where he can have the advantages of the school and enter regularly when there is a vacancy? I think the boy would be glad to sleep on the bare floor and would think it a privilege to do so, for the sake of the advantages of the school." He hoped that Moody could meet him, "see his face," and know that "he is born in Christ."

Moody relented and Howard Thurston was sent to Mount Hermon on September 15, 1887. He was student number 507. Considering that Thurston had been feeling the itch to run from New York, his admission to Moody's school was an astonishing second chance for a boy who had been holding on tightly but, much like poor Reddy Cadger, was ready to tumble onto the tracks.

"THERE IS SOME MISAPPREHENSION abroad for the plan of the school," Professor Henry Sawyer, Thurston's first headmaster, explained at a Mount Hermon building dedication in 1885. "It is not a reformatory; the fact that a boy is bad is no reason he should be sent to Mt. Hermon. It is not an orphan asylum. It is a school for earnest Christian young men who want to round out their education so that they can become of use in the world. . . . If we are going out into the world, the head, heart and hands need training."

Reverend Dwight Lyman Moody was a nineteenth-century celebrity in the world of evangelism. He was born in 1837 in Northfield, Massachusetts, founded the Northfield Seminary for girls there in 1879, and in 1881 he opened Mount Hermon Academy for boys, on a separate campus across town. Mount Hermon offered classes at high school level. Unlike the Moody Bible Institute (opened as the Chicago Evangelization Society in 1901), it was not intended to produce ministers, but to give a well-rounded education. In fact, in the 1890s, Mount Hermon dropped the Bible course study, as the school felt it was attracting an inferior grade of student. Moody felt that society needed "gap-men," good Christians who testified, worked in the world, and served between the laity and ministers. The application form to the school asked about signs of piety and pointedly inquired if the student wished to attend. "He has made it a daily prayer for months," Round explained in Thurston's application. Although the school was never intended as a reform school, it often accommodated hard-luck cases. Moody himself impulsively wrote on some applications, "Take this boy before the devil does."

The sprawling, new campus was beautiful and bucolic, with redbrick buildings surrounding the lush, hilly grounds. It was more idyllic than anything Thurston had seen in Ohio, more inviting than the city tenements or train yards that had served as his homes for the last six years. Still, he admitted that he "suffered at Mount Hermon. The change from the nomadic life to the prosaic life of a student seemed unbearable at times." He had already calculated the train schedule. "Night after night I debated with myself whether I would quietly leave the dormitory and catch the midnight freight that stopped at Mount Hermon. I attribute my resistance to the same comfort and strength that gave me the courage to kneel at my bed in the Bowery lodging house." Professor Sawyer once showed him a letter in his file from William Round, which had detailed Thurston's criminal career in New York. Sawyer was grandly making the point that no further punishment was necessary, but the memory of that letter, and his status as an outsider, haunted Thurston.

At Mount Hermon, he made a little extra money by cutting his fellow students' hair and shaving them (a skill he learned from his father). He earned average to good grades. For example, his Bible courses began with excellent marks, but then faded to middling grades. Perhaps that was a sign of his expanding interests. He did poorly in singing (his voice had little modulation), but excellently in elocution (following the examples from Moody's soaring sermons, he learned to add pauses or draw out his words for emphasis). He failed geometry and struggled with algebra. He learned to juggle Indian clubs, heavy wooden pins that were swung in graceful movements around his body.

He was a star on the track team and intramural football team. He was also elected vice president of the Junior Middle Class (the equivalent of sophomore year).

During a special Christmas dinner at the school in 1890, at which young ladies from the Northfield Seminary joined the boys, Reverend Moody was on hand to join the small group for holiday toasts. After dinner, the students entertained themselves with songs, games, and recitations. There, Thurston performed his first public magic show. He grandly exaggerated this premiere, recounting later how he sliced off a student's head and enhanced the illusion with a large knife dripping with red ink. "Four women in the audience fainted." He also claimed to have reached into the pockets of Will Moody, the son of the evangelist, withdrawing handfuls of playing cards.

He didn't do these tricks. "The sleight of hand performed by Thurston added greatly to the evening's pleasure," according to the school newspaper, the *Hermonite*. There was no knife, no blood, and certainly no playing cards on the Mount Hermon campus. Thurston probably performed several discreet, polite coin and handkerchief tricks.

He attended the school until 1891, where he was officially designated "class of '93," meaning that he was two years from full graduation. He was twenty-one. More than likely, Mrs. Thomas had exhausted her funds after paying for Thurston's four years, and Round had now found a new project for the young man. His was not an unusual case. At that time, only ten percent of Mount Hermon students graduated. Thurston had endured a slow start with his academic work and many of his basic courses, like mathematics, elocution, and spelling, were necessary to his education but hadn't counted toward graduation.

On June 10, 1891, Thurston sent a note to Professor Cutler, the new headmaster.

Professor Cutler,

I come to bid you good bye and thank you for all that you have done fore me. I leave school to night but shall come for my baggage tomorrow morning. Prof one of

the chief desires of my life is to prove to Herman that all I have received here has
not been without effect. And that some day Herman may be proud that Howard
Thurston was ever under its care. Very respectfully,

H. Thurston

The misspelling of the school's name was not just odd or careless, but may
have been telling. His four years at Mount Hermon had given Thurston a taste
for real education and respectful camaraderie, but he still longed for adventure
and was anxious to try his hand in the tawdry, delicious world of show business. He actually found his life's work through the effect of a very different
"Herrmann."

THREE

"THE MOTH AND THE FLAME"

hroughout his life, Thurston's press stories encouraged the idea that he had trained for the ministry or actually graduated as an ordained minister. Neither was true. His career in the ministry probably consisted of a few days of street corner mission work, in the Five Points district, when he was trying to impress William Round and Reverend Dooly with his piety. He certainly heard Dwight Moody preach. At Mount Hermon, Thurston took a course of Bible studies—perhaps planning to become a preacher—but gradually his choices shifted to other areas. When he left the school, Round may have suggested that he continue his education at the University of Pennsylvania in Philadelphia, studying to become a medical missionary. But this next step would have depended upon Round's continuing largesse as well as Thurston's academic achievements—failing to graduate from Mount Hermon, he would have needed to pass entrance exams in Philadelphia.

William M. F. Round had moved on to a different project. In 1887, while serving the New York Prison Association and petitioning for Thurston's education at Mount Hermon, Round had also served as the corresponding secretary for the Burnham Industrial Farm in upstate Canaan, New York. Burnham was a reform school for adolescent boys, a project perfectly suited to Round's theories about rehabilitation. In 1891, William Round was the superintendent of Burnham Farm. A flyer boasted of the institution's success:

> Burnham Industrial Farm is no longer an experiment, but an entire success. Boys from slums, from county jails, and from families of wealth and position who could no longer control their erring sons [have been] trained to earn an honest living as respected, honest boys. Firmness and love and careful training have won the boys to better lives.

When Thurston left Northfield, Massachusetts, in the spring of 1891, he stopped in Canaan to visit William Round, who promptly recruited the young man to his cause. Round had introduced a new program to accept younger boys, aged nine to twelve. They were organized in a special "family" called the Lambfold and housed in a loft above the dairy on the Burnham grounds. He asked Thurston to become a charter member of a new fellowship called the Brotherhood of St. Christopher, and asked him to take charge of the Lambfold. Perhaps Round appealed to Thurston's Christian charity, or perhaps he simply mentioned the considerable investment he, and his mother-in-law, had made toward Thurston's education. Thurston realized that his future was still tied to Round and that he was obliged to repay the loan.

In December 1891, after he had been at the Burnham Farm for over six months, he wrote to his old headmaster at Mount Hermon, Professor Cutler, "I came to the Burnham Industrial Farm when I left the school last June. I have joined the Brotherhood of St. Christopher, an organization to train young Christian men for institutional lives, that is, to work or take charge of other institutions. The time of service is three years. The brothers receive no salary, only a small fee for necessary things. Most everything is furnished us by the Farm. I suppose you are somewhat acquainted with the Burnham Industrial Farm."

He later remembered that he earned five dollars a month at Burnham, and his time there was productive, as he helped obtain a herd of cattle for the boys and raise funds for a new silo and gymnasium. But the duties at Burnham Farm satisfied him only in that he had no other plans for his future. As he wiled his days in Canaan, New York, weeding the onion field or driving the horse cart, he decided that he'd had enough of the peaceful, institutional life of the country.

He lasted eighteen months at Burnham, certainly not the three-year term that he had pledged. It seems that Round's tenure at Burnham, and the Brotherhood of St. Christopher, were slowly unwinding. Thurston had reached an elevated position within the hierarchy, but, "being sort of an independent individual, I had an idea how things should be run and I tried to run the institution," he later recalled. "Anyhow, I didn't agree with the rest of them, so we decided that I would leave." When he departed on January 5, 1893, a cold, snowy day, all the boys lined up. Thurston bid them an affectionate good-bye, then climbed into a sleigh and was carried to the train station.

William M. F. Round played an essential role in young Howard Thurston's life, but in his later biographies, Thurston included his name with only passing references. He was merely "a noted philanthropist" who worked at the Prison Association and then offered the boy work. Thurston was always embarrassed by his connection to the head of the Prison Association—it raised obvious questions—and he felt guilty by disappointing this important patron.

THURSTON WAS LUCKY when he left the Burnham Farm and traveled through Albany, New York. There he happened to see a bright lithograph advertising Herrmann the Great, the Mephistophelean magician from his youth who had so inspired him. Thurston left the train and ran to the Hermanus Beeker Hall, where he bought a ticket for the show.

That night, Herrmann's performance was even more marvelous than Thurston ever remembered. Thurston waited by the stage door, but didn't have the courage to actually speak to the magician. Instead, he followed Alexander and Madame Adelaide Herrmann to the Keeler Hotel, asking for a room as close as possible to the great man.

Howard spent a sleepless night, pacing the corridor, trying to work up the courage to knock on Herrmann's door, and listening at the keyhole. He wondered if he should give up any further studies and follow his heart to pursue a career in magic.

Having overheard at the theater that the Herrmann company was traveling to Syracuse the next day, Thurston arrived at the train station in the morning to see the magician one last time. He opened the station door and was surprised by the great magician himself, pacing the lobby floor in a fur-collared coat, flourishing a gold-topped cane. As the Herrmanns walked to the trains, Thurston impulsively bought a ticket to Syracuse, paying the extra dollar for a Pullman car. He sat as close as he dared to the magician, watching him smoke one perfumed Persian cigarette after another, lighting each from embers of the previous cigarette.

In Syracuse, he waited through the week as the show was moved into the Weiting Opera House and rehearsed. Then Thurston bought a ticket and watched the show again on January 13, studying the finer points of Herrmann's magic. He had read the details of the tricks. He had studied Herrmann's clever bits of misdirection. He made his decision. He would become a magician.

MAGIC SHOWS were a staple of American theater, an established genre that attracted audiences in every major city. Like a circus, the nature of the show was family entertainment, not cloying or childish, but a mildly comic combination of verbal jests and visual wonders. And like a vaudeville show, musical revue, Wild West, or minstrel show, it had developed its own traditions and fashions—especially in America, where magic shows were designed to tour from city to city. They played in medium-sized theaters, of five hundred to a thousand people, and were organized in two or three acts. The show often started with small sleight-of-hand tricks, showing off the performer's skill and personality. A topical theme was spiritualism. The magician might re-create a séance onstage or produce apparent manifestations in a curtained cabinet.

Then a variety act or two might be included to offer a change of pace: a different magician, or an acrobat or comic. As the show proceeded, the scale of the mysteries gradually increased. Here the magician included cabinet illusions, the disappearance of a lady, or a levitation illusion. The show might conclude with a short comic sketch, or an illusion staged with operatic sensibilities and spectacle—a cremation or a decapitation.

A show like Herrmann's was complicated to perform and difficult to transport, depending upon trains to major cities. His performances would feature three or four changes of scenery and special curtains. The magician invariably dressed in formal evening clothes. A small group of male assistants, who helped move the cabinets or bring the props onstage, would be dressed as pageboys or bellboys; the magician's wife often took the part of the principle assistant, with several elegant gowns and exotic costumes to match the illusions.

Large or small, any magic show was designed around the magician and always accentuated the magician's personality. Robert Heller was known for his droll patter and wit. Dr. Lynn, from England, indulged in deliberately silly, polysyllabic words and ridiculous presentations. Harry Kellar, a solid and dependable Pennsylvania-born magician, was never especially funny or chatty but chose his words carefully and emphasized the amazing marvels. And Alexander Herrmann, the public's favorite, was wry and devilish, a European roué who seemed especially exotic to Americans. He managed to convince his audiences that his magic was both skillful and effortless at the same time, and his patter sparkled with amusingly tortured French-English that kept the theater bubbling with laughter.

Herrmann was considered a respected man of the theater, a professional on the level of Edwin Booth or Joseph Jefferson. He was born in Paris in 1844, into a German Jewish family of great magicians; his father, Samuel, and his oldest brother, Compars, were both professionals. Alexander appeared as an assistant in his brother's show; Compars and Alexander performed for Abraham Lincoln in Washington, D.C., in 1861.

Working on his own in the 1870s, Alexander Herrmann was billed as Herrmann the Great. Our modern image of a magician, the tall, angular man in silk stockings and a swallowtail coat, the goateed performer who flexes his long fingers and mumbles fractured bits of French, is Alexander Herrmann.

Herrmann's sleight-of-hand tour de force that opened the show, a long sequence titled A Bouquet of Mystic Novelties, consisting of amazing manipulations with his kid gloves, cards, coins, bouquets of flowers, and rabbits. Another Herrmann specialty was card throwing. The magician had a knack for scaling ordinary playing cards, hurtling them individually through the air with a quick snap of his wrist. He could deliver cards to specific seats in the theater, even up to the balcony as spectators shouted their approval, or send them careening off the filigree plasterwork in the dome of the theater, which earned wild cheers.

His pretty, redheaded English wife, Adelaide Scarsez, had appeared as a dancer in Paris. In the 1880s, when Thurston first saw Herrmann's show, she played the part of the "slave girl," levitated over the stage with her elbow touching a vertical pole.

By 1893, when Thurston found Herrmann in Albany, the magic show had swelled to spectacular proportions. He still included his Bouquet of Mystic Novelties and The Slave Girl's Dream. But his new illusions included Ya Ko Yo, the transposition of a Chinese assistant from one suspended wooden cabinet into another, and Herrmann's marvelous spirit séance. "He duplicated, absolutely and convincingly, all of the manifestations of the so-called spiritual cabinets," a Boston critic commented on the new wonders. "In a word, he gave an amazingly elusive, delicately droll and vastly amusing exhibition of powers that two centuries ago would have given Herrmann a very warm berth indeed."

IN LATER NEWSPAPER ARTICLES and his autobiography, Thurston managed to enhance the simple story of encountering Herrmann from Albany. In Thurston's improved version, he was traveling to the University of Pennsylvania, having vowed to continue his education and become a medical missionary. Watching Herrmann's performance in Albany reminded him of his interest in magic. That night, he was racked with self-doubt. Should he continue his education or become a magician? He finally decided upon traveling to Pennsylvania and starting college, but at the train station he stumbled across Herrmann again.

> I heard the guard say to Herrmann, "Syracuse, eight-twenty."
>
> My train left for Philadelphia about the same time. Now comes the strange part of the whole incident, which bears out what I have often said, that a man is not his own master in certain critical moments.

I went to the ticket window, laid down a twenty-dollar bill, and asked for a ticket to Philadelphia. I placed the ticket in my pocket and counted the change.

"You've made a mistake," I said to the agent. "The price to Philadelphia is five dollars and twenty cents, and you have charged me only two dollars and eighty cents."

He replied in a gruff voice, "You said Syracuse!"

I looked at the ticket—then at Herrmann.

"All right," I said, "I'll go to Syracuse!"

God knows I asked for a ticket to Philadelphia, so the sin rests with the ticket seller!

Gazing at my ticket in a dazed sort of way I walked slowly toward the gate. I boarded the train for Syracuse. . . .

Fate had cast the die for me. There was no use in trying to thwart destiny. Had I been a free agent I should have been in Philadelphia at that moment, making arrangements for my future work as a medical missionary. But I was not a free agent.

It was probably Thurston's brilliant publicity agent, John Northern Hilliard, an experienced magician, who later concocted this version of the story. Elements of the account seem especially suspicious because they so nicely echo the story of Jean-Eugène Robert-Houdin's introduction to magic. Hilliard had known Herrmann and was an avid reader of magic history.

Robert-Houdin was the great nineteenth-century French magician, an inventor and performer who enjoyed a brief, spectacular career in Paris and in tours of Europe. His innovations were copied by his contemporaries. His colorful autobiography, *The Confidences of a Prestidigitator*, published in 1858, inspired generations of important magicians. In his memoirs he recounted an incident from 1826, when he was about twenty years old, training to be a watchmaker.

I went into a bookseller's shop to buy Berthoud's *Treatise on Clockmaking*, which I knew he had. The tradesman being engaged at the moment on matters more important, took down two volumes from the shelves and handed them to me without ceremony. On returning home, I sat down to peruse my treatise conscientiously, but judge my surprise when I read, "The way of performing tricks with the cards, how to guess a person's thoughts, to cut off a pigeon's head, to restore it to life," et cetera. The bookseller had made a mistake. Fascinated, however, by the announcement of such marvels, I devoured the mysterious pages. . . . How often since have I blessed this providential error, without which I should have probably vegetated as a country watchmaker!

Robert-Houdin's memoirs are filled with fictional embellishments, and none was more convenient than this tale: his nineteenth-century readers would have wondered why a young man, born to a good family and trained in a respectable field, would be drawn to the disreputable world of conjuring.

It's unlikely that Thurston was actually traveling to the University of Pennsylvania. He must have left Canaan, New York, without any real prospects and was lucky to cross Herrmann's route. It's easy to see how the combination of allures—the train travel, magic show, impulsive change of schedule, and obsessive desire to see one show after another—provided delicious reminders of his most carefree childhood adventures. After years of supervision and responsibility at Mount Hermon and Burnham Farm, encountering Herrmann must have seemed empowering.

By retelling the story as Robert-Houdin did, with a heavy dose of fate to excuse his irresponsibility, Thurston left his decision in someone else's hands. It made the incident more memorable, more dramatic, and more flattering for him, who, at twenty-three, was now expected to act like an adult.

Besides asking what elements were added to the story, we might wonder what elements were left out. Thurston's account of shadowing Herrmann sounds perfectly accurate, right down to the gold-topped cane and Herrmann's chain-smoking. But after leaving Mount Hermon and Burnham Farm (where he assertively clashed with the decision-makers), Thurston was no longer the hopelessly shy, socially intimidated adolescent portrayed in his autobiography. His intention must have been to plead for a job with Herrmann. More than likely, at the Albany stage door, at the hotel, or on the train to

Syracuse, Thurston cornered the magician, pulled out his playing cards, performed a few flourishes, and offered his services as an assistant. Under these circumstances, Herrmann certainly would have dismissed him. Magicians avoided magic-mad amateurs; only dependable, experienced professionals were considered for such important jobs. And Thurston, humiliated by the rebuff, would never have admitted it.

HIS WEEK of high living, following Herrmann across New York state, must have exhausted Thurston's limited funds. He took a train back to Detroit to spend the winter with his father as he planned his professional career.

William Thurston had remarried the year after Margaret's death. His new wife, Emma Dearth, was seventeen years his junior. The couple moved to Detroit, Michigan, with Emily, one of Emma's daughters by her previous marriage. William worked as a tailor, making women's clothes, and the Thurstons ran a boardinghouse.

Howard lasted only several weeks with his family. As he assembled some magic props—a small case with rubber balls, thimbles, and seven decks of cards, his stepmother thought that his plan to be a magician was disappointing and his father found it merely laughable. "My father and I did not get along well, so finally I left," Thurston later said. When the weather was warm enough to travel, Howard put on his only suit of clothes, picked up his valise, and walked to the front door, announcing that he was "going to start." William Thurston thought his son was joking. Howard nodded, and then dropped his voice, admitting, "I'm broke." His father grandly put his hand in his pocket and brought out a quarter. "Here," he said, "never let it be said that your father didn't help you." Thurston never forgot his father's cruel joke.

Howard Thurston spent fifteen cents on a streetcar to Wyandotte, Michigan. At six o'clock that evening, he gave his first professional performance, standing on a box in front of a store, trying to catch the eye of people hurrying home from work. It was such a failure that the next day, when he walked to Detroit, he remembered his prayers and asked God for guidance. As he looked up, he saw a pitchman selling wire potato peelers. The man showed him how the peelers were made and boasted of how much money he managed to procure. That evening, Thurston visited a hardware store, bought a few supplies, and sat in his cheap hotel room, twisting up potato peelers.

He headed to Cleveland for his debut as a potato-peeler-selling magician. He had read that Sells Brothers Circus was working there, and he hoped to get some work on the circus grounds. The activity of the circus provided a steady stream of customers, and Thurston gradually became adept at his card-trick, ball-trick, handkerchief-trick, potato-peeler act.

Sells Brothers Circus wasn't interested in card tricks and didn't want a potato-peeler salesman, but they were impressed with Thurston's smooth voice and slick mannerisms. He became a talker for the sideshow, the man who stands out in front and coerces the crowd into the tent. He followed the show through the Midwest and into Wisconsin and Minnesota, then jumped to other small carnivals if they could offer him a spot performing magic.

Throughout the early months of 1893, outdoor entertainers were drawn, as if magnetically, to Chicago. The World's Columbian Exposition was to open that spring, and attractions and concessionaires were being assembled. It was a beautiful world's fair of imitation white marble palaces, offering many important innovations—the modern Otis elevator, Edison's kinetoscope, Tesla and Westinghouse's alternating current dynamo, which illuminated the fair buildings at night—as well an astonishing array of new products—Cracker Jack, carbonated soda, and the hamburger. The precise mixture of exotic displays and unabashed fun served as an inspiration to a young Walt Disney, who attended that summer. The twinkling domes and colonnades that surrounded the Jackson Park lagoon also provided the dream of an imaginary city called Oz; author L. Frank Baum attended the fair as well.

But one of the fair's most lasting legacies was the Midway Plaisance, the world's first midway, a collection of popular American fairground shows, exhibits, and mild con games, scrubbed clean and lined up in a mile-long approach on the western edge of the fairgrounds. Young Harry Houdini came to Chicago looking for a place to feature his magic act; instead, he donned greasepaint and played the part of an Indian fakir in the Algerian and Tunisian Village. Thurston couldn't sell his card tricks, but he was able to find employment as a talker for the African Dahomey Village, a little further down the midway.

The Dahomey Village was the work of Xavier Pené, a French entrepreneur who had provided African performers for fairgrounds. Like many sideshow attractions, the lure of the show was the promise of lasciviousness, concealed within an overt cultural appeal. Photos suggest that special shows at the Dahomey Village allowed audiences to ogle the bare-breasted native women.

The crowning jewel, the astonishing attraction of the midway, was the original Ferris wheel. Houdini and Thurston spent the days of 1893 listening to the roar of the wheel's engines and the whooping cheers of its crowds. It was the creation of engineer George Ferris, intended to best Paris's Eiffel Tower of 1889. At 264 feet tall, it was positioned precisely midway in the midway, a hulking, awe-inspiring, animated marvel. Its thirty-six train car–sized cabins each accommodated forty people.

At the base of the Ferris wheel was another attraction that has become enshrined in American folklore: The Streets of Cairo. There, a Syrian-American dancer named Farida Mazar Spyropoulous danced the scandalous belly dance, twisting and undulating in a provocative display. It was a hit, jamming the Streets of Cairo and making a star of the dancer. Her stage name was Fatima, but she became famous under the nickname Little Egypt. The melody that accompanied her gyrations, played on Oriental flutes, has become equally famous as "The Snake Charmer Song," often starting with the lyrics, "There's a place in France / Where the ladies do a dance." It was the first "hoochie kootch" show.

Thurston was just two years from his good Christian education, but he pitched the Dahomey maidens and witnessed Little Egypt's performance. As a showman, not a preacher, he greedily admired the simplicity of the dance routine and the long line of customers waiting to glimpse any sort of indecent display. When his twenty-one-year-old brother Harry came out to the fair, Howard and Harry prowled the midway together in search of business opportunities. Harry, of course, studied all of the exotic dancers and introduced himself to many of them. The "hoochie kootch" inspired the Thurston brothers, just as it revolutionized the sideshow business in America.

WHEN THE FAIR CLOSED in October 1893, the Dahomey Village moved to Coney Island in New York for the next season, and Howard Thurston moved with it.

In the spring of 1894, he left Coney Island and headed back to the Midwest to find a good circus engagement. Now his magic show consisted of card flourishes, some ball and handkerchief tricks, and a new finale in which he reached down the collar of a spectator's coat, withdrew scarves and a laundry line of baby clothes, and finished by producing a large black-faced doll. It guaranteed applause, and sent the audience away guffawing, but Thurston still hedged his bets by buying a box of can openers. It was always best to end the show with a little sales pitch.

In Logan, Ohio, Thurston shared a torchlit spot on the city street with an itinerant tattoo artist named David Lano. When Thurston went into his act, Lano stepped back and watched. He was impressed. Lano explained that he was traveling with the Hurd and Berry Great London Sideshow, a ragtag assembly of freaks and variety acts.

Lano brought the magician back to the fairgrounds and introduced him to Tom Hurd, the owner. Thurston was told that they had been looking for a magician because the sideshow was carrying a nicely painted banner advertising "Anderson, the Great Wizard of the North." "There it is," Hurd told him, unrolling the banner. "If you want to be with it, you get six dollars a week and grub. That's if you can wiz." Thurston joined the show in Logan. He remembered that he "sat in the train with my chest puffed out like a pouter pigeon's, because at last I was a professional traveling magician."

They performed thirty or forty shows a day, every fifteen minutes, interspersing his performances with Lano, who was a puppeteer; Pop Samwell, with his troupe of trained dogs and monkeys; Big Hattie Boone, 465 pounds of feminine charm; Mademoiselle de Leon, the Circassian Beauty; Thardo, the knife thrower; Coffee, the skeleton dude. . . . Within weeks, Berry had proved an undependable drunk, so Thurston was pressed into service as the talker. "Gentlemen, as a special service to the gentlemen here today, I'm obliged to point out that Big Hattie Boone is available and willing to marry. The man who gets her, if she's worth her weight in gold, will end up having the whole mine!"

For months, Thurston overlooked the hardships. He was thrilled with his work as the Wizard of the North, and exhilarated by tents filled with audiences. Years later he remembered:

All the members of the company ate and slept in the tent. We had breakfast at 8 o'clock and supper at night, with a cup of coffee and sandwich between times without skipping the performances. The tattooed lady and the snake charmer received extra pay for the cooking. An oilcloth was spread over one of the freak platforms and this was our table. The food was not of the best quality, but the fresh air and the hard work gave us huge appetites. I have since eaten all over the world, but as long as I live I shall never forget the smell of coffee coming from the cooking tent in the early morning.

But late that year, friction within the sideshow troupe combined with Thurston's growing sense of self-importance: "The two managers were no help at all." He was now a better talker than the owner and could take charge of just about any aspect of the show. In the winter of 1894, as the company traveled through the Allegheny Mountains, Thurston led a revolt against the managers, Hurd and Berry, splitting the troupe in half.

The new company—the Great Country Circus—worked in rented storefronts or public halls. They talked their way into the towns, convinced the residents to come to the performance, and relied upon borrowed lanterns to illuminate the show. "I sold tickets," Thurston wrote, "'worked straight' in the opening comedy act ('feeding the comedian' as it is called), did an exhibition of [Indian] club swinging, lectured on the freaks, did an occasional talk outside the hall, acted as ringmaster for Pop Samwell's trained animal act, did a magical turn, and worked in the concluding sketch." If Thurston had been half as clever, or experienced, as he thought he was, he would never have tried to start his own show in the middle of winter, stranded in tiny Pennsylvania towns. It was miserably cold—Thurston could barely perform his manipulations; the audience, wrapped in coats and furs, could barely applaud.

As spring brought warm weather, it also brought the new manager a renewed determination. He needed reinforcements. He wired Harry Thurston in Chicago, urging him to join the show and help with its management. He knew he could count on Harry. Harry would be hardworking, clever, tough, and fiercely loyal to his brother. Most of all, after his fascination with the Columbian Exposition, Howard suspected that Harry would like a taste of real show business.

Howard was right on every count. And it was a decision he'd regret for the rest of his life.

FOUR

"THE MYSTIC FOLLIES"

 arry Elias Thurston was born in Columbus, Ohio, on November 3, 1871. He was two and a half years younger than Howard, a few inches taller, and a little heavier. The brothers shared a natural intrigue with deception. In Harry's case, it began and ended with con games, business expediencies, or little white lies to carry him through the day—he could never be bothered by the meticulous rehearsal to turn tricks into magic. Harry was a city boy, whose show interests ran from dime museums to gambling parlors. The "hoochie kootch" shows of the Chicago midway were perfectly suited to his tastes.

Harry idolized his older brother and was drawn to Howard's exciting lifestyle, but he had none of Howard's personal charms. Harry was Howard without the wealth of experiences, or perspective. But he was also Howard without the contradictions. Harry was simply a tough customer.

Howard needed just this sort of discipline behind the Great Country Circus, his loose collection of acts that was struggling through Pennsylvania. He also needed quick cash, and Harry brought a pocketful of money to save the day.

In Williamsport, Pennsylvania, the brothers made arrangements to rent a local tent and drivers. Under the big top the little circus took on a new luster, but rain limited the number of performances, and the local sheriff moved in to attach the circus's possessions. Harry studied a map. They were midway between New York and Pittsburgh. He knew a nice little dime museum in Pittsburgh, operated by Harry Davis, that just might be looking for a big attraction. The Thurstons dashed to the Western Union office and wired Davis, offering a sale price of $150 a week for their show, promising a collection of marvels, including "the world's greatest magician," and concluding, "answer immediately." Then they returned to the Great Country Circus tent and waited nervously.

At eight o'clock that night, Davis finally wired his response. "All okay, open Monday." Fortunately, Harry had saved just enough money for two bottles of whiskey. They got the sheriff good and drunk, then snuck out of the tent with their possessions, running to the train station.

In Pittsburgh Thurston borrowed a dress suit from John Harris, the treasurer and box office attendant at Harry Davis's establishment. The show ran for three weeks, but it was a victim of its own success. After a long, hard winter, most of the troupe saw their profitable Pittsburgh appearance as a chance to finally escape, using their profits to run back to other sideshows.

BOTH HOWARD AND HARRY had developed their own ways of making money. Howard regularly purchased boxes of cheap jewelry, watches or brooches that were flash-plated with a thin layer of gold. He also purchased one expensive watch—an exact match—made in real gold with a quality movement. He used his skills as a pitchman to lure his customers, and his skills as a magician to make the sale. The buyer examined the quality watch, studied the movement, and admired the gold. Howard invisibly switched it for a cheaper watch—the simple work of some palming—just before the sale. This little con game was especially useful when the brothers were pressed to pay a hotel bill or a fine. Invariably Howard's "family watch" came out of his pocket as a tear came to his eye. After apparently weighing this painful option, he would finally agree to offer the watch as security on a loan, switching the watch and skipping out of town.

Howard's smooth good looks and placid demeanor earned him many female admirers. He cultivated a wardrobe of elegant clothing—silk ties, navy jackets, crisp white shirts, and straw hats—so that he always looked prosperous and desirable. He taught his brother Harry how to "tish" the girls; it seems to be the only sleight of hand that Harry ever learned, his kind of deception. While propositioning a showgirl or dance-hall floozy, Harry would smile, pull a five-dollar bill from his pocket, fold it into a neat bundle, wrap it in a piece of tissue, and then discreetly tuck it beneath the lady's garter. This little gesture usually earned a special favor. The next morning, the lady discovered that the bill had been switched for a piece of paper. The showgirls in cities like New York or Chicago were already on to this trick, but Howard and Harry discovered that it still worked in Pittsburgh or St. Louis.

With the Great Country Circus disbanded, Harry had no work, and he returned to the Chicago to search out dime museums. Howard realized that his best prospects were still on the road. Through the fall and winter of 1894, he jumped from one small show to another, performing magic in the sideshow or working as a pitchman with another new product. First, he tried selling hot dogs (a delicacy that had just become a fairground favorite) and carpet cleaner, which could be mixed in big batches in a hotel bathtub. But he was always more comfortable working with a partner. He teamed up with a showman named Sam Meinhold, who played the zither to accompany the magician. The partners headed south for the rest of the winter, first with Colonel Routh Goshen's Circus (Goshen was one of Barnum's giants), and then on their own.

When Thurston and Meinhold presented their sideshow in a small Georgia town, the local constable assembled a list of fines and charges, designed to extort money from anyone who stumbled through the community. Thurston couldn't pay the fine. Howard and Sam were marched into court that morning, and Howard began addressing the judge with a long, impassioned plea, detailing the unfair way they were treated. He concluded:

We are strangers to you, and I know you want us to leave your beautiful city feeling that we have been fairly treated and that your honor and the honor of your fair city have not been debased by the actions of unscrupulous officials. Who knows, your own boys may be in similar positions sometime.

He paused, noticing that everyone in the courtroom was speechless. They stared back at him, awaiting his next words, apparently blindsided by the sideshow worker's unexpectedly pure rhetoric. Thurston pulled his handkerchief from his pocket, wiped his eyes, and continued with a voice that trembled with theatrical emotion.

I am glad this thing has ended so happily for us all and that we can leave the city feeling we have your friendship and good wishes. I want to thank you for your kindness. I want to bid you all good-bye, and I hope to see you all some day.

He and Sam pushed their way through the court and out the door. No one raised their voice or attempted to stop them. "I had been the accused, I opened the case, did the pleading, closed the case, returned the verdict and acquitted myself," Thurston later wrote. "To borrow an expression from my own profession, I had forced a card on everyone in that room."

It was another incident in a small, deeply segregated Georgia town that left the strongest impression on the young magician. As they were preparing their show in a small hall opposite a train station, Thurston and Meinhold heard a train rumble through town, and the sudden screams of a boy. The magician dashed across the street to the station as a crowd assembled. There, an adolescent black boy lay screaming on the tracks. The train had run over his legs and nearly severed them completely.

The assembled crowd, a group of mostly black faces, was horrified by the scene. Thurston admonished them to pick up the boy and carry him to the drugstore. "I'm a magician. I'll put the magician's curse on all of you unless you help at once!" A few volunteers carried the boy across the street; he was bleeding profusely and sobbing. There was nothing that the local doctor could do for him. Thurston knelt by the side of the boy. He tried to comfort him with a showman's trick, simple suggestion, telling him that he would take away all his pain. "Rest and sleep," Thurston repeated. They were the same lines he would use, years later, while performing the Levitation Trick. The boy looked into Thurston's face, and asked, "Are you Jesus?"

Thurston hesitated, and then answered quietly, "Yes."

He told the boy to close his eyes, repeating that the pain would leave. As he looked up, he saw the stunned crowd outside the drugstore kneeling in prayer. "The boy was dying," Thurston remembered. "With a feeling I hope I shall never experience again, I walked slowly through the praying Negros and awe-struck whites, and climbed the stairs." He walked back into the little hall and then performed his magic show.

It was a story that Thurston told for the rest of his life, as if puzzling through it, attempting to reconcile the way his deep honesty and dishonesty could combine for the benefit of an audience. "I felt that it was right to tell the boy that I was Jesus." This also demonstrated the essential difference between the brothers Harry and Howard Thurston. Harry was a master of the simple con game. But Harry could never have bamboozled the Georgia court, nor comforted the dying boy. He never would have tried.

IN 1896, Howard Thurston was personally awestruck by a different kind of deception. Although he fancied himself an expert magician, his peripatetic fairground work meant that Thurston was an outsider to the world of magic. When he witnessed a young midwestern magician, T. Nelson Downs, perform an act with coins and playing cards, Thurston was surprised to see something new—genuinely unique—using just a few cards. Downs showed a fan of five cards and, one by one, made them disappear at his fingertips.

Thurston stumbled through an approximation of the trick, trying to re-create Downs's movements. It wasn't until he traveled through New York City later that year that he was able to track down the full story of the disappearing cards. It was Dr. James Elliott's trick. In fact, as any magician of the time could have told you, it had to be Dr. Elliott's.

James William Elliott was born in Maine in April 1874; he was the same age as Harry Houdini. He was famously devoted to magic. When rehearsing a new move, he would rent a room—separate from his apartment—with nothing in it but a table, a chair, and a deck of cards. No distractions. He'd lock himself in the room with instructions that he was not to be disturbed. And then, for four or five hours at a time, he would rehearse. He might then leave for a meal or a short walk, and then return and resume his rehearsals—analyzing each maneuver, solving minute problems, and repeating thousands of repetitions so that the magic became second nature to him.

He studied medicine at Harvard, and then attended Bellevue Hospital Medical College in New York City—which brought him in contact with the New York magicians.

Thurston arranged to meet with Elliott in New York, and found a big man with patrician pride and a "sweet, forceful character," according to one of Elliott's friends. Thurston and Elliott must have formed an instant bond. Elliott was a churchgoing Christian. Thurston was able to recount his years at Mount Hermon in Massachusetts with Dwight Moody. Then Thurston pulled out a deck of cards and demonstrated his sleight of hand. At that time, he performed the standard collection of sleights and flourishes, concluding by passing his hand over the face of the deck to make one card change into another. He presented these slights masterfully, for his years on the sideshow platforms had been a trial by fire for these delicate maneuvers.

Thurston knew he passed the test when he saw Dr. Elliott dip his fingers into his vest pocket and remove his own deck of cards. Elliott took a few steps back and stretched out his right arm. At his fingertips was a single playing card. He moved his hand up and down slightly, a sort of exaggerated wave. And the card disappeared. It was the same thing he'd seen Downs perform. Elliott held his hand flat, his fingers straight, so Thurston could see his empty palm. He repeated the action and the card reappeared at his fingertips.

Thurston shook his head and exhaled in surprise. It was amazing. He suspected what must be happening, even if he didn't know how.

Elliott began again, pulling a chair close to Thurston and speaking with the tone of a professor. It was a move that he had titled the Backhand Palm (which later became known to magicians as the Back Palm). A single card was held horizontally at the fingertips, between the thumb and the middle two fingers. By bending his knuckles in, against the back of the card, and clipping its corners between his fingers, Elliott could suddenly open his hand, transporting the card to the back of his fingers. His palm was empty, his fingers held tightly together. In that position the card was pinched against the back of his hand.

Elliott then demonstrated his improvement, an amazing somersault that invisibly transferred the card from the back of the hand to the front. In required a specific series of moves—the hand didn't just turn over, but rolled closed with a slight flourish. As this happened, Elliott twisted his wrist so that his knuckles were momentarily pointed away from Thurston. In that position, he was able to straighten his fingers, pushing the card back against his palm. He finished the move, showing the back of his hand. Reversing the motion, the card smoothly slid around his knuckles and was concealed behind his hand again. It required a specific knack and a neat sense of touch. Thurston's hands were ideal for the maneuver, with long, muscular fingers.

Backhand palm was a ridiculous name, of course. Before this time, if a magician concealed a card in his hand, he palmed it, holding it in his cupped palm with the back of his hand facing the audience. The art was in the naturalness of this motion. So it's only logical that to palm a card, you use the palm of your hand. But Elliott's misnomer indicates the unexpected and innovative nature of the discovery. There was no good way to describe it. It was a way of palming a card while your palm was empty.

The move hadn't started with Elliott, but with a Mexican magician who wandered into a Bowery magic shop on June 2, 1892, and showed the proprietor, Otto Maurer, how he could make a card disappear. Maurer showed Dr. Elliott and Harry Houdini, and each of them began performing the maneuver. To Elliott goes the honor of refining it. Before Thurston saw it, Elliott's achievement had already spread, like wildfire, to a group of top magicians: Barney Ives, Alexander Herrmann, Billy Robinson, Servais Le Roy, Lawrence Crane, and T. Nelson Downs—all professionals who were in a position to march onto the stage with it.

These magicians swooned over it, but only a few performers used the Back Palm; even then it was merely a fussy little interlude in the middle of a rarefied vaudeville routine. It had little impact with audiences and might have languished as a mere novelty. Houdini, who had tried to perform as a "King of

Cards" several years before, boasted about performing the move, and even tried to take credit for inventing it. Ultimately Houdini had no use for the Back Palm—his act was now devoted to escapes.

To be successful, the Back Palm needed a champion—someone who would make it special for an audience and, in the process, make it practical. This is where Howard Thurston, the carnival worker and part-time confidence man, had the advantage.

IN CHICAGO, Howard and Harry Thurston settled on a new business plan. Thurston's Original Oddities was a midway show, according to their letterhead, offering "Original World's Fair Oriental Dancers . . . Turkish Orchestra . . . Beautiful Maidens of the Orient . . . Life in a Turkish Harem." They were running a "hoochie kootch" show.

Based on the success of Little Egypt and the exotic dancers at the 1893 Columbian Exposition, the kootch show (to use the sideshow slang) became a new attraction at fairgrounds. It was cheap to produce—aspiring dancers could be recruited, costumed, and enhanced with a few pennies' worth of dark greasepaint. Besides, they didn't really need to be good dancers. They just needed to wear abbreviated costumes and shake their hips.

The secret of the show was to promote it as vaguely cultural or exotic—to give the small-town gentlemen an excuse to queue up and pay their dimes. Once inside, the show was as efficiently lascivious as the crowd insisted or conditions allowed. Costumes could always be buttoned up, or gyrations slowed down, if there was the slightest indication of trouble from local lawmen. Of course, that was part of the con game: local lawmen could be bribed by a special audience with the exotic women.

Howard and Harry offered colored lithographs to advertise the show, promising that it would be "billed like a circus." Howard performed as the talker out front, to "run 'em in and run 'em out," the carnival phrase for coercing the crowd into the tent, and then efficiently ending the show and pushing them through the exit so that the new group could enter. "She's sensational . . . sen . . . sa . . . tion . . . al!" Howard intoned from the bally platform. "She's the world's best Oriental dancer, brought to you direct from the midway of the Chicago World's Fair. She twists, turns, and vibrates in ways that you never thought were possible. Let her show you! She can move every muscle, every bone, each and every part of her body!"

The show moved up through the Midwest, booked as a special attraction with fairs and carnivals. Howard insisted that his small group of dancing girls and musicians wear their makeup and exotic costumes whenever they were traveling by train, to advertise the attraction.

As Harry counted the receipts, Howard would slip into the tent and stand onstage, performing his card manipulation act. He was now adept at the Back Palm, testing each of Elliott's moves in front of his audiences. In many ways, it was the perfect audience, for no one was there to watch card tricks. The crowd of men, shoulder to shoulder inside the tent, hooted, whistled, or impatiently stamped their feet, waiting for the girls. If Thurston could learn to impress them with his card productions, he could impress anybody. He spent every available moment, that fall of 1896, waving his hands up and down, tracing arcs around his body, twisting his wrists, and then deftly plucking playing cards from thin air. His training with Indian clubs, from his Mount Hermon days, was an inspiration—big, graceful movements of his arms concealed the smaller manipulations with the cards, and also enhanced the trick, creating a poetic flow to his motions. He was slowly becoming the world's greatest card manipulator.

HARRY AND HOWARD overspent on their attraction, and the following season they decided to consolidate their show with the DeKreko Brothers Congress of Eastern Oddities, a traveling tent carnival—George DeKreko had been the manager of the Streets of Cairo exhibit from the Chicago World's Fair. This left Harry without a job, so he returned to Chicago dime museums. Howard planned the new season, contracting the dancers, musicians, and canvas men. In August 1897, as Howard was getting ready to go back on the road, he traveled from a meeting with Harry to Cincinnati for a new stock of cheap jewelry.

When the train traveled through Indianapolis, a young girl boarded, carrying her tiny tin trunk. Howard struck up a conversation. She explained that she was on her way to visit her aunt and was now a trained dancer—this was an exaggeration, as she had just learned a castanet dance and won an amateur talent contest. Howard explained that he "employed a number of dancers." Another exaggeration, for those girls only shook their hips. He convinced her to join his show.

Born in September 1881, Grace E. Butterworth was just fifteen years old, pretty and petite, with green eyes and a mass of blond curls. She was instantly in awe of Thurston, captivated by his handsome features, his commanding voice, and his amusing sleight of hand, which he used to entertain her on the train.

Grace was also sweetly naïve. When they arrived in Cincinnati and found a hotel, Thurston signed the register, "Howard Thurston and wife." She asked him, "When is your wife going to join us, Mr. Thurston?"

In fact, Thurston was awestruck by Grace's chaste, girlish charms, and he surprised himself by acting the perfect gentleman. He paid for her own hotel room and began introducing Grace as his sister. They traveled to Sparta, Wisconsin, where he rejoined the DeKreko Congress of Eastern Oddities.

The brother and sister act was good cover, as it prevented Grace from being recruited for the kootch show. Meanwhile, realizing that a detective was on his trail, Thurston began to arrange their marriage. It was the masterful work of a con man. On August 14, 1897, he wrote a letter to Grace's widowed mother, Lida Butterworth, in Indianapolis—Grace had conversationally provided the details of her family. The letter started with an obvious untruth. "I suppose Grace has told you about me and spoke of our relations to each other," and quickly moved on to, "We want to be married . . . we love each other. Am awaiting most patiently for a favorable reply."

But Thurston didn't want a reply; he arranged to have the letter sent from another town, so Mrs. Butterworth would be unable to trace the couple. Grace, of course, knew nothing of the letter.

Over dinner several nights later, he sweetly mumbled to Grace about how he loved her, and then kissed her on the cheek. She responded indistinctly, "Oh, I like you a lot." The next day, as they walked through town, Thurston steered her to a Seventh-day Adventist church. He interrupted the service to suddenly announce, "We want to get married!" The minister stopped his sermon and questioned the couple briefly. Thurston claimed that Grace was sixteen, the legal age to marry in Wisconsin. After a perfunctory exchange of vows, the minister pronounced them man and wife. Grace had not discussed marriage, but was now too astonished to object.

"Never the straightforward way for him," Grace later explained. "He played so many angles that he was always imagining a great many that were not there."

THE DEKREKO SHOW folded in the next town, Rhinelander, Wisconsin, and Howard and Grace organized their own small show. Grace was a quick study and a determined performer, learning the twists and turns of a kootch dance, as well as the skillful steps of a buck-and-wing, to augment her castanet dance. He billed her as Texola—he later explained that his grandmother had once seen the strange name in a dream and always considered it a good-luck charm. Grace also played the piano to accompany his act. And, of course, she learned her part in the "selling the watch" routine, which Howard still employed, as necessary, to skip out on a hotel bill.

Grace realized that Thurston was a mass of contradictions. In Duluth, Minnesota, he was thrown in jail because of his associations with a dealer in cheap jewelry. Thurston charmed the jailer, even if he failed to talk his way out of the charge. Grace visited him daily, until other friends raised the bail and transported him safely out of town. Grace noticed that Howard never returned to Duluth.

Although they were now man and wife, Howard could be strangely solicitous or shy. Shortly after their wedding, he bought her a doll and yards of gingham to make dresses for it. He also continued their "brother and sister" act in the beer halls, reasoning that it made Grace's dancing seem more desirable to the local men.

Of course, the pretense actually provided a world of trouble. At a honkytonk in Minnesota, Grace was expected to "work the house" after her dance, offering drinks, and maybe much more, in the private wine rooms. Thurston solved the problem by having a local friend whom he trusted sit with Grace in the wine room, buying bottles of beer so that she reached her quota of sales. In Montana, a group of toughs threatened to hang Howard—one of them had peered through the window of their boardinghouse and had seen him in bed with his "sister." Grace raced to their room and produced the marriage license.

Grace was awed by Howard's magic, his hard work and self-control. Her husband rose early each morning to practice, often standing before the mirror for hours at a time, repetitively running through each movement of the card routine. He was also meticulous about his hands. After spending months together, his wife realized that the "medicine" that he applied to his hands to soften them every night was actually his own urine. Thurston would wave his hands through the air until they were dry, and then wash them off before retiring for bed. Grace didn't comment. She found his habits and obsessions "strange and amusing."

REDUCED TO THESE small-town productions—in storefronts or beer halls—Thurston's act now started with a few welcoming remarks and moved on to the back-palming routine. He would reach into the air, producing single cards or causing them to magically pass from one hand to the other. He combined the moves with traditional palming, so that it seemed as if he could effortlessly pluck cards from any direction. His hand movements were sweeping and graceful, with a dancelike quality that quieted the crowd and established his credential as an expert magician.

Thurston demonstrated card throwing, a favorite trick from the Herrmann show. He held a card at his fingertips and spun it out toward the crowd. In a small room, the card snapped against the wall with impressive and frightening force. The crowd whistled appreciatively. Thurston then delivered cards to specific spectators, or snapped them against lamps or door frames around the room.

Depending on the length of the show, he proceeded with some classic card tricks. Cards that were selected by spectators ended up in his pocket. Other cards, named by the spectators, magically changed into different cards. If the audience was a small one, Thurston might step down to the spectator to demonstrate some fancy shuffling, ending by dealing himself the four aces. Finally, three or four cards were selected by the audience and shuffled back into the deck. Thurston placed the deck upright in a goblet and waved his hand over it. One by one, the selected cards seemed to climb up and out of the deck, so he could pluck them free and toss them to the audience.

By this time, Thurston's engaging patter and easy manner had completely charmed the audience. For his big finish, he brought up a local celebrity—it was best if it was the sheriff or mayor. Thurston looked into the man's sleeves, deftly reaching inside to withdraw a fan of cards. More cards were pulled from his coat pocket, followed by a pair of red long johns, and ladies' stockings and underwear. He opened the man's coat and pulled out a wash line strung with baby clothes. Finally, Thurston grabbed his assistant's shoulders, turning him so he was standing in profile to the audience. The magician reached straight down the man's coat collar, withdrawing a live duck. "Why, it's good old Socks, my pet duck! You weren't trying to . . . No, he must have taken a fancy to you and crawled into your hip pocket!" The appearance of the duck, squirming and flapping as he climbed from the coat, invariably made the victim whirl and fight, struggling to keep his coat on, then jumping from the stage and returning to his seat. Thurston could depend on gales of laughter to take him off the stage, and then bring him back for bow after bow.

When the Thurstons arrived in Belt, Montana, a boomtown next to a brand-new mine, they carried their trunks to the honky-tonk saloon. The bar had been stripped of glass, and the sheets of tin were ominously filled with bullet holes. Despite the tough clientele, Howard and Grace were a hit, and best of all the Belt audience showed their appreciation by throwing silver dollars. The next morning, over breakfast, Thurston told his wife about a new trick he'd wanted to try, an improvement on the old Rising Cards.

All day, he and Grace worked out the new routine on the Belt stage, fidgeting with the apparatus and planning every move. It was the most elaborate trick he'd attempted, relying on special preparation and Grace's hard work.

That night, as Thurston wrapped up his card routine, he told his audience that he was about to try an especially challenging trick. He shuffled the deck in his hands, then stepped into the audience, asking for five or six cards to be selected. They were replaced inside the deck, and Thurston boldly offered the cards to one of his spectators, asking that they be shuffled.

Unlike the traditional Rising Card Trick, Thurston didn't bother with a glass goblet. He returned to the stage and simply held the deck in his left hand, at arm's length. He waved his other hand over the top of the deck. "What was the name of the first card?" he said, pointing to a man in the audience. "Five of hearts!"

"Fine, fine. . . . Let's see the five of hearts." There was a pause, and then the five seemed to climb out of the deck. But now, it didn't simply push its way up; it rose, straight up in the air, levitating through the air for about a foot and a half, into Thurston's empty hand above the deck. The magician stopped to look at the card, then scaled it out to the audience, delivering it in the lap of the man who asked for it.

There was a long pause, and then a sustained burst of applause.

Thurston stepped to a different spot on the stage and called for the second card. This one was the jack of clubs. "Well, then, let's see if the jack is listening!" He snapped his fingers. The card soared out of the pack, straight up into his hands, and was then propelled into the audience.

Thurston breathed a sigh of relief. With the first two cards, he knew the trick was a hit. Grace, watching from the wings, clapped her hands in excitement.

For the third card, Thurston paused, waving his fingers over the deck. He was now relaxed and playful. "Up, up, up, up!" he called. It was a little verbal trill, his voice rising in inflection, that he'd heard Dwight Moody use in his sermons. "I can see him now," Thurston later wrote, "as he raised his voice and arms in describing the ascension of Elijah to heaven in his chariot of fire." The card sailed upward, through the air. Moody's words were now the perfect accompaniment to his magic, a mere card trick turned into a nearly religious experience.

"By the time he had caused the other cards to rise, and had thrown them to those who had called for them," Grace remembered, "the audience was on its feet, cheering." Silver dollars rained onto the plank flooring, and the audience grabbed Thurston, pulling him from the stage, lifting him to their shoulders and carrying him to the bar to offer drinks.

With the introduction of the Rising Cards on that night in 1897, Howard Thurston had achieved his boyhood dream, after more than a decade of hard work. He'd assembled the pieces of a magnificent new magic act. But the struggle had landed Howard and Grace precisely at the bottom of the entertainment ladder—in dives like Belt, Montana. "Up, up, up, up" was now Thurston's admonition to himself. Ironically, he had lost sight of any way to rise to the top.

FIVE

"DISINTEGRATION OF A PERSON"

he Rising Card trick became mythologized by Thurston's retelling. He claimed that he invented it in Boulder, Montana; as he was setting up the act, a fight broke out in the saloon and a bullet pierced the curtain, smashing the goblet in his hand. Thinking quickly, he improvised a new method for the Rising Cards, which didn't need the goblet.

His fictional story was assembled from events in Belt, Montana, where the Thurstons did witness an argument and fatal gunfight in the saloon. But his new card routine had nothing to do with the gunfire, it was the result of deliberate planning and rehearsal. The key part of his fiction was the word *invent*. He didn't invent it, he read it in a book.

New Era Card Tricks was a collection of the latest ideas in card tricks, compiled by August Roterberg, a respected Chicago magic dealer. Thurston bought the book when it was published that year, 1897, and poured over the contents as he and Grace traveled through the West. The book was filled with inspirations for new tricks, not just the standard sleight-of-hand routines that had been popular for decades, but fascinating descriptions of how card tricks were being brought to stage shows, using new routines and techniques. *New Era* contained the first written description of the Back Palm. Roterberg didn't mention Thurston—he didn't know him at the time—but he praised Houdini and Elliott for their handling of the amazing new maneuver. He also omitted Elliott's technique for showing both sides of his hand; the neat bit of sleight of hand that Thurston was using, as Roterberg wrote it, was "too difficult to describe."

Later in the book, Roterberg included the Cards Rising Through the Air, an improvement on the old Rising Cards routine. The trick had been invented by Carl Soerenson, a magician from Hamburg, Germany, but, oddly, Roterberg published it without any credit.

Soerenson's secret involved a thin, invisible black silk thread stretched horizontally across the stage, just over the magician's head. At either end, the thread passed through a small pulley or eyelet, and was then attached to a small bag of shot, to hold the thread under tension. In this way, the thread was a sort of invisible clothesline.

Certain cards had small clips on their backs, attached to the upper corners. In waving his hands over the pack, the magician contacted the thread, pulling it down. He then slipped it beneath the clips on the back card. By releasing his grip, the horizontal thread smoothly lifted the card, so it would soar into the magician's waiting hand. The rest of the trick was accomplished by the traditional magician's fare: forcing cards and palming cards.

Like any good trick, it probably didn't appear suddenly, as if by magic, in Boulder or Bolt, but was worked out through trial and error as the Thurstons traveled west. As Howard grew confident with the new trick, he and Grace discovered ways to improve it. By placing several horizontal threads across the stage, Thurston could change his position, moving closer or farther from the audience. Grace also suggested a simpler system of weights offstage and a neater cardboard flap on the back of each card. Magic is like any work of art. The tiniest, subtlest brushstrokes are perceived by the viewer and influence our impression of the entire picture. Their final flourish—a wonderful touch that would make the trick uniquely Thurston's—was still months away.

A GOOD NEW TRICK like the Rising Cards might have inspired the couple to reverse course, heading back east. But instead, Howard and Grace had set off in the direction of the Klondike, where gold prospecting had created boomtowns starved for entertainment. They were first tempted by stories of the goldfields and performances that had been rewarded with piles of gold nuggets, but by the time they'd reached Montana, Howard and Grace had met entertainers who had just escaped from the Klondike. They shook their heads over the primitive conditions and the dangerous men, telling the couple not to bother. Instead, Howard suggested that there were small mining towns in the western states, towns that the railroad didn't reach, where money could be made.

Grace was now an important part of their success, not merely standing next to her husband and handing him the props for the card act, but as "Texola, Coon Songs and Comedy Buck Dancing." Buck-and-wing was a flashy form of early tap dancing that had its roots in African-American performers. She bought her early lessons from a black dancer named Deyo in Montana. In many saloons and beer halls, it was the pretty, shapely Grace who the managers wanted in the show—they reluctantly agreed to also take the magic act. Grace had become a tough professional on and off the stage. She learned the formula of steps and smiles that would charm her audience and encourage tips. She also became adept at another kind of tap dance, taking a subservient role, flattering her husband and soothing his ego or quieting his temper when he felt ignored by the audience.

In Butte, Montana, the Thurstons shared the bill with Clare Evans and Mabel Maitland, a husband-and-wife dance team. They quickly became friends. Clare was a tall, thin, handsome Texan who performed in blackface with buck-and-wing dancing. Mabel Maitland was the daughter of a Seattle sea captain. Double-jointed, she performed an acrobatic act, and also teamed up with her husband for some dances. Grace noted that there was very little musicality to Mabel's performances; she "could not carry a tune in a roll of music, and had to watch her timing carefully." Evans and Maitland were recruited to join the Thurstons for their tour of smaller mining towns. Even more important than their dancing, Clare Evans was an expert horseman and had saved a little money, which he volunteered to finance their adventure. The couples bought a narrow-gauge wagon, reasoning that it would be easier to maneuver through the rough mountain trails, and a team of four sturdy ponies. They stocked the wagon with a tin Klondike stove, pans, kettles, cups, dishes, and sleeping cots, as well as their theatrical trunks and costumes. On the side of the wagon they painted their names and advertised "Thurston's Original Oddities, High-Class Specialty Artists . . . A Show of Great World Interest and Educational Value."

The wagon set off, pointed west, from Butte on July 1, 1898. It was a ridiculously naïve plan—three dancers and a confidence-man magician setting out as explorers—that became evident just three days later, when they started across the Great Divide and encountered snow. They hadn't brought a compass or a map; they hadn't thought to include any heavy clothing or boots.

A rancher advised them to turn back. "The country is rough enough for men on horseback. With that wagon and the women folks, you'll never make it." But the women remembered the clientele in the wine rooms that they'd left behind and voted to keep going. Whatever they found ahead, it would have to be better than that. The Evanses and Thurstons slowly negotiated up the slushy mountain trails; Clare drove the team as Mabel, Grace, and Howard walked next to the wheels with chocks so they could block the wheels as they began to skid and slide.

The weather warmed, from winter to summer, as they descended the mountains. Grace recalled that they "crawled" through the west, following rivers or railroads for any sign of civilization and stopping at any outpost and soliciting the local saloon to put on a performance: Southern Cross, Sula, Medicine Springs, Darby, or Hamilton, Montana. Thurston was right. The locals were often starved for entertainment. But he was wrong about the receipts. The audience could only offer bags of flour, lard, or canned food in payment. The four performers, often starved, were happy to accept the food.

Like many entertainers, Thurston came to live for each show, becoming more animated and engaged as he heard the audience assembling on the other side of the curtain. Grace, Clare, and Mabel would stand in the wings, marveling at his easy grace in front of a room full of strangers. He quickly convinced each person in his audience of his friendliness, talent, and quick wit, then worked hard to earn their applause. But during the days, as the performers set off for the next town or foraged for their next meal, Thurston grew nervous and irritable, barely speaking to his companions. Grace felt that the source of his frustration was deep—he was contemplating his stalled career. Now nearly thirty years old, Thurston realized that the inebriated cheers from each small Montana town left him with a sort of egotistical hangover, reminding him each morning why he was just a failure. Grace sensed that her husband had not only lost his patience but had never exhibited any personal faith. "If he had developed faith, he could have avoided the fretful bitterness that irritated him more and more with every passing day."

In one Utah town, the group was surprised by the wonderful provisions that had been offered in payment for their show—bags of oats, ducks, chickens, jerked beef, canned fruits and vegetables, sacks of cabbage, potatoes, beets, and onions. Grace looked down at the bags of groceries and began to imagine recipes for stew. Howard just sulked. "It's an insult. We're a good show. We ought to be living in good hotels and playing big theaters."

Just like his father, Howard felt sullen and confused after business failures. When his mood darkened, he accused Grace of flirting with other men at the saloons. And, like his father, he struck back by literally striking out, opening his hand and swinging at his wife. She didn't understand the significance of the gesture; she was smaller and faster than Howard, so she easily dodged the swings, giggled, and returned to put her husband at ease by jollying him through a conversation. But Clare saw what happened. The tall Texan had no tolerance for that sort of behavior. He became especially solicitous of Grace and was quick to remind Howard that he was watching.

IN UTAH, during a sudden thunderstorm, the troupe took refuge in an empty church. They hitched their ponies, lit the potbellied stove, and moved their cots inside for a peaceful night of sleep. The next morning, the church doors burst open and a crowd of Mormon men arrived to throw them out. In the midst of the shoving and yelling, Howard jumped atop his cot and held his arms out—in his white nightshirt, he looked almost angelic. Perhaps this is why the men froze for a moment and listened to the intruder.

"Gentlemen and brothers, let me introduce myself and extend apologies,"

Howard began, raising his voice to a smooth purr—part carnival talker, part evangelist. "I am Howard Thurston, and this is my wife, Grace. The others are members of my famous traveling company. We took refuge in your godly house against the sudden coming of His gracious rain. I intended to leave a substantial sum on the pulpit in the morning to help you further His good works. Perhaps we can join in a moment of prayer with the added strength of numbers." Realizing that he had seduced another audience, Howard paused briefly and then poured on the charm. "Coincidentally, I happen to be a theologian, and have often admired and studied the work of Joseph Smith. . . . I graduated from the Dwight L. Moody School. I wonder if anyone in the assembly is familiar with that blessed institution?"

As Grace, Clare, and Mabel settled uncomfortably into the pews, they listened to hours and hours of fervent prayers, Bible quotations, and fulsome blessings. The couples stayed another night, and the next morning they hitched their ponies to the wagon and left. Of course, there was no "substantial sum" left behind. The magician's skill at misdirection ensured that the offer had been neatly forgotten.

The trail became even more dangerous. One afternoon, as their wagon negotiated the walls of a canyon in the Unita Mountains, it skidded out of control on the hard trail. The performers attempted to lash the wheels, pulling on the wagon to stop it, but it continued to slide, careening around a curve and almost overtaking the ponies, who danced nervously in front of it as their hooves tripped and slipped on the rocky path. Clare pulled mightily on the ropes from the back but ended up being dragged. "Keep her going straight!" he called out. "We'll skid her to the bottom!" But by the time the wagon had hurtled to the canyon floor, bumping across a wide ditch and settling to a stop, they realized that Howard had been thrown from the wagon onto the trail.

They found him several yards away, lying prostate and moaning in pain. Luckily, they ended up a short distance from an abandoned ranch house. They carried Thurston inside and carefully placed him on his cot. He was badly bruised on the side of his body and had cracked two ribs. Grace bandaged him tightly with strips torn from a sheet. "He seemed so helpless," Grace remembered, "like a small boy whose world had been smashed to pieces." He could not raise his arms; he was unable to perform the card act or even rehearse his moves.

She sat by his side, nursing him back to health, offering bits of available food, "motherly tenderness, firmness, and a great deal of secret prayer." Thurston's own prayers had been confined to conning religious men. When he was broken, helpless, and frustrated, he couldn't imagine praying for help.

The spooky, empty ranch house in the hidden valley seemed analogous to their situation. They had reached the bottom, quite literally, and were now at the end of their money, at the end of their luck, in an abandoned spot far from the notice of anyone else. As Grace explored the house, it seemed haunted by some sudden tragedy—the rooms were still filled with clothing, furniture, and remnants of food, and in the farmyard she found the pitiful skeletons of cows, some with the skeletons of their unborn calves. On the kitchen door was pinned a note. "Gone with John. Goodbye. Ruth." The note chilled Grace. She considered how lucky a wife would have been to have such a home, and why she might have left it. In many ways, the house represented her dream of security.

AS CLARE AND MABEL searched for food, Grace sat by Howard's side for days. His nerves were soothed, and his ego satisfied, by detailing his life story to his wife. She dutifully filled the pages of her diary. He spoke honestly about his days of crime as the Nim Kid, his arrest in New York, and his time at Moody's School and Burnham Farm, before he rediscovered Alexander Herrmann's wonderful show. Thurston's long monologue seemed confessional and redemptive. "Grace, I guess sometimes I haven't been really kind or honest with you, but you've stuck all the way," he admitted. "I truly love you." She wrote those words, too, as it had seemed to come from such a desperate, vulnerable place in his heart. He promised to build her a real home when he found success in his career.

After five days, the group decided that they needed to leave and try to find a doctor. Howard was barely strong enough to consider the journey. Using wheel chocks and straining against leather straps, they began the slow, laborious climb out of the canyon. Thurston was confined to kneeling inside the wagon, holding on to the curved stays over his head and silently wincing with pain. "He would stare with disgusted resignation," Grace recalled. "I knew he considered this a low point in his life."

When they reached a town, they found a local doctor who examined Howard and applied new bandages, advising him to rest for several days. Clare went off to arrange a performance in town; a local rodeo guaranteed a crowd of people. Thurston couldn't present his act—his arms were still too sore. But he dressed and agreed to "run-'em-in-and-out" for the three shows, energetically gathering a crowd, promising marvels inside, and then shooing the audience so that the next group could be accommodated.

His sideshow duties rejuvenated him. The next morning he resumed rehearsals of his card act. He positioned his mirror low on the side of the wagon so he wouldn't have to lift his arms. Then he lit a cigar, one of the strong dark cheroots that he preferred, clenching it between his teeth and puffing like an engine. He methodically repeated his sequence of moves—cards appearing, and then disappearing—for hour after hour, cigar after cigar. Grace was delighted to see his determination.

Thurston returned to the act in Diamondville, Wyoming, a brand-new mining town that smelled of lumber and sparkled with silver nail heads against sheets of black tar paper. He could sense the silver dollars and gold nuggets that seemed to clatter in the pockets of the residents. "Here's where we get ours," he coolly announced to the troupe of entertainers. That night the card routine drew cheers, and Socrates the duck's appearance from the volunteer's coat nearly started a riot. The troupe added to their bankroll, traded their wagon for a proper stagecoach, and replenished their supplies—new linens, new pots and dishes. But shortly after that, the cold weather began to set in and they grew impatient with their life on the road. Passing through Denver, Thurston secured bookings at a local variety theater, the Alcazar. It sounded exotic and elegant. It turned out to be another miserable honky-tonk wine room, even if Thurston had made special arrangements so that the ladies were spared the usual duties of fraternizing with the customers.

The crowd at the Alcazar was not just enthusiastic, but insanely, danger-

ously wild, drunk, and determined to have a high time in their low-life surroundings. At the end of Mabel's act, some of the men lunged for her, dragging
her into the audience with loud whoops. Clare burst out of the wings and
jumped into the crowd, swinging his fists. Days later, Evans and Maitland decided to leave Denver. They'd been offered a booking at an East Coast dime
museum that they just couldn't resist—a real city, a real salary. Howard and
Grace reluctantly said good-bye. Clare Evans took Grace aside and warned
her about Howard's temper—he was a good man, but she had to keep her
eyes open.

Thurston and Texola were precisely back where they had started nearly a
year earlier. Howard sent to Cincinnati for another box of cheap watches and
returned to the usual con game: Grace resumed her tearful act of parting with
a worthless watch in lieu of paying the hotel bill. In a small town on the Ar-
kansas River, the magician befriended a red-bearded local policeman named
Britt, who was an amateur performer and a show business ham. Britt arrived,
at the end of the engagement, and apologetically explained that he had instructions to attach the Thurstons' theatrical trunks, since the couple had
failed to pay their bills. Thurston rose to the occasion. "Britt, we are a bit short
on cash, but I've wired for two hundred dollars, and it's being sent to Lamar,
where we will play tomorrow night." He charmed the constable into following
them so they could pick up the money. Of course, the money wasn't in Lamar,
and the couple earned almost nothing at the local saloon. Thurston flattered
the stagestruck constable into traveling to the next stop, Cripple Creek, even
borrowing money from him for their train tickets. He was a sucker.

When they arrived at Cripple Creek, and the Western Union agent informed the magician that no money had been wired, Thurston feigned aston-
ishment. He earnestly explained to Britt that he now realized the problem. The
money must have come to Lamar, after they'd left. He urged Britt to go back
and retrieve the cash, promising him a little extra money for his trouble. But
Britt was starting to come to his senses. "I hate to ask this, Mr. Thurston," he
said, "but maybe we ought to wire Lamar to make sure the money's there."

Thurston smiled. He thought this was an excellent idea. He went to Western Union and sent a wire, explaining that the Lamar operator would wire the

answer to their next engagement, in Colorado Springs, before they worked their way to engagements in Helena and St. Louis. When the trio arrived in Colorado Springs, Thurston walked to the telegraph office and asked if he had a wire waiting. And, as if by magic, there it was. He handed the form to Grace and Britt, carelessly catching a corner of the paper so that it tore away. The telegram was correctly dated and addressed to Howard Thurston. It read, "Yes, $200 received via wire for you. Operator Lamar."

Grace was dumbfounded by the message. The appearance of that money seemed to be the most incredible miracle her husband had ever accomplished. She knew that they weren't due any money. Howard grandly autographed a note empowering Britt to pick up the money, and then escorted the relieved lawman to the station. As the couple were finally free of the lawman, watching his train depart for Lamar, Grace turned to ask her husband, "Where did you get that telegram?"

"Maybe someone sent us two hundred dollars," Howard shrugged.

But she knew her husband too well. "What's the grift?"

He opened his hand; he'd been palming the torn corner of the telegram, identifying that it originated in Cripple Creek. Thurston had sent the message to himself, from Cripple Creek to Colorado Springs, and then torn away the address line.

Of course, there were no jobs in Helena or St. Louis. Thurston rattled off those cities to throw poor Britt off the scent. "Don't worry," Thurston told her. "Britt won't want his fellow citizens to know what a stagestruck fool he is. We'll never hear from him again." The couple picked up their trunks and set off for Denver.

They were broke again. They contemplated selling the apparatus and costumes for a few dollars. "There's one prop we don't have to sell," Howard said, eyeing his pet duck in his specially built carrying case. "We can eat him as he is." Howard and Grace couldn't actually bring themselves to kill and dress poor Socrates, but a friendly local butcher agreed to the deed. Socks had the last quack. As an experienced professional, flapping and strutting onstage, he had become tough and stringy. For years after that, Howard and Grace laughed about the most miserable day of their careers, "the day we ate the duck."

THE THURSTONS HAD SECURED another booking at a Denver honky-tonk. Howard later claimed to be working at the Alcazar, but the couple was probably appearing at a less reputable, unnamed spot in the city's red-light district. A magician named Hellmann, a student of Alexander Herrmann, was also appearing in town. He stopped in to watch the young card manipulator at work and admired his new Rising Card trick.

Days later, the Herrmann the Great company arrived in town for an engagement at the Tabor Grand Opera House, Denver's leading theater. Here was another chance for Thurston see a real magic show, and perhaps another opportunity to find work from a great magician. Thurston plotted a way to attend the performance; his busy schedule of shows at the local saloon prevented him from buying a ticket.

The Herrmann show had changed. In December 1896, Alexander Herrmann, Herrmann the Great, the charming, satanic performer who had inspired Thurston in his youth, succumbed to a heart attack as he was touring through New York state. He was mourned by the world of magicians and Broadway theater professionals. His widow, Adelaide, was determined to carry on with the show, and assistants and managers agreed to remain with the Herrmann the Great company, continuing their tours. Adelaide wired to Leon Herrmann, Alexander's twenty-nine-year-old French nephew, offering him the starring role.

Alexander had actually intended Leon as his successor, and Leon was a trained magician, performing in salons and the Folies Bergère in Paris. But his principle qualification seems to have been the family resemblance. Leon had thick black hair and a goatee. His uncle was known for his bubbling personality and bonhomie, as well as his hilarious French-accented English. By contrast, Leon spoke very little English. He was bloodless onstage, haughty and difficult offstage. Worst of all, he had never seen his uncle's show. When Leon Herrmann arrived in America, in January 1897, he knew less about Herrmann the Great than almost any theater fan in the country.

The new show was cobbled together from Leon's own tricks, Adelaide's special illusions and dance routines, and some of his uncle's favorite effects. In an effort to introduce Leon to the American public and offer him a primer in magic, the show had taken an uncomfortable step backward, offering old, tried-and-true features from Herrmann's warehouse.

In Denver, Hellmann met his old friend Billy Robinson on the street. Robinson had been a longtime assistant and confidant of Alexander Herrmann and was now the stage manager of Leon and Adelaide's show. During the course of their conversation, Hellmann raved about the wonderful new Rising Card trick that he'd seen Thurston perform. Robinson listened intently, twisting the tip of his mustache, and admitted that the trick sounded interesting. He explained that he wouldn't have a chance to go and see it—there's just too much to do with the Herrmann show—but if Hellmann saw the young man again— his name was Thurston, right?—Robinson would like to meet him.

That was the coincidental sequence of events that led to October 22, 1898. On that day, Thurston played his part in an astonishing performance and a controversial meeting of four of the world's greatest magicians. The incident displayed his distinctive mixture of ignoble confidence games, personal desperation, and a masterful talent to amaze and surprise.

SIX

"THE APPOINTMENT"

illy Robinson was one of the most important magicians produced by America, but the public almost never heard his name. He was born in 1861 in New York into a theatrical family, and then learned magic from the inside, by working at Anthony and Francis Martinka's famous Manhattan emporium of magic—a store and workshop that created the specialties for magicians around the world.

Robinson teamed up with a saloon showgirl, Olive Path; her diminutive size earned her the nickname Dot. Their early act landed them positions with Harry Kellar's touring magic show, where Billy presented his own magic, worked as an onstage assistant, and supervised the show backstage. Dot took part in Kellar's illusions. The duo became renowned magic assistants. Billy was discreet, dependable, and knowledgeable about every aspect of the theater and magic. Dot was the perfect size for wriggling through a trapdoor.

They were so good that the Robinsons were hired away from Kellar by Alexander Herrmann, America's greatest magician. The Robinsons admired Kellar for his hard work and professionalism, and Herrmann for his instinctual talent and offstage bonhomie. For several seasons, they were traded and back and forth between Herrmann and Kellar, like prized players on a baseball team.

Something about these frantic seasons, and Robinson's heady work between the two rivals, hardened his personality. His knowledge of both shows—all the secrets—compromised his discretion and involved him in espionage. Herrmann began including copies of Kellar's illusions; Kellar quizzed his employee about Herrmann's tours. Robinson, once the dependable figure behind the scenes, became both valued and feared for this treachery. He gradually achieved the lofty reputation of the man responsible for each magician's success.

Billy and Dot Robinson had been traveling with Alexander Herrmann when he died, and they were quickly recruited for the new Herrmann show, starring Adelaide and Leon. They found Adelaide to be suspicious and manipulative. More than likely, her tough business sense was inspired by her late husband's careless spending and lavish lifestyle, which had left her with a raft of unpaid bills. "[Alexander Herrmann] was all right," Robinson wrote to a friend. "He made friends, and his wife made them into enemies for him. She used everyone for a sucker."

The situation was even more uncomfortable when Leon arrived. He was younger than Billy Robinson, far less experienced in magic, and completely unfamiliar with his uncle's specialties. Leon chafed at the magic lessons from his American associates. Billy and Dot resented the way they were supposed to teach this imposter to impersonate Herrmann the Great. Robinson confided to a friend that Leon was "one the dumbest fellows I ever saw." The show was still titled The Herrmann the Great Company, trading on Alexander Herrmann's famous reputation, but there no longer was a "Great" holding the troupe together. By the time the company reached Denver, the atmosphere backstage crackled and sparked with tension.

IN THE LOBBY of Denver's Tabor Grand Opera House, Howard and Grace ogled the colorful lithographs. One, titled "Leon Herrmann's Art of Palming," portrayed a montage of Leon's hands in various positions, manipulating balls and coins, concealing them in his hands. Thurston pulled out a deck of cards, stood beneath the poster, and began his sequence of manipulations. Perhaps, he thought, he could attract some admirers in the theater lobby.

Even better, Herrmann might challenge him. He wasn't sure exactly what he was doing, but he was desperate to steal a few rays of Herrmann's spotlight. Some passersby watched his performances, but Herrmann's company was too smart to call attention to the upstart magician. Thurston dashed back to the saloon for his own performances and returned to entertain Herrmann's patrons before the evening show.

During one of these impromptu shows, Grace noticed a man standing at the back, coolly admiring Thurston's manipulations as he twisted the tip of his mustache. The man pushed his way to the front of the crowd and offered his hand. "You're the one doing the Rising Cards at the local joint," he said. "You've seen it?" Howard asked. The man shook his head. "No, I didn't have a chance. But I hear you've got something, a real corker. If you come by tomorrow afternoon, I'd like to talk to you about it. I'll be backstage. I'm Billy Robinson."

As Grace and Howard hurried from the lobby to their own show, Thurston was dumbfounded. "Billy Robinson!" he kept repeating. "He's supposed to know more about magic than any man living. They call him the magician maker!"

The next day, Thurston arrived at the theater alone and was led to a small workroom under the stage, where Billy Robinson was surrounded by props—the cloth covers, metal stands, and bouquets of silk posies—that were used in the Herrmanns' show. He was repairing a secret compartment in a metal vase, holding solder against a red-hot tool. Billy stopped his work and signaled for Thurston to draw up a chair.

"I see you're a student of Dr. Elliott," Robinson said. Thurston nodded mutely, surprised to be plunged into a discussion of card trickery. "I can tell those moves are from Elliott, by how you transfer to the front palm. It's the right way to do it." Billy picked up a deck of cards and plucked a single card off the top. He then performed a short sequence of back palming, effortlessly, perfectly, rotating his empty hand in the air. "It's the thumb that covers the movement, isn't it?" Robinson drawled. He had been one of the first to be taught by Elliott, one of the first initiates to the precious new maneuver. Thurston swallowed hard. He had spent the night rehearsing various propositions and boasts about his card routine, but Robinson quickly pulled the rug from beneath him.

"So, tell me about your Rising Cards," Robinson said.

"Well, I'm sorry that I can't actually do it for you right here," Thurston started. He stood, acting out the sequence of moves. He demonstrated how he had cards selected, and returned to the deck. Then he struck a dramatic pose, with his hand held over the imaginary cards. As he reached the crescendo, he said, "The card rises straight up, right up through the air into my hand." Robinson nodded perfunctorily, looked down at his soldering, and returned to work.

"Yep, that's what I thought," he said. "It was in a German book some years ago, and then in Roterberg's book. A horizontal thread and a hook card. It's interesting because the thread is horizontal. . . . A nice touch." Thurston smiled. He couldn't argue with the magic expert, who must have been familiar with Roterberg's *New Era Card Tricks*; Robinson had even contributed a trick to the contents of the book.

"Well, I won't say if you're right or wrong," Thurston tried equivocating, his voice dropping as he slid back into his chair. "But I am sure you know the trick."

He'd just failed as a magician. There was a long pause as he watched Robinson drip solder onto the metal vase. Thurston now switched to the con.

"You know, if I can show my trick to Herrmann, maybe I can sell it to him. That is, if I needed to make a little money, you'd understand. . . ."

Robinson looked up at him. With Grace back at the hotel, Thurston needed to develop his own sob story. "I won't forget your kindness," he continued. "I am hard up. My wife is sick, and right now we're working in a dive. I must have some money and this might be my chance. . . . You won't spoil my game, will you?"

Billy smiled. "No, of course not. You won't get him to your saloon, but you could perform it on our stage. Tell him you'll do it this afternoon. Tell him you talked to me. Herrmann's staying at the Palace Hotel."

A great assistant, a loyal assistant, would have protected the magician. After all, Billy Robinson's job was to advise Leon Herrmann as an expert in magic.

But he had more sympathy for the destitute card magician, the total stranger. He might have thought it would be funny, or humiliating, if the sophisticated Paris magician were to be fooled by a published card trick.

The secret of any great con game is the moment when the mark, the victim, constructs a con game in his own mind. The hotel managers accepted Thurston's cheap watches because they greedily thought they were taking advantage of a desperate young man who had stupidly offered a precious, jewel-encrusted watch in exchange for a modest hotel bill. That's the point at which the mark becomes complicit, and the success of the confidence game is assured. When Thurston left the Tabor Grand that afternoon, Robinson was ready to serve as the accomplice. Or maybe—this was the most wonderful part of the plan—it now seemed to be Robinson's con game, and Thurston was the accomplice.

THURSTON PICKED UP GRACE, and they both ran to the Palace Hotel, asking for Mr. Herrmann. The magician met them in the lobby, bowing with courtly grace. Thurston was momentarily dumbstruck. Leon showed a definite resemblance to his wonderful uncle, the same dark eyes and expressive, bobbing eyebrows. But something was wrong; it was as if he were a burlesque actor playing Herrmann. Leon spoke with an impenetrable French accent and made himself clear only with a series of cartoonish, exaggerated gestures—shrugging, frowning, or spreading his fingers and then slowly separating his hands, as if he were holding an ever-expanding balloon.

Leon Herrmann was intrigued to hear about the trick, but puzzled when Thurston explained that he couldn't perform it there, at the hotel. He offered to present it on Herrmann's stage.

Herrmann grimaced. "Eem-poss-ee-buhl! On my stage? Ziss iss eem-poss-ee-buhl!"

"Mr. Herrmann," Grace interrupted, talking slowly. "You might think that we would need to move your equipment or touch any of your props. But we wouldn't." Thurston added, "Mr. Robinson will supervise everything." Herrmann reluctantly agreed, telling the couple that he would come to the theater that afternoon.

As they dashed from the hotel, Howard surprised his wife by making a sharp turn and careening through the doors of the Denver Post building. Once his heels reached the shiny terrazzo floor, Thurston stopped, smoothed his hair, stepped over to the man behind the desk, and politely asked for the city editor's office. "I have a news story," he announced, catching his breath. The man pointed his thumb at the newsroom upstairs. Howard and Grace bounded up the stairs and pushed their way through the door.

The editor listened to Thurston's boast and suggested that it would only be a news story if the great magician would actually admit that he was fooled. He thought it was unlikely. But Thurston's enthusiasm won him over, and he agreed to supply a reporter, who could hide in the wings and watch the impromptu performance.

Howard and Grace circled back to their hotel room and filled their pockets with their special playing cards, a package of small brads, and rolls of fine silk thread. On the way to the Tabor Opera House, they stopped at a hardware store to buy a tack hammer. They couldn't pick up their tools at the honky-tonk, as by now they'd missed the afternoon performances and couldn't risk the wrath of the manager.

STANDING ON Leon Herrmann's stage that afternoon, Thurston was momentarily transfixed. There was Alexander Herrmann's gold-leaf Louis Quatorze table, the one he'd seen the magician use when he was a boy. Thurston knew that the surface was adorned with a sophisticated system of trapdoors and secret compartments. Pushed to one side was the distinctive Artist's Dream illusion, and hanging from one edge of the framework was Herrmann's blazing red Mephistopheles cloak. Bolted to the floor, behind the back curtain, was a frame of metal that had been carefully wrapped in canvas. Thurston knew that it must have been the secret device used in Trilby, the levitation illusion he'd seen, in which Madame Herrmann took the role of Svengali's beautiful protégée. The darkened stage seemed haunted by visions from Thurston's youthful dreams; the scenery smelled of layers of turpentine and paint, the legacy of seasons on the road, and the wooden floor creaked mysteriously under each step. "So charged was the silence with the personality of the man, all that I remember," he later wrote, "is that as I stood there, around the paraphernalia that had once belonged to the master of all magicians, I was suddenly over-whelmed with a sense of unreality."

Thurston regained his senses with a familiar "tap, tap" sound. Grace was using the tack hammer to pound several brads into the edges of the scenery. She had begun to stretch threads across the stage for the Rising Card trick.

They waited, walking in tight circles, whispering to themselves. Herrmann didn't show up.

The reporter balked; he'd been waiting in darkness at the side of the stage, but wondered if the meeting would ever happen. Billy Robinson assured Thurston that Herrmann must have taken an unexpectedly long dinner. He would have to arrive for his own show that night.

If they were going to perform it just before the show, it meant that the audience would be arriving in the auditorium. Herrmann would be standing on the stage, just a few feet from the trick. Thurston thought it was still worth a chance. He located the electrician, working in the wings. "I'm going to need your help. I can't have the stage brightly lit." The electrician stepped away from the tall iron control board studded with porcelain handles. "Tell me what you need, young man."

"I'm going to call for lights. And I want you to bring up the borders. Slowly. Very slowly. I'll call for more light. Just keep them coming. But when I put my hand in my pocket, like this, I want you to hold the lights right there. No matter what I say. Even if I call for more light, you hold it right there. Understand?"

"I watch for your hand in your pocket," the electrician repeated.

"I can't thank you enough," Thurston told him. He pulled his hand from his pocket and tossed the man a ten-dollar gold piece. "Get yourself some cigars and a good drink after the show."

A little after seven-thirty, the stage door swung open with a loud clatter and Thurston heard the sound of raised voices. The company manager, Edward

Thurnaer, had just been told about the planned show onstage and he was loudly protesting. They wouldn't be able to delay the curtain. But Leon Herrmann dismissed him with a wave of his hand. "Yes, yes, I know. If zee man is here now, I will see ziss treek!" Leon, his wife, Marie, and his aunt Adelaide, were still in their coats and hats. They pushed past Thurnaer and strode grandly onto the stage. Grace gasped to see the group pass beneath the stretched threads. Madame Herrmann's feathered hat almost snagged, but fortunately no one noticed the threads. A small group of stagehands and assistants followed the magician onto the stage, as well as Billy Robinson, who stood at the back of the group.

"Mr. Herrmann!" Thurston greeted him like a long-lost friend. Thurston maneuvered the group so they were standing with their backs to the curtain. He could already hear some of the audience, beyond the drapery, arriving to take their seats. He knew that, in a matter of minutes, Herrmann would be pressed to go to his dressing room to change and apply his makeup, and Robinson would need to set the stage for the performance. He felt his heart racing.

"Let me have some light!" he called out to the electrician. The overhead rows of glass globes sparked with golden pinpoints, then glowed with a cool blue illumination. "More light," Howard called out. The lamps grew brighter. Thurston pushed his hand into his pocket. "Still more light!" Thurnaer looked nervously at his watch. "We need to hurry," he said. Herrmann made a casual gesture, flourishing his fingers above his shoulder, as if dismissing the remark.

Howard froze, with his hand in his pocket, "as if he were waiting for a streetcar, without a care in the world," Grace recalled. "Brighter lights!" he called again. The electrician now understood the ruse. He yelled back, "You've now got all the power I can spare for you, young feller!"

He asked four people to withdraw cards from the deck that he was shuffling in his hand. They each looked at their cards and then replaced them in the deck. He stepped back several paces. Grace watched from the wings as he gestured casually with his hand over his head, contacting the first invisible thread. He smoothly lowered it to the edge of the cards.

Thurston asked for the name of the first card chosen. "It was the ten of diamonds," Marie Herrmann told him. "Ten of diamonds, come forth," Thurston called. And the card sailed up smoothly through the air. He caught it, and then tossed it forward, spiraling it into the hands of one of the attentive spectators.

He repeated the trick with each card, deliberately stepping to different positions on the stage. One of the stagehands, attempting to throw him, called the wrong card. Thurston knew that the man was trying to fool him; he said that he'd return to that one. He asked Herrmann for his card. "Zee ten of clubs!" "Up, up, up," Thurston exhorted. The ten rose smoothly to his hand, and he stepped forward to present the card to the magician.

The young magician now took a spot several paces closer to his audience and asked again for the last card. "I was pulling your leg. It was really the jack of hearts," the stagehand admitted. He had barely finished speaking the name of the card, and the jack of hearts sailed through the air into Thurston's hand.

A few stagehands applauded. Robinson quickly turned away. "Fifteen minutes! Let's strike this, and set the entrance drop! Props!" And the group scattered to the wings.

Grace reached up, snagging the threads and pulling them free of the brads. She noticed Herrmann was taking several steps toward Thurston, with an expansive gesture, twirling his hand in the air. She suspected that he was guessing at the secret and feeling about for threads. But she was too fast; he just missed them.

Thurston moved Herrmann toward the reporter in the wings. "Did you like the trick?" he asked. *"Très bien."* Herrmann shrugged. "Did it mystify you?" "Yes, M'sieu." Thurston smiled and looked up at the reporter, who nodded. Relieved, Thurston followed up by whispering a few technical details to Herrmann. Yes, the trick was accomplished with threads, he told him, horizontal threads, and a special way of preparing the cards. Herrmann nodded. He was now uncomfortable with the discussion, which was going on too long. He was anxious to get to his dressing room. "Do you want to buy the trick?" Thurston called after him. "Mmm, ees poss-ee-buhl. Call for me at zee hotel!"

Madame Herrmann pushed her way past the young magician. "Very nice. Now please get off the stage. Please!"

He glanced back over his shoulder. The stage had been transformed into an elegant drawing room, ringed with tables full of bright scarves and shiny metal vases, in anticipation of Herrmann's show.

The stage door slammed on Grace, Thurston, and the reporter and they were suddenly startled by the calm. Howard took a deep breath of the cool air. "Sure, we'll print it," the reporter told him nonchalantly. "He said you mystified him. That's what my editor told me to get. I got it."

AT THREE the next morning, Howard and Grace were pacing outside the newspaper office, waiting for the early edition of the Sunday paper. When the first copies were brought down to the office, he flipped through the pages to find his prize. He had two columns. A neat pen sketch showed Thurston, in profile, performing the Rising Cards for Herrmann and his group; the French magician was distinctive with his homburg and waxed goatee. The headline proclaimed, "Herrmann, the Magician, Mystified by Another Magician." Thurston groaned. His name didn't make it into the headline. But the reporter had done his job; the story was succinct and accurate, ending with a brief summation of Thurston's résumé and the statement, "He had mystified the mystifier."

Late that morning, Thurston foolishly stopped by the Palace Hotel to meet with Herrmann. Drunk with the excitement of the previous night, he had remembered that Herrmann invited him to talk about buying the trick. By the time Thurston arrived, Herrmann had seen the newspaper and realized that he'd been double-crossed. The meeting, such as it was, must have consisted of some brief, Parisian-accented American obscenities. Thurston slunk back to his room. "How did it go?" Grace asked. "It didn't," Thurston growled. "Leave me alone!"

They bought stacks of papers and spent the morning cutting articles to send to agents and theater managers, but they heard nothing from the East Coast agents and remained in the Denver area for months, circling through the same mining towns, honky-tonks, and sideshows, anxiously checking the mail every day.

By early 1899, Thurston had decided upon his plans. He would have his own magic show, one of the world's greatest magic shows, in ten years. It would be the sort of show to rival Herrmann. He could only do it if he were a success in New York. Howard and Grace counted their money, packed their bags, and headed east.

THE BACKSTAGE SHOW at the Tabor Grand Opera House had been a magnificent con game. When Herrmann was fooled, it was because he had been fooled by the sneaky little touches—the multiple threads, the little show with the electrician, Grace's deft work in the wings. Most of all, he was fooled because he couldn't imagine that his own stage could have been prepared to deceive him, with his own stage manager supervising.

That strange backstage performance changed the fortunes of every magician who was there.

That night marked the beginning of the end for Billy Robinson, who had acted duplicitously with the Herrmanns. Oddly, he never mentioned the newspaper reporter who had been hidden backstage. It was Thurston's inclusion of a reporter that should have angered Robinson. If Thurston had really wanted to sell the trick to Herrmann, if he needed the money, there would have been no reason to contact a reporter.

Robinson must have known about the reporter all along—as the stage manager, he must have seen him. Was Robinson's intention to humiliate Herrmann? He later complained that Thurston had been ungrateful, and Herrmann vindictive. "I done it all against Herrmann's wishes, also our manager's. They raised hell to think I would do such a thing. Well, I had hell every day for months, and all on account of doing a good turn for a dirty loafer." Early in 1899, he and Dot quit the show. It was the best decision Robinson ever made.

After the Robinsons left, the Herrmann show rattled apart. Less than a year later, Adelaide Herrmann had lost all her patience with her nephew and developed her own act. It made her a star and began a long successful career for this famous woman magician.

Several years later, Leon adopted the billing "Herrmann the Great," promptly generating a lawsuit from Adelaide. Herrmann the Great was the title of her husband, she insisted. The judge was confused by the case, reasoning that Herrmann was Leon's real name and he could use his own discretion if he wanted to call himself great. Leon put together a shorter act and then returned to Europe several years later. He was just forty-two years old when he contracted pneumonia and died in Paris in 1909.

When Thurston walked out of the Tabor Grand, he was only months from real stardom. The *Denver Post* article disappointed Thurston, but he and Grace managed to concoct a billing, "The Man Who Mystified Herrmann," from the headline. It proved to be just enough of a boast to call attention to the handsome new card magician, the modest snowball that began rolling down the hill. By the time they arrived in New York in 1899, they were in the middle of a new sort of avalanche, called vaudeville.

SEVEN

"THE MAGICIAN'S ASSISTANT"

arry Thurston settled back in his easy chair and lifted a glass of beer. "To my big brother, the great magician!" He then let out a small laugh that made Howard and Grace slightly uncomfortable. As Howard tipped his glass, he realized that problem was inevitable—Grace had to meet Harry sometime. But Harry's freewheeling conversation had worked Howard to the edge of his seat: he would ask about Howard's business—the take in the mining towns, or the sideshow attractions in Denver—and then suddenly lose focus, interrupting the answer with some embarrassing story from their past. "Remember how we tished those showgirls in St. Louis?" he'd chuckle. "I worked with that little blonde from the kootch show. The one you liked. She's still got some moves, lemme tell you!"

A warm spring breeze was blowing off Lake Michigan, and Harry's downtown apartment offered a beautiful view of Chicago. But Grace couldn't take her eyes off her strange brother-in-law. He definitely resembled her husband, and even spoke with the same warm, nasal hum. But Harry was fatter, coarser, and nastier. His words were slurred and sprinkled with street slang; his interests were narrowly focused, from dime museum attractions to petty crime. He exhibited all of Howard's worst traits, and Grace waited, in vain, for any of the redeeming qualities. "During the years that followed I never became friendly with Harry," Grace wrote, "and he never showed much enthusiasm for me, either. Proving, perhaps, that first impressions are important."

Harry had returned to the Midwest and worked for a season as a bill poster for Ringling Brothers Circus. He settled in Chicago and began buying interests in dime museums, the cheap little urban sideshows that had served as the last refuge for his big brother: ten, twelve, sixteen short shows a day, in quick rotation. Harry's dime museums naturally focused on the Oriental kootch dancers and supplemented the shows with games of chance and slot machines.

Harry was making money, and a reunion with him was a small sacrifice to inspire his largesse. Howard hinted about a little loan, and discreetly asked about booking their act in the Midwest. Harry was only too happy to help; his check, and his promise that he knew the slickest agents in Chicago, were his upper hand in a friendly game of sibling rivalry. Thanks to Harry, a Chicago agent gave Howard and Grace a short tour of small cities through Illinois, Indiana, Michigan, and Ohio.

With their new bookings, Thurston ordered fancy new posters from the Donaldson Litho Company of Newport, Kentucky. The pretty one-sheet stone lithograph was printed in full color and portrayed the scene backstage at the Tabor Grand, as Thurston performed before Herrmann with his Rising Cards. Their new letterhead advertised "America's Premier Card Manipulator," "The Man Who Mystified Herrmann," as well as "Texola, Comedy Buck Dancer."

They arrived in New York City in the summer of 1899 and settled into a cheap boardinghouse on Lexington Avenue. Harry Houdini was also in New York that summer and renewed his acquaintance with Thurston. Houdini's career had almost paralleled Thurston's, from their earliest meeting at Chicago's Columbian Exposition. They had both been mired in small-time show business—Houdini had toured with a circus and specialized in dime museum shows—and were poised for imminent success. Houdini was naturally circumspect of Thurston, who had been working small towns out west, virtually unnoticed by any other performers. After Houdini's own failure as the "King of Cards," it was typical of his personality that he scoffed at Thurston's achievements and still felt possessive of the Back Palm and card flourishes.

Even worse, the New York agents continued to doubt Thurston. The sleight of hand impressed them, but invariably he was told that card tricks were far too small and cheap for the stage—it was the sort of thing only suitable for a garden party or a men's clubroom. Thurston realized that the act needed an audience; if only the agents could have seen how it worked for the rough-and-tumble miners in the tar-paper saloons of Montana, they would have been convinced.

Grace's blackface tap-dancing act was an easier sale. A pretty, perky little minstrel was still fashionable at the end of the century. She was offered a job at Heck and Avery's, a New York dime museum, and Howard reluctantly agreed that she should accept.

Thurston spent his evenings sitting in Union Square, waiting for Grace to finish her turns, deftly practicing his card sleights with his arm tossed over the back of a park bench. He was there in July, on his thirtieth birthday, feeling sorry for himself, surrounded by the twinkling electric lights that outlined the theaters on Broadway, and imagining his own name illuminated brightly. He felt all the more foolish for reaching middle age with such adolescent fantasies. Thurston recalled watching the Broadway swells pass him by, "wishing I could go to Dennett's, for a cup of coffee or a plate of griddle cakes; but I did not have enough money even for this indulgence." One evening, a stout man with a sparse brush mustache and tortoiseshell glasses, stopped and introduced himself. He hadn't recognized the magician, but he recognized the card moves. He was a fan of magic himself, a writer for the *New York World*. John Northern Hilliard was Thurston's age; he shared his recollections of great magicians he had seen and offered encouragement for Howard's efforts.

Thurston received another invitation to audition for two agents, this time on a Monday morning at the roof garden at the New York Theater, on Forty-fourth Street. Here was the same problem; he'd be facing another empty theater with a couple of silent, cigar-chewing faces staring back at him, trying to decide if the act was funny, or original, or big enough to entertain.

Thurston put a small ad in the Sunday paper: "Wanted, 1000 men. $1 for 1 hour. Apply 10 a.m. Monday Morning. The New York Roof." When Grace heard about the plan, she knew that it was coldhearted. She told Howard it "would be hard on a lot of men looking for work." But she realized that the ad was a good idea, concluding, "It's a hard world."

When Howard and Grace arrived at the New York Roof the next morning, the seats were filled with noisy men and the lobby buzzed with even more hopeful applicants. The agents were huddled behind the curtain. "What's going on here?" they asked Thurston. "We're supposed to be using this theater, but those men told us they'd read an ad in the paper offering them work." Thurston blinked slowly, the picture of innocence. "Well, I certainly can't imagine! But then, you're auditioning some new acts, aren't you? That's an old amateur night trick, filling up the theater. These non-professionals will try anything to get attention."

The agents decided to cancel the audition. "No, no. I'll handle it," Thurston told them, shooing the agents into the auditorium. He walked onstage. "Gentlemen, there is some sort of misunderstanding." The crowd grew quiet. "Until the man in charge arrives, I wonder if you'd like a little entertainment?" They cheered. He performed the act—the card manipulations, the Rising Cards, and the duck finale, with their new Socrates—winning laughter from the crowd and gratitude from the agents. They reciprocated with some out-of-town bookings.

BUT THE MAN Thurston had set in the crosshairs was Walter Plimmer, a British theatrical agent who booked vaudeville. He was younger than Thurston and was a notoriously tough judge of talent. He was also impossible to see and wouldn't return messages. One day in August 1899, Thurston grew tired of waiting. He and Grace walked past the secretary into Plimmer's office. He slammed the door as Grace spun around and turned the lock. Plimmer looked up with his eyes wide. Thurston had already pulled the cards from his pocket and begun his manipulations. "Good afternoon, I'm Howard Thurston."

"Yes, Thurston, I know. Another magician. I've seen it a hundred times."

"No, you haven't seen me a hundred times. You wouldn't see me once. But you're going to see it now." As he spat out the last few words, he was pumping through his card manipulations.

The agent leaned back, watched, and was impressed enough to let Thurston continue: cards disappeared at his fingertips, tumbled from his hands, changed into other cards, or were effortlessly propelled across the office, snapping against the window behind the agent.

Plimmer smiled and began scrawling on a piece of his stationery. "I can't use you right now. But tomorrow, take this note downtown to Tony Pastor."

Grace and Howard walked out in a daze, giddy and celebratory, weaving down the sidewalks back to their apartment. After their years of struggle, it couldn't really be that easy, could it? The right audition in the right office, and they'd suddenly heard the most magical name any variety act ever heard: Tony Pastor.

TONY PASTOR didn't actually invent vaudeville. It was forged out of the saloon variety entertainments, dime museums, and minstrel shows of nineteenth-century America. Pastor was one of a number of producers who worked hard to distill the very best and scrub clean everything else. But his acquaintances usually awarded him the honor because it made a better story. In a field of monsters and cads, Tony Pastor was beloved, an entertainment phenomenon and a New York institution.

He was born Antonio Pastor in New York City in 1832 and worked for Barnum as a child prodigy singer, and then performed as a blackface minstrel, a clown and ringmaster in the circus, a trick rider or clog dancer. He was short and stout, with a long mustache and wavy black hair. By most accounts his dancing was slightly ridiculous and his voice was merely a raspy baritone. But he learned how to act a song, "putting it over" with exaggerated gestures and a graceful, friendly personality. In 1861, he managed his own theater and hosted the shows each evening. He was always the star. An evening might begin with Pastor's latest songs. He specialized in funny or sweetly romantic ballads, as well as stirring patriotic tunes in support of the Union troops. Then the show would offer some variety acts and conclude with a comic afterpiece, a short parody of a popular play or opera. He marketed his shows to women, eliminating the worst qualities of the beer halls, the loose waitresses, blue humor, smoking and drinking. He was a fine judge of talent and had inspired instincts about the public's tastes. Pastor is credited with discovering a generation of important stars, including the era's most famous chanteuse, Lillian Russell.

As New York's theater district gradually moved uptown, to more respectable neighborhoods, Pastor relocated to better surroundings, out of the Bowery and on an inevitable march up Broadway. In 1881, he finally settled into Tony Pastor's New 14th Street Theater, just off Union Square in the basement of Tammany Hall.

The word *vaudeville* was a hybrid to describe the new phenomenon and brand it as a new product; it was probably derived from the French phrase for "voice of the city." Tony Pastor himself avoided using the word for most of his career. He thought it sounded sissy and French. He preferred calling it variety. By the 1890s, his gradual innovations had been acquired by vaudeville entrepreneurs in uptown theaters, who systematized and popularized the entertainment.

By 1896, it was Pastor who was racing to keep up and fill the seats at his thousand-seat theater. He adopted the latest vaudeville trend, continuous entertainment. This was a sort of all-day buffet of talent, in which a collection of dazzling acts followed, one after another, in cycles of performances from about noon to eleven p.m. Patrons could pay for a ticket and watch the whole cycle or any part of it. It was hard on the acts, but an attractive novelty for the public—entertainment as a factory assembly line. By July 1899, Pastor included American Vitagraph features on every bill, a few short subjects courtesy of the latest fashion, the motion picture.

When Howard and Grace walked into his office, Pastor's esteemed status had led them to anticipate some sort of titan, the toughest, most judgmental producer of all. "He could point you toward the big time, or doom you to the sticks," Grace believed. Instead, they found the elder statesman, a sweet sixty-seven-year-old, sitting behind his desk in a small office of framed pictures and Victorian knickknacks. "You want an engagement?" he asked. "Billy tells me you're the best magician he's seen." Thurston nodded. Pastor smoothed his brush mustache. "Come to rehearsal Monday at ten o'clock." Quickly, Grace spoke up. "You realize that we're two acts. I sing and dance in blackface. Can I come, too?" Pastor smiled. "Yes, my dear, you come too." He turned back to Howard. "How much do you want for the act?"

Thurston had been advised by Clare Evans to always place a high value on his services, "if you want a manager to appreciate your work." Thurston had rehearsed this moment and knew that he wanted to ask for the top price. "Eighty dollars."

Pastor looked at him, Thurston recalled, "with a quizzical smile and a twinkle in his kindly eyes."

"Young man, I have offered you an engagement. I don't know what you can do, but from your looks I think you're all right. As you're a stranger in New York, your name will not add a cent to my business," Pastor started. "Besides, I can engage all the well-known acts I want at eighty dollars. Fifty dollars is all that I can pay you. But I'll give you a contract for eighty dollars, and charge you thirty dollars to put your name on the billboards. If your act's a success, you can show the contract to other managers and it will establish your price."

"BY NOW, I was a capable entertainer in my own right," Grace later wrote. "I was always adequate, the kind of act managers will keep on when they're too lazy to book another." But since Grace had secured her own solo act at Pastor's, Howard needed a new assistant for his show. On Saturday, he borrowed eighty cents from his landlady and placed a small ad in the newspaper for a young man, a "colored assistant."

Thurston was following in the tradition of his idol, Alexander Herrmann. Herrmann had always featured a black assistant whom he nicknamed Boomsky, relying on him for exaggerated comic reactions or burlesque physical humor. For example, it was Boomsky's job to borrow a hat from a man in the audience, and then "accidentally" trip on the way back to the stage, falling on the hat and crushing it. Herrmann would upbraid the assistant. Boomsky would roll his eyes with comic chagrin. The magician then proceeded with his trick, miraculously restoring the hat. Boomsky was a theatrical role filled by a number of African-American performers; the last was a young man named M. Hudson Everett, who continued to work with Adelaide and Leon Herrmann.

On Saturday night, exactly one boy responded to the ad, knocking timidly at Thurston's door in the rooming house.

His name was George Davis White. He was then twelve years old, the oldest son of Mary (Helen) Davis and Tolliver White. His father may have been a freed slave from Virginia. George was born on February 2, 1887, in New York City, and had received a public school education. His family lived uptown, on Sixty-first Street; his brothers worked as elevator operators in apartment buildings. Thurston found George to be bright and serious; he had no hesitation about getting to work or learning the details of the act. The magician offered the boy room and board, and fifty cents a week, and the next day George was given a quick education in magic. Grace stitched a costume for him, showed him how to hold each prop and stand onstage.

There was also quite a bit to do backstage. Howard and Grace had recently added an important new improvement to the Rising Card trick. Now, instead of having cards selected by the audience and shuffled back in the deck, Thurston stood on the stage and had spectators call out cards—any cards—that they wanted to see rise from the deck.

This meant that George, hidden backstage, was ready, next to a large cloth banner that had been sewn with fifty-two pockets; each pocket contained a playing card that was a duplicate of Thurston's deck. As he heard the cards named, George quickly plucked them from the banner, stacked them in a packet, and then walked onstage, under cover of handing Thurston a handkerchief to wipe out the goblet. He secretly delivered the duplicate cards to the magician, who palmed them onto the top of the deck. The subterfuge made the trick even more amazing and quickened the pace at a large theater like Pastor's; Thurston no longer had to step off the stage to have cards selected. Now Thurston was starting with the cards in the goblet and then ending with them held in his hand.

"Careful, don't look up at the audience. Smile. Look only at Howard,"

Grace drilled George as he ran through the maneuvers. "Don't take the focus from the magician. Step to the back. Always behind him. Use your left hand, the closest hand. Never turn your back."

All Sunday, they paced back and forth in the rooming house, repeating each step of the act: George's entrance, how to style (a flashy, quick way of taking a bow), arranging the packet of cards, delivering the duck load, invisibly, to Thurston. Throughout the day, George barely spoke a word. He listened to each instruction, nodded, and repeated the actions perfectly, meticulously.

The next morning, August 21, 1899, Grace and Thurston pulled their trunk down the street and George followed, lugging the duck in his crate. As they turned the corner to see Pastor's Theater, Howard absentmindedly asked, "Have you ever been in a theater before?" George answered, "No, sir."

Thurston almost stopped on the street to give him a short lecture on stage fright, but then thought better of it, realizing how lucky they were. George had never even considered being nervous.

THURSTON AND GEORGE walked mechanically through their rehearsal and then retired to the wings to double-check each prop before their twelve-thirty premiere. Grace was scheduled to start on the dinner show; her engagement at the dime museum overlapped Pastor's engagement for one week, so she dashed between the theaters to honor both contracts. At Tony Pastor's, Thurston faced the problem of music for the act. He'd never carried sheet music, using whatever Grace could pound out on the piano, or the local band would choose from their repertoire. When asked what he wanted, he had always simply said, "A waltz." He said the same thing to Pastor's house orchestra, a notoriously ragged collection of Pastor's old friends who seemed to specialize in popular melodies played out of tune.

That morning, he was the third act on the bill at Tony Pastor's, a safe spot that didn't promise too much to the audience. As Thurston sauntered onto the stage for his premiere, the orchestra swung into "Zenda Waltzes," a featherweight tune that had been written by Frank Witmark four years earlier, for a play based on the popular novel *The Prisoner of Zenda*.

Howard struggled through the act. He hesitated on a few of the early moves, and then began to fret about the mistakes, stumbling over his lines. He broke out in a chilling flop sweat that quickly soaked through his collar and left his hands trembling as he walked offstage. There was a smattering of polite applause.

"My God, Grace," he told her in the wings. "I muffed it."

She knew better. She knew that the act was fine and her husband's nerves were frayed. "It's fine. It's just all new. You'll have them jumping on the tables tonight." Little George, however, was precise and unflappable, moving with an admirable, otherworldly detachment. He circled back around the curtain, holding the duck. Without any need for congratulations or any prompting, he quietly went about preparing the props for the next show and re-sorting the cards.

Grace was right. By the evening show, Thurston had steeled himself, managing to sweep every bit of his experience—the carnival platforms, beer halls, and lantern-lit performances in general stores—onto Pastor's New York stage. "Then, too, George's ease had a tonic effect on me," Thurston recalled. That night, the card manipulations drew stunned silence. The Rising Cards inspired gasps. The card throwing earned cheers. When he finally finished the show by pulling handfuls of cards and a string of baby clothes from a spectator's coat, the audience stamped their approval. Socrates the duck, pushing his way to the top of the man's collar and flapping his wings as he tumbled onto the stage, stopped the show with peals of laughter, and then loud applause. George chased the duck, scooting after it with arms outstretched, then holding it high so it flapped its wings manically, just as George had been trained. Thurston took three steps, approaching the footlights, turned his chin upward, toward the balcony, and offered a deep, self-satisfied bow.

Tony Pastor himself followed Thurston from the wings into his dressing room. "Well done, my boy. Fine job."

Howard Thurston was always prone to finicky superstitions. At Pastor's, he adopted two more that served him well. His song was now "Zenda Waltzes," and he insisted that it always accompany his card routine. And George White, a new lucky charm, guaranteed success. George was alongside him onstage—his principal assistant—in every performance for the rest of his life.

THURSTON WAS HELD OVER at Tony Pastor's, and then offered work, through the agent William Morris, on leading vaudeville circuits—Proctor, Keith, or Orpheum. With the benediction of Tony Pastor and the ironclad contracts of the fashionable new vaudeville chains, Thurston had leapfrogged over virtually every other magician in America.

Early vaudeville, from the 1880s, had been about songs, dance, and sketch comedy. It also accommodated short, sensational variety performers like jugglers or acrobats—transplants from the circus. But magicians were never an easy fit. The great tradition of magic in America, as personified by Heller, Dr. Lynn, Herrmann, or Kellar, was the tradition of the "great man," a performer who enchanted the audience with a long, full program of marvels. The magician's skills took time to develop, required tables filled with apparatus, and often indulged in chatty patter to make his points.

It was tough to boil it down to twelve, fifteen, or twenty minutes for a vaudeville bill. The first vaudeville magicians, like Imro Fox, Fredrick Eugene Powell, and Carl Hertz, performed short versions of the "great man" act, squeezing together a little of everything to remind their audiences of other popular magicians. Leon Herrmann ended up with the same approach to vaudeville, and so did his aunt Adelaide, the "great woman" in the field.

But as vaudeville became a real commodity in big cities through the 1890s, there was a need for new acts and a desire for new fashions. The trend was toward specialists, handsome young men in tails who marched onto the stage, used very little apparatus, and presented a narrow range of marvels in a simple, memorable act—striking, precise, and crisply modern.

That's why Martin Beck, the manager of the Orpheum circuit, told Houdini to stop performing magic tricks and to concentrate on the handcuff and locked trunk escape that made his performance unique. It was Beck who pulled him from the dime museums and put him on the vaudeville stage. He made Houdini an "escape artist," and then made him a star.

T. Nelson Downs, who Thurston had seen demonstrating the Back Palm, had spent his youth as a telegraph operator in Marshalltown, Iowa, learning sleight of hand with the coins in the cash drawer—stacks of silver half-dollars performed flashy somersaults in his hands, or disappeared and reappeared at his fingertips. Magicians told him that he was mad to concentrate on an act with just coins; those small tricks were considered only suitable for drawing-room performances. They were proved wrong. Tommy Downs's "The Miser's Dream," twelve minutes of dazzlingly pure coin manipulations, premiered at the Hopkins Theater in Chicago in 1895. He was billed as the "King of Koins."

Thurston was now exactly at the right place, at the right time. And he had the right act. His flashy new letterhead listed the elements of his vaudeville routine, "Time of act, twenty minutes; Twelve minutes in one (that is, in front of the front curtain, allowing the stage to be set for the next act); Elegant photos for lobby, Special lithographs; Assisted by Colored Attendant," and included an odd boast, "Not a Magic Act." It was important that these new acts were perceived as much more than traditional magic—a bold new sort of art. An early reviewer noted, "Howard Thurston is a thorough artist, and presents his performance in a very neat and a very entertaining manner. You do not know, you cannot imagine, how he does it."

HOWARD AND GRACE moved down the street to a pretty apartment on Lexington Avenue. Thurston had full-length triple mirrors installed, so that he could rehearse. According to Grace, "he arose at five each morning and spent two or three hours before the mirrors, his teeth clamped on one of his midget cigars, repeating the sleights over and over again." She had hoped that success would bring him relaxation. It didn't. He was still nervous, and unpredictably jealous of Grace's affections, becoming temperamental if she spoke to another man, suspicious of how she spent her money or what she said about her husband. Adding to the tension was the boorish Harry, who arrived for an extended visit, basking in his older brother's success and sniffing around for business prospects in New York.

Grace's success in vaudeville, her independence, contributed to Howard's fears. After the couple joined some show business friends for a late dinner, Thurston ended the party with some impromptu magic, managing to pick the men's pockets. He returned their wallets with a laugh. Later, Grace complimented him on the feat. "They should have met the Nim Kid," she told him, referring to her husband's early days in a crime gang. Thurston scowled. "I want you to forget all about that. Forget about our past, the western trip. Now I want to show the public the right picture." After a pause, he asked her about the pages in her diary, his long, confessional autobiography. Where were they? She realized why he was asking and changed the subject.

On another evening, after Grace had been trapped in an argument with Harry, she overheard him in the next room growling to Howard. "She's so damn smart. I'd like to wring Grace's neck." She couldn't clearly hear Howard's reply. For years, she wondered about how he responded to his brother.

Howard and George left for bookings in Canada and then toured on the Orpheum circuit through most of 1900. They returned back through Keith's theaters in Boston and New York and played the New York Roof Garden (where Howard engineered his audition) in September of that year. Grace often joined him, working as his stage manager. When Howard grew temperamental, she stayed home in New York or went out and found her own vaudeville bookings.

By the end of 1900, Howard was being bombarded by telegrams from Charles Morton, the manager of London's Palace Theater, asking him to commit to a four-week engagement. Thurston avoided responding. But Morton was insistent, and after months of resisting the manager's offers, Thurston announced that he and George would go to London and fill the dates.

Grace had been waiting to see if she would be invited to London; when she heard that she wasn't, she dutifully packed her husband's trunks for the voyage.

In fact, Thurston didn't believe that he'd be gone for very long. He felt that four weeks was excessive and petitioned Morton to reduce the contract to two weeks, in case the card act didn't click with London audiences. Thurston had so many good offers in America that he was afraid to leave the country for very long. Audiences wanted to see him now, and they could be fickle.

In October 1900, Thurston didn't realize that his associates—Houdini, T. Nelson Downs, and Billy Robinson—had already beat him to London, and all three of them had become stars. London had developed an insatiable taste for magic, and now they insisted on seeing "The World's Premier Card Manipulator." There was a growing prestige, a sense of royalty, with these unique performers. Thurston's fame meant that he had been summoned to "The Palace."

EIGHT

"ORIGINAL CARD PASSES"

 very vaudevillian knew the phrase "The boat sails Wednesday." It became a punch line symbolizing the vagaries of the business, but it originated—so the story was told—in the strange contrast between vaudeville and music hall. Vaudeville was strictly American. Music hall, the British version, had its own traditions and fashions.

Willis Sweatnam was a popular comedian who made the transition from minstrel shows to vaudeville. He received a good contract for music-hall work in London. Determined to make a hit, he opened on Monday night with some of his best material, rapid-fire American dialect jokes. He didn't get a single laugh. He walked offstage in silence. The music-hall manager came to his dressing room to offer solace.

"Mr. Sweatnam, I'm afraid your sort of humor isn't suitable for England. Now, you shouldn't take it personally, but of course, you'll have to be canceled. The boat sails Wednesday, and you can still book passage."

"You haven't seen my best material," Sweatnam insisted.

"But I fear it won't be acceptable for our audience's taste. Now you'll find that the boat sails Wednesday and . . ."

Sweatnam wouldn't give up. "Don't be hasty! I've got lots of material. I've been doing this for years. I'll put together an act that will have them cheering. I can prove it."

The manager reluctantly agreed. "You may go on the next show, but please remember, the boat sails Wednesday."

Sweatnam huddled with the orchestra leader, deciding that he needed good straight lines, like a minstrel show. The conductor was happy to help.

"Look, I'll walk out on the stage," Sweatnam told him. "I'll ask you, 'Why is an old maid like a green tomato?' And then you'll say, 'I don't know, why is an old maid like a green tomato?' And then I'll say, 'Because either way, it's hard to . . . mate . . . her!'"

They planned a long list of straight lines and jokes, the conductor placed his script on his podium, and it was time for the second show.

Sweatnam walked onstage. "Maestro," he growled, "I wonder if ya' can tell me . . . Why is an old maid jus' like a green tah-may-ter?"

The orchestra leader responded, loudly, "I don't know Mr. Sweatnam, why is an old maid like a green toe-maaah-toh?"

Sweatnam paused just a moment, realizing that he was doomed. "Maestro," he shouted, "the boat sails Wednesday!" And he walked offstage.

THE PALACE THEATER of Varieties was built in 1880 near the busy intersection of Charing Cross Road and Shaftsbury Avenue in the West End of London, an imposing gingerbread of red brick and arched windows. It was Britain's leading music hall, a former opera house that was now devoted to pure variety. By the turn of the century, the music hall had become big business, dominated by producers and circuits of performers. While vaudeville signaled an end to saloon entertainments—eliminating the smoking and alcohol—music hall had always been organized around the bar, attracting customers with the acts, and then serving them drinks.

Charles Morton, the manager of the Palace, sat at a small table in the orchestra pit. If an act saw him lift his hands and tap them together, it was his sign that he was satisfied. If not, they could expect the worst, and his vengeance was swift. He ran the show like a military operation. Morton didn't abide any lateness; when the act heard its music cue, it had to be ready to step onstage immediately, or it was dismissed.

Even stranger was the claque system. Each act had money deducted from its salary to pay for a group of stooges, their claque, positioned in seats throughout the auditorium. The claque applauded on cue and naturally encouraged more applause from the rest of the audience. Acts were always suspicious that the claque weren't really doing their job, but instead were merely "patty-caking." The London music halls developed an early taste for magic and an appreciation for the distinct acts of the specialist. T. Nelson Downs, the convivial midwesterner who manipulated coins, had arrived at the Palace Theater of Varieties in May 1899 and was held over for a long engagement. At that time, Downs's encore was a short trick, producing cards at his fingertips by using the backhand palm. Technically, he had beat Thurston to London with this move, but the public always remembered Downs by his billing, the "King of Koins," and his feat of catching hundreds of silver half-dollars from the air, not his brief card manipulations.

Chung Ling Soo, a Chinese magician, premiered at the Alhambra, another London variety theater, a year later, in April 1900. The magician was tall and bald; he worked silently with a bland smile and exaggerated comic or dramatic gestures. His assistant was Suee Seen, a tiny, delicate Chinese maiden. His act consisted of startling novelties. He caught goldfish in the air, at the end of a fishing line, and produced an enormous basin filled with water and ducks from beneath a shawl. Soo's Oriental-inspired magic was a startling novelty and fascinated the London audiences.

Theater professionals knew the truth. Chung Ling Soo and Suee Seen were actually Billy and Dot Robinson, the erstwhile assistants to America's great magicians. After leaving Herrmann, they developed their act by copying a genuine Chinese magician named Ching Ling Foo, who had toured America in the last years of the nineteenth century. Shaving his head and wearing a long braided queue, dark makeup, and embroidered robes, Robinson completely submerged himself in the role, on- and offstage, and Chung Ling Soo became a music-hall star.

And then, on July 2, 1900, Harry Houdini premiered in London at the Alhambra. Early in 1900, Houdini's career was just beginning to attract audiences in vaudeville, but his new manager, Martin Beck, boldly calculated that a European success would jolt Houdini into stardom. It was a good plan, but Beck and his partners had bungled the deals. There were no actual engagements in place when Harry and Bess Houdini boarded the ship.

In London, Houdini scrambled for attention. He arranged a special demonstration at the Alhambra for policemen from Scotland Yard and members of the press. The newspapers featured stories on the amazing young American who could escape from handcuffs and leg irons. The Alhambra booked him for a two-week engagement; during his first week, Houdini shared the bill with Chung Ling Soo, who was just completing his run at the theater. When Houdini was a hit, the booking was extended through the summer. His abilities were framed with a sense of challenge and triumph, and the nature of his act—the little man daring the world to hold him—seemed far beyond mere magic tricks. The *Times* offered an enthusiastic review, concluding, "Mr. Houdini frankly admits that his feats depend on trickery, but that does not lessen their cleverness or interest."

The fashion for specialization inspired a number of performers. Servais Le Roy, an inventive Belgian magician, instructed his wife, Talma, to perform an act in imitation of Downs. She appeared as the "Queen of Coins." George Stillwell performed magic with handkerchiefs. Allan Shaw specialized in both cards and coins. Even P. T. Selbit, a young British magician who was just starting his career, worked as the "Card and Coin Demon," although Selbit later found success by inventing a series of large-scale illusions.

BY THE TIME Thurston arrived in London, at the end of October 1900, all he could think about were the lucrative offers that were waiting back in America. He was anxious to get back on the boat. As he settled in at a theatrical boardinghouse, he now felt contrite about leaving Grace in New York. He guiltily sent a number of wires that reported, "All is well. Home soon."

Charles Morton welcomed him to the Palace and was anxious to see the famous card manipulator at work. But after Thurston and George's first rehearsal, Morton wanted cuts. He insisted on a brisk seventeen minutes; no more. The finish with spectator on the stage and the duck wouldn't be necessary, he told Thurston perfunctorily. "Thank you, but we'll just need your card manipulations, the rising cards and card throwing routines." This meant that most of the act was completely silent, with Thurston barely speaking at all; only a few lines were left at the start of the rising cards.

On his opening night, November 5, 1900, Thurston feared that his finely tuned act had been pushed and pulled in the wrong directions. He stepped to the footlights feeling slightly sick to his stomach. The audience seemed uneasy as well, watching intently, but suspicious of the young American in the swallowtail coat. Thurston reached out, produced a card at his fingertips, and then another and another, twelve in all, one by one, handing them to George in a wide fan. When he finished this first trick, the modest start to the act, he was met with a loud round of applause that cascaded over the polite clap-clapping of Thurston's claque. He was stunned. The audience had been watching closely, and they approved. "It's all right, George," Thurston said.

As the act continued, the Palace rumbled with applause and the audience cheered each effect. His new finish, card throwing, inspired increasing yells of "Bravo" and made spectators in the stalls stand so that they could watch the cards flying into the balcony. London had never seen anything like it. Thurston scaled individual cards to boxes, a single card aimed perfectly at each box on the first tier, and then he circled back and delivered cards to the second tier of boxes. The audience was still cheering when he then let loose a fusillade of cards, rapid fire, in the direction of the theater's dome. The response was even more enthusiastic than his premiere at Tony Pastor's. The audience brought him back for bow after bow, and the entire orchestra of forty musicians stood and applauded as well—this was considered the ultimate compliment for a music-hall artist.

The next day, Morton welcomed the magician to his office and slid a new contract in front of him. Thurston was still woozy from the audience's response. He'd quickly forgotten all his misgivings and had to admit that Morton's edits to the act were exactly right for the crowd. He agreed to stay at the

Palace for six months. And as a final compliment, Morton offered to let him pick his own time on the bill. Thurston chose to go on at 9:25 each night. Every day in the newspapers, the show at the Palace was advertised with Thurston's name prominently featured and the starting time of his act. He costarred with over a dozen of the finest stars of vaudeville and music hall, including W. C. Fields, who was then presenting a tramp comedy and juggling act. The show concluded with selected films from the American Biograph Company.

Of course, George White's experience in show business was very different from his boss's. He traveled in steerage, stayed in inexpensive boardinghouses, and lived frugally, devoting his time to preparing all the elements of the show. Using Herrmann's comic Boomsky as a model, Thurston had intended George White to play the part of the comical Negro, indulging in stereotypical reactions. Early in their career together, Thurston even billed him as "Keno," as if he were a character in the act.

Grace sewed George a new costume, which she sent on to London. It was a handsome, jade green bellman's uniform, with gold epaulets and lots of brass buttons. George cleverly avoided any stereotypes or cartoonish gestures. "The 'darkie' boy is possessed of a most expressive countenance," wrote a reporter for *The Black and White Budget*, a popular British magazine, after meeting Thurston and George. "He does not, however, use such words as 'sah,' 'yo,' and 'fo,' he is not constantly singing 'The Swanee River.' He is much like one of our own boys."

Another London reviewer commented on George's appearance during the act. "The young black attendant moves about with silent, feline step, more a machine than a man, all admirably appropriate to the character of the performance. . . . When he smiles, golly, it's huge!" George was learning the power of slow, restrained motions on stage. When he punctuated one of Thurston's tricks by looking out at the audience and suddenly smiling, it was a bit of precise timing, providing another sharp jolt for the audience to applaud, far more effective than Thurston's claque at the Palace. George became adept at disappearing and then reappearing on stage—ignored and almost invisible to the audience, and then suddenly present for a moment of misdirection.

———————

GRACE HAD TIRED of waiting in New York and booked herself with a theatrical stock company that was playing in Massachusetts. But Thurston was anxious to see her again, to share his success. A telegram sent to New York was forwarded to Grace on the road: "I want you to join me." She had already decided that she would not be won back so easily. But her resolve lasted exactly one hour, when a second telegram arrived: "Ticket at No. 1 Broadway. Sail on Minnihaha January 21."

When she arrived in February, Grace was thrilled at Howard's success and stardom. His 9:25 performances left him time to accept private bookings at clubs and salons in London. If he arranged his schedule carefully, he could supplement his income with two or three well-paid shows each night. Edward, the Prince of Wales, was a fan of variety as well as magic, visited Thurston several times backstage, and chatted with Grace. Thurston offered the prince brief lessons in sleight of hand, showing him how to back-palm a card.

As the famous American magician, featured in newspapers and magazines, Thurston was also in demand at parties, banquets, and balls, and Grace enjoyed mixing with high society. He was invited to a private party thrown by the Shah of Persia, where he pulled a duck from a spectator's collar and dropped it in the shah's lap. Thurston was also invited to the home of Baron Rothschild and performed his act. Rothschild returned the favor by performing some of his own favorite card tricks. "[Howard] fitted in as if he had been born to dukedom or educated at Oxford," Grace marveled. "He could not spell a word longer than 'cat,' but he could talk like a man with a doctor's degree." She credited his smooth skills from being a confidence man. Now, instead of charming the customer to sell a cheap watch with paste diamonds, he was selling himself. "Howard Thurston's a great man," W. C. Fields remarked to Grace. "Only one I ever knew with complete confidence in his own con."

Grace also discovered that her husband had been charming some female admirers. She found herself in several awkward situations—accepting backstage visitors, or perfumed letters delivered to their hotel room—that made her suspicious of his affections. One night, as Grace waited in Thurston's dressing room at the Palace, a beautiful, dark-haired woman appeared, insisting that she was going to dinner with her "Howie." "You'd better run along dear," Grace told her, "before you get your eyes scratched out. I'm Mrs. Thurston."

THURSTON ALSO HAD his own souvenir playing cards printed, with his portrait in an oversized heart, for the Palace Theater. These were special throwout cards that he used to propel into the audience at the finish of his act. By using slightly heavier cardboard than normal playing cards, the cards could be thrown even farther.

He also produced *Howard Thurston's Card Tricks*, a slender book that was published in London early in 1901 to capitalize on his success. The cover showed Howard and George in the midst of their act. The book contained explanations of the Back Palm as well as the Rising Cards. All was supposedly written by Thurston, but it was actually the work of William Hilliar, an American magician and manager who was in London working with T. Nelson Downs. The previous year, Hilliar had written a similar book for Downs, describing his coin tricks.

The book was nicely illustrated by Sidney Tibbles, the brother of English magician P. T. Selbit, and the section on the Back Palm provided a detailed account of the maneuver. But the explanation of the Rising Cards was a fraud. Hilliar invented another method to accomplish it, using a black thread on a spring-wound reel concealed in the performer's coat. It looked good in print, but this arrangement couldn't have duplicated Thurston's masterful effect. Instead, the little book satisfied curious readers, made some money, and helped to throw magicians off the scent of the real secret.

Thurston's Card Tricks also started a series of nicely sanitized, highly exaggerated biographies of the magician. In this little booklet, and later interviews and articles, Thurston was standardizing his imaginary life story. He was now a nephew of U.S. senator John Mellon Thurston of Nebraska. His father was now the vice-consul in Algiers, where, at the age of three:

Thurston was stolen by the Mohammedans, and for three years all of North Africa was hunting for him in vain. Strange as was his sudden disappearance, his return was even stranger, for three years from the very day he was kid-napped, he was mysteriously returned to his parents—how it was never ascertained. While in the hands of the Mohammedans, they never once mistreated him, nor did they seek ransom, though large sums of money were offered for the boy's return. The only thing which seems to have affected the boy was that, at times, he would sit for hours in silent meditation, no one ever fathoming his thoughts. As a child of six, he began to show powers which appeared to those about him little short of miraculous.

So much for the Nim Kid. These stories were usually ignored as press puffery typical of many performers. Houdini's official biographies contained similar foolishness. But it was more specific exaggeration that raised the ire of the magicians, especially Houdini.

Thurston had sent a copy of his card book to Houdini, who was then making headlines with his escape act in Berlin. Houdini noted that Thurston had simplified the story of his Rising Card performance in Denver. He now fooled Herrmann the Great, and all of his staff, with his amazing trick. He had been appearing at the nearby Orpheum Theater at the time, and Herrmann was at the Tabor Grand.

Houdini had his doubts. He couldn't calculate how Thurston had ever mystified Herrmann the Great (Alexander Herrmann), who died in 1896. Houdini wrote to his friend Billy Robinson, Chung Ling Soo, for clarification. Robinson was appearing in Vienna at the time, and replied to Houdini's letter. No, he insisted, it was Leon Herrmann, not Alexander. "He says he fooled The Great Herrmann. He did not," Robinson wrote. And no, Robinson was certainly not fooled as well. "I gave him a black velvet set instead of a light scene, so the thread could not be seen. Ask him if he remembers that, and then he will change his mind about fooling me."

When Thurston arrived in London in 1900 and discovered that Billy Robinson—now Chung Ling Soo—was a star, he may have tried some quick fence-mending. In an interview for an English magazine, he credited William Robinson with important help during his early career. Thurston must have known that Robinson would see this as a peace offering.

THURSTON TOOK short breaks in his Palace contract to work other English cities, and Grace found work for her own act in short runs at English music halls. When Queen Victoria died in January 1901, entertainments stopped in England during the mourning period. Thurston and Grace accepted offers from the Continent. He opened at the Winter Garden in Berlin, where Thurston's "Zenda Waltzes" was played by a fifty-two-piece orchestra—including twenty-one violins. Thurston performed a private show for the Kaiser, and in April went on to Copenhagen, where Howard and Grace met four monarchs—King Christian IX of Denmark; his son King George I of Greece; Edward VII of Great Britain; and Tsar Nicholas II of Russia—who were riding through a park in a carriage. It was a celebration of King Christian's birthday. Thurston later reported that he greeted the rulers by reaching out and producing four playing cards, the four kings. The tale of Thurston's trick seems to have been a publicity boast, and it became an official part of his enlarging biography.

In July 1902, Howard and Grace appeared with their own acts on the bill at the Folies-Marigny in Paris for one month. Then they returned back to England to appear in Douglas on the Isle of Man. Thurston returned to London for another long run at the Empire Theater.

In London, they settled in at a theatrical boardinghouse near the British Museum, at Number 10 Keppel Street—a home away from home for many American vaudevillians. Filled with successful, extroverted performers who were experiencing London as a great adventure, the house had the atmosphere of a party. At times the Thurstons were joined there by the Houdinis, T. Nelson Downs, W. C. Fields, and a host of other performers, like Charles Aldrich, a quick-change artist; Fred Stone, the famous song-and-dance man; and Everhart, who performed a beautiful juggling act with wooden hoops.

Thurston's busy schedule left him moody and unpredictable. He now needed a frame of dark curtains surrounding his bed, a sleep mask, and earplugs, in order to get a full night's sleep. He second-guessed Grace's motives, even her laughing conversations with the Prince of Wales or the fun, flirtatious atmosphere at 10 Keppel Street.

Howard and Grace's marriage was crumbling. Thurston's dark moods often ended in arguments, or noisy chases down the stairs, out the front door, and through the street. When Howard bought a new gown for Grace, it inspired a laughing remark from W. C. Fields: "I wish I'd seen you first, before that card tosser caught you." Thurston marched his wife back up the stairs, told her that her flirting was a disgrace, and had her remove the dress so that he could burn it, bit by bit, in the flame of the gas jet. He left her sitting on the bed, sobbing, and marched out of the flat. Hours later he returned, proffering an apology and a new set of diamond earrings.

On another occasion, when Thurston's temper raged and he lunged for her, Grace grabbed a chair and swung it, knocking him to the ground. Thurston stumbled from the room, quiet and contrite, then returned with a bandage on his scalp. He never mentioned the incident. "Looking back," Grace wrote, "I wonder if I should have broken more chairs."

Grace had become inured to the bickering and threats, and was surprised when one of her friends at Keppel Street, a young dancer named Jimmy Polk, pulled her aside and told her, "Everybody knows what goes on. He hits you."

GRACE PLAYED dates through England while Howard and George returned for a quick trip through midwestern cities in America in the spring of 1902, fulfilling long-standing engagements on the Orpheum circuit. In June, they met back in Paris to begin another tour of the Continent. Thurston was calculating how long he'd have to work, how much he'd have to earn, to take the next step.

In fact, Howard Thurston was never really a vaudevillian. Unlike many of his contemporaries, he hadn't been seduced by the new trend in entertainment. In 1900, most stars in vaudeville or music hall could only imagine long, lucrative careers; the circuits were expanding and the public couldn't get enough of the acts. But Thurston saw his act as a means to an end. Perhaps it was a unique bit of business acumen or his natural restlessness. More than likely, he had fixated on his childhood dream to become a great magician with a great, elaborate show in the Herrmann tradition. In vaudeville, there really was no place for a great magician, just "another magician."

It would be a dozen years before the cracks began to appear in vaudeville; twenty years before vaudevillians began to see the end of the road. But by 1902, Thurston was scheming his way out. His plan was to develop an elaborate, star turn in vaudeville that consisted of innovative large illusions. This would be his first step toward his own show.

In the early years of the twentieth century, London was a magnet for the greatest magicians of the world. In Piccadilly was the famous Egyptian Hall, a creaky Victorian theater painted with faux Egyptian hieroglyphics and scarabs that accommodated a small audience of just 275 people. Since 1873, the theater had been operated by John Nevil Maskelyne, an inventive magician and impresario, and his partner George A. Cooke, who often played the assistant in Maskelyne's magic.

Maskelyne and Cooke's Egyptian Hall was a laboratory of great magic, responsible for many of the finest new illusions. The performances were organized around a sort of repertory company of magicians, and American performers like Alexander Herrmann, Harry Kellar, and even Billy Robinson had pillaged Maskelyne's latest ideas for their own programs.

The new century seemed to instill a new energy at Egyptian Hall. David Devant, Maskelyne's new partner, joined the company in 1893. He provided a perfect mixture of the new style of magic—stark, pointedly elegant manipulations with a handful of ivory billiard balls—with the traditional Maskelyne specialties—ingenious optical effects or stage illusions worked into scenes or playlets. Most important, Devant was a warm, ingratiating performer with a natural flair for comic patter. He quickly became the ideal of the new generation of magicians. Maskelyne kept Devant busy working at Egyptian Hall or managing the provincial tours through Great Britain. Thurston and Devant quickly became friends. They were close in age and shared similar tastes, hardheaded about the business of magic but artistic in their approaches.

Another important presence at Egyptian Hall was the German magician Paul Valadon, who was hired in 1900 to fill the program when Devant was working outside of London. Valadon's specialties were billiard balls, in the style of Devant; back palming, in the style of Thurston; and Chinese magic, in the style of Billy Robinson.

But Thurston was most interested in the incredible, inventive illusions featured at Egyptian Hall. The most puzzling of these was John Nevil Maskelyne's levitation of "the Entranced Fakir," introduced in 1901. Set within a short farce about a visiting confidence man and an Indian fakir, the highlight of the evening was when the robed fakir, played by George Cooke, floated horizontally out of a coffin, rising into the air. Unlike the awkward, mechanical levitations performed by magicians, Maskelyne had really seemed to conquer the force of gravity. Cooke floated far from any scenery or drapes, on a brightly lit stage, and Maskelyne paced around the floating man throughout the effect. At the climactic moment, the magician passed a solid metal hoop over the floating man, proving that he was not using any wires.

It was easy for magicians to think that it had all been done, that the finest mysteries had already been invented or performed, that the glory days of magic were in the past. But the Entranced Fakir reminded Thurston that the very best magic, the most incredible illusions, had yet to be invented. Here, in 1901, John Nevil Maskelyne had managed to create a totally new illusion that bamboozled Thurston completely.

When he discreetly asked his friend, Devant, about the miracle, Devant smiled. "Howard, that's one of Mr. Maskelyne's very best efforts," he said. "Of course, I can't talk about it. But I have seen the mechanism. Do yourself a favor and don't think about it. It's nothing that you could ever use. Much too complicated for your sort of show."

Of course, Devant's advice just steeled Thurston's resolve. "Maybe you're right," he told Devant, "but you don't know what sort of show I'm going to build."

HOWARD AND GRACE rented a flat in Torrington Square, and Thurston opened a workshop near Bedford Square, hiring several carpenters and scenic artists to build his illusions. Thurston had collected files of new ideas; he selected a dozen original effects and combined them into a new act. For eight months in 1902, he worked evenings performing at private parties or in music halls and spent his days at the shop, supervising the new effects or rehearsing each sequence of moves. Grace stuck by his side, realizing that he desperately needed her help to organize the new enterprise, assisting off and on the stage. She recalled that, at one point, they were employing eight people, laborers or artists, as well as another seven or eight special engineers for the illusions. This time he wouldn't make any mistakes by scrimping on the production or underestimating his abilities. Each illusion, each piece of scenery and costume was striking and brand-new. The act would be adorned with full orchestrations and a cast of six, plus Grace and George. Soon the rumor of Thurston's lavish new act spread through the London theatrical community. "I am inclined to think it will be a winner," T. Nelson Downs reported from London.

Thurston had miscalculated the amount of work involved and the costs. After several months of work, he had spent the $10,000 he had put aside for the new act—a princely sum for magic props—and was now borrowing money to finish the production. Thurston sent a note to his fellow vaudevillian, Harry Houdini. "We never know our luck until we try, therefore I take the liberty to ask you to loan me five pounds," he wrote. The amount translated to about $25. "I would do the same for you if you needed it." Houdini sent the money. An urgent telegram was sent to his brother Harry in Chicago for a much larger loan. "My future success depends upon you," it began. Harry scraped together the profits from his dime museums and cabled the money to his older brother in London.

With the quick infusion of cash, Howard rented the Princess Theater in London on December 15, 1902, for a trial performance. Grace sent telegrams to theatrical managers and vaudeville agents. After ten years of performing with playing cards, just three years from the misery of a Union Square park bench, Thurston was now ready to make his premiere as the world's greatest magician. Or maybe it was a simple case of his complete confidence in his own con.

NINE

"THE REVERSED GIRL"

irst the audience noticed the colors. As the timpani drums rolled, the theater curtain ascended on a blaze of vibrant colors that filled the stage from corner to corner—electric bulbs had been tinted to produce warm gold and rose-colored light. The scenery was painted in bright, pure colors to resemble the courtyard of a mysterious Oriental palace, with a view of a formal garden beyond the walls. Tiny, twinkling electric lights outlined the edges of the palace. Glowing, golden suspended lamps hung overhead, surrounded by swags of peacock blue silk. Revolving color wheels, concealed above the stage, gave the impression of flickering flames in each lamp.

And then the audience at the Princess Theater in London noticed the Great Thurston. He was standing, with his arms crossed, draped with a long cape of dark green velvet and embroidered gold. His costume was a fantasy of the mysterious Orient: a colorful green-and-maroon-striped turban, a short velvet riding coat, high riding boots of embroidered bloodred Moroccan leather, bright green jodhpurs, and a maroon silk cummerbund.

The London public had become familiar with Thurston, the handsome young America in his black formalwear with his long locks of brown hair. But now, he was suddenly presenting himself as a swashbuckling star of a Scheherazade story, the romantic prince welcoming us to his palace. It was no longer a music hall, but a fairy tale.

The orchestra began a bright march. George entered, dressed in a green silk tunic, and removed Thurston's cape. Another pretty female assistant, dressed in silk harem pants, offered her shawl, twirling as it was pulled from her shoulders. Thurston waved the shawl in the air, draped it over his arm, and reached beneath it. He emerged with a large brass bowl filled with water. He placed it on a table, and a ring of fountains spurted up from the bowl.

He reached beneath the shawl a second time, and his hand emerged with another brass bowl filled with fire. He produced a large porcelain platter, which floated in the air in front of him. He smashed it with a small hammer to prove that it was solid and heavy.

Thurston stepped to a table that supported a tall high hat. He twirled it in his hands, showing it empty, and then reached inside. His fingers emerged with a pastel-colored balloon that seemed to fill the interior of the hat. He released it from his hands and it floated up to the ceiling of the theater. Thurston repeated the trick, shaking the hat gently and dislodging a second balloon that floated away. He produced four large, gas-filled balloons from the empty hat.

Then he picked up a small gilded ball, the size of a small globe, and carried it into the audience. It remained suspended over his fingers as he passed a hoop over it. Thurston returned to the stage, with the golden ball floating between his hands.

Thurston followed with several more unusual effects. George entered holding a tray. Thurston produced a dozen eggs, one after another from George's mouth. The trick became more and more ridiculous with each egg. Then eggs seemed to be produced from George's chest, his back, and his elbow. For the finale, a real chicken appeared to push its way through George's chest, tumbling onto the tray.

The orchestra began Thurston's lilting favorite, "Zenda Waltzes," as the magician and George presented the popular card act—card manipulations, the Rising Cards, and the finale with Socrates the duck.

Next came one of Thurston's most amazing accomplishments. He picked up a simple coconut shell, half of an empty coconut. Thurston stood on a small stool to isolate him from the stage floor, alongside a table that supported a basin of water. He dipped the shell into the water, filling it, and then tipped the shell over the basin, pouring the water out again. He repeated the motion, filling and emptying the shell, even slower this time. The third time he filled the shell with water and turned it upside down, holding it over the basin. The audience was amazed to see a torrent of water gushing from the shell. It poured, and poured, until water ran over the side of the basin and was caught in a metal sluice, running down to another tall metal vase. Within seconds, this was also filled with water, which poured down into a third can. Just as the audience began to suspect that the water might have been coming from concealed hoses, up through his boots and then down his sleeve, Thurston lifted his feet from the raised stool with a few delicate steps. There was no explanation for the deluge. As a perfect climax, Thurston held his other hand aloft, and a blaze of fire burst from his fingers.

Grace entered and reclined on a low Moorish sofa. The orchestra hit a chord and barely paused before the woodwinds began a sinuous, mysterious Oriental melody. Thurston stood above her and, with a ripple of his delicate fingers, she rose slowly into the air. When she was about two feet above the sofa, resting peacefully in space, he passed a metal hoop over her, from head to feet. She descended back to the sofa again. Admittedly, Thurston's feat was not as miraculous as Maskelyne's incredible levitation at Egyptian Hall—that one still eluded him—but this version, titled the Aga Levitation, was a good fit in his mysterious Oriental act.

The finale involved several large illusions. The music quickened as Thurston produced a statue of a lady atop a table, and then slowly the statue turned into a real person. Four harem ladies stood on a raised platform above the stage. Thurston covered the platform with a cloth, pulled it away, and the ladies had disappeared.

The entire cast rushed onto the stage for the final bow as the light wheels played on the columns, turning them rainbow colored, and twinkling water fountains spurted into view across the stage. Thurston took a long bow as the audience kept applauding, one curtain call after another. He was happy, relieved, vindicated, and proud.

WHO CREATED THURSTON'S ACT? Years later, Thurston described his weeks of work at the shop near Bedford Square, insisting that he had invented each of the illusions and had even sought to patent them. But Grace recorded that Thurston greedily collected plans and drawings from other magicians, as well as designers in Paris, assembling his new act from their best ideas.

Certainly, stage technicians were responsible for some of the wonders. "It was the first magic show to make extensive use of electricity," Grace recalled. "Electric motors turned on many of the illusions, and sparkling filaments and fountains were part of several tricks." Thurston also used chemicals for the fire effects, compressed air and pumps for the production of the balloons and the floating ball—which was held aloft as it tumbled and turned within a stream of air—and hydraulic systems for the flowing coconut. All of these were unusual and extravagant for magic shows in the early 1900s.

It's unlikely that any of the illusions were Thurston's ideas. He was never inventive, although he highly valued the process of invention and used to exaggerate his own creations—perhaps this was a result of his father's failed career as an inventor of household knickknacks. The magicians who later worked with him found that he had a surprisingly tin ear about evaluating new ideas. But as a performer, he had wonderful instincts about presenting these illusions for an audience.

A number of the illusions were clearly the work of other magicians. Only a handful of clever performers could have supplied these ideas. Servais Le Roy, a creative Belgian magician, was not in London then and met Thurston for the first time about a year later, after the new act was complete. Neither Maskelyne nor Devant would have offered suggestions, as they were busy with their own shows. Charles Morritt, an inventive Yorkshire magician who had worked with Maskelyne and would later work with Devant and Houdini, might have met with Thurston and offered new illusions. But none of the highly scientific or experimental Thurston illusions feel like Morritt's sort of magic.

There are three likely candidates: Horace Goldin, the American illusionist; Percy Tibbles, the young London magician who worked under the name P. T.

Selbit; and Fergus Greenwood, a British illusionist who appeared in music halls with the stage name Fasola.

All of them were at the start of their careers and would have been enthusiastic collaborators, flattered by Thurston's attention. Horace Goldin (his real name was Hyman Goldstein) was the most experienced of the candidates. A Polish immigrant to America, he had started his career in dime museums, often working alongside Houdini. Goldin premiered at London's Palace Theater of Varieties in July 1901, with a magic act performed at a breakneck pace. He prided himself on his inventions, although he'd borrowed some of his best ideas from other magicians. Goldin's creations were later featured in Thurston's show.

Selbit's brother illustrated Thurston's book on card magic, and the magicians met when Thurston was working at the Palace. T. Nelson Downs suggested that at least one of Thurston's illusions—probably the coconut shell—had been shown to him two years before Thurston's premiere by Selbit, who had a working model in a barn in London. Within several years, Selbit began specializing in large illusions and Thurston featured many of his greatest effects.

Fasola had been assembling his own illusion act. We know that he discussed an idea with Thurston around this time, an illusion with a cannon and a nest of trunks, which was later featured by Fasola and Goldin, and then used by Thurston. But the most telling indication may be fashion: Fasola, like Thurston, performed wearing a turban and silk jacket, as an Indian prince. It was an unusual choice for a magic act, and suggests that Thurston had been influenced by Fasola's suggestions. Fasola remained a close friend and confidant of the magician, and Thurston soon came to depend upon Fasola for new ideas.

THURSTON'S LAVISH new act was a hit with the agents. Paul Keith, the son of vaudeville impresario Benjamin Franklin Keith, saw the performance at the Princess Theater in London and negotiated Thurston's appearance at Keith theaters on the East Coast, starting the next spring. Grace and Howard hosted a late-night dinner for the cast and crew, and Howard offered a toast to everyone who made the Great Thurston possible.

But the next day, Thurston's dark moodiness returned. He roared at Grace, accusing her of encouraging other men and flirting with the vaudevillians at Number 10 Keppel Street. In the middle of his tirade, he reached out for her neck. She ducked, ran from the apartment, and hailed a cab for Keppel Street.

Thurston arrived during dinner, while Grace sat at the table surrounded by her friends. He was calm and composed, quietly asking if he could speak to her in the lounge. Alone with his wife, Howard mumbled an apology. He wanted her to come back to the flat, as they had a special private show that night. Grace told him that she wanted a divorce.

She avoided him for three days, convinced that he could deftly talk her into returning—the con man's relentless salesmanship. She ignored his messages and left the house early in the morning to dodge his visits. She then booked passage for New York on the first available ship. When she arrived, she raced upstate to the home of Charles and Addie Champlin; Charles, a kindly theatrical producer, had employed Grace in his road companies. There was already a stack of telegrams from Thurston waiting for her. Somehow he had anticipated that she'd go to see the Champlins—or perhaps he had simply blanketed all of her friends with urgent messages. She burned the telegrams without reading them.

When she looked back on their marriage, Grace suspected that Thurston's conflicts stemmed from his early life, his mixture of criminal activity, the Bible classes at Moody's school, and the years of "handling the suckers" in carnivals and sideshows. "Feelings of guilt and anxiety were with him always," she later wrote. "He had a reasonable understanding of right and wrong, but I think that he spent his life worrying about the exact location of the dividing line. He carried his own torture chamber inside him, and those in close contact with him often writhed on the rack of his moods and outbursts."

Grace Butterworth Thurston, "Miss Gracie Texola, American Singer and Buck Dancer," was just twenty years old, on her own after four years of marriage, a hardened show business professional, experienced and insightful beyond her years.

———

THURSTON TOOK MONTHS to adjust his new act, perfecting the devices that were built in London. He omitted the card manipulations and the levitation, as a shorter act was easier to sell. Not everyone was charmed. When he opened at Keith's Boston Theater on May 4, 1902, an unnamed reviewer for *Mahatma*, an American magician's journal, complained about the elaborate elements of the act.

> It is unlike any other act of magic ever produced here, too much depending upon the stage electrician and not enough on the efforts of Mr. Thurston himself. There is nothing in the entire act which would require a great amount of skill in the operator, and much is dependent on mechanical devices. When Mr. Thurston becomes actor enough to carry out his ideas and presents them without appearing to be one of his own mechanical pieces, he will have a good act. It is on the whole a strange performance, and leaves one in doubt as to its excellence in its present condition.

The review was disappointingly accurate. The act had plenty of magical things, but not much magic. Even more frustrating, in sheer logistics—cutting trapdoors, installing electrical circuits, and testing the lighting effects—Thurston's new effects were too complicated for a touring show. He realized that the novelty of the act would buy him time as he added more material. Most important, he put the card manipulations back into the program and consulted his files on new illusions.

The show played Philadelphia and then Keith's Union Square Theater in Manhattan, opening in June for three weeks. Thurston couldn't resist sauntering into the square and sitting on the same park bench—where he sat feeling sorry for himself, practiced his sleight of hand, and met John Northern Hilliard—just three years earlier. Now his name was in lights across the street, on America's leading vaudeville theater.

A newspaper reporter enthused about the good-looking young man who

(ABOVE) Thurston, left, and Houdini shared a rivalry and cautious respect as they competed for the public's attention. *(Mike Caveney Egyptian Hall Collection)*

(RIGHT) Howard Franklin Thurston, formerly Willie Ryan or The Nim Kid, on the track team at Mount Hermon Academy. *(Mount Hermon archives)*

(BELOW LEFT) Alexander Herrmann was America's greatest magician in the last years of the nineteenth century; Thurston followed him across New York. *(MCEHC)*

(BELOW RIGHT) The Dahomey Village at the Columbian Exposition, 1893, was a ragtag exhibit of African natives; Thurston was the talker in front. *(Author's collection)*

(RIGHT) Grace Butterworth was an amateur dancer who was recruited for Thurston's ambitious plans. *(Rory Feldman collection)*

(BELOW RIGHT) An early posed photo shows Thurston pulling a duck from a spectator's coat. His father, William, was the man; George White stands at the side. *(RFC)*

(BOTTOM LEFT) Thurston's lavish illusion act featured costumes and scenery that seemed to be taken from an Oriental fairy tale. *(MCEHC)*

(BOTTOM RIGHT) Beatrice Foster, Thurston's second wife, was the floating lady featured in the illusion titled Amazement. *(MCEHC)*

(ABOVE) In India, when no theater was suitable, Thurston purchased his own tent to present the show. *(Ken Klosterman collection)*

(RIGHT) Harry Kellar sold his show to Thurston, and treated the business venture as an act of royal succession. *(MCEHC)*

(BELOW) In 1907, during his season with Kellar, Thurston's act was simple and austere; only in later years did the magic become spectacular. *(RFC)*

KELLAR THE WORLD'S GREATEST MAGICIAN
THE PEERLESS CONJURER AND THURSTON

(Above) Thurston's Waltz Ride, at Coney Island, consumed years of time and thousands of dollars in research. *(David Sigafus collection)*

(Right) With his new wife, Nina Leotha Willadsen, and his adopted daughter, Jane, Thurston became a proud family man and father. *(RFC)*

(Below) Charles Thurston's murder came as a shock to his brother Howard, who had been busy monitoring Jane's and Leotha's illnesses. *(Jay Hunter collection)*

The Thurston show, circa 1918, showed Leotha's artistic touches and Thurston's fondness for bigger, more spectacular illusions. *(RFC)*

Thurston's associates and fellow magicians. Left to right, top row: Gus Fasola, Theo Bamberg, Guy Jarrett, Grover George; bottom row: John Northern Hilliard, Harry Jansen (as Dante), Raymond Sugden (as Tampa), and Herman Hanson.

(ABOVE) During Thurston's famous Levitation of Princess Karnac, Mohammed and Abdul chanted the theatrical "prayers" as Thurston evoked the spell. *(MCEHC)*

(LEFT) Jane Thurston joined the show in 1928, adding song-and-dance routines as well as her own theatrical magic. *(George Daily collection)*

(BELOW) Thurston introduced the Sawing in Half illusion, as invented by Horace Goldin and redesigned at Thurston's shop by Harry Jansen. *(MCEHC)*

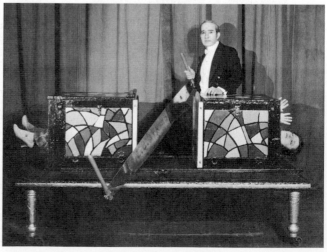

(ABOVE) Harry Harris, Jane Thurston, Leotha, and Howard; it was an unhappy situation, and in this photo, only the young groom managed a smile. *(JHC)*

(BELOW LEFT) Thurston with his cast; the ladies appeared and disappeared. Fernanda Myro, the floating lady, is at the bottom. *(GDC)*

(BELOW RIGHT) In Iasia, Thurston and Cyril Yettmah's masterpiece, the princess disappeared while hanging over the audience. *(JHC)*

(LEFT) The redoubtable Harry Thurston, after his face-lift, plotted his own career as a magician under canvas. *(MCEHC)*

(RIGHT) Howard's marriage to his assistant, Paula Hinckel, caused a distinct rift within the company and alienated Jane. *(RFC)*

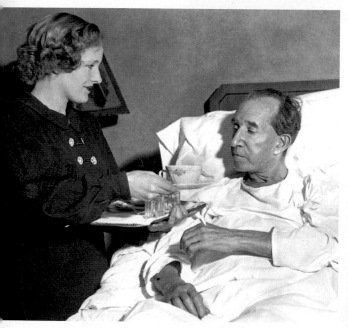

(ABOVE) Jane vowed to carry on the show after Howard's stroke in Charleston, West Virginia, but Harry Thurston stepped in and closed the show. *(MCEHC)*

(RIGHT) Loyal George White performed the "broken wand" ceremony for "The Governor," and later toured with Dante's show. *(JHC)*

portrayed the eastern prince at Keith's, and Thurston reciprocated with a string of press puffery. "He is the nephew of United States senator Thurston." Or, sometimes, the son of Senator Thurston. "He is a native New Yorker, for he himself will admit that for many years he was [a resident of] Brooklyn." Or a native of Boston, or Detroit, or Columbus, depending on whom Thurston was talking to. "For a fact he was educated for the ministry at the Moody School at Northfield, Massachusetts, but just before being ordained he attended a progressive euchre party in Brooklyn and there beheld a parlor pest doing tricks with cards."

Thurston moved the act to the theater at Willow Grove amusement park, near Philadelphia, for the summer. It gave him a chance to perform for a long, leisurely run at night and work on new illusions at a nearby shop during the day.

He added one of Fasola's suggestions, an illusion that the two magicians had discussed in London. A large, colorfully painted trunk was hanging over the edge of the stage, above the orchestra pit. It was there, in front of the curtain, when the audience arrived and remained in place through the show. Near the conclusion of the act, Thurston brought one of his assistants to the edge of the stage. He cautioned the audience to examine the lady's features and remember them so they could identify her when they next saw her. In order to help the identification, he borrowed a handkerchief from a man in the audience and tied it around the lady's arm.

Now the assistant was lifted to a table and covered with a screen. She disappeared, in the style of many other vaudeville illusions. But there was a unique surprise.

The trunk was quickly released, and it slid down a loop of rope, bouncing onto the stage. Thurston pulled out a ring of keys and unlocked the trunk, and two assistants threw open the lid. Inside was a slightly smaller trunk. Using a long pole, which was slipped through two loops of rope on the trunk, the assistants lifted it straight up and placed it on the stage. This trunk was unlocked, revealing a third trunk inside. With the pole, this tiny trunk was also lifted out and placed on the stage.

When Thurston unlocked it, he found the missing lady inside. She stood and was marched to the edge of the stage, where the spectators could identify her and the borrowed handkerchief could be returned.

The Nest of Boxes had been an old trick from the early Victorians. In the original version, a small box, the size of a jewelry box, was shown. A borrowed watch or ring disappeared, and then was discovered inside the group of nested boxes. Fasola's spectacular variation, using a person, was so good that it quickly became embroiled in a battle of magicians. Horace Goldin claimed that the trick was his, and even filed a patent for the mechanism to accomplish it. Fasola and Goldin became locked in pointless charges and countercharges within the world of magic.

AT WILLOW GROVE, another priority was to improve the levitation illusion. From his file of ideas, Thurston pulled out sketches of a levitation that combined the Aga—the lady floating horizontally into the air—with an older idea called Astarte—a special metal corset that allowed her to pirouette in space. Harry (Henry) Couzens, Thurston's mechanic, was entrusted with the job of creating the steel device. It was one of those awful jobs that needed jewelry-like precision in certain spots, and crude, solid work in others, the sort of mechanism that a stage carpenter could quickly repair with a hammer. After months of work, Thurston announced that there had been an eighth-inch mistake. Henry would have to rebuild the mechanism one more time. Couzens took off his apron, tears welling in his eyes. "That's enough for me, Mr. Thurston, I quit. You're impossible to please. You're losing your money and I'm going crazy."

After thinking it over, Couzens returned and finished the job the next day. On stage, the illusion was always called Amazement. Backstage—where every trick with an exotic title is given a nickname by the stagehands—they called the trick "Henry."

Now the lady was hypnotized and placed in a low coffin on low legs, which was wheeled to the center of the stage. Thurston stood behind the coffin and gestured over it. Slowly, the lady rose from the coffin, straight in the air, until she was floating just in front of the magician's chest.

The assistants removed the coffin, allowing the audience to appreciate that nothing was holding her in the air. Thurston held his arms straight over her, as if holding her aloft by the sheer power of his gestures.

The setting brightened with colorful shafts of light, demonstrating that Thurston and the floating harem girl were isolated in the center of the stage. And then, strangely, she began to revolve. Her rigid body turned a horizontal axis from her head to her feet. It was as if she were slowly twisting and tumbling. First she seemed to roll forward, and then she stopped, lying in space upside down, with her face and toes pointing toward the floor. Then her body twisted backward, making several smooth revolutions in the air. Thurston was handed a large, solid metal hoop. He swept it across her floating body twice and then tossed it to an assistant, who took it down to the first row of the audience for examination.

The coffin was replaced and the lady slowly descended into it. Thurston's assistants lifted her to her feet; the magician clapped his hands and she awoke.

The weird illusion of Amazement was always noticed by newspaper reviewers and earned special praise for Thurston.

IN 1903, Thurston took the magic show back on tour through vaudeville theaters in the Midwest, and then returned to Willow Grove for another long run and experiments in the workshop. He still wasn't satisfied with the act and enhanced it with a number of cabinet illusions. His months on the road allowed Thurston to evaluate every trick carefully. What was the audience reaction? How did each piece of apparatus hold up backstage? How long did it take to prepare in each city? Gradually, he was working out the most elaborate and temperamental lighting effects and fountain effects, pruning the show down to the best tricks.

The last addition to the show was an amazing new illusion called Dida. Contrary to Thurston's claims of originality, Dida originated in Germany several years earlier and had worked its way to London, where it made a minor hit at the Alhambra, and then appeared in New York vaudeville. Thurston might have seen it himself, or copied the apparatus from accounts of the London show. A large, low horizontal glass tank was wheeled onto the stage and then filled with water from buckets. Thurston covered the tank with a sheet, which was pulled away seconds later, disclosing a lady assistant, wearing a bathing costume and submerged in the water. She stood and stepped out of the tank. Thurston took his bow, and then asked if the audience would like to know how he did it. Invariably the audience answered yes. He returned to the tank, repeating his motions. He covered the tank a second time and pulled the cloth away to produce a second lady. Despite Thurston's disarming presentation, the audience still had no idea how it was accomplished.

When Houdini reminded Thurston of his loan of twenty-five dollars, Thurston responded with a cheery note. "I am delighted to hear of your continued and great success. The name Houdini will live forever in the history of magic. Now, about the five pounds you loaned me. . . ." Thurston begged him to wait. He was still scraping together money for his new show and had been addressing debts of "over $3,400 since I returned to America." He had been busy paying back other debts, and presumably Harry Thurston was also clamoring for his money.

IN MAY 1904, Harry Kellar brought his show to the Grand Opera House in Philadelphia, just before Thurston reopened at Willow Grove amusement park. After Alexander Herrmann's death, Kellar was regarded as America's greatest magician. But in style, he couldn't have been more distinct from Alexander or Leon Herrmann.

Kellar was tall and bald, with rounded shoulders, big, fleshy hands, and a continual twinkle in his eye. His charm consisted of his familiar, avuncular style.

His childhood had been a neat match for Thurston's, a boyhood on the streets. He had been born Heinrich Keller in Erie, Pennsylvania, in 1844, the son of German immigrants. When he was eleven, he ran away from home, first to Cleveland and then to New York City. A benefactor, Reverend Robert Harcourt, befriended the boy and offered him an education if he would pledge his life to the ministry. Magic intervened. Young Harry saw the Fakir of Ava's magic show. The fakir was Isaiah Hughes, a Buffalo, New York, magician. The boy ran away to join the fakir as an assistant, and those years provided his education in magic.

Keller—later spelled Kellar, to avoid comparisons with the magician Robert Heller—had a rough-and-tumble education in traveling shows. He toured through the Midwest with his own magic show, then joined the Davenport Brothers as their stage manager in 1873.

The Davenports were stars, and represented a particular American phenomenon: spiritualism as entertainment. In the late 1850s, these two brothers developed a novel act in which they were tied into a large wooden cabinet, a sort of armoire, and apparently produced spirit manifestations, an actual séance onstage.

Of course, the Davenports were frauds. Kellar learned their secrets, and then set out with William Fay, another Davenport employee, with their own spirit cabinet act.

In partnership with other magicians or on his own, Kellar traveled extensively—through Europe, South America, India, and Australia. By 1885 he returned to America and took on Alexander Herrmann. By now, Kellar was a seasoned show business professional and a daunting adversary, famous for hardheaded resolve and an explosive temper. Their rivalry was genuine and acrimonious. Kellar thought that Herrmann was a ridiculous, dandified fraud, and he insisted on calling him Niemann—he believed that Alexander was not actually a member of the famous Herrmann family of magicians. Herrmann, tired of his rival's outbursts to the press, insisted that Kellar's name not be mentioned in his presence. Billy and Dot Robinson, working between the two magicians, just added a level of espionage.

Kellar specialized in bringing marvels to his audience, working hard to beg, borrow, or steal the greatest magic for his shows. He was neither comical, nor especially adept at sleight of hand, the way Herrmann was. Instead, he carefully memorized his patter and rehearsed several sequences of small magic, which gave the impression of manual dexterity. Many of Kellar's finest mysteries had originated at Egyptian Hall in London. Kellar made regular pilgrimages to Maskelyne's theater, where he examined the latest illusions. He sometimes offered to buy them, but in any case he never took no for an answer, and often went back to America and produced his own copies of them.

In spite of his determination, Harry Kellar seemed confined to Herrmann's shadow. The public could regard only one magician at a time as "great"; perhaps this was a result of the ever-present fantasy of a magic show—that the magician on stage is a unique person with unique secrets. It wasn't until 1896, when Alexander Herrmann died unexpectedly, that Kellar ascended to the status of America's great magician.

Kellar's 1904 show was a revelation to Thurston. He still included a number of his solid, late-Victorian marvels. For example, Kellar presented favorites like his Spirit Cabinet routine, inspired by the Davenports, or his popular mind-reading routine with his wife, Eva Kellar. But for the 1904 season, he was also featuring new magic like the Crystal Ladder—a large, showy coin trick taken from T. Nelson Downs—as well as the Demon Globe, a ball that rolled up a plank by itself, and the Dying Enigma, in which he colored a number of white silk handkerchiefs. These last two tricks were creations of David Devant, from London. Thurston might have been proud of himself by befriending Devant, but the wily Kellar had vaulted over him; Kellar was bringing some of Devant's best feats to his American audiences.

The real surprise was Kellar's latest levitation. Kellar had been performing levitation illusions for over a decade, gradually evolving and improving them from season to season. But in the 1904 version, the Levitation of Princess Karnac, a pretty Indian princess was levitated high over the stage, isolated from any scenery. American magicians were dumbfounded by the illusion and wrote glowingly of Kellar's new invention. When Thurston watched it, he realized that the new levitation was astonishing, enchanting, and somehow strangely familiar. He'd seen it before, and he'd seen it in London. Thurston realized that Kellar's illusion was nearly identical to John Nevil Maskelyne's amazing levitation from Egyptian Hall.

As a magician inspired by Alexander Herrmann—his boyhood idol—

Thurston had sometimes considered Kellar to be a second-rate talent. But watching him in Philadelphia, Thurston had to give the old wizard his due. Somehow, Kellar had assembled a wonderful show and had even finagled the Maskelyne levitation out of London. Thurston realized that Kellar was still a formidable competitor.

KELLAR ADDED Paul Valadon to his cast in the fall of 1904. Valadon was the German sleight-of-hand artist that Thurston had seen at Egyptian Hall. As Kellar had worked with guest stars in the past, Valadon seemed to fit nicely into the formula. Thurston even considered working with Kellar. He wrote to him in February 1905, and Kellar responded with the fascinating information that "next season will probably be my last on the road; at least, that is my present intention." Thurston made arrangements to meet with Kellar that summer in New York. But the meeting didn't take place. Thurston realized that his show had grown to a scale that meant he could no longer be an act or even a costar. By the summer of 1905, Thurston already had his eye on a larger prize. He had announced that he was finished with vaudeville and would now open his own magic show, following in the footsteps of Herrmann or Kellar.

Thurston had been booked by theatrical manager H. B. Curtis for an Australian tour. In 1899, Curtis had brought another promising young American magician to Australia, Oscar Eliason, who performed under the name Dante. Eliason had a highly successful, artistic show inspired by Alexander Herrmann. Unfortunately, after one season in Australia and New Zealand, Dante was accidentally shot in a hunting accident and died. He was just twenty-eight years old.

Curtis was anxious to recapture his success with Dante and wanted Thurston in Australia. But when Thurston arrived in San Francisco, he found that Curtis, desperate for cash, had first booked him for five weeks at the Fisher Theater, a vaudeville establishment in the city. Thurston had no option but to play out the contract. He paid off Curtis, and then discovered that the actual tour had been something of a fraud. Curtis was not welcomed in Australia. Several years earlier, after bringing a minstrel troupe to Australia, the manager had skipped out on the company without paying them. The Australian authorities were waiting for him.

Thurston was determined to bring his show to Australia. He pawned his baggage with the steamship line for transportation, borrowed money from his new employees, and sent the obligatory telegram to brother Harry for some emergency funds. On June 11, 1905, he left the shores of California on the *Saratoga*, destined for Hawaii and then Australia, accompanied by George and four technicians, above a hold containing dozens of crates of scenery and magic. As Howard and George stood on the deck watching the sunset, Thurston absentmindedly reached into his pocket and took out a silver dollar to practice his sleight of hand. He intended to flip it into the air and shoot it into his sleeve. Instead, the coin caught on the edge of his sleeve and tumbled onto the deck, rolling into the water.

Thurston froze, and then instinctively reached back into his pocket, feeling for another coin. George saw the expression on his face and knew something was wrong.

"What are we going to do, Governor?" George asked. "Don't worry, George. Never worry," Thurston sighed. That had been Thurston's last coin. He now had the largest magic show in the world, but he didn't have a cent to his name.

ALSO ON BOARD was a nineteen-year-old actress named Beatrice Foster, small and slender with alabaster skin and a great crown of brunette hair. She was one of the two ladies Thurston had brought to take part in the illusions. Foster was a stage name, her mother's maiden name; she was born Beatrice Fleming on November 3, 1883, in New York City, but friends called her Tommy.

Beatrice came from a theatrical family; her grandfather, an English-born playwright, wrote and produced an early "Uncle Tom's Cabin" show, and cast it with members of his family. Little Beatrice first appeared on stage when she was two, and then went on to specialize as Little Lord Fauntleroy. For five years, her family sent her to the Academy of the Holy Angels, a convent school for little girls, in Fort Lee, New Jersey. When she was sixteen, she returned to the stage, working in vaudeville plays. Thurston had first met her in 1900, when she was working in one of Edwin Milton Royle's short plays; Royle was a Broadway leading man, playwright, and lyricist. Later Beatrice applied when Thurston advertised for assistants during the Willow Grove experiments. She was then twenty, the perfect petite size for magic, with dark eyes and a sharp profile. Beatrice quickly became the unlucky assistant who was strapped into Henry's metal corset and turned upside down over the stage, and then propelled into the tiny, airless trunks before they were tipped, jostled, and unlocked.

She took it all in stride, as part of the job. Beatrice had relinquished her acting career, no longer dreaming of stardom. She was happy to become a magic assistant and was game for any adventure. On the *Saratoga*, she was leaving for the adventure of a lifetime.

TEN

....

"A STREET SCENE FROM THE ORIENT"

 hurston spent his voyage making plans. By the time the company landed in Honolulu, at the beginning of July, he had wired one of Australia's most successful theatrical managers, George Musgrove. Musgrove had seen his show in America, and Thurston optimistically announced to Hawaiian reporters that the manager would be representing the show in Australia.

When Thurston arrived in Sydney, his first concern was George White. At the end of the 1890s, the Australian Labour Party had championed a White Australia policy, barring any additional non-Caucasians from entering the country. On board the *Saratoga*, Thurston made arrangements with one of the officers to let George wear a uniform and join the crew on the deck, where immigrations officials might overlook him. Thurston then arranged a little signal, a sort of magic routine, to sneak George onto the dock. When the man from Australian immigration joined the ship, and Thurston had him distracted in conversation, the magician mopped his brow with his handkerchief. George took his cue and disappeared into the crowd with the stevedores—it was his usual act of accomplishing something while becoming invisible. He arranged to meet Thurston hours later outside of Tattersall's Hotel in Sydney.

Thurston had scraped together some money and booked a grand room at

Tattersall's, which he could not afford. Then he arranged for George, the cast, and the crew to stay at nearby theatrical boardinghouses. His first priority was a special performance—not magic, just bluff—for the Australian theatrical managers. A group met him at the famous marble bar at Tattersall's, where everyone took turns buying rounds of drinks. Thurston plied them with stories of his success, his reviews from New York and London, and his state-of-the-art apparatus. A Mr. Collins represented George Musgrove. Another manager, Edwin Geach, had been responsible for Dante the magician's tour of Australia several years earlier.

When it was time for Thurston's round of drinks, he ordered champagne and cigars for the group, and then tipped the waitress lavishly with a casual gesture. Pushing the extra money into the waitress's hand pained Thurston, and at the moment of truth he almost weakened. But he noticed the raised eyebrows around the table and realized that his plan worked perfectly. They thought he was rich. Geach offered a generous contract to handle an Australian tour, and Thurston was happy to accept. He knew that Geach would be familiar with the technical requirements of a magic show.

In fact, Geach had a number of good ideas. He booked Thurston into Sydney's Palace Theater and supplemented the show with Allan Shaw, a Canada-born coin manipulator who had traveled to Australia with Thurston, a cello soloist, and a comic singer. The final feature on the show was an Edison motion picture projector, which Thurston brought from America for the tour. He had selected several short, comic films, *A Touch of Nature* and *The Lost Child*.

Geach set the opening for July 22, 1905, and advertised it extravagantly in the newspapers: "What Irving is to drama, Melba to opera, The Great Thurston is to magicians, absolutely the greatest living exponent." It was a nerve-racking opening, with repairs and adjustments being made throughout the day and until the curtain time. Realizing how difficult the show had been to mount, Geach was horrified to hear the orchestra repeating the overture, as the crowd stamped their feet in anticipation. He rushed backstage to find Thurston still onstage in his work clothes, adjusting a prop. The manager marched his magician into the dressing room, insisting that he put on his tuxedo and makeup for the performance. Once Thurston had been pushed onto the stage and the performance began, any of Geach's fears were quickly dispelled. The orchestra began the "Zenda Waltzes," and Thurston started his faultless manipulations. The audience swooned with each new marvel. Geach knew that he had a star.

Thurston appeared for four weeks in Sydney and was then held over several additional days. The company moved on to Melbourne, where they opened at the Athenaeum Hall on September 2. This theater was a particular challenge, as it had only a concert stage and needed extensive work to accommodate Thurston's scenery, trapdoors, and electrical effects. Again, the crew worked until the show time; in fact, the audience arrived to hear hammering behind the curtain. The opening-night show was interrupted several times when the lights failed unexpectedly. Thurston patiently waited, chatting with the crowd, and when the lights flickered on again, he resumed the show.

"There isn't so much patter," a reviewer noted favorably. "No magician has used less in a show. He has a strong personality and holds his audience firmly." His eloquence was admired; his rich voice with a nasal twang, combined with his neat Americanisms, were considered enchanting. An Australian magician recalled a friend who had been studying public speaking.

> His instructor said, "Go and see that clever conjurer at the Athenaeum and take particular note of both his diction and his delivery." My friend went, but unfortunately for his teacher, came away crazy to learn conjuring, and with little interest remaining for his elocutionary studies.

In Adelaide, a reviewer admired Thurston's marvels but chafed at the conventions of a magic show:

> He frequently appeals to the audience for assistance in various ways. The same old springboard is run out into the front seats and Thurston calls upon onlookers to shuffle and select cards, lend him handkerchiefs, to temporarily hold apparatus, and to go on the stage with him while he pulls a duck, baby socks and other articles out of their clothing, and eggs from their jaws. When will there appear a magician who will entertain without disturbing the peace and

dignity of his paying patrons? Why would a man who boasts of having 5000 pounds worth of accessories want a cheap linen handkerchief from his audience?

HOWARD AND BEATRICE had arranged a little deception that made their travels together much easier. By the time the ship landed in Sydney, the ship log recorded her as "Mrs. Thurston," and she was introduced this way to the press. It was an odd twist on his earliest days with Grace, when they denied they were married and insisted that they were brother and sister. Adding to the complication was the fact that Howard was still married. After their final argument in London, Grace had been anxious to leave, but she never actually filed for divorce.

Howard explained to an interviewer in Australia, "I am not a club man," insisting that he didn't drink and rarely socialized. "The only day I go out is Sunday, and then I take Mrs. Thurston to church. The rest of the time I work."

Curiously, much of his appeal in Australia was to members of the opposite sex. Reviewers noted the high proportion of women in attendance, explaining that his marvels held a "strange fascination for womenfolk." Perhaps the attraction is represented in photographs published in Australian newspapers— Thurston's handsome, placid face and dark-lidded eyes staring out from a formal portrait; or his proud pose, gazing upward, arms crossed, in his embroidered Oriental jacket and neat turban. He embodied the dashing, romantic prince of countless fairy tales, and his movements on stage displayed a balletic elegance. "The Napoleon of Magic," his billing proclaimed. "Thurston is a married man, and he passes all his letters on to his wife," a Perth reporter warned his female admirers. Presumably, Beatrice had become suspicious of his fan mail, just as Grace had in London.

IN MELBOURNE, Thurston first met Servais Le Roy, who was then touring Australia with his own one-hour magic show. Le Roy's career had neatly crisscrossed Thurston's; he had been taught Dr. Elliott's Back Palm in New York just before Thurston learned it, and may have been the first performer to use it on an English stage. By the 1890s, he was an established performer in London. In 1905, he was also touring through Australia with an impressive show, Le Roy, Talma and Bosco. Talma was his pretty wife, the coin manipulator, and Bosco was a fat comic sidekick.

Servais Le Roy was four years older than Thurston, born in Belgium in 1865. Le Roy always looked the part, a small, athletic, dapper man with a wave of blond hair and a long waxed mustache. On the stage he was charming and impish, an instinctive performer. He could seemingly do anything—intricate sleight of hand, split-second comedy, and physical illusions. Most of all, he was ingenious. His magic was all of his own creation, and astonishingly novel. One of his greatest feats, which he was then performing in Australia, was his version of the levitation, titled the Garden of Sleep. Talma, his wife, reclined horizontally on a table. She was covered with a large silken cloth. Then she floated into the air, high above the performer's head. The table was removed from the stage. Le Roy passed a hoop over the floating lady—now a standard bit of business for these levitations. His surprising climax came when he gripped a corner of the cloth and pulled it away. At that moment, the lady seemed to visibly disappear in midair.

Le Roy and Thurston pledged admiration for each other's work. Le Roy envied Thurston's natural grace, but he realized that few of his illusions were original. Thurston took note of Le Roy's brilliant innovations. In fact, he was too proud to admit it, but Le Roy had fooled him with many of his effects.

But as he traveled through Australia, the magician that Thurston heard about most was Dante—the young man who had reached such renown, and then died tragically. Dante seemed to haunt the public's memory, and reviews often compared the two magicians. Thurston even visited the magician's grave, sending back a photo to an American magician's magazine. Thurston realized that he'd succeeded when he read, "Dante was a marvel, and it might be thought he reached the top of his profession, but Thurston goes one better." The reviews also document how the show was undergoing changes as he moved from city to city in Australia. Some of these were the rotating guest stars hired by Geach. For example, George Stillwell, who performed a magic act with silk handkerchiefs, replaced Allan Shaw. Then American comedians Maude Amber and Winfield Blake joined the company. They presented a fast and funny act burlesquing operas. As new motion pictures were rented, they were billed as the latest features with the Edison projector. But Thurston also improved his tricks. "Mr. Thurston is gradually adding to his program as he gets his budget of wonders unpacked and placed in position," a newspaper explained. Two of his most successful were the small tricks called Mysterious Dice and Eggs Extraordinary.

Mysterious Dice was an import from American magic dealers. Thurston showed a large wooden block, like a large child's block, painted with spots like a die. He had an accompanying box, a small horizontal coffer that was exactly twice the size of the die; it consisted of two compartments, side by side, and accompanying doors.

Thurston started by placing the die inside a tall opera hat and explained that he would make it disappear. The die was then taken from the hat and placed in one of the compartments of the box. The doors were closed. Thurston then indulged in a silly comedy of errors, showing the box empty by subtly tipping the box from side to side. He opened one door, and then closed it again, tipping the box before opening the door on the opposite side.

Of course, the children in the audience took the bait, gradually voicing their disapproval. Thurston identified two of the loudest boys, inviting them up on stage. He asked them to open the box and remove the die. They rushed to the box and opened the doors, only to find that the die was really gone. Thurston showed that it had returned to the hat.

He then kept the smaller boy onstage. He showed an empty hat and demonstrated how he was able to make eggs by magic. He asked the boy to blow on his hand, and then dipped it into the hat, producing an egg. He handed it to the boy, and repeated the procedure, showing another egg. As Thurston increased the pace, the boy crossed his arms, to collect the stack of eggs, and struggled to keep up. At one point, Thurston produced an egg and then held it at arm's length, waiting for the boy to take it. The magician looked in the opposite direction, supposedly oblivious to his helper's predicament, forcing the boy to reach for the egg. The audience giggled throughout the boy's trial and roared as he finally began dropping eggs that smashed on the stage.

From city to city, the egg trick got better, as Thurston indulgently tried different gags and combinations. It would finally come together several years later as the Boy, the Girl and the Eggs. Thurston's ultimate formula was the addition of a little girl, who took each egg from Thurston and then relayed it to the boy. Each transfer, from hand, to hand, to hand, increased the potential laughs.

In Australia, Thurston began using a phrase in his programs, "Howard Thurston is the originator and inventor of every illusion he presents." It was pure hyperbole, particularly unsuited to Thurston, who was always dependent on other magicians for his ideas. But the egg trick was the exception. It was a brilliant bit of situation comedy, refined and perfected during his world tour.

Some of his other new magic included the Man in Red, a disappearance and exchange illusion, and Incubation Thurstonia, the production of dozens of barnyard birds, inspired by one of Le Roy's popular tricks. Chang Ling Sing, A Cantonese Conceit, was a sequence of Chinese magic with Thurston in Chinese costuming. Ah Sid was the production of a small Chinese boy from within a tall rolled piece of matting. These new features were prominently printed on the bill when Thurston's show returned to the Sydney Palace during the Christmas season at the end of 1905.

SHORTLY AFTER the company arrived in Australia, Howard had wired his brother Harry, encouraging him to join the company. Like his big brother, Harry's marriage had dissolved, and he was now ready for a welcome distraction, a reminder of his years with the sideshow or the circus. Always anxious to attach himself to his brother's successes, Harry found the tales from Australia especially irresistible. Howard brought him onto the show as the business manager. As the company was headed to different countries, Thurston reasoned that it would be a good idea to have a tough, trusted negotiator. For Harry, it was a big adventure, as well as an opportunity to look after his business interests—after years of steady loans, he was now an investor in the Thurston magic show. Harry left San Francisco on the *Ventura* and arrived in Sydney at the end of January, joining his brother in Brisbane in February 1906.

Thurston performed in the towns of the goldfields, Kalgoorlie, Coolgardie, and Southern Cross, then moved on to Hobart, Tasmania, and up the coast through the mining towns until the finish of their tour in Townsville. The brothers had been busy trying to book dates through the Far East, with the help of Louis (Doc) Henry, a colorful, seedy old show business character. Doc Henry had made promises and issued vague threats about the competition. In Melbourne he had tried to lure Le Roy to India "before Thurston." Le Roy turned him down. Doc Henry then sold himself to Thurston as an advance man.

Geach considered Thurston a friend, not merely an investment, and he tried to discourage the tour of China. It was notoriously difficult to arrange contracts in the Orient, he warned, especially a profitable combination of dates, from city to city. And quality theaters that could support Thurston's show were few. But Thurston was determined. The company traveled for two weeks to Manila in the Philippines, opening at the Zorrilla Theater on April 5, 1906. They crossed the bay to Cavite, and then Hong Kong and Macao. Thurston remembered the city as a microcosm of the Orient.

> Filth, poverty, wealth, its crime and brutality, its beautiful silks and its foul cotton rags, its fish and opium, all huddled together in a space so small that living there was like being caught in the midst of a pulsing, swaying, clamorous crowd. And over all was the unforgettable and indescribable odor of the East.

Howard was enchanted with the exotic spectacle. "I had never been happier in my life," he wrote. It had all of the exciting jangle of a busy midway, the tempting mixture of money and adventure that had filled his dreams as a boy. Winfield Blake, the actor working with Thurston, didn't share his fascination with Macao. "It's nothing but a big, bad smell," he told Thurston.

There they played for several days at the Portuguese Club, and then a wealthy owner of a gambling club approached Thurston; he wanted to hire him for some private performances. The businessman offered to build a special theater, near his house outside of Macao, just for his show.

Charlie Holzmueller, a young stagehand from San Francisco, had been hired as Thurston's machinist, and he was dumbfounded to watch this special theater erected in forty-eight hours. "There wasn't a nail driven in it." Maude Amber called it the Aladdin Theater, as it had seemed to appear by magic. They performed three or four shows in the special structure. Holzmueller recalled that it rained during all the performances. The muddy grounds, combined with the springy stage—bamboo and fresh-cut lumber—made the large, heavy illusions difficult to perform.

They were relieved to return to a traditional Chinese theater, the Tai Ping, in Hong Kong. The latest films from Edison were waiting at the docks. A short film of the devastation from the San Francisco earthquake was of special interest to the American cast and crew. A number of them were from San Francisco and had received wires from their families while they were traveling. But the Chinese weren't interested in the news footage. They preferred the short comedies, particularly one that involved a small baby crawling into a doghouse.

In Hong Kong the film was a hit, but Thurston encountered a new raft of problems with the magic—he had to slow down the pace of his performance, to allow the audience to chat about each illusion after he performed it. He allowed extra time for the translator, who seemed to elaborate on every simple phrase. Finally, he found it necessary to include careful excuses why women were appearing on his stage—or even worse, in bathing costumes—during the performance. Traditionally, women did not appear on a Chinese stage. When Thurston stopped to kiss the hand of Beatrice when she emerged from the water tank, the audience voiced a loud cry of disapproval. Thurston insisted that the women in his show were necessary, and the illusions depended upon them performing in a hypnotic state. That was enough to deflect the critics. The extra time for translations, discussions, and pantomime demonstrations of hypnosis, Thurston recalled, meant that the Tai Ping Theater show ran from nine o'clock in the evening to three in the morning.

Harry left the show in Hong Kong, traveling back through Japan and arriving in Vancouver, British Columbia, late in May. He'd indulged his sense of adventure and, within several months, had his fill of show business. More than likely, he'd also bristled at his older brother, the star, who made all the decisions and actually left nothing for the "business manager" to manage. Harry didn't want to argue. He bid his good-byes and good luck. He made his way back to Chicago.

Thurston faced more personal problems when he appeared at the Lyceum Theater in Shanghai, starting on June 1, 1906. Before one show, Beatrice and Howard shared a long, loud argument. George White and Charlie Holzmueller didn't know the cause of the squabble, but Thurston didn't resolve it before he stepped onstage. Beatrice, taking matters into her own hands, walked out just before the second act. She timed her exit precisely to cause the most impact— Amazement, Thurston's revolving levitation, was her special number, and she was the only person who could perform it.

Backstage, Thurston flew into a rage but resolved to carry through with the show. He grabbed Charlie, telling him to get word to the electrician out front. "Tell Percy to run an extra film, and we're going to rehearse someone else." Looking around, Thurston had spotted a slender stagehand, a Chinese boy hired that week in Shanghai, who was just small enough to fit into the metal harness. It was his only possible solution.

The boy was bolted into the steel harness and given a little extra padding around the hips to fill it out. Then he was thrown into the princess's costume and hurried to the stage.

As the film flickered out front, Thurston nervously rehearsed the steps of the levitation. Fortunately, the stagehand had spent the last few performances watching the trick from the wings and could repeat all of the action—being hypnotized, falling backward, and remaining expressionless during the routine.

When the motion picture screen lifted on the scene, the audience instantly recognized the boy as native Chinese. "In their amazement a lot of them just stood up in their seats, gaping," Holzmueller recalled. They had excused a lot of Thurston's magic as mysteriously foreign: the fairy-tale Arabian scenery and costumes, the cast of flamboyant Americans, and Thurston's apparent ability to hypnotize, or otherwise control, his weak-minded assistants. But the inclusion of the Chinese boy onstage, in the middle of this fantasy world, suddenly made the illusion seem dangerously real and challenging.

He played his part perfectly, and Thurston had to stifle a laugh when he saw the boy's accurate impersonation of Beatrice—fluttering his eyes, or pretending to fall asleep, cocking his head to one side with a sweet smile on his face. As the boy floated in the air and began to revolve in space, the Shanghai audience was held spellbound. After the trick concluded, they brought the performers back for one bow after another—both the boy and the magician. Thurston and his new princess finally stepped into the wings, inspiring even more whoops of congratulations from the crew, who had been watching the scene anxiously. The surprising ovation soothed Thurston's temper.

At the hotel with the rest of the cast, Beatrice heard about the Chinese stagehand. The next day she returned for the show. As she was slinking back through the stage door of the theater, feeling embarrassed, Thurston sidled up to her. "Tommy, these Chinese are a funny group. Of course, I want you back in the show. But I have to listen to the audience, and I'm afraid that they liked it better without you," he teased. "Wasn't I lucky to find that out?"

Despite the incident, Beatrice Foster was now an essential, irreplaceable part of the show, and Thurston couldn't afford any arguments. He was running the occasional advertisements in the American theatrical journals *The New York Dramatic Mirror* and *Billboard*, boasting of his success overseas and noting that "Miss Foster" was his chief assistant. He had dropped the husband-and-wife act, especially if Grace or any of their friends could read about it.

The Thurston company traveled to Kobe and Yokohama, Japan. Then they returned through Hong Kong to Saigon for a week of engagements, passed through Singapore, and headed to Batavia, and then Surabaya, Java, in September 1906. In Java, the show traveled from the wharf with the heavy crates piled high on twenty oxcarts. The following month they performed in Rangoon, Burma. In Calcutta, India, they opened at His Majesty's Theater on October 22, 1906.

HOWARD THURSTON was fascinated by India, and over his months of travel he had been anticipating his tour there. Howard had been told that the famous Indian fakirs, the street magicians throughout the country, would show him marvels unseen by any Westerner. He passed word among the Calcutta magicians that he would welcome them at his hotel. A number arrived, but he was disappointed in their magic. "Many of them were very clever at sleight of hand," he wrote, "and had highly developed personality and showmanship." But invariably, they relied on a small set of skills like palming or misdirection, as they crouched on the ground. He asked if any of the magicians could perform the famous Indian Rope Trick, in which a rope rose in the air and a boy climbed to the top. Most of the fakirs had never heard of it, and none could show him. In search of anything that he could use in his performances, Thurston auditioned performers during his free time in Calcutta. Finally, he was told that the very best magicians would come to see him. They arrived, dressed in bright, theatrical costumes, and proceeded to show him their best routines. After the show, they explained that they'd learned them in Chicago, when they worked at the 1893 World's Fair, a little farther down the midway from Thurston's platform at the Dahomey Village.

Eventually, Thurston was told that the mere street fakirs were not the keepers of the secrets, and he and his company were introduced to a yogi, a holy man, who was supposedly capable of self-levitation. Talking through an interpreter, the yogi solemnly informed Thurston about his careful ritual; the yogi needed to spend five days in the mountains, living on nothing but lamb's blood and engaging in prayer. Then he could sit cross-legged, breathe deeply, and rise into the air. If Thurston would pay the man's meager expenses, he promised a demonstration. Thurston paid him and awaited his return.

Winfield Blake laughed it all off, pointing out how the only thing that the yogi managed to raise was a donation for the lamb! Beatrice found the promise ridiculous. She'd now seen too many fakirs with their elaborate promises and disappointing tricks.

But Howard seemed convinced by the wizened old wizard, and over the weeks, he gradually talked himself into believing the man's powers. "If this man can do it, if he can really accomplish this, then I have to learn it. I'll stay here in India and learn his secret, copy his diet and his prayers, even if it takes years," he told his company.

Thurston was a canny enough con man to have recognized a swindle, but his ecumenical education at Dwight Moody's school had morphed into a very

different point of view. If Grace Thurston's account was correct—that her husband had developed no personal faith to sustain him in difficult times—it
suggests that his principle education from Mount Hermon was the pose of a
sophisticate and a young man of faith. By the turn of the century, Thurston's
London society shows and New York vaudeville successes had allowed him to
rub elbows with real society. There he saw that Moody's open-minded acceptance of other religions had been supplanted by a new fashion, Madame Bla-
vatsky's Theosophy. The root of true religious wonders, according to Theosophy
salons, could be found in India, and manifested in the occult. Thurston's pro-
fessed interest in these phenomena was a sign that he had erased his past as a
hard-boiled carnival talker. If Thurston didn't really believe in the marvels of
Indian magic, he had learned the value of this pose and learned to con himself.

The cast was surprised by their boss's willingness to trust the yogi; it seemed
incredible to them that he might be willing to forgo his career for such ridiculous promises. Inevitably, the yogi failed to return for the demonstration, and
Thurston realized that he'd been taken for a handful of rupees.

In fact, the newspaper reviews made it clear that the greatest magic in India
was Thurston's performance at His Majesty's Theater. The sleight of hand was
more astonishing than any fakirs; the levitation feat, Amazement, was more
imaginative than the usual Indian legends. There they played to European
audiences—not to the natives—and worked to capacity crowds for four weeks
before moving on to Bombay.

The show then returned to Calcutta, where they settled at the Classic
Theater for twelve weeks. At the Classic, Thurston quickly learned a new set
of taboos. The trick in which he pulled eggs from the mouth of a boy from the
audience earned him murmurs and shouts. Hindus considered the egg un-
clean. Even worse was a cute little routine called Feeding the Baby, in which a
piglet seemed to slurp down a big bottle of milk. Pigs were considered offensive
by many in the crowd, and during an early performance, when Thurston's pig
jumped from the stage, the audience scattered for the exits. George chased the
squealing piglet into the auditorium and removed it from the theater before
Thurston could lure the Indians back inside.

Planning ahead, Howard hit on an ingenious scheme. He commissioned a tent to be made in Calcutta, a three-post monstrosity that seated two thousand people. His company located a Chinese tentmaker who was willing to take on the job, and Thurston supervised the work, producing a perfect replica of the wonderful American circus tents of his youth. The name "Thurston" was painted in large letters on the big top, and an American flag flew on the center pole. This way, the Great Thurston show would be guaranteed to find audiences even in the cities where a theater was not available—Lall Bagh, Benares, and Lucknow. It was a return to the old Thurston Brothers tent show days—the circus and sideshow business that he had shared with Harry.

IN CALCUTTA, Thurston caught up with his mail. Letters from fellow performers or back issues of *The Dramatic Mirror* kept him abreast of the latest news. Thurston was contemplating his return to the United States and anxious to read about his competition. Journals like *Mahatma* and *The Sphinx*, American periodicals devoted to magic, had been regularly reporting on Thurston's world tour. Howard's British friend P. T. Selbit was now editing a London magazine called *The Wizard*. Harry Houdini, a sensation in vaudeville with his escape act, was now a prominent part of the magic community as the editor and publisher of a New York periodical, *The Conjurer's Monthly*. Houdini included reports of Thurston's success in India. "Rumor has it that Howard is making several fortunes in the Orient," Houdini reported, "and he has great prospects of making more money than any magician that has ever 'gone the route' through India." No doubt Houdini's positive notice was inspired by the fact that Thurston had finally sent him a check for twenty-five dollars, repaying the loan from London.

But as Thurston sat in the bright sun at a table outside of the Continental Hotel, reading through the journals, he was struck by the latest news from America. Even in faraway India, he could piece together the scraps of information, from one article to another. It was now clear what was happening with Harry Kellar and Paul Valadon.

Thurston began to feel sick to his stomach, helplessly double-crossed. Kellar was now retiring and had made his decision. He was about to name Paul

Valadon as his successor. Howard Thurston—with one of the largest magic shows in history and a fat scrapbook filled with rave reviews—would return to America consigned to second place.

IN ALLAHABAD, near the end of Thurston's season in India, the company had moved the crates into a big, dirty old theater. Charlie Holzmueller and George White were cutting the necessary traps in the stage. They'd sawed through the holes and then jumped down about five feet, onto the dusty subfloor, to finish the job, when the manager of the theater came running to the stage. "Get out, get out! Hurry! There are cobras underneath the stage!" Charlie and George scrambled out of the hole, and the performances could only be accomplished, night after night, with a small brigade of Hindu boys under the stage with lamps and sticks, to drive away the snakes. That way, the assistants and the girls in the show were able to crawl around in relative safety, making their magical entrances and exits.

Thurston watched the near accident and shook his head. It seemed eerily significant. He knew that it was time to go home. But he had no idea what sort of show business snakes he'd find beneath his feet.

ELEVEN

"THE LEVITATION OF PRINCESS KARNAC"

agicians didn't get to pick their successors any more than they were allowed to select their competitors. It's true that the American public seemed to accept only one great magician at a time. But there was no tradition of the heir apparent until Alexander Herrmann hinted, in 1896 interviews, that he might be retiring soon and that his nephew Leon was capable of taking over the show. With Herrmann's sudden death, it was incumbent upon his widow, Adelaide, to turn that hint into a royal succession, to lavishly promote Leon, fulfill the dates, and keep the show rolling.

It was, of course, a cold business decision, and not an actual inheritance. And the public rejected it. Leon Herrmann never succeeded to his uncle's lofty status. Harry Kellar fulfilled the role of America's great magician.

In turn, Kellar had his own cold business reasons for choosing a successor and mythologizing the process. Kellar was now in his late fifties, with a comfortable bank account. He was looking forward to retirement. He loved to travel and adored fishing. His show had been carefully established as a theatrical entity—not only the props and scenery, but also the contracts with theater managers, agents, assistants, advance men, newspaper editors, and poster printers. Kellar was in a position to sell the show, and its all-important relationship to the public, by officially endorsing a successor. He could make money by selling the properties, as well as earning a weekly fee from the next magician.

Thurston may not have realized what Kellar was considering when he had his first exchange of letters in 1905. But by 1906, Kellar was in the midst of his second tour with Paul Valadon. And suddenly, all of the pieces fit together.

It was Valadon, the German sleight-of-hand artist, who had supplied Kellar with mechanical details for Maskelyne's incredible levitation from "The Entranced Fakir." He'd seen the equipment backstage and could describe it to Kellar. That's how Kellar had his own version of the levitation just months before Valadon joined his show.

The timing was too coincidental. And as if to prove it, Kellar followed up, the next season, by extracting more information from Valadon and introducing another longtime feature from Egyptian Hall, Maskelyne's comical illusion sketch, "Will, the Witch, and the Watchman." In London, Valadon had costarred in both "The Entranced Fakir" and "Will, the Witch, and the Watchman," suggesting that he had reconstructed these illusions for Kellar. Valadon's part in the show was gradually increasing, and he had achieved equal billing with Kellar. He was being groomed as the successor.

Thurston first felt betrayed. He had sent wires to Kellar, asking him to consider him for future business opportunities. But now he realized that as he'd spent two years of hard slogging through Australia, the Orient, and India, Kellar had spent those same two years introducing Paul Valadon in the finest, plushest theaters across America. Thurston realized that he was helpless; the entire con game was being played on a level far over his head. If he had followed through with Kellar, could he really have been named as his successor? Probably not, for Valadon had already, secretly, earned that position through his treachery.

THE FIRST ONE to figure out the game had been John Northern Hilliard, the congenial reporter and magic fan whom Thurston had met on the park bench in Union Square.

In 1904, when Valadon joined the Kellar show, Hilliard reviewed it for the

Rochester Post Express. In previous years, Hilliard had been tough on Kellar. He considered him an inferior magician—almost completely inept when it came to clever sleight of hand. But the addition of Valadon seemed to round out the program beautifully, and Hilliard's 1904 review offered a fulsome endorsement of the show.

> Mr. Kellar has attained perfection in his own particular line, and we have no
> hesitation in doffing our hat and hailing him as the Grand Old Man of Magic.
> Mr. Kellar, as we have explained many times, has certain limitations as a con-
> jurer. He is not a manipulator, but essentially a magical entertainer, and in this
> field, he stands absolutely alone.

Harry Kellar was famously temperamental off the stage, a colorful buffoon of a man who could alternately explode in profanity or offer friendly pats on the back. If a piece of equipment failed him onstage, he was likely to take it into the back alley and break it to bits with an ax, or throw it into the wings, where it often raised a bump on the head of his assistant, Fritz Bucha. The next day, Kellar would apologize profusely. He knew Bucha's shoe size, and invariably bought a pair of expensive shoes as a peace offering. By the end of the season, Bucha used to joke, he was carrying a trunk filled with new pairs of shoes.

Kellar had been braced for another bad review from Hilliard, but was so thrilled by his praise that he typically overreacted, trying to recruit him as his friend. Kellar told Hilliard that he needed his help. He had been using an awkward paragraph in his program to promote his new levitation:

> Absolutely new in principle, it is the outcome of experiments extending over a
> number of years, and in which more than ten thousand dollars have been ex-
> pended. Experts who have witnessed the mystery declare it to be the most in-
> explicable mystery that has ever come within their expertise.

Instead of crude boasts, Kellar needed real poetry with some two-dollar words, which he knew Hilliard could deliver. Hilliard agreed to write the program note for fifty dollars, and delivered a sparkling paragraph:

The most daring and bewildering illusion, and by far the most difficult achievement Mr. Kellar ever attempted. Absolutely new in principle. The dream in mid air of the dainty Princess Karnac surpasses the fabled feats of the ancient Egyptian sorcerers, nor can anything more magical be found in the pages of The Thousand and One Nights, and it lends a resemblance to the miraculous tales of levitation that come out of India. The illusion is acknowledged by critics and historians of the goetic art to be the profoundest achievement of either ancient or modern magic. Its perfection represents fifteen years of patient research and abstruse study, and the expenditure of many thousand dollars. The result of these labors is a veritable masterpiece of magic, the sensational marvel of the twentieth century, and the crowning achievement of Mr. Kellar's long and brilliant career.

Kellar thought it was very good, but suspected that it should be longer. It was hardly worth fifty dollars. So he sent Hilliard a check for twenty-five dollars, voicing his disapproval.

In their escalating argument, Hilliard managed to tweak his final draft of the paragraph, substituting the word "obtuse" for "abstruse." The new sentence read, "Its perfection represents fifteen years of patient research and obtuse study . . . ," which was now a nice insult to Kellar. Hilliard reasoned that Kellar, with his cursory grade-school education, would never notice the difference. Kellar didn't notice, proudly printing the paragraph—and the word "obtuse"—in every program for his show for over a year. It was sweet revenge.

HILLIARD WASN'T EXAGGERATING when he described the Levitation of Princess Karnac as a masterpiece of twentieth-century magic.

It was the brainchild of John Nevil Maskelyne, who had been experimenting with different levitation devices throughout his long career. By 1900, there had been two distinct innovations in the illusion. The first secret was that the floating person could be supported with a strong, steel horizontal bar that supported a cradle, a metal support beneath the lady. This bar generally extended straight back from the lady, passing through a slit in the curtain where it attached to some upright gantry or lifting mechanism. Nevil Maskelyne, John Nevil's son, had invented a clever twist on this, quite literally. By inserting a tight bend in the bar just behind the lady—it was a sort of dog leg or, to use the popular magical term, a gooseneck—a hoop could apparently be passed over the floating person. In fact, the hoop passed over one end, head to toe, where it was now linked onto the bent metal behind the lady. By casually sliding the hoop along the tracks of the gooseneck, behind the lady, it could be maneuvered back over her head and then passed back across her feet. The hoop was now unlinked from the metal support. It was this clever move—passing the hoop twice, while it was secretly linked onto the support between each pass—that created the illusion.

Maskelyne's second innovation was a series of thin wires, used to suspend the lady on the cradle. Rather than using two or three thick cables to hold up a person, an array or fan of extremely thin steel wires could be used, if the multiple tiny connections could be carefully arranged so that every single wire supported part of the load. Each wire would be about the thickness of a sewing thread. If the wires were chemically dulled, and the lights on stage were carefully arranged, they were virtually invisible.

In 1901, Maskelyne was able to combine these ideas into an incredible invention. The assistant reclined on a steel cradle. Just behind the cradle, hidden from the audience by the floating assistant's body, was Nevil Maskelyne's shaped gooseneck, a piece of wrought iron. Two bundles of fine wires picked up the cradle on the upstage side of the gooseneck—the side away from the audience. Above the stage, the ends of the wires were attached to a steel grid hidden behind the curtains.

Of course, this didn't quite work. Hung in this way, the cradle would have tipped, spilling the person forward onto the stage. Maskelyne ingeniously solved this problem by using the wires going up as a fulcrum. Then, another group of wires, pulling down, were attached a few inches further upstage on the cradle.

The wires going down passed through a narrow slot cut into the stage, where they were attached to a steel-framed box of weights. By adjusting the weights, Maskelyne had created a sort of invisible lever on stage, and the cradle could be perfectly balanced. By lifting the entire system with an offstage winch, the lady seemed to levitate.

The assembly—the floating assistant, steel cradle, weights, and grid—weighed over four hundred pounds. Maskelyne increased the number of wires to accommodate the weight. In Kellar's version of the illusion, for example, he used two bundles of fine wires to lift the apparatus—a total of fifty-four wires—and another bundle of thirty-two wires extending down through the slit in the stage to provide the counterweight. A wonderful combination of physics, metallurgy, engineering, and mechanics, the illusion was ultimately enhanced with great dollops of theatrical fantasy.

ONCE HE had been cheated out of his twenty-five dollars and his hackles were up, John Northern Hilliard discovered the truth about the Levitation of Princess Karnac, that it had been purloined from Egyptian Hall. The crowning achievement of Kellar's career was actually his most brazen bit of espionage.

Surprisingly, it took a year before this became apparent. Few magicians had actually seen both levitations, and as they occurred in different settings on stage, it was difficult to compare them directly. Even Maskelyne was confused when he heard about Kellar's illusion. Maskelyne's only solution was to have the steel wires delicately looped around projections on the cradle, and the trick took days to set up on stage. In fact, Kellar had hired the Otis Elevator Company to develop the illusion; they were responsible for engineering the wire connections, allowing Kellar to pack the illusion in cases and move it from city to city.

In December 1905, Hilliard reviewed Kellar's new show for *The Sphinx*:

Although Mr. Kellar naturally claims the really wonderful levitation as the offspring of his own brain, it is really none other than the Maskelyne Levitation, which for several years puzzled the habitués of Egyptian Hall. I make this statement advisedly, for I have it on unimpeachable authority that this is the Maskelyne illusion. . . . The brain of John Nevil Maskelyne is responsible for yet another feature of the Kellar program, the cabinet trick known as Will, the

Witch and the Watchman, including the insufferably tedious dialogue and its lamentable and pathetic attempts at humor. This was a deadly bore as presented by the insufferable actors of Egyptian Hall, although the trick itself is mechanically clever. Mr. Kellar would have shown better judgment had he rewritten the sketch and enlivened it a little for American audiences.

In the middle of this wholesale pan, there is another Hilliard twist of the knife: he knew very well that Kellar was not capable of rewriting anything or evaluating a script.

Kellar performs his handkerchief tricks as atrociously as ever. . . . He introduces a ridiculous card trick, during which he harangues his audience on the idiotic subject of forcing a card. . . . His patter is so absurd [that] I was about to call it asinine. . . . Paul Valadon is the feature of the Kellar show this season; indeed, he was last year.

Kellar reddened by the time he'd finished the review: Hilliard again. The magician ripped the magazine to shreds, erupting in a long string of profanities.

THURSTON COMPLETED his two-year tour at a theater in Delhi, India, in March 1907. Several days before their last engagement, one of the sheets of glass in the water tank, Creation, cracked when the water poured inside was too hot. Charlie and George located a large mirror in the theater lobby and brought it backstage, scraping away the silvering on the back so that it could be used to replace the glass. The repaired tank was used for the two final performances.

In an effort to economize, Thurston sold a number of illusions that were particularly heavy, or broken, or unusable. For example, the hastily repaired Creation tank never left India. He also sold stacks of his lithographs that had been produced for the India tour. The company traveled back to Bombay before splitting up and going in their separate directions. Standing on the docks at the end of his long adventure, Thurston spoke, surrounded by his loyal workers. His voice cracked with emotion. "I want to thank you, but I also want to tell you what you've done for me," he said. "I landed in Australia two years ago completely broke. And right now, I can sign a check for fifty thousand dollars." There were cheers and hearty pledges of friendship. Maude Amber and Winfield Blake returned to Australia. Doc Henry remained in India. George White and Charlie Holzmueller supervised the return of the remaining equipment to the United States, arriving in May 1907. The props and scenery were sent on to Chicago, where Harry Thurston was ready to warehouse them.

Harry had returned to Chicago with a handful of gems and a trunk of Oriental knickknacks. Of far more value was a practical inspiration from the Great Thurston show—the Edison motion picture machine that was featured at every performance. Harry used his profits from the tour to open the Five Cent Theater on South State Street, one of the city's first permanent movie theaters. Harry remarried and settled down with his new wife, Isabel. He was becoming an influential businessman in Chicago's famously crooked First Ward, a hotbed of nasty, big-city political intrigue. Harry fit right in.

HOWARD AND BEATRICE took a more leisurely route back to America, stopping in London. In 1904, Maskelyne had moved his theater from the Egyptian Hall in Piccadilly to St. George's Hall, just off Regent Street. Maskelyne's new partner was David Devant, Thurston's good friend.

John Nevil Maskelyne, the old man of British magic, was of the same generation as Harry Kellar, and over the years they had squared off in a simmering rivalry. But Devant and Thurston were both a generation younger, bristling with new ideas and anxious to develop a new style of magic. Although Maskelyne had always been too stubborn and high-handed to negotiate with Kellar, Devant saw his job as expanding the Maskelyne and Devant franchise, and retaining a cool, diplomatic relationship with all his fellow magicians. These important British magicians found a new ally in Thurston: he was now cash rich from his world tour and had an opportunity to buy some of the greatest magic in the world.

Thurston was interested in three of Devant's recent illusions. The Problem of Diogenes was the production of a man from the interior of a sealed barrel. The New Page involved a tall, narrow cabinet, just large enough for a person. An assistant was strapped inside, against the back wall. When the doors were opened seconds later, the assistant had turned upside down. And finally, Thurston negotiated a price for the Mascot Moth, Devant's amazing new vanishing lady illusion, in which she seemed to shrivel up and disappear as she was standing in the middle of the stage. Devant arranged a contract and pushed it past the old man; the prices were high and the terms strict. For example, the New Page was £52, plus £4 per month rental ($260 plus $20 per month), and the Mascot Moth was £104, and £8 a month ($520 plus $40 per month).

Thurston's contract for the Mascot Moth was particularly significant. Kellar had already managed to produce a poor imitation of Devant's illusion for his 1906 show. Devant's original Mascot Moth depended upon an ingenious mechanism and split-second timing. Kellar's version, titled the Golden Butterfly, had none of this sophistication. A number of Kellar reviews noted that the lady had obviously disappeared through a trapdoor in the stage. Frustrated by this especially tricky trick, Kellar had given up on it. By negotiating a price for Devant's original version, Thurston had officially trumped Kellar's best efforts.

Thurston and Devant vowed to keep each other informed of their best ideas and exchange material for their shows. Devant especially intrigued his American compatriot by telling him that he had solved the problem of the legendary Indian Rope Trick, the boy who disappears on the rope. Devant was already having the intricate mechanism built in Brighton.

Before Thurston and Beatrice left for London on May 11, 1907, they had added one additional person to the company. Bella Hussan was a charming old Mohammedan fakir whom Thurston had imported from Bombay, the very best native magician he had seen during his travels. One of his specialties was a juggling feat with a long bow, like an oversized violin bow, that supported three wooden balls. As Hussan held the bow diagonally, pointed upward, and spun his body in a circle, the balls climbed the bow in various puzzling configurations. He was engaging on the stage but, according to Thurston, "we had to teach him half of his tricks; the best thing he did in his act was to wrap his turban around his head."

ONE OF THE GREAT PUZZLES of American show business was the sudden transaction, in May and June 1907, when Paul Valadon was pushed aside and Thurston quickly stepped in to inherit Harry Kellar's show.

For three seasons, Kellar had teamed with Valadon, featuring his skillful manipulations on stage and exploiting his knowledge of Maskelyne and Devant's illusions. Kellar had hinted in print that he would be retiring and that Valadon would take over the show. At the end of 1906, Kellar even told a St. Louis paper that he may "put a big spectacular show on the road next season, featuring Paul Valadon." *The Sphinx*, the magician's journal, seemed set on this idea, promoting Valadon as Kellar's successor.

There had been friction backstage. Eva Kellar, Kellar's wife, was often featured in the show in a mind-reading act she performed with her husband. She didn't like Valadon, and was even frostier to Valadon's wife, who worked as his assistant. Compounding the problem, both Eva Kellar and Paul Valadon drank, and then allowed the alcohol to saturate their arguments. "Mrs. Kellar was an awful souse, and a battler, one of those kind that just has to win a decision off of somebody each day." Guy Jarrett, a stagehand and magic show insider, was repeating the gossip that he had been told. "One day Mrs. Kellar was dishing out some of her grandest, with the Valadons on the receiving end, and Valadon broke, and passed it back to her, plus."

If the story is true, it must have happened long before the end of the tour, for Mrs. Kellar left the show in the spring of 1906 for an extended vacation to her hometown of Melbourne, Australia. When she was there, she was told about Thurston's success in Melbourne earlier that year—perhaps she even saw newspaper clippings.

Back in the United States, according to Jarrett, Mrs. Kellar "came in one evening, all in a dither, and excitedly explained to Harry [Kellar] that she had found a successor to take over the show."

But the story can't be that simple. In February 1907, just after Kellar and

Valadon had performed in Baltimore, Henry Ridgely Evans, a friend of Kellar's and a Baltimore author on magic, contributed an article for a British publication. Evans speculated about Kellar's retirement. "Who will be Kellar's successor? Go ask the Sphinx, and perhaps the stone monster will tell you," Evans wrote. This was a joke on *The Sphinx* magazine, and their endorsement of Valadon. Evans had a different opinion. "If you ask me, I say Howard Thurston, by all means. I predict that upon Thurston, Kellar's mantle will fall." In February 1907, with Thurston touring in India, this was a shocking prediction, and it suggests that Kellar may have just provided the hint to his friend Evans.

In April 1907, Harry Houdini repeated the speculation in his own magazine, *The Conjurer's Monthly*. "What do you think about Kellar's retiring? Is Valadon going to succeed him? Would you like our opinion? From all signs and indications, the dark horse in the race seems to be Howard Thurston." Houdini had also been hearing rumors.

THURSTON LATER CLAIMED that the partnership with Kellar had been set, by telegram, before he left India. But this story is also much too simple. Thurston could not have had his deal when he contracted to purchase illusions from Maskelyne and Devant, because he made tentative arrangements for the Mascot Moth, an illusion that Kellar had just produced. He also wrote that when he returned to New York, he raced to Blaney's Theater in Brooklyn to see one of Kellar's last performances that season and to greet the master from the front row. But this was also untrue. Howard and Beatrice boarded the *Etruria*, from Liverpool to New York, on May 11, 1907, and only reached New York on May 20. Kellar and Valadon's last engagement had already taken place in Atlantic City two days earlier, on May 18. Thurston never saw Kellar's show after 1904 and never watched one of Valadon's performances in America. When he later wrote of these events, Thurston must have realized that his fast-paced negotiations, behind the scenes, looked unpleasant and suspicious.

When they finally sat down to dinner in May 1907, the two magicians must have made an instant connection. In many ways, they had shared the same childhood, selling newspapers in midwestern cities, contemplating the ministry, and sharing remarkably similar tours, a generation apart, through Australia, the Orient, and India. And Kellar's decision probably involved a combination of elements—personalities and temperaments, Kellar's impatience, Eva's reports from Australia, as well as Thurston's occasional telegrams. But the ultimate reason for Thurston's success with Kellar is much simpler: money.

Valadon had agreed to slowly pay off Kellar's show. Thurston was willing to pay for Kellar's show. When Kellar told a St. Louis newspaper that he would consider producing "a big spectacular show . . . next season . . . starring Paul Valadon," it suggested that Valadon was not in a position to buy Kellar's show, but would be hired as an employee and would be working off the investment. More than likely, this was the reason for the protracted seasons with Valadon. But Thurston now had all the money he needed and was ready to write a check to Kellar. He didn't need Kellar's investment. It would be a perfect way for Eva and Harry Kellar to start their retirement, and a comfortable, flattering way to contract a successor.

THEIR CONTRACT was dated June 8, 1907, and Thurston was to pay $7,000 for all the illusions, props, and scenery, as well as permission to perform the famous levitation. Thurston agreed to credit Kellar for the illusion whenever it was presented. In exchange for his work on next season's tour, Thurston would receive $150 per week. Thurston would take possession of the show at the end of the next season, in June 1908, and if, at any time in future, he desired to "strengthen the show," he could arrange for Kellar to take part, when convenient.

According to the contract, Thurston would also engage Dudley McAdow for five years; he had been Kellar's manager for sixteen years in conjunction with Stair and Havlin, a theater chain. And if Kellar desired, Thurston would not prevent him from establishing a permanent magical entertainment in a large city. Kellar had long fantasized about establishing a permanent magic theater, the way Maskelyne had with Egyptian Hall in London.

Once the contract was in place, the partners finalized the arrangements of the next show. George White would be Thurston's principle assistant. Beatrice

Foster was to assist both Thurston and Kellar, taking the role of Princess Karnac in Kellar's famous levitation. Thurston hired his own assistants and technicians, and two identical twins, the Terry brothers, which allowed him to produce some very surprising illusions. Bella Hussan would be included on the bill with a short act.

Thurston contracted for Devant's barrel illusion, Diogenes, and the New Page, but did not purchase the Mascot Moth, as Kellar had now warned him off of it. Kellar, in turn, wanted to purchase Maskelyne's latest feature from London, the Spectres of the Sanctum, an elaborate séance effect in which a ghost slowly materialized in a cabinet. Thurston facilitated the contract with Maskelyne and Devant. After stealing dozens of Maskelyne effects for his show, this was the first one Kellar had ever paid the inventor to use.

Kellar would tour one final season, splitting the performance with Thurston. And Kellar would finally, unequivocally, introduce Thurston as his successor. The swift transaction gave the impression that Paul Valadon, the loyal soldier, had been unfairly treated, as he was left scrambling for vaudeville dates. It seems that Valadon suffered the surprise that awaited many spies—once the game becomes treacherous no player is actually safe.

THE NEWSPAPERS BILLED the show as "Kellar and Thurston, The World's Greatest Magicians, Presenting All That Is New in the World of Magic," but their rehearsals in Yonkers, New York, suggested trouble. Kellar was a perfectionist who never took chances with his magic. The Spectres of the Sanctum was a complicated trick of lighting and reflections, using an array of electric bulbs and a large sheet of mirror that slid onstage, invisibly, in a special metal track. It called for meticulous drilling, but Kellar wouldn't give up the stage until it was perfect. Thurston was left cooling his heels.

After days of work, just as Kellar was satisfied with the Spectres, and Thurston was bringing his own staff on the stage, the city electrical inspector arrived and explained that the Spectres' light sockets needed rewiring. All the rehearsals stopped again, and Thurston waited patiently until Kellar's trick was perfect. Thurston's first shows were awkward and underrehearsed, but Kellar seemed to take it all in stride. "It's all right, Thursty," he told his new associate. "It was all my fault, but don't worry."

Thurston could be temperamental, but he tended to fall into black moods and sulk. Kellar's temper was something completely different, a source of continual amusement to the people around him. He exploded in firework displays of profanity, stomped, screamed, and then slinked back into the theater for mumbled apologies and pats on the back. At a dinner at the Astor Hotel in New York, Kellar ordered baked potatoes for himself, his wife, and the Thurstons. When the waiter bungled the order and delivered small boiled potatoes, Kellar erupted in fury. "Eva, look at that! Thursty, look at that!" He stuck a fork in the potato and held it over his head, rushing through the dining room and calling out to anyone who would listen. "You call that a baked potato? A baked potato?"

At the end of the dinner, Kellar had been deflated again, as sheepish and foolish as a schoolboy. Thurston noticed that he left a generous tip. "I am a fool, Thursty. I am a big fool. But I don't mean any harm, do I?"

WHEN THE SHOW played in Rochester, New York, John Northern Hilliard wrote another review for the *Post Express*.

> Mr. Howard Thurston made his initial bow to a Rochester audience as a master magician. . . . This season he is the feature performer with his own program, and challenges attention as the most skillful sleight of hand performer and worker of illusions on the stage today. Curiously enough, since the death of Alexander Herrmann, America has had no representative magician, save the hanky-pank men of vaudeville, the clumsy performer of unwieldy mechanical illusions, or the itinerant performers of the streets, the parks, or the fairs. When Alexander Herrmann died, magic in America died. . . . This period of dubiety has passed, however, for Howard Thurston has taken up the wand of the dead magician, and claims the honor of successor by right of skill and fitness. . . . Thurston, in a word, has arrived. He is the master magician of the day. . . . Among those who also appeared was Mr. Kellar, who performed his usual little

bag of tricks, the same that he has been doing for the last quarter of a century. He made a brief speech announcing his retirement from the stage at the close of the present season, which was warmly applauded.

The next day, Kellar showed the article to Thurston. As Thurston read it, he braced himself for the gale. Instead, the old magician surprised him by seeming remarkably sanguine. But that night, as Kellar was standing onstage, he happened to spy Hilliard sitting in the audience, and this lit the fuse of his temper. Thurston was standing next to Barney, Kellar's longtime assistant, as they watched from the wings. Kellar sauntered offstage to prepare the next trick, and Thurston noticed the magician approaching him. Kellar was red with rage.

"There he is, Thursty! There he is!" he mumbled. Kellar grabbed Barney by the throat and began shaking him. "Help me, Barney! Help me! Help me think of something to call that god damned miserable son of a bitch who's sitting there, just sitting there in my god damned audience!"

Thurston was dumbfounded, but Barney was long accustomed to his boss's strange rages. Barney collapsed to the floor with laughter as Kellar turned and walked back onto the stage with a loud harrumph. If only he could have thought of some of those two-dollar words to berate Hilliard.

TWELVE

"MAGICIANS PAST AND PRESENT"

n December 1907, when Kellar and Thurston appeared at McVicker's Theater in Chicago, Houdini was appearing in a local vaudeville house. Thurston made arrangements for Houdini's wife, Bess, to have a box seat—Houdini was busy that afternoon at his own theater and planned to attend later in the week. But Thurston accidentally offended Harry by inviting Dr. Wilson, the editor of another magic magazine and, at that moment, one of Houdini's archrivals. Houdini was happiest when he was embroiled in melodramatic alliances or competitions. When he heard that Wilson had been at the show, he chafed at Thurston's insult and wouldn't attend McVicker's Theater.

Houdini, a magazine editor—publishing *The Conjurer's Monthly Magazine*—was happy to report on Thurston and Kellar. But he privately had his doubts about Thurston's new role. His fellow vaudevillian, the coin manipulator Tommy Downs, encouraged Houdini's skepticism. "I note what you say regarding Thurston and Kellar," he wrote to Houdini, "all that B.S. about Kellar retiring in favor of Valadon I never believed. Kellar will never retire, he will die in harness, same as Herrmann did."

Downs voiced the opinion of many magicians, that Kellar simply wanted a chance to push Thurston out of the picture. "Kellar is a foxy Pennsylvania Dutchman and is probably afraid of Thurston as a possible competitor," he confided to Houdini.

Both Downs and Houdini were passing judgment from a lofty, rickety perch. The vaudeville circuits had provided a false sense of security for many twelve-minute marvels. Houdini had anticipated that his handcuff act was just a short-term novelty, but he was ambitious and clever enough to keep expanding the scope of his act, adding bigger challenges and grabbing more headlines. He freed himself from a straitjacket, and was about to introduce an escape from an oversized milk can, filled with water. By 1907, he had become one of vaudeville's genuine stars. In contrast, his friend Thomas Nelson Downs had proven to be a one-trick pony, and that trick was the Miser's Dream—plucking half-dollars from the air. After his act had been seen, and then imitated, around the world, Downs returned to Marshalltown, Iowa, looking for the next good idea. He was having trouble finding it. "As far as I am concerned, I have no ambition to be styled 'The Great.' The game is not worth the candle. I don't see what Kellar wants with Thurston," he wrote to Houdini, still grumbling about Thurston's tour. "Thurston is a case of lucky boy, falling into Kellar's show. I know at least a half-dozen magicians better qualified. I don't believe he will succeed with the public. Thurston is a nice fellow, but not a genius and not original."

Neither Downs nor Houdini understood that the relationship, and the creation of America's next great magician, was no longer about Kellar's stubbornness or Thurston's originality. Thurston and Kellar had come to admire each other. One afternoon at McVicker's Theater, as the magicians arrived at the stage door, Thurston suddenly remembered something. He led Kellar down the alley, examining the long expanse of dirty bricks. Thurston located the dim scratches of two initials: HT. He explained to Kellar that twenty-three years earlier, he had been working as a newsboy with Reddy Cadger in that alley, waiting for the bundled first editions of the *Chicago Tribune*. They were hungry and cold, huddled on the iron grate above the warm air of the *Tribune* pressroom. Thurston had watched a group of swells, in their silk hats and furs, leaving the theater. He vowed, one day, to perform there, and scratched his initials on the side of the building. Kellar's eyes twinkled with recognition. It was as if Thurston had been describing a chapter from Kellar's own childhood.

KELLAR AND THURSTON performed their last engagement together at Ford's Opera House in Baltimore on May 16, 1908. The entire tour had been organized with a magisterial sense of inevitability, a royal succession, and the final performance provided the emotional climax. At the finish of the show, Kellar threw his arm around Thurston's shoulder and walked him forward. He thanked his public for their support, recalling his forty-five-year career as an entertainer and his most famous feats—summoning the spirits in his old cabinet act, growing rose plants inside a cardboard tube, and transmitting his thoughts to his beloved wife, Eva. While touring the faraway lands, he'd been proud to bring sophisticated American mysteries to the people of the world. Thurston noticed him leaning more heavily on his shoulder. As he began to predict a glowing future for his young associate, Kellar turned to look at his successor and his voice cracked. Kellar paused, and then solemnly handed over his wand to Thurston with a deep bow—the symbol of the magic being passed from one generation to the next. The band played "Auld Lang Syne" and ushers rushed down the aisles with floral tributes, filling the stage with wreaths of bright roses.

> *We two have run about the slopes,*
> *And picked the daisies fine.*
> *We've wandered many a weary foot,*
> *Since auld lang syne.*

As the audience stood as a group and sang one final chorus—"We'll take a cup of kindness yet, for auld lang syne!"—the notes rang through the theater. Kellar wiped his eyes. Thurston turned away, surprised to find that he, too, was looking out at the audience through shimmering tears. He stepped back, allowing the old master to indulge in one final bow at the footlights, and the curtain fell.

The next day, the company took the train back to Philadelphia. Kellar and Thurston sat in the train car and talked. Kellar seemed tired and morose. After the warm reception of his last performance, he was saddened to contemplate the end of his career, but his colorful recollections seemed to enliven his spirits. He had worked hard over every one of his illusions. He spoke fondly of each piece of apparatus, every routine, the careful string of words that had been refined for the introductions, and the sequence of maneuvers. They'd all been labors of love. Thurston realized that these prized mysteries were, in many ways, the children that Kellar had never had.

"He was the kindliest and biggest hearted man I ever knew," Thurston recalled. He attributed Kellar's blunt, decisive manner to the many challenges he encountered through his career. Kellar had been endowed with thick, awkward fingers, a speech impediment, and very little natural grace to enhance his stage performances, but he had overcome every challenge. "Kellar was the last of the old-school magicians," Thurston wrote years later. "Mystery came first with him. Entertainment was not considered."

As a sign of his devotion to Kellar, and the slippery, fluid qualities of his own biography, for several years Thurston changed his childhood story, insisting that it was a performance of Kellar, not Herrmann, that had initially inspired him in Columbus. This not only omitted the awkward reference to Herrmann, Kellar's longtime rival, but it completed the father-and-son analogy with some poetic publicity.

In his year of touring with Kellar, Thurston had seen the old wizard at his most stubborn, argumentative, and old-fashioned. But he also understood how, above all else, Kellar had been devoted to magic. He fussed over it, defended it, and loved bringing it to his audiences.

THURSTON'S YEAR on the road with Kellar had been a financial drain. Anxious to make the best impression, to hire his own assistants and technicians, during his months on tour Thurston's payroll had been $350 a week, but he had been receiving just $150 from Kellar. In fact, he'd never learned how to budget a show. He insisted on what he wanted, and was constantly at odds with his managers, like Dudley McAdow, to balance the books.

Thurston's sudden fame led to a number of impulsive purchases and more than a few terrible investments. For example, he had paid $15,000 for nine acres of property in Cos Cob, Connecticut. Thurston had imagined a restful, elegant country estate outside of New York City, something that would remind him of Mount Hermon Academy. The property in Cos Cob fell short of his ideal, although it was certainly rustic. The land was at the corner of Bible and Hardscrabble streets—one could not imagine a better intersection to summarize Thurston's early career.

"It is indeed a farm," reported one friend after he visited it, "he has horses, cows, and chickens." The farm was supervised by a foreman and was always on the brink of disaster. Thurston joked that the property was distinguished by having the largest rocks in Connecticut. The farmhouse, situated on a bluff, was called Hillcrest, and a few small buildings around the property provided space for his twelve mechanics and carpenters to live.

His first priority was the barn, which was converted into a forty-by-hundred-foot workshop, complete with a blacksmith shop and woodworking facilities. Thurston also set up his own rehearsal stage so that he could test scenery, lighting, and new illusions. Thurston had vowed to replace the old-fashioned elements of the Kellar show. Kellar had always conducted a leisurely show, filled with benign chat and emphasizing the small tricks. Every year he had tried to include two or three large illusions—a levitation or disappearing lady—to vary the procedure and entice the press. Thurston wanted to turn that formula on its ear, with a bigger, flashier show. He eliminated all of Kellar's material except the Spirit Cabinet and the famous Levitation of Princess Karnac.

Perhaps Thurston's greatest extravagance was the formation of the Thurston Amusement Company, an enterprise designed to franchise Thurston's success, indulge his interest in invention, and occupy his brother Harry, who was now underfoot in New York City. The letterhead explained that Howard was president and Harry was the manager, "Constructors of Original Riding

Devices for Parks, Automatic Games, Novel Features for 5 and 10 Theaters." In other words, they were in the dime museum business.

> Howard Thurston, the World's Famous Magician, Has Invented the Greatest Money-Making Device Ever Exhibited at Parks, Fairs, Carnivals, Penny Arcades, Etc.
>
> Five beautiful illusions combined in one. Nothing objectionable. For men, women and children.

The Maid of Mystery, their first product, was an elaborate coin-operated arcade device. It sounded like the perfect combination of Harry and Howard's interests. A tall, five-sided kiosk was equipped with five small windows, one in each side. A spectator could stand at each window and place a penny in a slot. A timer opened the window for ten seconds, allowing each spectator to peer inside. Each spectator was allowed to spy a sideshow illusion; although it wasn't specified, presumably this was a variation on the usual effects, like a living half-lady or disembodied head. The Thurstons' brochure did the math: "Net profits larger than a 5-cent Theater. Earning capacity, 5 cents every ten seconds, 30 cents a minute, $18 per hour, $180 for 10 hours, $1,260 per week."

Another idea that Thurston had been toying with for some time was a spinning amusement ride for carnivals and parks. A circular track contained individual cars; each was like a large canister, just the size to contain a couple standing together. As the cars revolved around the track, they also spun like a top, giving the riders a wild, whirling thrill.

Each of these ideas had been easy to draw on a scrap of paper and sounded exciting and profitable. But each required months of work and experimentation with a staff of metal workers, engineers, and then patent lawyers and salesmen, before the idea could be evaluated in the marketplace.

Thurston's last project, and maybe the most important of all, was to take the necessary steps to marry Beatrice Foster, now officially billed on his programs and posters as the "Queen of Magic." Howard hired an attorney and filed to divorce Grace at the end of 1907, noting that they had been separated for four years.

IN THE AUTUMN OF 1908, Howard Thurston took his new production on the road. A special series of brightly colored stone lithographs advertised the show with extravagant scenes. Thurston hired the Strobridge Lithographic Company of Cincinnati, which had created Kellar's artistic posters. For more than a decade, Kellar's posters had incorporated images of tiny red devils, perched on his shoulder or whispering secrets into his ear. Now these little devils, presumably the helpmates of the magician, became the property of Thurston; they were seen scampering across his advertising materials.

One of Thurston's most impressive new posters portrayed Kellar bestowing a scarlet "mantle of magic" on Thurston's shoulders as Mephistopheles stood to the side and watched. Each poster included the words "Kellar's Successor," and "Mr. Kellar says Thurston will be the Greatest Magician the World Has Ever Known."

The show now opened with a striking image, reminding the audience of Thurston's progenitors. The curtains raised on an enormous upright book with the title *Masters of Magic*. Two assistants stood at the sides and opened the cover, like a door. On the first page was a full-length, life-sized image of Philippe, the nineteenth-century French magician. They continued to turn the pages, revealing Heller, Herrmann, and Kellar. When the final page was turned, the assistants revealed Thurston, standing stationary within the frame of the book before stepping out and beginning his act.

Bella Husssan worked for part of the season, and Thurston also filled out the program with a European vaudeville act, Paul Kleist, who performed a pantomime clown magic act. Thurston added illusions with boxes, ducks, crystal lanterns, and trunks. And now the show closed with a series of big, fast, impressive magic—oddly shaped cabinets and cases that filled the stage with color and action. The Lady and the Boy was probably inspired by Devant and Fasola. Thurston introduced it by explaining, "My object in presenting this effect is to demonstrate the possibility of passing a living person through space on a well-lighted stage!" Two assistants, a young lady and a young man, stood on a large platform. A curtain covered them for an instant, and they both disappeared. One reappeared in a locked case beneath the curtain. The other assistant emerged from a suspended cabinet on the opposite side of the stage.

Before the applause had subsided, Thurston was introducing the final feat. "We shall conclude our evening's entertainment with our most interesting illusion, entitled the Flight of Princess Kiyo, or the Triple Mystery." This was a combination of three sensational surprises. Two large boxes were shown empty and nested together. Thurston clapped his hands, and Beatrice Foster popped out of the box. She stepped over to an Egyptian mummy case, entered, and closed the door. The case was lifted into the air on cables.

Thurston took a blank revolver in his hand and fired it into the air. With a crash, the panels of the mummy case fell open. She was gone. Now Thurston called attention to the brightly painted, square trunk that had been hanging over the audience's head since they entered the theater at the beginning of the show. The trunk slid down a loop of rope onto the stage, and inside Thurston's nest of three trunks, Beatrice emerged.

The critics praised Thurston's sensational efforts, but "The World's Greatest Magician" was broke. Late in the season, when ticket sales were slow in Canada, he wired his brother Harry for more cash—anything he could pull out of the amusement company or personal funds he might have on hand—to keep the show open. When he limped across the finish line in April 1909, at New York's Metropolis Theater, he transported the crates back to Connecticut and began rehearsing the next season's show.

THURSTON WAS CONVINCED that his show needed new features every year, and he was eager to prove his versatility and creativity to his audiences—despite his depleted bank account. For the 1909–1910 season, Thurston had planned even more new sensations, and had been horse-trading to get the material. Thurston sent his friend David Devant the details of his egg trick, titled The Boy, the Girl and the Eggs. The trick was now a complete comedy routine in his show, and the previous season, when he performed it in Washington, President Roosevelt's young son, Quentin, was the boy recruited to drop the eggs. It was a perfect routine for Devant's breezy style. Thurston wrote:

This trick will create as much talk as anything I have ever seen performed on the magic stage. If you cannot get seven minutes of good solid laughter from the trick, let me hear from you, and I will do what I can. I am anxious to get good small comedy tricks, and I hope that our exchanges from time to time will prove satisfactory.

In return, Thurston desperately wanted David Devant's version of the Rope Trick, and he went so far as to have posters printed announcing it. Unfortunately, the trick proved too complicated for Devant, and the result was disappointing in his show. Thurston scrapped his plans for it. Another sensational illusion, the Witch's Cauldron, was based on an illusion of Billy Robinson's. It was built at Cos Cob but never used, as it was too difficult to install on stages.

In exchange for a duplicate of his Coconut Trick for Gus Fasola, Thurston obtained some of Fasola's best ideas. Thurston wrote to Fasola:

Remember, Gus, that you and I are the two best friends possible for two magicians to be, and that we have given our word to assist each other to the best extent and not to hold back any secrets.

Fasola's new trick was called the Lady and the Lion, and Thurston's shop was kept busy building it through the summer of 1909. The final result proved to be a fantastic illusion, a stage-filling marvel that generated headlines across the country.

On the left side of the stage was a curtained cabinet, roughly the size of a large closet. On the right side of the stage was a sort of square, four-post framework, consisting of a plywood top and a platform. Thurston invited a gentleman to step on stage; he asked him to tie his handkerchief around the wrist of his female assistant, so the man would be sure to be able to identify her later.

The lady entered the cabinet to the audience's left, and Thurston drew the curtains around both enclosures. He fired his pistol. Both sets of curtains were ripped away from the cabinets. The lady was now discovered on the opposite side of the stage, sitting inside an enormous suspended birdcage to the audience's right. In her place, on the left, was a strong steel cage containing a growling, pacing lion. The man from the audience, standing near Thurston and watching the action, saw the lion and invariably dashed back to his seat.

The trick was accomplished with an array of ingenious principles taken right from Fasola's show—false compartments, collapsible containers, flaps, traps, and special concealments. The entire sequence depended upon the smooth, instantaneous operation of a number of mechanical devices, and the cooperation of the lion, which was hidden in the back of the cabinet until his sudden appearance. Thurston provided the final touch. As he positioned the man at the side of the stage, he whispered under his breath, "When you see the lion, run like hell. I'll tell you when to run." The lion appeared, and as the audience cheered, Thurston added one final sotto voce growl in the direction of the man: "Run!" His exit, which seemed so unexpected, provided the laugh to punctuate the mystery.

DURING HIS SECOND SEASON, Thurston finally had an opportunity to meet Paul Valadon when their paths crossed. Valadon had faced a difficult year. After he left Kellar's show, his wife had died, in April 1909, and Valadon and his son were then touring smaller vaudeville theaters. He had added a levitation illusion, and even worked under the name Briscoe, in an effort to draw more attention to his act.

When they met, Valadon was impatient and chilly with Thurston, seeing no reason to be gracious to the new "World's Greatest." But Thurston applied his confidence man's charm, flattering Valadon with compliments and easing him into a good humor. Thurston provided passes, so that Valadon could see his new show, and asked him to take note of any improvements that he could make.

Valadon was perplexed by the new material. He was only two years older than Thurston, but his sensibilities were trapped in the era of Kellar's slow, serious Victorian conjuring. Thurston's flashy new tricks—the cabinets, cages, and containers that now filled the stage and punctuated the show with the bangs and crashes of slamming doors—merely annoyed him. Afterward Thurston took him to dinner and asked for suggestions. "Herr Valadon, is there anything that my show needs?" Valadon glared at him. "Thurston, you need another *box*!"

In fact, many magicians thought that Thurston's quick, pyrotechnic changes to the show were a sign of desperation, not expertise. "Thurston is not a magician," Dr. James Elliott wrote to Downs. Elliott had given Thurston his lessons in the Back Palm, and now considered that he had turned his back on real magic. "His only hand work was what I taught him with cards. Then on come the boxes, lion cages, refrigerators, ash cans, ladders, water tanks, and other huge affairs. God only knows what you can call them. He carries an army of assistants and the railroad and hotels are happy."

UNFORTUNATELY, it was only a matter of time before Kellar began to have his doubts. Harry and Eva Kellar had just retired to a pretty house in Los Angeles, when, on March 28, 1910, Eva Kellar died of a heart attack. It was within a year of Mrs. Valadon's death.

With Eva gone, Kellar increasingly turned to his other love, magic. He visited the local magic shops and attended meetings of the Society of American Magicians, bestowing genial praise and pats on the back to amateurs and professionals alike. He became the beloved old master of magic. In particular, Kellar spent his time fussing and fuming over the state of his child—the show that he had sold to Thurston.

Kellar was enough of a showman to understand that Thurston would present the magic with his own style, and he didn't object to the inclusion of big illusions. But Kellar was particular about the quality of each piece of the show. He now feared that many of Thurston's new ideas were slapdash and careless, designed to provide production value instead of mystery. Florenz Ziegfeld, the Follies producer, was famous for insisting that his girls wore expensive French silk underwear—not because the audience would see it, but because the girls knew it was there. Similarly, Kellar had once purchased a prop from a magic dealer and found that the inside of it had not been painted. "No one sees it," the dealer told him. "I see it," Kellar snarled.

It was a line drawn in the sand. Thurston was the sort of magician who did not paint the insides of props. He used to tell colleagues, "Magic comprises only about thirty percent of a magic show." To him, the tricks were only a small part of the formula. The rest was showmanship, presentation, stage deportment, and all those indefinable elements that intrigued an audience. But these were fighting words for Kellar, who had devoted his career to the finding the finest tricks and always making them shine.

Kellar began petitioning Thurston in subtle ways. He recommended tricks that he'd seen, or magicians who might have good ideas for the show. When he felt Thurston brushed off his suggestions, Kellar would, in turn, buttonhole his friends and ask them, as a personal favor to him, to use their influence over Thurston.

In 1910, Kellar hit on a plan. Theodore Bamberg, a third-generation magician from a famous Dutch family, who was living in New York, was established in vaudeville under the stage name Okito, performing an Oriental magic act. He was also a builder of magic equipment, famous for his meticulously built apparatus and his old-world perfectionism. Bamberg had known Thurston for years; he had worked with him in Paris just after Thurston's success at the Palace Theater in London, and he admired him.

Kellar felt that it was a perfect fit. Theodore Bamberg could join the show performing his hand-shadow act, creating the silhouettes of people or animals with his hands held in a spotlight. It was a perfect novelty for a magic show and wouldn't compete with any of Thurston's magic. And behind the scenes, Bamberg could make sure that the magic was up to Kellar's standards. Kellar ended the proposal with an arm around Bamberg's shoulder. "I know I can count on you, Theo."

Finally, Kellar had a spy on the inside.

BUT FOR THURSTON, it was the spies on the outside that were creating the problems.

Charles Joseph Carter was four years younger than Thurston, born in Pennsylvania and trained as a lawyer, before he decided to become a professional magician. He was pudgy and authoritative, an unlikely showman, but he was also tough and impervious to insults. Like many of his generation, he had constructed his show by modeling Kellar's performances.

Carter followed Thurston through Australia and India the year after Thurston, playing many of the same theaters and capitalizing on his successes. "Carter possessed no originality whatsoever," wrote magician and critic Charles Waller, "but he was nevertheless a really good presenter of magic. He was almost the last of the old-time magicians. In later years, his show moved too slowly for the times." Carter made most of his money overseas. After his first world tour, he returned to America for new material.

Fritz and Carl Bucha were two brothers who had served as backstage mechanics for Kellar. They continued working with Thurston during his first season, but in 1908 they left the show. Thurston wasn't surprised. They were old associates of Kellar, and Thurston now had his own men to supervise the work backstage.

What neither he nor Kellar realized was that Carter had hired the Buchas away and paid them to build copies of the Kellar and Thurston marvels, based on their own experience with the show. The Levitation of Princess Karnac and the Spirit Cabinet were secretly duplicated in a New York shop. After four years of working with these devices, Fritz and Carl knew them inside and out.

Kellar's wonderful levitation, developed and improved by Otis Elevator Company, had been a mystery to many magicians. But the Bucha brothers had personally adjusted every bolt and spring on the precious levitation illusion, oiled the winch, and tightened the wires. They could reproduce it faithfully for Carter.

Both Kellar and Thurston were left flat-footed when the rumor was reported, and then Carter took the new illusions on his second world tour in 1909. When Kellar heard the news in Los Angeles, he secretly fumed, but by rights he couldn't really complain. He'd obtained the invention through a similar bit of trickery and now had to swallow his pride. "Carter had the nerve to telegraph me for the stuff to blacken wires," Kellar wrote to Thurston. The chemical to dull the shine on the steel wires was an important part of the secret. "I didn't even answer him as I might have said something I should have been sorry for."

Similarly, Thurston felt helplessly removed from the controversy. Kellar's dealings—with Maskelyne, Valadon, and the Bucha brothers—had all been arranged long before Thurston joined the show. Now he was a victim of those old relationships, and powerless to repair them.

IN MAY 1910, Howard's divorce from Grace had been finalized and Howard and Beatrice decided to get married. Thurston told the press, "We agreed that if, after seven years, we should find we cared for each other as much as we did, then we should be married. That time expires and we are to keep our agreement." It made for an attractive, romantic story—America's Greatest Magician and his floating princess—that ignored the fact that he had been waiting out a divorce decree.

If their marriage would provide a bit of calm rationality in the middle of his chaotic life, it was probably intended just that way. It was just weeks after Eva Kellar's death and Valadon's dwindling prospects, just as Thurston was trying to simultaneously rein in his businesses and expand his show. Unfortunately, before Howard and Beatrice were able to set the date, Thurston had to deal with another woman—an amazing, headline-making Neapolitan who had supposedly mastered the art of levitation. When Thurston met Eusapia Palladino, it was a controversy that he didn't need.

THIRTEEN

"DO THE SPIRITS RETURN?"

n a bright, warm, Sunday afternoon in Manhattan, Howard and Beatrice sat on the sofa in an uptown apartment, waiting patiently for something amazing to happen. It seemed incredible, impossible, that they were about to attend a séance. Wasn't that supposed to be happening in the middle of the night, in a dark parlor?

After they'd been ushered into the apartment, Thurston realized that he would have only a few moments before the others arrived. He jumped up and began searching the room, instructing Tommy to follow his lead. "Look for anything out of the ordinary. Threads, batteries, electrical wires along the walls. And don't forget to turn back the carpet," he whispered.

Just as he had finished feeling the edges of the wainscoting, he heard the floorboards creak in the next room. The Thurstons froze as the door swung open and a small cluster of people entered. Hidden in the middle of the group was a tiny, elderly woman, wrapped in a long black taffeta skirt with a high-necked white blouse. Her face registered a deeply lined, permanent scowl.

"Howard, let me introduce Eusapia Palladino," Hereward Carrington said. Carrington was a friend of Thurston's, an author and amateur magician. Thurston and Beatrice bowed to the medium as she mumbled something in Italian. A man at her side translated. "Yes, she says it is a pleasure to meet you." But

Thurston noticed, from her expression, that she probably had said nothing like that at all.

Palladino was shaped like a fireplug and conducted her séances with a haughty attitude. She sat at the end of a small, rectangular wooden table that was a permanent part of the act. Howard was invited to sit at one side of the table, holding her hand to the tabletop and—she instructed him—placing his foot alongside of hers. Beatrice was positioned to the other side and held her other foot and hand. Palladino gave a few other instructions in Italian, which she reinforced by stamping her feet, coming down on Thurston and Beatrice's toes. It was obviously important to her that their feet always remain in contact.

The séance circle was completed with others sitting at the sides of the table. Carrington closed the drapes, but Thurston was surprised to see that the room was barely shaded. The sunlight ricocheted around the bright walls, allowing everyone to clearly see Palladino's every breath, the slight twitching of her hands, and the nervous stamping of her feet.

"She needs to reach her spirit contact," Carrington narrated in a whisper. But within minutes, neither Carrington nor the lady's translator was able to keep up or offer any explanations. A séance with Palladino was famous for being unsettling and emotional. The little lady shut her eyes tightly, cursed, whispered, cried, complained, pulled her hands away, beat at the air with her fists, then roughly grabbed the hands of the people next to her.

Thurston noticed how Palladino's process was oddly untheatrical. It didn't offer any of the comforts of a neat sermon, the prayers or talks about loved ones coming back to visit. In fact, his Spirit Cabinet provided a far better show, without any of the pretense of a real séance. Every night, Thurston stood in front of the empty cabinet, his fingertips held gently to his temple, calling upon the ghost of Katie King, the famous spirit guide. And every night, on cue, as the first violins played pizzicato, the gauzelike ghost appeared, sweeping through the cabinet. Katie King rattled a tambourine, drummed on the cabinet with a cane, and then disappeared as the doors were flung open, providing a gasp from the audience.

With Palladino there were no actual ghosts, just suggestions. She settled into a trance, suddenly froze, threw her head back, and stiffened her arms.

Gentle rapping noises reverberated through the tabletop. These became louder, as if the legs of the table were vibrating. The table shook gently, from side to side. Her hands—along with Howard and Beatrice's hands—pushed down firmly on the tabletop, as if she were defying it to stay in place. But the table wouldn't obey. It jumped an inch, and then another, rising slowly until it was several inches in the air, with all four legs off the floor. As Thurston looked down, finding the medium's hand still pressed against his own, the table fell back to the floor with a thud.

THURSTON HAD BEEN LURED to the apartment by Hereward Carrington, who was in desperate need of publicity. Carrington was born in England and immigrated to the United States as a young man. He had been hired by Thurston to add publicity material and tricks to the latest editions of his souvenir books, sold in the lobby at his performances. During his time with Thurston at Cos Cob, he had engaged the magician in long discussions about psychic phenomena. Carrington had gradually come to believe in the reality of the supernatural, and he found Thurston surprisingly open-minded—Howard started his conversations with Moody's ecumenical education and then peppered his stories with the marvels of the Indian yogi that he had almost witnessed.

In conjunction with the British Society for Psychical Research, Carrington had recently become the manager of Eusapia Palladino. She had already enjoyed a long career in Europe. She was born in 1854 in Naples and had baffled respected scientists like Professor Cesare Lombroso, Oliver Lodge, Pierre and Marie Curie, Camille Flammarion, and author and spiritualist Sir Arthur Conan Doyle.

She first visited America in 1908, and when Carrington brought her back in 1910, they were hired for a number of séances for scientists and magicians at Columbia University. Joseph F. Rinn, a boyhood friend of Houdini's and an investigator of psychic frauds, supervised the tests and warned everyone what to watch for. The Columbia committee wasn't impressed. It was apparent that the Neapolitan medium was extremely skillful in several devious tricks. For example, in the chaotic atmosphere of the séance room, she could move her feet together so that one foot could do the duty of two—contacting one spectator with her toes, and the other with the heel of the same foot. Once this occurred, her remaining foot was free. She gradually worked the leg of her table onto her toe, and then pressed down with her hand, forming a sort of "human clamp." This was how the table levitated at Columbia University.

When a published exposure was imminent, early in May 1910, Carrington quickly arranged the séance for Thurston. He was sure that if the magician were impressed, his credentials would cancel out the other lesser-known magicians like Rinn. Fortunately for Carrington, Howard and Beatrice had been fooled, and fooled badly. While the Columbia exposures were running in the newspapers, Rinn challenged Palladino to a test séance, to be conducted in an office at the *New York Times*, and offered her $1,000 if she could produce phenomena under special test conditions. At Carrington's urging, Thurston offered a counteroffer:

> I have been a conjurer all my life and have always been able to expose all mediums producing physical phenomena in the past. I am so far convinced that this medium can produce genuine table levitations that I agree to forfeit $1000 to any charitable institution named if it can be proved that Mme Palladino cannot levitate a table without resort to trickery or fraud.

Thurston's offer was silly. As Rinn pointed out, "A complete negative could never be proved. The fact that he is a magician does not mean that he may not have been fooled at the sitting which inspired his offer." Still, Rinn seemed to appreciate Thurston's point of view. "Magicians generally regard mediums as frauds," he later wrote, "although Howard Thurston did lean slightly toward a belief in Spiritualism. He told me, however, when he was on my Palladino committee, that he inclined that way only tentatively because he had witnessed some phenomena that he could not explain."

Palladino didn't help her cause. As she negotiated the terms of the challenge, she confessed to fraud. "You see, it is like this: some people are at the table who expect tricks, in fact, they want them. I am in a trance. Nothing happens. They get impatient. They think of the tricks, nothing but tricks. I automatically respond. But it is not often. They merely will tell me to do them. That is all," she admitted to the stunned reporters. Many of her admirers, faced with her exposures, had postulated that, as her powers waned, she had resorted to more and more fraud. "All mediums trick, all!" she said. "And it is not so easy to catch them. I say this from personal experience. All!"

The final séance was scheduled for the evening of May 24. Thurston, Rinn, and the other magicians, scientists, and reporters waited in the newspaper office. At the last moment Palladino refused to show up. The next day, she responded to reporters with "a choice array of Neapolitan expletives," insisting that she would not go through with the test. In fact, she wouldn't even perform for Thurston, who had supported her. She asked, "Am I a prize pig, to be made an exhibition of, to have persons bet on what I can or cannot do?" Palladino feared that, if she had been successful at the *Times*,

the next day, the next week, somebody will say that one of the magicians helped me produce my phenomena, and that I paid him to do it. No, I am not going to be caught that way. And for that reason, I do not wish Mr. Thurston to be at the table when I give my séance in the Times Tower. In Europe, I have only the greatest scientists for my investigators, and not the jugglers of the country fair.

Thurston later clarified his point of view:

Of course, Palladino is a trickster. She will even acknowledge it herself and many of her methods have been made public in the magazines. Nevertheless, she is able to do some things which are not explained by trickery or magic. I myself saw her levitate a table and I am positive that it was done without mechanical means. On the other hand, she will often resort to trickery in this very matter of table levitation when she cannot get control of the other power, whatever it may be. It seems to me that it is a great deal better to believe in it. I think the world would be a great deal better off if more people would devote their time to studying this psychic force. Such a study is more likely to be of use than airships, for instance. It doesn't seem to be that they will ever be of practical value.

Thurston had begun a curious dance, postulating the supernatural even when the circumstances disappointed him. Palladino not only admitted that she cheated, but hinted that Thurston might be accused of cheating for her. Just like his encounter with the yogi of India, he was capable of twisting his arguments like pretzels, ultimately believing his own con.

He had also overstated his qualifications. Like most magicians, he was not an expert in all deceptions, but only knew what would work on a stage, in his own show. Palladino's erratic séances, which proceeded in fits and starts, and her odd technique, squeezing the table while lifting it, were hardly part of a magician's arsenal.

The quote is especially interesting as Thurston's psychic researches predated Houdini's; it was another three years before Harry Houdini would discover his crusade against fraudulent mediums and turn this issue into a prominent part of his career. Still, Houdini may have been in Thurston's thoughts when he made the dismissive remark about "airships." Just months earlier, Houdini had been grabbing headlines with his new hobby, aviation. That spring, he had become the first man to fly over the continent of Australia.

JUST FOUR DAYS after the failed séance, on May 28, 1910, Howard and Beatrice walked to the Marble Church at Fifth Avenue and Twenty-ninth Street in Manhattan and were married. During the publicity about Palladino, Beatrice had been called alternately "Mrs. Thurston" by some observers and "my assistant" by Howard. In fact she had been both since 1904, and the couple finally formalized their relationship.

It was a rare, pleasant moment of stability. No one understood that Thurston had mastered the amazing illusion of seeming to move forward, while he was actually sinking in debt. His businesses were deeply in the red, and the continual salaries kept him scrambling for money. Thanks to Harry Thurston,

Howard's new partner in the amusement company was now William H. Swanson, who ran a Chicago film exchange and had formed Rex Studios, which was later one of the small studios that would be merged into Universal Studios in 1912. In the summer of 1910, Thurston's bills seemed endless. He needed money to file the patent for his amusement park ride, to develop new illusions, and continue a venture with scenic designer and melodrama writer Langdon McCormick. And he was still looking for cash to pay for the changes to the property at Cos Cob.

Houdini had just returned from Europe, with tales of a triumphant world tour. Thurston quickly asked for a loan of $250 to $300. Houdini turned him down, with pleasure, meticulously explaining how he'd been slighted in Chicago years earlier. Like many of Houdini's associates, Thurston was stunned by his ability to carry a grudge. Thurston wrote to Houdini:

> I am glad of our talk today; the talk has done much to explain matters between us. I am indeed sorry to have offended you in Chicago and I assure you it was not intentional. I have always had the greatest interest in your career and it has been a pleasure to think of you as a friend. I must confess I was disappointed and somewhat hurt today to learn that you would not do for me what would have been a pleasure to have done for you, had the positions been reversed between us.

THE NEW FEATURE for the 1910–1911 season was the Great Automobile Surprise. During the course of this three-minute pantomime, Howard and Beatrice arrived onstage in a two-seat roadster, an Abbott-Detroit 30. Howard got out of the car and entered the door of a café. Two robbers then appeared, dressed in long coats and masks, stealing Beatrice's purse as she sat in the car. The robbers were distracted for a moment; when they returned to the car, they found that Beatrice had mysteriously turned into a policeman, who now attempted to arrest the robbers. Thurston returned to the stage and was overpowered and tossed offstage. When the robbers removed their disguises, they were revealed to be Thurston and Beatrice, who stepped back into their car and drove into the wings.

These exchange illusions became a fashion for magic shows, introduced by vaudeville magicians and quick-change artists Fregoli and Lafayette, and Thurston's friend Servais Le Roy. The secret involved overdressing, with costumes that could be quickly stripped away, and then switching one actor for another at the edges of the scenery. The exchanges were designed to go unnoticed because of misdirection—other action onstage that momentarily distracted the audience. Magicians referred to these tricks as "raincoat and whiskers dramas," indicating the shabby costumes necessary for the exchanges. One of Thurston's critics called them "leg drop comedies," as the characters seemed to hover around the leg drops (the vertical curtains at the sides of the stage), waiting for their chance to switch for another person.

Thurston's auto trick was exactly the sloppy sort of magic that Kellar had feared. Spectators returning to see the show a second time would surely be able to follow the action and discern the secret; for Kellar, this was an anathema. Bamberg pointed out the flaws, but Thurston was stubborn, insisting on the big picture, the qualities the scene would bring to his show. Bamberg and Thurston spent many late-night meetings at Bamberg's workshop in Brooklyn, plotting every sequence of action to make the illusion as effective as possible.

Theodore Bamberg had been the perfect choice to work with Thurston. He loved magic and was both grand and discerning about its fine points. Offstage, he could come across as stuffy and patrician; he was hard of hearing and spoke with a clipped German accent, making him seem remote. "Theo acted as a brake on Thurston's impractical impulses," his son, magician David Bamberg, later explained. "It was a hard job that required tact, as Thurston had a strong will, but Theo's common sense and inventive genius was what Thurston needed most."

When they were finished planning the trick, Theo was given the role of the policeman in the little scene. They had both been right. There was not much mystery, but the big picture was very effective. The entrance of the car drew applause. The scenery and action were unlike anything else in the show, earning favorable reviews. And Thurston had managed to wring out several nice commercial endorsements: Abbott-Detroit were happy to provide the car; Miller Tire paid to have Thurston's throw-out cards imprinted with their logos. "Mr. Thurston uses Miller Standard Tires," the program now read.

Thurston was dogged and driven in surprising ways. He never stopped fidgeting with the Spirit Cabinet and the Levitation. Perhaps it was an effort to establish these illusions as his own. Or maybe, once they were established in his show, Thurston understood that he had to keep incorporating new surprises for his audiences. He suggested to Bamberg that they conclude the Levitation by adding Servais Le Roy's trick, in which the lady is covered with a cloth, floats in the air, and disappears. It started another long, simmering argument with Theo. "Und vhy vood you choose to take diss great illusion, und just stitch on anodder trick? Do you stitch on anodder pair of pants mitt your best trousers? Does dott make 'em look bedder?"

BEATRICE MISSED SECTIONS of the tour, staying home in Connecticut, and friends noticed that she avoided social dinners hosted by magicians' clubs. Thurston offered her apologies, explaining that she hadn't been feeling well. Her absence put an extra strain on the show, and the couple's relationship. Fortunately, a group of Italian pantomime clowns, the Monte Myro Troupe, had joined the show. In 1900, they had been featured by Siegmund Lubin, an early film producer, in a short motion picture. One of Monte's daughters, Lucille Myro, was exactly the right size for Thurston's illusions. She was less than five feet tall, rail thin, and pretty, with magnetic, dark eyes. She was given the stage name Fernanda, and became Beatrice's understudy, filling in as the lighter-than-air Princess Karnac, and her odd, exotic features suggested an Oriental princess.

The name Fernanda seemed to fit the illusion as well. Thurston had vaguely referred to the assistant: "The young lady comfortably rests in mid air." But now he gradually began to incorporate the new name; something about the sharp triple syllables made it irresistible. Thurston's neat baritone transformed it into a poetic chant that rippled throughout his routine: "Rise, Fernanda, rest, Fernanda, dream, Fernanda. Dream of the banks of the Ganges."

KELLAR CONTINUED pulling strings behind the scenes. He wrote to Karl Germain, a clever Cleveland Lyceum performer, urging him to contact Dudley McAdow and "join forces with Thurston. . . . I do know that it would be the strongest magic show in the world." Germain was elegant and artistic, a famous perfectionist on and off the stage, but he was a friend of Thurston's, and he ignored Kellar's offer, telling an associate that there was something "rotten in the state of Denmark."

Dudley McAdow, Kellar's longtime director, left the show in 1912, at the end of his prearranged five-year contract. Like all of the Kellar associates, he'd become used to the old system and was uncomfortable with Thurston's business. Charles Carter instantly hired him to direct his upcoming U.S. tour. Presumably, any scrap that fell from Kellar or Thurston's table, or could be pried away, was a delicious treasure for Carter's magic show.

Kellar followed up with another clever recommendation for the 1912 season. Guy Ellsworth Jarrett was a thirty-one-year-old magic builder and sideshow performer who had recently arrived in New York from San Francisco. Born in Ohio, he had operated a sideshow in California, and then joined T. Nelson Downs when the coin magician briefly attempted a vaudeville illusion act. Downs wasn't successful, but magicians noticed Jarrett's new illusions. When Kellar met Jarrett in New York City during one of his annual visits east, he thought he'd found an ideal addition to Thurston's show.

Jarrett was an interesting contrast to Bamberg; he had no airs about classic magic, nor did he fuss over lacquer or catches. Jarrett loved innovative secrets that challenged the audience and he loved dependable apparatus. Kellar used to have a rule about how magic apparatus had to be made: "Make each piece of apparatus twice as strong as required, and then double that strength." Jarrett produced well-made props and had developed a knack for hiding people in impossibly small spaces.

Still, Jarrett continually clashed with Thurston, and the arguments started at the shop in Cos Cob, even before the show went out on the road. Jarrett agreed to build several of his own illusions for the tour. He suggested a small wooden cabinet that would produce nine people; Thurston was carrying a group of nine Arabian acrobats, the Haja Hamid Troupe, as a variety act. The cabinet would allow Thurston to make them all appear.

Jarrett's illusions were famous for how small they looked, and the secrets depended upon tight little spaces that he had measured carefully. He allowed exactly eight inches of space for the bodies of the acrobats, squeezed in between two false panels in the cabinet. When Jarrett left the shop at the end of one day, Thurston added an additional twelve inches on the plans, telling the carpenters that he wanted to be sure the cabinet was big enough. Jarrett returned and saw the completed cabinet, stopping all the work. "It looked like a garage," he later remembered. He cut apart the carefully doweled panels, reassembling them to the correct size. "I can't remember a single time that Thurston was ever right."

Perhaps the most incredible of Jarrett's creations was called the Bangkok Bungalow. Thurston showed a small, narrow, two-story dollhouse, picking it up and putting it at the side of the stage. It was about the size of an orange crate on its side.

Jarrett stood atop a small pedestal. "I call your attention to this young man. He is the most remarkable man I have ever met," Thurston told the audience. "He can be in two places at the same time. I would like to have you take a good look at his handsome countenance so you will know him the next time you see him." The assistants held a cloth in front of Jarrett for a few seconds. When the assistants pulled the cloth away, he was gone.

"Now I want you to watch him and trace him, and see where I place him, for I'm going to hide him and you're to find him! Here he is, in the Bangkok Bungalow!"

Thurston now picked up the little house, lifting it effortlessly. He mumbled out of the corner of his mouth, as if talking to someone inside. "Yes, he says he is in there. He wants to get out."

The assistants now brought in a low platform on wheels, with upright posts and curtains hung around the sides. Thurston placed the house in the curtained cabinet, and the drapes were closed. Seconds later, they were opened again, and Jarrett was back, standing next to the house.

"Now, the next effect is the most astonishing of all."

The cabinet was turned so that the curtains obstructed Jarrett. The assistants marched onstage, pulling away the curtains, one section at a time, and showing that he had disappeared again. Thurston stepped over to the cabinet and lifted the house in his hands, walking it to the wings and tossing it to an assistant offstage. Meanwhile, the audience noticed a suspicious lump in the last curtain on the cabinet. They'd located the missing assistant.

Thurston returned to the stage, as if proudly taking his bow. But he now noticed the murmur through the crowd. He turned back to the cabinet and pulled away the final layer of curtains. Jarrett had completely disappeared. "Where is he?" Thurston asked, as if he had puzzled himself.

"Here I am!" Jarrett shouted. He jumped high into the air, and as the spotlight hit him, he was standing in the center aisle of the auditorium.

The entire illusion took just a few minutes, and Jarrett's magical transportation seemed to occur in split seconds. Like the very best Jarrett mysteries, the Bangkok Bungalow involved a series of clever principles to throw the audience off the scent. The most amazing part of the routine involved the little house. It was just large enough—barely—to contain Guy Jarrett, curled up inside. Even though Thurston's routine suggested that the house was just a part of the con game, for the final phase of the effect Jarrett actually hid inside the house. It was sixteen by eighteen inches square, and twenty-eight inches high, carefully constructed of thin wood and metal to give Jarrett as much room as possible inside.

As the assistants entered to remove the curtains, one of them held a metal hook at the end of a long, thin piano wire that was hanging from the grid of the theater. When the scene was carefully lit, the wire, like the wires used to fly actors in aerial ballets, was completely invisible to the audience. The hook was clipped to the top of the house. An offstage counterweight, on the other end of the wire, allowed Thurston to lift the house and carry it as if it weighed only several pounds. When he placed it in the wings, he was actually taking Jarrett offstage, though no one could possibly believe it.

Jarrett emerged from the house and ran around to the front of the theater, sneaking down the aisle in darkness as Thurston completed the trick. A few simple wire loops provided the shape in the curtain, suggesting that Jarrett was still hiding on the stage. "The people never notice me," Jarrett explained, "for they are so intent upon the bulge in the curtains on the cabinet. My speed was incredible." When Jarrett finally appeared in the auditorium, the audience had been completely conned.

JARRETT LASTED just one season with Thurston. He didn't have much regard for Thurston or his magic. In addition, he was angered that his name was never included in the program and that he wasn't paid any extra money to build the illusions in Connecticut, before the tour had started. Jarrett never understood that Thurston was pinching pennies with all of his employees.

But Guy Jarrett's failure also represents a missed opportunity. He should have developed a perfect rapport with the magician. Both were Ohio boys who learned their skills as carnival talkers, performing the roughest form of magic and promoting a number of uncouth shows. Jarrett wore these experiences as a badge of honor. Thurston had completely erased them from his history; as the boss and the star of the show, he now adopted a pose of superiority and sophistication to retain the upper hand.

Years later, when Jarrett wrote about Thurston, he recalled him as maddeningly cool and confusingly pretentious. "Thurston did not play the market," Jarrett wrote. "No wine, women or song came into his life," efficiently proving how little Jarrett knew about his employer. If Howard had dropped his guard, confessed his financial worries, and laughed about his sideshow days, he probably would have found a lifelong ally in the mercurial Guy Jarrett.

Kellar's spies in the Thurston show didn't provide him any peace of mind. Instead, they just gave him excuses to indulge his colorful temper. The old showman naturally played to his audience. "Kellar was so disappointed with the way Thurston botched up the show," Jarrett wrote to a friend, "he would take me out to eat somewhere and sit and cuss." After Jarrett's season with the show, he worked in the back room of Clyde Powers' Mysto Magic Shop on

Broadway. When Kellar visited the shop, Jarrett showed him a new fishbowl production that he'd just invented. Kellar was so delighted with the craftsmanship that he paid thirty-five dollars, buying it for Thurston. He asked Jarrett to deliver it to Thurston when he next passed through New York.

Thurston arrived and Jarrett proudly showed him the prop that Kellar had bought for him, but Howard dismissed it. "Oh, I already have a bowl production, so if it's the same to you, I'd rather take the same amount in little accessories that I can use in the show." Jarrett waited until he saw Kellar again before pulling him aside and whispering, "I'm going to tell you something, and you are going to be sore as hell." And, of course, he was. "Did he think I was just making him a present of a lousy thirty-five bucks?" Kellar roared. "I wanted him to have one good small trick in his show."

Jarrett somehow had retained access to Thurston's workshop in Whitestone; more than likely he had befriended the assistants and was allowed to visit and take a look at their latest projects. In 1915, when Thurston was developing a special illusion for the Miller Tire Company—an automobile tire that seemed to float in the air—Jarrett saw the awkward invention in Thurston's shop. He made a few suggestions about improving it, which were promptly ignored, and he retaliated by selling his own version of the floating tire illusion to Kelly Springfield Tires. Of course, this served to ruin the novelty of Thurston's illusion for Miller. It was an act of commercial espionage that hopelessly corroded Jarrett's relationship with Thurston.

When Kellar met Bamberg in his workshop, and heard about Thurston's plans for new illusions, he reddened and then quietly reached over to an ashtray. "You see this match?" he growled to Bamberg. "I wouldn't waste it to burn down the whole damned Thurston show!"

FORTUNATELY, Kellar was unaware of the real problem: Thurston's debts had already surrounded him like a roaring inferno, licking at every investment and threatening to engulf his career. In August 1912, Thurston mortgaged the entire show to Hyman Fish, a New York commission salesman, for a quick $1,000. Included in the loan was a full accounting of the show, including the crates containing Kellar's levitation, the props from Maskelyne and Devant, the Lion Cage, electric equipment, backdrops, tools, and Thurston's personal trunks. Mr. Fish now owned it all, until Thurston paid it off—nearly one hundred cases, baskets, and crates—a train-car load of specialized equipment, the parts and pieces of the America's greatest magic show.

Hyman Fish is a surprising name. He was convicted by the New York State Supreme Court in early 1915 for forging a set of books in conjunction with another 1912 loan, then charged again for perjury during the case. He was a loan shark. Apparently Fish was unrelated to Thurston's business. When the magician found him, it was for the same reason anyone went to a loan shark: they'd reached the limit from friends, associates, and family members.

Howard Thurston had returned to America just five years earlier with $50,000—and he was a millionaire by today's standards. Now he was forced to pawn one last property. And, of course, he couldn't let any of his partners or acquaintances know what he'd just done, or have anyone in show business gossiping about such a loan. The situation suggests that Thurston may have simultaneously, dangerously, mortgaged the show for similar loans.

"Don't worry, George. Never worry," Thurston habitually advised his loyal assistant. Now he knew that he had to keep his eyes forward, trusting that one of his business ventures would succeed. Something would work. Something would finally pay off. After all, it couldn't get any worse.

FOURTEEN

"THE PIERCING ARROW"

hen Thurston appeared at the Imperial Theater in Chicago in January 1912, he heard a knock on his dressing room door, and George White's voice. "Governor, there's someone here to see you." The door opened slowly, and a sad, skeletal figure, wrapped in an oversize dress coat, tottered into the room. Thurston stood and quickly pushed his chair toward his guest. It was only when the old man looked up and smiled that he recognized Paul Valadon.

He'd been brought from the Cook County hospital so that he could see the show, but now Valadon was offering apologies. He wasn't sure he'd be able to stay, and felt weak and dizzy. He was suffering from tuberculosis, penniless and homeless. The doctors told him that his only hope would be to move to a southern climate, but . . . Valadon simply shook his head. It seemed to Thurston as if he'd completely given up.

That afternoon, Thurston sent a letter to *The Sphinx*:

My brother magicians, there is a duty before us, and it appeals to this higher and broader nature. It is to extend a hand of sympathy and assistance to a dying brother. An old war-horse has fallen by the wayside. I have no hesitancy of telling you the sad truth. The recent death of his beloved wife has helped to hasten the lowering of the final curtain of this once brilliant performer. It is our duty to help him, and perhaps we may be able to save him.

In conjunction with Dr. Wilson, the editor of *The Sphinx*, Thurston established a Valadon Fund for his welfare. Thurston was the first contributor, offering $50, and then additional money as the months progressed. Members of Thurston's company offered several dollars more, including one dollar from George White. Kellar contributed $100. When the cause was promoted by Will Goldston, a British magic editor, contributions were made from Maskelyne, Devant, and the performers who remembered him from Egyptian Hall.

Could Valadon have been a success with Kellar's show? World War I would have sealed his fate with the American public, as Valadon's German accent always identified him as an outsider. His style might also have doomed him; he had a classic approach to magic, favoring the purely Victorian wonders. His contemporaries, like Devant, Thurston, Bamberg, and Downs, had been working hard to modernize their shows.

Valadon and his young son, Paul Junior, were able to move to Phoenix in February, but their bad luck continued. In August 1912, the hotel they were staying at caught fire, and Valadon escaped the building with only his nightshirt. He was taken to a local tuberculosis hospital. Dr. Wilson warned his readers that his health was perilous and that further contributions should now be sent directly to the magician in Phoenix.

After his long illness, Valadon died in April 1913. He was forty-six years old, leaving an orphaned thirteen-year-old son.

The Valadon Fund had seemed to tap into the admiration, and the deep-seated guilt, that surrounded Valadon within the magic community. He had been a fine, skillful performer whose ambition had pushed him within the cogs of a grinding show business machine. Professional magicians sent their contributions glumly. They knew, with some embarrassment, that the tragedy was both personal and professional. The world of magic was to blame.

For Thurston, the sight of Valadon sitting in his dressing room was particularly haunting. Thurston believed in dreams and omens; he realized that he might have been gazing at his own future. Valadon had almost become America's Greatest Magician. Even more sobering, America's Greatest Magician had become almost as destitute as Paul Valadon.

ON FEBRUARY 6, 1913, Al Jolson ran onto the stage at New York's Winter Garden Theater in blackface makeup. He danced down the runway, rolled his eyes, joked with the audience, and pushed aside the ragged plot of *The Honeymoon Express* so that he could stop the show with his latest songs. It was this show that introduced his comic song "The Spaniard That Blighted My Life," as well as the perennial hit "You Made Me Love You." Fanny Brice and Gaby Deslys were also in the star-studded cast, and the new Shubert musical was a roaring success by offering a little bit of everything, adding up to a long, wearying evening in the theater.

But the *New York Times* reported that it was a novel special effect that started the audience cheering.

> To comprehend the psychology of that peculiar composite, the theater crowd, is extremely difficult. For instance, the first-night audience at the Winter Garden is probably as sophisticated an assemblage as may be encountered anywhere. For its edification and delight, the highest salaried artists are trotted out, there seems to be no limit to lavishness in dress and incidentals, and the effort is always to provide an infinite variety of the newest things in song and dance. . . . Yet it was for none of these that the audience made its greatest demonstration. What moved the Winter Garden audience most was a representative of a race between a train of cars and an automobile. And this, be it said in justification of the crowd's enthusiasm, was really quite remarkable.

The Mile a Minute effect—that's what it was called—was created by Langdon McCormick and developed by Thurston's company. McCormick was an American playwright and scenic designer who had specialized in extravagant, melodramatic stage effects, the crashing, flaming, roaring spectacles. As McCormick sometimes worked in London, his association with Thurston may have dated from Thurston's early act, advising him on the fountain and fire effects. McCormick's sort of sensation melodramas had fallen out of fashion by 1913, but short, flashy special effects had recently become part of the formula in Ziegfeld and Shubert reviews on Broadway. McCormick and Thurston had patented the effect, and Thurston had sold Mile a Minute to the Shuberts for their latest review.

It wasn't really magic, but an element of theatrical hokum that added to the witty show. In *The Honeymoon Express*, the plot had worked its way around to a chase between one character in an automobile and another character in a train. A motion picture screen descended, showing a short film of the actors boarding the train and jumping into the car, bidding their farewells. The film screen was raised, and the audience was now looking at the set of a train station exterior, to one side of the stage. An elaborately painted backdrop showed a mountain in the distance, with winding paths extending down from its peak. The Winter Garden orchestra started a quick gallop, and the audience noticed two tiny pinpoints of light at the top of the mountain. They maneuvered around the winding road, suggesting the tiny headlights of a car. Shortly after this, another tiny lamp appeared, as if the train had reached the crest of the mountain and was following down the tracks, approaching the audience.

The music quickened. The tiny lights descended the mountain. As they did, they seemed to grow in size, and the headlights of the car spread farther apart. Finally, they reached the bottom of the mountain as full-sized headlights. "From the first faint glimmer of distant lights way up on the mountain side, through the devious turns of the road and down to the valleys, it could all be seen and heard," the *Times* reported. There was a rumble offstage and a roar of wind. The backdrop was raised, and the lamps were revealed as real auto headlights and a real locomotive lantern—the car and the train were now side by side. They charged forward, squealing their brakes, and stopped at the edge of the stage as the audience cheered. The actors bounded from the vehicles, and the plot of *The Honeymoon Express* was neatly resolved.

McCormick and Thurston's effect was actually simple. The two headlights were provided with mechanical irises, allowing them to be made smaller or larger. Similarly, they were handheld, mounted on a hinged arm, so the lamps could be brought close together or spread apart. Stagehands stood on raised platforms, holding the headlights just behind the translucent painted back-drop. They traced the path of the road, gradually opening the irises and spreading them apart. A single locomotive light was handled in a similar way. As the stagehands lowered the lamps to the stage, additional carpenters had pushed on the prop car and locomotive just behind the curtain. The lamps were then smoothly placed on the fronts of these vehicles, giving a seamless effect. The stagehands and carpenters ran for the wings, and the curtain was lifted, showing the completed effect.

Unfortunately, the success of the effect created a problem for Thurston. Another inventor of scenic effects, Lincoln Carter (not related to the magician, Charles Carter) smelled the profits from *The Honeymoon Express* and insisted that he had already patented that effect, for an 1898 melodrama called *The Heart of Chicago*. Through 1913, he pelted Thurston's attorney, Thomas MacMahon, with threats and challenges. MacMahon urged the magician to settle with Carter, but Thurston optimistically held out. He desperately needed the money from the Shuberts and was afraid to have them omit the effect or cancel the show because of the legal action.

When Carter's patent papers were finally examined, his game was finished. In *The Heart of Chicago*, he had used a prop locomotive that approached the audience from the back of a darkened stage. In his patent, the lamp on the front of the locomotive grew in size, giving the impression that the train had been traveling a much longer distance—that was the only similarity to Mile a Minute. Carter had accomplished it with a surprisingly clumsy device. A round glass covered the front of the lamp. This was covered with a layer of lampblack—soot. A small sponge on an arm pressed against the glass. As the glass revolved, the sponge wiped off the soot in a widening spiral, giving the impression that the lamp was enlarging. Carter could not patent the idea of a racing locomotive; he could protect only his actual devices, like the one used to enlarge the spotlight.

For the magician, the lawsuits provided a white-knuckle chase even more thrilling than the Mile a Minute effect. As late as November 1913 Thurston had still been avoiding creditors, and his show was almost attached in Pittsburgh for a $500 note, past due. But early in 1914, Carter finally withdrew his claims and the Shuberts paid Thurston in full for *The Honeymoon Express*, which had run for months in New York and on the road. Thurston had spent extravagantly on attorney fees and patents, but *The Honeymoon Express* raced across the finish line by delivering a bundle of much-needed cash to Thurston and McCormick. The magician was able to pay off the loan on his show to Hyman Fish and temporarily right his wobbly bankbook.

ANOTHER WELCOME SUCCESS was Thurston's amusement park ride, now completed, patented, and delivered to Luna Park at Coney Island. The first model had cost over $25,000, the equivalent of nearly half a million dollars today. It was called the Thurston Waltz Ride. According to one of Thurston's friends, its gyrations "caused many a loving couple, under the delusion that they were waltzing, to throw up their hot dogs." It was renamed Tango Waltz Ride, as confusing as that seemed, to capitalize on America's obsession with the tango, and then sold to Magic City in Paris, Atlantic City, and Riverview Park in Chicago, where Harry Thurston supervised the installation. Thurston's advertising claimed that it was the "Best, Newest, Safest, Cheapest Ride Ever Invented." It was hardly the cheapest, and after years of work, Thurston couldn't have realized much of a profit.

Thurston's next invention was inspired by the *Titanic* disaster of 1912. He proposed a special ship that could be turned into a series of lifeboats. The deck was built with double thickness. If the boat sank, large wedges of deck could be released, so they could float away as oversized rafts. It was a ridiculous idea, but he obtained the patent and proudly turned it over to the U.S. government as a special lifesaving device. A thank-you letter from Charles D. Hilles, one of President Taft's secretaries, was later featured in Thurston's souvenir books, with the headline, "Thurston Inventions Benefit Humanity . . . Gives His Knowledge and Creative Genius to His Fellow Citizens."

Howard was delighted with the publicity, but his obsession with invention seemed to be aimed directly at his father, William Thurston, who was still living in Detroit. He'd never had any faith in his son's abilities and had even insulted him by offering a quarter toward his career in magic. Now Thurston made sure that William read of his lifeboat patent. This was William's comeuppance: his son was not only a famous magician, but he had surpassed his father as an inventor.

AT THE SAME TIME, John Northern Hilliard was busy reinventing Thurston. Howard's journalist friend from Rochester had holed up in a writer's colony in Carmel by the Sea, California, writing the magician's biography for him. "I have got to write the story of your life, because the book is in my blood, because it is part of my actual existence." He refused an offer to write a Thurston newspaper serial on Indian magic, as it didn't interest him. And he turned down an invitation to travel with the show for a few weeks; as much fun as it might be, he was receiving a small stipend from his newspaper and his expenses were covered. Hilliard was luxuriating in the process of simply writing.

Hilliard had been critical of Thurston for the silly ballyhoo and exaggerations he'd used in his souvenir books—claiming that he'd been abducted as a child, or was related to Senator Thurston, or fooled Herrmann the Great. Instead, Hilliard wanted to lightly dramatize the real events. Thurston had trusted him with stories of his early life, riding the rails and traveling with the races. When Howard and Tommy read Hilliard's first chapters, they were gripped by the colorful scenes but embarrassed by some of the language. "Many minister friends would be greatly shocked," he wrote to Hilliard, by the words "damn and God damn." Hilliard sulked, and then put aside the work. He had considered each word to be realistic and perfectly chosen.

At the end of July 1913, Howard and Tommy left for a monthlong trip, visiting England, Paris, and Budapest. Thurston was able to promote his Waltz Ride to amusement parks and discuss business with David Devant. The previous year, Devant had been invited to appear on the first Royal Command Variety Theater performance—a select group of music-hall artists performing before the King and Queen—and Devant scored a success by performing Thurston's Boy, Girl, and Eggs routine.

In the hands of Thurston and Devant, the trick was now a minor master-piece. As the little boy escorted the little girl onto the stage, the orchestra played the "Wedding March." Once on the stage, Thurston would ask the little boy what he wanted to be when he grew up. "A policeman," he would answer. And then he'd ask the little girl. "A policeman's wife," she'd respond. Thurston accomplished this neat trick by whispering the responses to the children, tim-ing his instructions so that they were unheard as the audience laughed at some previous joke.

Maskelyne and Devant had been having their own financial difficulties at their new theater, and Devant was shrewdly looking for investors. He pro-posed establishing a permanent theater of magic in New York and told Thur-ston that they had already been approached by "two quarters" about this sort of deal, but, of course—the smooth salesman's touch—they preferred to col-laborate with Thurston and Kellar. Remembering the clause in his contract with Kellar, in which the older magician could set up his own theater, Thur-ston sent on the proposal. Kellar shot it down instantly. He had "no present intention of going into the permanent theater scheme," and then concluded with an admonition. "Take my advice and don't get entangled with Devant or any other English showman."

Thurston had intended to secure several Maskelyne and Devant illusions for his show but couldn't arrange a deal. Devant's recent feature, the Window of a Haunted House, looked wonderful in Devant's music-hall show illusion, but Thurston discovered, to his embarrassment, that he'd already purchased and performed a crude copy of the trick for his previous season. He didn't know it was Devant's idea. When they discussed the matter, Thurston took it out of his show.

Howard may have originally intended the trip as a long-delayed honey-moon, but their marriage was waning before the trip even began. Beatrice had moved out of their home in Cos Cob by the beginning of July, and after they returned from Europe at the end of the summer, she remained at the Hotel Walton in Philadelphia. In September, Howard received a report from the hotel detective that his wife had been staying in a room that adjoined and shared a bathroom with an insurance doctor, Olin M. Eakins. Their "dress, conduct, and the conditions of the rooms" suggested that their relationship was adulterous. In October, Thurston filed for divorce in Bridgeport.

Thurston's attorney, Thomas F. MacMahon, added this to a long list of problems that he was then juggling for the magician. "Why don't you answer my letters regarding your divorce matter?" MacMahon asked in a letter. Thurston had been paying Beatrice twenty dollars weekly and wanted the payment reduced to ten. "Mrs. Thurston came into my office and made a scene the other day because she hadn't received money from you," the attorney wrote. "She wants her notes paid."

MacMahon had been busy trying to finagle Thurston into deals and simultaneously out of trouble. He seemed genuinely confused and humiliated by his client's frustrating decisions and changes of focus. The Lincoln Carter case was a good example of Thurston's meddling; he had ignored requests, complicated deals, insisted on changes, and then jeopardized his business associations when he impulsively grabbed for a settlement. He also complained about Mac-Mahon's neglect. "All of your ugly letters can be answered very easily and with gentlemanly calm," MacMahon responded. The attorney provided the details of his meeting with Beatrice, the latest advice on the *Honeymoon Express* injunction, and information on the foreign Waltz Ride patents, but much of it was news that Thurston didn't want to hear. MacMahon pointed out that they were about to make $1,900 on the French Waltz Ride, and spend about $2,200 on the French version of the patent, a foolish decision. MacMahon was suffering from stomach problems, and ended one letter by warning Thurston, "It is such letters as you write, proving you lack the confidence in those supporting you in every direction, that chills your friends."

When his friends noticed that Beatrice was no longer traveling with the show, Thurston explained that she was under doctor's care in New York; it's not clear if the remark was intended as a sardonic joke. The divorce was granted on April 24, 1914. Beatrice had started her relationship with Howard Thurston as a seasoned professional and finished the same way. The "Queen of Magic" had not only been featured in his show, but was the original assistant in many of his important illusions. Shortly after the divorce was granted, she married Dr. Eakins and retired from the stage.

———————

ONE OF THURSTON'S new effects, the Spirit Paintings, was astonishing. A stack of blank canvases were shown and examined by the audience. A bright electric light was placed behind two of the canvases, held upright in a frame, and members of the audience selected a subject for a painting, or a personality for a portrait. As the audience watched the back-lit canvases, a picture seemed to slowly materialize, from misty colors to sharp, clean lines and colors. When the canvases were separated, the finished work of art—fully painted and dry—had materialized.

It was an amateur magician, David P. Abbott, who had discerned this secret from two Chicago mediums, the Bangs Sisters. The Bangses' phenomenon was a brazen fake; the ladies manipulated the frames as they held them in front of a bright window. Abbott's secret worked its way to England, where it became a sensation in P. T. Selbit's music hall act. He featured it throughout America in vaudeville. Abbott showed the secret to Thurston and Bamberg when they visited him in Omaha, Nebraska. Spirit Paintings was a perfect mystery, designed to make audiences scratch their heads—the visual, puzzling sort of marvel that Bamberg loved.

Unfortunately, the next season Thurston's new effects were just more *Sturm und Drang*, those monstrosities that made Theo Bamberg wince. For example, the Vanishing Piano was a Fasola inspiration. An upright piano sat on a low wooden platform. An assistant sat at the piano and began playing. She was covered with a curtain, and the piano and player were lifted high above the stage. Thurston fired a pistol. The music stopped, the curtains and their framework fell to the stage with a crash, to reveal that the piano and assistant had disappeared.

The Boy, the Girl, and the Donkey was even sillier, and more spectacular. Two assistants, a boy and girl, led a donkey down the aisle of the theater and up to the stage. There, the donkey was coaxed inside an enormous cabinet, painted with Egyptian hieroglyphs. Once the donkey was inside, the boy and girl instantly followed. The curtains were closed at the front of the cabinet and the prop was given a turn. When it was opened, all three had disappeared. The most wonderful surprise came just seconds later, when the boy, girl, and donkey instantly reentered at the back of the auditorium.

The box part wasn't very interesting at all. The cabinet simply had a false back that was large enough to hold the human and animal assistants—the kind of "garage" that had horrified Jarrett. But Thurston had hired twin girls, twin boys, and twin donkeys. . . . Or nearly twin donkeys: he needed animals of a specific size to fit in the box, and in 1914 an animal broker wired him, "Nature doesn't make mature animals according to your specifications; smallest matched pair available forty-two inches ground to top shoulder. Price, forty dollars." Three sets of twins, a ridiculous extravagance, explained the miraculous reappearance at the back of the theater.

Thurston asked his friend Karl Germain to paint the cabinet with colorful Egyptian hieroglyphs. When the show returned to Cleveland, Germain made a habit of visiting backstage after the show and touching up the painting. One evening, he found himself alone on the stage with Thurston's lion. As he walked by the cage, the lion's paw shot through the bars and grabbed Germain's sleeve, ripping it to shreds, just missing his flesh.

Thurston now had numerous reasons to look for new ideas, and reasons to be always looking over his shoulder, with an eye on his competition. Charles Carter was eagerly filling his show with magic from the Kellar and Thurston shows. He now had his own lion illusion and was touring America. Harry Houdini seemed to have tired of his escape act and toured England briefly at the end of 1913 with a magic act, including a disappearing pony. His English magic tour was a flop. Audiences weren't interested in watching Harry Houdini, with his reputation as an escape artist, performing magic tricks. But to Thurston, who was wary of Houdini, it sounded suspiciously like the first steps toward some real competition.

When he heard that Houdini was returning to the United States with a new illusion, Walking Through a Brick Wall, Thurston hurriedly had Bamberg rebuild one of his small tricks—a neat little effect in which a pencil or a wand was pushed through a small square of fabric—into a gigantic piece of apparatus to accommodate a person instead of a pencil. Bamberg objected, pointing out that it would be a bad trick, and it was. But Thurston wanted to be ready to steal a little of Houdini's thunder if he managed to score a hit.

One winter morning in Indianapolis, as he traveled with Thurston in 1918, Bamberg arrived at the theater and found the stage brutally cold. Thurston was onstage rehearsing in dress gloves, to keep his hands warm. Bamberg called to him, "Don't forget to take your gloves off." Thurston responded, "Nothing doing, Theo. I keep them on." Bamberg was amazed to see him present the first part of his show, including his intricate card routine, wearing gloves. In this, Thurston was years ahead of the times; a generation later, it became fashionable for magicians to perform card manipulations wearing gloves.

Bamberg worked for three seasons with Thurston before returning to vaudeville. He admired Thurston as an engaging performer and a magnetic personality. But he also was mystified by Thurston's strangely tin ear with magic; Thurston always fancied himself an inventor, but always depended on other people to lead him to a genuinely new idea.

PERHAPS IT WAS Theo Bamberg who even led him to Nina Fielding, Thurston's third wife.

As the story was told, the show was playing in Ottawa, at the start of World War I. Howard and Theo were lounging in the hotel, feeling lonely, when Bamberg began flirting with a pretty woman and her little girl. She'd just seen the Thurston show and was anxious to meet Bamberg and Thurston, but her little girl had not seen the performance because, she told Thurston, "my mother won't let me." The magicians amused the little girl with pocket tricks, and the mysterious lady revealed that she was a widow and her husband had been a victim of the war.

The story can't be even slightly true. Neither the year nor the situation was correct. So, here's another story. Thurston was performing in Montreal; he supposedly saw a pretty lady seated in a box during his show. She loaned a monogrammed handkerchief—N.F. for Nina Fielding—and there was a mix-up in handkerchiefs as it was returned to her. The lady seemed amused, returning to the show and then inviting Thurston to perform at a children's birthday party. That one's not true, either.

Or there was the story that he met her in Atlantic City. Or on the steps of an Asbury Park, New Jersey, hotel. . . .

The lady's name was actually Nina Leotha Hawes Willadsen. She was born in 1885 to George Hawes and Ellen Fielding Hawes. It seems that this was Ellen's second marriage, as Nina had an older half sister, Emma, who was born in Nova Scotia. Her mother was Canadian, but later claims—that Nina was the daughter, or niece, of the former premier of Nova Scotia, William Stevens Fielding—were untrue.

She had a short career in the theater, working under the name Nina Randall, playing comic supporting parts in several Broadway productions, including Florenz Ziegfeld's musical for Anna Held, *Mam'selle Napoleon*. Nina had sparkling dark eyes and a pleasant smile, with broad features and a square jaw. She was too large to be a Ziegfeld showgirl, or for that matter, one of the slender waifs that Thurston pushed through trapdoors or balanced on the levitation cradle. In 1908 she was married to John R. Willadsen, an experienced theater manager, who had been responsible for running one of the most successful Broadway shows of all time, *Abie's Irish Rose*. This probably signaled the end of her stage career. They lived in Weehawken, New Jersey, just across the river from Manhattan, where he built his wife a three-story brick apartment house, on Oak Street near the waterfront. The couple occupied one of the five apartments, with a maid. In July 1909, Nina gave birth to a pretty, blond daughter, who was named Jane Jacqueline, and John Willadsen called their home "Villa Jane."

Thurston knew Mrs. Willadsen from New York show business circles, where they may have attended parties together, and it's very possible that their relationship preceded their own divorces—this might be the reason for constructing innocent fictions about how they met. By the summer of 1914, both Nina and Howard were recently divorced. He was America's greatest magician, a prominent figure in the theatrical world. She was a minor star of the stage, now a wealthy and attractive lady of independent means who owned an apartment building. Articles around this time refer to her as "not engaged in the theatrical profession." As their relationship became more serious, his letters were concerned with disappointing her.

> My past experiences have been so sad that I had become reconciled and had about given up hopes of ever obtaining that peace and joy to be formed only with the [union] of two souls. . . . You will discover so many things in me that may not please you, and I fear that those things may gradually change your feelings for me.

We can imagine the list of problems: his unpredictable temper, his criminal past, his shaky finances, failed marriages, and a tie to low-life show business that he could never quite shake—Harry Thurston was always nearby to draw him back. Thurston's first two marriages had been with very young women who had been longing for the spotlight. He may have reasoned that the time was right to pursue one of those wealthy, independent socialites who used to visit his dressing room early in his career. If he had started the relationship with this cold, calculated business plan—a confidence game—then he fooled himself. Thurston fell head over heels in love.

There's a strange desperation in Thurston's love letters. He was awed by Nina's Broadway connections and social status, and also intimidated by her worldliness. She had her own money and property and was accompanied by a young daughter, a maid, and a number of independent women. The assembled retinue seemed to not only impress Thurston but throw him off balance; he had always been ready with a deception or a brash bit of self-confidence—"Never worry, George!"—but now seemed so helpless that he could only rely on the truth. In October he wrote to Nina. He called her "Leo," short for Leotha, or his "Love Girl":

> Here are two people whose lives have been entirely different. You are giving up friends, position, family and all and everything, even your dreams of worldly

comfort and luxury which are laid at your feet at every side. With only one answer. I love.

Even after they resolved to be married, at the last minute Thurston was fretting over her social status. He wrote on October 24, 1914:

I know your dinner was a success. . . . I know you were the most beautiful lady present. I am anxious to see you in evening dress. It will probably be the last special dinner you will ever give in your old home. Things are surely changing for you. It is a complete change in your life and entirely different from what you ever expected. And I really believe you will enjoy the change of living. If it is in my power to make you do so, I am sure you will. Only twelve days more then you will belong to me and I to you.

Thurston and Leotha were married on November 5, 1914, in a simple ceremony at Niagara Falls.

LEOTHA'S INFLUENCE on the show was immediate. The famously meticulous producer, Ziegfeld, was the inspiration, and John Willadsen, her first husband, provided the example, for she now fulfilled some of the duties of a company manager. Leotha insisted on new scenery and suggested new costumes from Lenore Schulz, a seamstress and friend of Leotha's. Thurston's new wife offered an attention to detail that Thurston had always lacked—the complaint of Kellar, Bamberg, and Jarrett. Whenever she visited the show, Leotha watched from the front row or a box.

Thurston acknowledged her in the audience with their own special "love code," a simple gesture of holding up his hand and crossing his first two fingers as he smiled in her direction. Leotha sat with a pad of paper balanced on her knee. She would scribble notes—a drape that had not been hung straight, a hinge that squeaked, a costume that needed pressing, or an assistant who needed a haircut. This pad was then handed backstage to Thurston at the end of the show for a formal critique. A visitor to the show recalled a typical "school session":

Thurston lined up the assistants and crew to talk over the mistakes that had been made. This was most annoying to everyone who wanted to get the hell out of the theater, but they had to go through with it . . . a daily harangue and the snide side comments.

A smudge on an assistant's pants would start a chain of finger pointing. If the assistant had brushed against a dirty prop, was it the assistant's fault, the wardrobe department's fault, or the property man's? Every problem was addressed and solved for the next performance. The process was later expanded, adding pads backstage to record problems during the performance. These school sessions—reading and discussing Leotha's notes—made everything better, and her influence gradually pushed away the last cobwebs of Kellar's stodgy Victorian magic show. Thurston's production was put on a trajectory where it could compete with Broadway's touring reviews.

Bamberg noticed a new efficiency to the production. For a Detroit matinee, Thurston's show arrived late at the theater, at one p.m. for a two-thirty matinee. As the trucks were being unloaded, there were already people in line at the box office. Theo objected that it would be impossible to have the show ready. Thurston smiled. "Watch my system, and time exactly when the curtain rises." Thurston's fourteen assistants worked in a sort of precise ballet: the show's switchboard was brought backstage, backdrops were unloaded and hung, and tons of apparatus was uncrated and assembled. Thurston stepped into the dressing room just three minutes before the show, knowing that George White had unpacked his clothing and makeup. The curtain went up twenty-five minutes late; illusions in the second act of the show were still being assembled backstage during the first half. Theo was dumbfounded that this massive show could be handled so efficiently.

Like all of the magician's friends, Theo noticed that this marriage was different. Leotha's independence seemed to earn her special respect from her husband. Unlike his previous wives, she didn't rely on him for friendship or her career. He listened to her advice and doted on her wishes.

And then there was the little girl, Jane, whom Howard formally adopted. He was delighted to suddenly become a father. He wrote letters to his "Jane

Girl" nightly, sent trifling gifts back from the road, or, failing that, enclosed dollar bills or funny poems. On stage, he increasingly found opportunities to mention her during the show. "What is your name?" he'd ask a little girl from the audience. "I have a daughter named Jane. She's a little younger than you are. She takes after her dad. I suppose you take after your dad. All nice girls take after their dad." And then Thurston would glance over the footlights at the little girl's father. "Don't they, Dad?"

The audience laughed. If Jane was in the audience, she giggled with delight at being mentioned from the stage. Thurston intended it as a simple joke, of course, and never realized just how much little Jane would take after her dad.

FIFTEEN

"BIRDS OF THE AIR"

hen Fredrick Keating was a teenager, he ran away from home to join a magic show. He'd studied card tricks and fancied himself a card manipulator, and of course, Thur-ston was his idol.

Thurston rejected the boy several times, instructing his company manager to put him on a train and send him back to his mother. But when Keating left Peekskill Military Academy and arrived backstage in Bridge-port, Connecticut, dirty, hungry, and still in his military uniform, Thurston tried another tact. "Give him a dollar a day," he told his company manager, "and see that he damn well earns it!"

Keating earned it by painting props, distributing playbills, cleaning Thurston's shoes, and catching Fernanda as she fell through a trapdoor beneath the stage, so that seconds later, he could close her into a trunk that was shoved back through a different trapdoor. This was the understage action of the Triple Mystery, and it earned bruises for both Fernanda and Keating. He also washed the ducks—Thurston used a bit of Hindustani, calling him the keeper of the ducks, "my duck-wallah."

One of Thurston's opening tricks was called Birds of the Air. Thurston would stand on the stage and swing a long-handled butterfly net; a white pigeon would appear in the net, as if it became visible the moment it was caught. The bird was dropped into a small cage that George was holding in his hands. This was repeated, producing two more birds.

Birds of the Air was an ingenious mechanical trick using a trick net and trick cages. Thurston had devised a special finale to punctuate the mystery. He would step down into the audience, as if spotting an invisible bird over the audience's head. Standing in the aisle, he swung the net. His stooge, sitting next to him in a theater seat, had a pigeon concealed in his cap, holding it in his lap. When Thurston swung his net in a low arc, the stooge would drop the bird inside, so that the audience saw the bird as the net reached the top of the swing and was illuminated by the spotlight. One of Keating's jobs was to be that stooge, with a pigeon in his cap, sitting in his seat at the start of the show.

One evening, it all went wrong. Keating left the stage door with a bird in his cap and hit a patch of ice on the pavement. The cap flew from his hands, and the dove skidded on the ice. Luckily, its wings were clipped. He chased the bird around the ice, tumbling head over heels as he lunged for it. By the time he had the exhausted bird back in his clutches, the boy was scratched and panting. He dashed for the entrance of the theater, but Thurston's manager wasn't there to let him in. The local house manager didn't recognize him and wanted a ticket. The boy gave him a shove and careened through the lobby.

As Keating reached the back of the aisle, his heart sank. He was too late. The show had started. Thurston was standing in the auditorium, waving the net helplessly. "Anyone but him would have simply gone on with the next trick," Keating later wrote. "But not Howard Thurston."

"Welcome home!" he snarled at Keating as he took his seat. By now, of course, the trick was botched, but Thurston wouldn't give up. He signaled for the orchestra to stop.

Ladies and gentlemen, my show is more than a show. It's a big business. I run it that way. I have a large, efficient organization. This young man wishes to be my successor. He kept pestering me until I was kind enough to let him join my organization. Not only that, but I pay him!

By now, the audience was in on the game. They laughed at each line as Keating slouched lower and lower into his seat. Thurston pointed a melodramatic finger at the boy, and his voice hardened to a comically icy accusation.

I pay him to be in that seat at the right time, and he's late as usual! You see what I have to go through to bring you this wonderful show!

Thurston planted his feet, swung the net, and shouted, "Now!" Keating flipped the bird into the net and the audience erupted in cheers. Not a single person had been fooled, but each one had been privileged to watch Thurston's improvised lecture. "The audience loved it," Keating recalled.

Thurston always made them part of the show. There was a folksiness about him, to be sure, but [he was] no hayseed. You had the feeling of being at the home of a friendly and fatherly host whose table was as abundant as his heart. Young and old, peasant and patrician felt themselves honored guests.

Many people used the analogy of a minister, a man of great personal warmth and good humor, but also great dignity. Howard Thurston's show was now filled with bubbling humor, from start to finish, although Thurston never told a joke. He presided over a magical party.

For example, the Rising Card Trick now accommodated bits of unexpected humor. When Thurston had asked for the name of a card, a stooge sitting in the balcony loudly called for the joker. Thurston dismissed him, saying "No joker," as if he'd been caught, and couldn't perform the trick with the joker. But the man in the balcony loudly repeated the request, causing the magician to roll his eyes. "Yes, the balcony is filled with jokers," Thurston quipped.

Thurston asked the name of a small boy in the front row and had him stand on his seat. "I say, Gilbert," he started, "place your hand very gently on top of father's head. Now, don't disturb father's hair. You know, I want father to be happy. I want him to be proud of you and I want him to have a good time. Now raise your hand in the air and say, 'Rise, Ace of Clubs.'"

The boy did it, but nothing happened. "That's strange. Gilbert, just take a firm hold of father's hair. Hold tight because I want dad to be happy. Say, 'Rise, Ace of Clubs.'" The card started to appear. "Now Gilbert, just pull on father's hair. Pull, pull, pull, pull, pull!" And as the little boy pulled, he seemed to make the magic, causing the card to float out of the deck.

When the joker rose from the deck, Thurston instructed someone else in the front row to tell the card to rise. "Go down," the voice from the balcony interrupted. And, on cue, the card descended. "Rise, rise," Thurston countered. The card began to rise. "Whoa," the stooge yelled, and the card froze in midair.

Once Thurston had established his conflict with the mysterious man in the balcony, the situation led to further comedy. An hour into the show, when Thurston was presenting the Spirit Cabinet, the lights were lowered to a mysterious blue haze. "I shall now present the spirit that controlled Katie King more than forty years ago," Thurston intoned. A gauzy, luminous face appeared floating in the cabinet, sending a collective shudder through the audience. Thurston continued, with a hypnotic purr:

I say, when the lights are all down and the house is dark and no one can see, I shall cause the spirit to leave the cabinet and float over the heads of the audience . . . and it will rise and rise . . . and go up in the gallery . . . and land on the worst sinner in the gallery.

There was an uncomfortable pause, and then the stooge in the balcony yelled, "Turn on those lights!"

"A magician is an actor playing the part of a magician," the famous nineteenth-century conjurer Jean Robert-Houdin explained. Thurston had managed something even more remarkable. He played the part of a gentleman, businessman, entrepreneur, and a pillar of society who was a magician.

Thurston charmed his audiences as the dapper man in the tuxedo standing at the edge of the stage, with his hand raised in supplication—the gatekeeper between the comically ordinary, doubting rabble in the audience, and the rarefied wonders and profound magic just beyond the curtain. Howard Thurston was clearly part of both worlds, and the show consisted of him mediating between the two. What audiences may not have realized was that the real-world comments and reactions had been as carefully planned and plotted as the marvels of magic within the spotlight.

His audience assembled clues about his personality and came to their own conclusions about his respectability and probity, which was part of his incredible deception. Even young Keating, who worked with him for a season and befriended him in later years, got it wrong.

> He was a man of affairs, a leader of men, who could rub elbows as an equal with the builders of industry, Rotarian Resplendent. Henry Ford was his God, not Robert-Houdin. He did not produce fishbowls or cards or pigeons, he produced commodities.

His audience—indeed, even Fred Keating—could never have imagined him as a poorly educated street urchin, a carnival confidence man, a failed performer whiling his time on a Union Square park bench, or a magician so desperate that he would pawn his entire show to a loan shark. Those were the real secrets. Once he proved himself a great magician, fame had insulated him from his past.

Keating lasted one season with the show, and did, indeed, learn a lot about magic. On Thanksgiving, as the show passed through Trenton, New Jersey, Leotha, Jane, and Howard hosted Keating's mother at a local restaurant. The Thurstons knew that she had been ill; they planned the entire day carefully and treated her grandly—inviting her to the show, where she was presented with roses and introduced to the audience as the "mother of the future world's greatest magician." After the show, Thurston told her confidentially, "If Fredrick wants to be a magician, let him. Neither you nor anyone else can stop him." Keating's mother died shortly after that meeting. "I think she died happy," Keating later wrote, "because she had sensed something of the beauty, of the drama, of what I saw in magic."

DURING HIS SEASON with the show, Keating also learned about his boss's sense of humor. Howard Thurston was an inveterate practical joker, and his magisterial presence only made the situations funnier. For example, shortly after Keating joined the show, the boy was sent on an urgent mission from backstage. He dashed down the street, one theater to another, to locate the "key to the curtain," so that they could begin the performance. Every theater manager seemed to play straight man to Thurston's practical joke, listening earnestly to the boy's request, sadly noting that their key wouldn't fit, and sending the frantic boy to the next auditorium.

Thurston's patter often displayed his sense of irony. "Surakabaja," the Hindustani word that Thurston uttered endlessly during the levitation, was, his friends recorded, an unprintable, and physically impossible, command that he had learned in India. One of Thurston's scripted lines explained, "Surakabaja means, among other things, that those who love shall be loved," which was a sly acknowledgment of the real meaning. Similarly, in one illusion his script refers to the lady assistant as "Eileen." But there was no Eileen in the cast. The trick was accomplished when the lady would secretly lean out of the way to avoid a sharp blade; hence "I lean."

He similarly used words that he had learned in his Masonic initiations, sprinkling his patter with impressive-sounding spells and winking at all of his brother Masons.

IN 1915, Thurston finally managed to sell the farm in Cos Cob at a loss. Leotha Thurston searched for a home closer to New York City and located a cottage near the water's edge at Whitestone Landing, Beechhurst, Long Island, across the East River from Manhattan. When Howard saw the lot, he was shocked to realize that it was on the property owned by Alexander Herrmann, whose mansion had been across the street. To him it was one of those incredible premonitions. They moved into the cottage on the property and the following year built a large, three-story house there.

Beechhurst was a small suburban community that had become a haven for a number of actors and theatrical producers. Leotha supervised the grounds and the furnishings, splitting her time between the show and the family's new property. Jane was alternately neglected and spoiled. For most of the year, she was sent away to boarding schools—first to the nuns at Mount Saint Agnes College in Baltimore and then at the Academy of the Holy Child in Manhattan. Leotha offered the nuns gifts whenever she passed through town—candy, handkerchiefs, and, at least once, according to Jane's recollections, black silk negligees. Mrs. Thurston had a surprising, bubbly sense of humor to match her husband's, but Jane noticed that there was no joke intended by the presents. The nuns seemed very happy to accept these provocative garments.

Jane received daily letters from her mother and father; when she was old enough to write responses, her parents harangued Jane when they didn't hear from her—when she didn't report on her classes, or grades, or her health. "To my blue-eyed violet," Leotha addressed her letters, "From her brown-eyed Susan, Mother."

"Dear Jane Girl," Thurston used to start his letters, often counting down the days until they'd see her again. "Only two more days. Mother is here helping with the new water act. It is beautiful. Mother will call you Saturday. Love, love and a kiss. Daddy."

Her happiest times were the summers, when Jane's school was out of session and her father was home. Then the Beechhurst home became a beehive of activity. Illusions were repaired or built at a nearby warehouse. Blanche Williams, the sometime wardrobe mistress of the show, became the family's maid and nanny; Abdul, the somber dark-skinned Indian who prayed during the levitation, was the family's butler, answering the door with a solemn sense of duty and silently circling the rooms to polish the furniture. George White was available to play with Jane, perform songs on a guitar, apply bandages to her cuts and scrapes, and repair her toys.

Thurston indulged Jane with tricks, practical jokes, and stories about the little red devils on his posters. "Hocus Pocus" and "Conjurokus" were the good little devils, he told her, and "Beelzebub" was the one who made the trouble. Thurston's qualities as a father came naturally to him and seem to have developed from his work with children on stage—in many ways, each performance in which he invited a boy or girl on stage and then charmed them with his magic had served as an audition for his life with Jane.

"My greatest thrill is standing on the run-down [from the stage to the aisle of the theater], watching the swaying, happy children screaming with delight, and I often tell my audiences that our show is for children from four to ninety-four," Thurston wrote. "I think it is my deep affection for Jane which makes me delight so in the company of children. She has revealed to me all the beauty and glory of the child mind."

Since 1908, when he was called to entertain at the sickbed of a little girl in Atlantic City, Thurston regularly sought out orphaned or hospitalized children. He started traveling to the institutions with a suitcase of tricks, and then, by the late teens, turned the procedure on its ear. Now he offered special matinees at his theaters exclusively for these children, performing his full show of marvels. The children were brought in donated cars, buses, and ambulances; the aisles were often filled with children on stretchers. At a time when polio was still a scourge, it was not uncommon for individual hospitals or hospital wards to be devoted exclusively to crippled children. Thurston was eager to perform these benefit shows, and they earned him headlines in every city.

HARRY THURSTON had a different approach.

He owned thriving dime museums in Chicago, Indianapolis, and Cleveland. These were storefront assortments of seamy entertainment in the worst part of the city. "Freaks and strange people" were regularly featured on the program. Slot machines lined the walls. And initiates knew that they should ask for the back room, where the Maid of Mystery—the failed coin-operated attraction—had found an ignominious new home. Harry's solution was simple. Inside was a naked lady, who writhed and wriggled as the coin-operated shutters fluttered up and down. "She may have been wearing shoes," one fan of the attraction later speculated.

Harry and his wife, Isabel, and daughter, Helen, lived briefly in Cleveland but established their home in Chicago, where Harry bought and sold commercial real estate.

Harry and Howard Thurston had both started in show business as virtually the same person, sharing the same shady carnival businesses. But Howard's distinct skills differentiated him. Harry never really changed. He was something of a genius of downtown museums and strip shows, wearing every scar and stain from his career. He had become a big-city con man, a notorious wheeler-dealer in Chicago's First Ward, who skirted the edges of the law and paid off the police. One of his best friends in Chicago was Michael "Hinky Dink" Kenna, the notoriously crooked First Ward alderman who had organized the graft-ridden First Ward Ball.

Howard's success meant that he had been gradually repaying loans to his brother, although he still relied upon him to warehouse his illusions above one of Harry's Chicago dime museums. But Howard's success had also emboldened his brother, and Harry's advertisements gradually incorporated the word *magic* into various attractions. His new Chicago museum was titled Thurston's World Museum, and the publicity boasted that it was managed by the brother of the famous magician.

Howard resisted criticizing his brother—who had financed the show many times—but Thurston's World Museum was too much to endure. He sent a long letter pointing out his own efforts as a family entertainer, a Broadway star, and America's popular magician. Harry sent a grudging response to his older brother:

> Will say I closed the Thurston Museum a week ago and have got my old place back, the Royal. I call it Wonderland Museum. If I open the other place again I will never mention magic in any way if you think it hurts you in any way. I am doing fine. I am not running any kootch dancers at all.

The last statement, of course, was a mere technicality. Howard was happy to know that his little brother was flush; he didn't actually want to think about how he was making his money.

IN 1917, Kellar sent Howard Thurston a warm letter from Los Angeles, congratulating him on a full decade since their first association.

> Hearty congratulations on your splendid success. May it continue for many seasons to come. Don't mix up with any schemes outside of your own business.

Put away your money where it is absolutely safe and increase your store every year and you will at a near date awake one morning and find yourself independently rich. Good luck, old man.

It was wonderful advice from one of the few magicians who retired wealthy. Unfortunately, Thurston didn't follow it. One of his most costly schemes was about to leave the door open for his main competitor in the magic field, Harry Houdini.

It had started, innocently enough, with Thurston's special effects business. Capitalizing on their success with Mile a Minute for the Shubert show, Thurston and McCormick went on to produce the effect in a short vaudeville play. Thurston patented a smaller version, a race between a motorcycle and a car, and incorporated it into Thurston's 1917 show. It was a "raincoat and whiskers" play called *Villa Captured*.

During *Villa Captured*, George White played Poncho Villa, the Mexican rebel who was featured in newspaper accounts. George wore a handlebar mustache, a sombrero, and crossed bandoliers. The play was two simple scenes. A policeman raced to Villa's hideout to find the notorious Mexican bandit. Then Thurston's lighting effects portrayed the chase down the mountain. The motorcycle and car arrived onstage at the same time, but Villa seemed to have escaped. The characters tossed off their costumes, revealing that Villa, now in a magical disguise, had actually been captured.

Villa Captured meant very little in the magic show, but it inspired Thurston, who had been tinkering with different automobile effects. He patented an elaborate auto race, in which multiple autos would race around the stage, entering from the right, whizzing across the stage, and exiting on the left. A motion picture screen, in the center of the stage, synchronized the action, giving the impression that the audience was watching the cars as they reached the far side of the track, in the distance, and then returned for another lap.

It was just the sort of overblown, impractical idea they were looking for at the New York Hippodrome. The Hippodrome on Sixth Avenue was the largest theater in the country, an enormous white elephant that dwarfed almost anything that was put on its stage. At its premiere in 1905, the first production was titled *A Yankee Circus on Mars*, which allowed the producers to pitch a full-sized circus tent on stage as well as creating science fiction fantasy lands—that was the sort of desperate madness that was required to fill the stage. Later productions included earthquakes, a baseball game, Civil War battles, air battles, and even sea battles (when the massive stage was withdrawn, revealing the water tank). All of Broadway knew that the new producer, R. H. Burnside, was desperate for new ideas, any sort of sensation that could form the centerpiece for the next Hippodrome show.

Burnside had seen Thurston's auto race in *The Honeymoon Express*. Coincidentally, the Hippodrome had staged a show in 1907 called *The Auto Race*, which was something of a flop, as the actual race was just a disappointment. Now Thurston proposed something much more ambitions. His cars would be full-sized lightweight cars attached to long arms that moved at a center point, like the hands of a clock. Motors in the center of the stage were supposed to keep the cars spinning.

Thurston filed a patent for the new auto race, and the legal papers suggest numerous, desperate solutions to make the invention work. For example, the cars lost momentum as they reached the back of the stage, so stagehands were forced to push the cars up an incline so that they could gain speed before the arms pulled them around to their next entrance. The effect worked just fine in the scale of a model. That's how Burnside saw it and approved it. But when Thurston's mechanics returned to Whitestone and started building it full-sized, they faced an onslaught of mechanical problems.

In 1917, Guy Jarrett sent a note to Burnside with a very good idea: "Startle press and public alike by vanishing an elephant." Burnside instantly called him in. This was the perfect idea for the Hippodrome, who already had a group of performing elephants, often engaged for their elaborate productions. Jarrett demonstrated his trick with a model, a derby hat standing in for the elephant. He fooled Burnside with it, and Burnside considered the idea for several weeks. The temperamental Guy Jarrett probably didn't help his cause when he refused to leave Burnside with the model, making it clear that he suspected the producer would steal the idea. Burnside finally told Jarrett that he didn't need him, as he would be featuring the Thurston auto race. Those were the magic words that, to Jarrett, were like a red rag to a bull.

I told Burnside that he would need me more than ever, if he wanted the auto race to work. I had often seen Thurston and his clowns working on that thing, and I knew they would never make it work on a full-size scale. Men, time and worry went into it, but not a chance. So, there was no auto race in the Hipp.

Jarrett returned to the Hippodrome after the opening of the next show to razz the management about their failure. But they had the last laugh. Jarrett was surprised to hear, the next season, that a new show called *Cheer Up!* would feature Houdini and his Vanishing Elephant. Jarrett naturally felt that the idea had been stolen from him. But Charles Morritt, an inventive British magician, had also suggested the trick to Houdini. More than likely, the Hippodrome engagement was the result of a conversation between Burnside, quoting Jarrett, and Houdini, quoting Morritt.

Jarrett's idea had been for a Hippodrome production number, using hundreds of extras and elaborate scenery. Houdini's trick was pure magic show. An elephant was marched onto the stage and up a ramp into an enormous, garage-sized wooden cabinet. The doors were shut, the cabinet was given a turn, and the doors and curtains were opened, so that the audience could see through the cabinet and see that the elephant was gone. Houdini took a bow and the show went on.

It was, by all accounts, a terrible trick. Many in the wide auditorium couldn't actually see inside of the narrow cabinet, which was like looking down the barrel of a gun. The audience had to take Houdini's word for it, in his own distinctive phrasing, that "an-i-mile is gone!" But the trick received so much publicity, so many headlines and reviews across the country, that even publicity-mad Houdini was satisfied with the result. The Vanishing Elephant ran for nineteen weeks at the Hippodrome.

Thurston had heard all about it; he'd heard it was disappointing and that Houdini had failed to convince the audience. But the publicity had finally gotten the best of him, and he contacted Houdini a week before the end of his engagement, innocently suggesting that he and Leotha would like to see the trick. Houdini provided passes for the show, with enormous pleasure. He took Thurston's interest as another compliment.

Although a bad illusion, Thurston realized that Houdini wasn't playing it to the 5,200 seats at the Hippodrome, but the millions who read the newspapers. When *Variety* wrote "Houdini Hides an Elephant," Houdini had effectively won the battle. It made Thurston even more resolved to find new features, and bigger features, for his show.

Houdini used the publicity from the trick as a springboard for his ambitions. "Magic is now the vogue. My efforts are bringing it back into style," he wrote to Kellar. "'Twill make it good for Thurston and all other illusionists." But actually, of course, he was now including himself in the list of illusionists.

KELLAR HAD SPENT much of his retirement tinkering with magic. One of his pet projects was an improved version of the Levitation. He experimented with different systems to pass the hoop over the lady, but finally ended up rebuilding the prop from his show—his cherished secret—with a state-of-the-art winch and neatly forged steel. Kellar was even less mechanically minded than Thurston, but he got the job done by visiting Los Angeles machine shops and hounding them, having each little piece adjusted and rebuilt. A friend visited Kellar in Los Angeles and was astonished to find him in dirty overalls, adjusting the bits and pieces of the new levitation. He asked the old magician why he was building it. "For the pleasure," Kellar answered. "The work makes me feel happy." When he was finished, he packed it all in gleaming cases and stored it in his garage, for no particular reason and no specific show.

The original Levitation kept Thurston busy, especially through the years of World War I, when the fine wire was difficult to purchase. He sent a round of letters to friends and colleagues across the country—including Harry Thurston, Kellar, and even Fritz Bucha, his old assistant—asking them to visit local hardware shops and purchase all of the spools of wire they had in sizes 6 and 8.

The precious nature of the wire just compounded problems. One night a member of the crew, thinking he was settling a score with the magician, crawled out onto the theater grid during the illusion, some sixty feet over the floating princess. He sprinkled sneezing powder onto Fernanda's face. She resisted as long as she could, twitching her nose and contorting her features, but eventually she erupted in a violent sneeze. She nearly fell off the precarious cradle. When Thurston saw what was happening, he rushed across the stage, grabbing to keep her from falling onto the stage. She was unhurt, but it was too late for the apparatus. One wire snapped, and then another, and another. . . . The nature of the illusion meant that there was a domino effect with each wire as the load was shifted. Twenty wires had snapped and cascaded to the stage before the curtain was lowered and the trick stopped.

After the show, there was an extra special school session. Thurston lined up the crew and delivered a fusillade of profanity that, according to one visitor, "I have never seen equaled." When Thurston was provoked, he could recall every four-letter epithet that he'd heard from the carnival fairgrounds, and deliver them with a loud ringing oratory worthy of Dwight Moody.

KELLAR MIGHT HAVE UNDERESTIMATED Thurston's self-confidence and his resolve. Thurston continually tried to apply his formula—mixing fairy tale and challenge—to the levitation. By 1919, he had ignored Bamberg's advice and created a complicated mixture of illusions. He invited a committee of spectators onto the stage as the princess floated, and had them stand at the sides of the stage to watch the illusion. "This is such a strange, weird, wonderful affair and I am so anxious to convince you that she actually floats in space, that I shall ask onstage a number of ladies and gentlemen. Anyone may come." Thurston boldly ushered one or two of them around the floating lady as part of the Indian ritual. Finally they were all dismissed from the stage and the lady descended onto the Oriental couch. Thurston then continued with Le Roy's floating and vanishing lady: she was covered with a cloth and caused to float again. She disappeared as the cloth was pulled away.

Kellar had intended to give his levitation to Thurston, and Thurston hinted that he was expecting a new, expensive illusion from the master magician in retirement. But when Kellar heard about Thurston's new presentation, it was the old magician's turn to explode with profanities. He suspected that Thurston was exposing the trick to a handful of people every night, for beyond the glare of the footlights, the shine of the fine wires was visible against the dark wings of the stage. Even if the spectators didn't quite understand what they were seeing, the careless exposure was an affront to Kellar's great mystery and an insult to his fabled perfectionism. Thurston had reasoned that it was more important that a thousand people in the audience were dumbfounded; he was unconcerned if six or eight people might have a suggestion of how it was done.

Kellar was right, and the spectators could easily see too much. One of those spectators who walked around the levitation was magician John Hunniford, who remembered the experience years later. As Thurston escorted him to the back of the levitation, he gripped his neck firmly so that Hunniford couldn't look upward. As usual, Thurston had been directing the reactions on the stage.

He said to me in sotto voce, "When you leave the stage, walk backwards and scratch your head as though in bewilderment." [I] just couldn't help seeing all those fine silver wires. I considered this a bad piece of business. True, it was showmanship, but quite unnecessary.

Even worse, Kellar hated what had happened to the trick. The Oriental fairy tale had been a powerful image—the silk-wrapped princess, the methodical, trancelike procedure, and the Indian yogis who rushed onto the stage, knelt, and then chanted prayers throughout the ritual. Now, Kellar complained, there were just a lot of "crummy-looking people milling around on the stage." According to Jarrett, Kellar "could have killed him." David Bamberg, Theo's son, agreed that including the spectators "proved nothing and completely ruined the mysterious presentation; this was Kellar's main gripe." Kellar no longer had his own spies in the show, and Thurston was no longer taking his advice.

Part of Thurston's motivation seemed to be his love of the illusion; he was obsessed with wrapping the trick in his oratory. In his notebook is a long, fascinating, experimental script from 1920. Had he really tried such an elaborate presentation, it surely would have taxed Thurston's acting skills, with earnest recitations of Indian magic words, love spells, invocations, and challenges to the audience. It indicates his ideal mix of reality and fantasy—what he had been striving to create on his stage.

Unfortunately, Thurston's new presentation never reached his ideal and was never more than shambling and complicated. Through the 1920s he gradually simplified the routine, inviting just two spectators at the end of the effect and walking one boy to the floating princess to touch her ring and make a wish. In a later interview, Thurston came close to confessing his error:

> [In] my levitation trick, I could easily give up half an hour in talking, trying to convince the audience that it was a great feat. But I say very little. In doing the illusion almost in silence, the audience's powers of logic don't have a chance to get to work until the trick is over. They get a thrill even if they know there isn't such things as the miracle they are seeing.

Still, Thurston always took advantage of any friend who happened to be in the audience. Werner C. Dornfield was a young vaudeville comedy magician, known to his friends as Dorny. He once found himself invited onto the stage for Princess Karnac's ascent. Thurston took him by the arm and stood him behind the cradle—the place of honor, directly in front of all the wires. Then Thurston dramatically stepped away. "Look up!" he told Dornfield. Dorny did, and he saw the myriad wires disappearing into a system of shiny oiled springs in the dark grid. "Look down!" Thurston told him. He did, and saw a matched set of wires that passed through a narrow slot in the carpeted platform. Dorny felt a chill run down his spine. Those few seconds were some of the most astonishing he'd ever experienced in magic, a rare view of an incredible mystery, and he didn't want them to end. "Young man, in a loud voice, tell us, what holds her up?" Thurston asked.

"Well, I could have made him look like a bum, right there," Dorny recalled years later. "But you just didn't. I knew what I was supposed to do. I said, 'Nothing!' And the audience cheered."

SIXTEEN

"THE GIRL AND THE RABBIT"

hurston's first Broadway engagement was in 1919 at the Globe, a chance at one-upmanship after Houdini's Hippo-drome vaudeville run. But it was also an unfortunate scramble.

Thurston had regularly played around New York and the boroughs, but an actual Broadway theater was another matter. In August 1919, Actors' Equity had declared its first strike, and forty-one of forty-five theaters were shuttered. The Globe, at Broadway and Forty-sixth Street, was forced to cancel its current show, *She's a Good Fellow*. The Shuberts were desperate for touring shows, like Thurston's, that weren't covered by Actors' Equity. Thurston already had a relationship with the Shuberts through *The Honeymoon Express*.

Thurston rushed his show into the theater before his usual season started, but when stagehands and musicians were called out, expanding the strike, the opening was delayed. On September 8, Equity accepted the terms of the show and Thurston's show finally ran. Even taking the strike into account, the *New York Times* sniffed about finding a magic show in one of Broadway's top theaters:

New York is quite likely to regard an exhibition of magic as a somewhat naïve entertainment in these times, but there are nevertheless a number of ingenious tricks in the repertoire of the veteran Howard Thurston, who has been carrying his show up and down the country these many years. . . . Like most magicians, Thurston is happiest when he performs, and saddest when he talks. Of talking he does quite a little and, since he was generally inaudible, there was a feeling that the entertainment was being unduly spun out. But the exhibition has its moments. Thurston's trick of levitation, while basically the same as that performed by previous showmen, is a particularly uncanny piece of work, and his picking of pigeons from the air was also an illusion well sustained.

The reference to his talking was odd, for most people found him perfectly clear and engaging. But Thurston always fussed over his voice and was not above stopping the show to step into the wings and spray his throat or ask someone in the audience to close the door so that he could avoid a draft. He sometimes complained that his voice was not at its best.

Houdini wrote to Kellar, "I am surprised to hear that Thurston will act as strikebreaker for the Shuberts. He ought to know better." Both Houdini and Kellar sided with the actors and were disappointed to hear that Thurston, and other producers like George M. Cohan, took advantage of the situation.

PERHAPS ONE TRICK that had disappointed the New York reviewer with "quite a little" talking was the Girl and the Rabbit. Thurston included it in his show as early as 1912, but after he became Jane's father, the trick took on a special significance. The presentation stretched and became more conversational, focusing on the girl's reactions and her relationship to her father in the audience—as if he were performing it to Jane every night. For most audiences it was a highlight of the show, a small bit of magic enhanced with Thurston's natural rapport with children. The Girl and the Rabbit gradually moved to a place of honor near the end of the show, proof of its success.

Thurston showed a simple trick with a handkerchief and concluded by reaching beneath it and producing a small brown bunny. As the children oohed and aahed, Thurston asked if there was a little girl in the audience who wanted to take it home.

Invariably a little girl bounded up onto the stage. Thurston asked her name and told her about his own daughter, Jane. He instructed the girl how to hold the rabbit. "It's very cold out. Would you like me to wrap him in a piece of paper and keep him warm?" George stepped onstage with a sheet of brown paper, and Thurston told the girl to wrap the bunny up herself—the animal was folded into the paper and the ends were twisted shut. "For Jane's sake, you wrap him up yourself." He handed her the bundle, but then stopped her as she left the stage. "Oh, you shouldn't do that!" Thurston held the bundle to his ear. "He's stopped breathing. Poor little fellow." He slowly unwrapped the paper. The rabbit was gone, and in its place the magician discovered a nice box of chocolates. He awarded this to the little girl and dismissed her from the stage.

The audience gradually realized that the performance had been taking place on the little girl's face. She was excited to receive the bunny, careful and mindful of all of his admonitions, fearful that the rabbit had been hurt, and then resigned when it disappeared. The little girl—like everyone in the audience—had seen it coming. Of course, it was just a trick. Of course he was not going to give her a real rabbit.

She took her chocolates with a shrug of visible disappointment and set off for her seat. "Don't let him wrap that up, little girl," the stooge in the audience yelled, and Thurston looked up, offering the noisy man in the balcony a dirty look. As the little girl reached her seat, Thurston told her to stop. "I see that you want a little rabbit. Do you know any gentleman in the audience?" The girl identified her father.

"Father, you don't mind if your girl takes a rabbit out of your coat, do you?" Standing at the edge of the stage, he instructed his volunteer to stand on her chair, reach down her father's collar and say, "Come rabbit, come rabbit, come rabbit." As the scene became more ridiculous, Thurston told her, "I think I had better do that for you. You know, I have a certain way of doing that." Thurston took the candy, tossing it to a nearby boy, and then reached down the father's collar, withdrawing another rabbit, this one snow white. He presented it to the little girl with an exaggerated bow. "Feed him oats, water, hay, and bread, and he will live forever." Thurston followed with free passes for the Saturday matinee. "Come back Saturday with your friend, take front seats, see the show, and see someone else get the rabbit."

Traveling with a menagerie of animals—pigeons, ducks, geese, chickens, and a lion—created its own problem. But finding a regular supply of small bunnies to give away to children was a continual source of frustration. Thurston told about arriving in a town and discovering, to his horror, that the last two rabbits had died on the train. He asked the theater manager where he could find someone who raised rabbits. Howard and an assistant were directed to a small farm out of town where rabbits were sold for food. At the farm, Thurston found an old Dutch farmer wearing wooden shoes. The farmer was leery of two city swells arriving in such a hurry, but Thurston patiently explained the situation: he needed tiny bunnies. The farmer sold him two. In gratitude, Thurston offered him a complimentary pass for his show in town. He pulled out the pass—theater folks always called them "Annie Oakleys"— and signed the front of it. When the farmer took it, he noticed the little red devils cavorting across Thurston's printed name and shook his head. "No, I von't sell dem," he said. "I vill not haff my rabbits in a thee-ater!"

THURSTON WAS DISAPPOINTED to hear that Harry Blackstone, a clever young American magician, had been copying several of his tricks, including the Girl and the Rabbit.

Blackstone was a full generation younger than Thurston, born in 1885 in Chicago. He was bold and pugnacious on the stage, a roustabout with a rumbling bass voice and a charming swagger—precisely the opposite of Thurston's ministerial presence. Blackstone was also garrulous offstage; he was suspicious of Thurston as a wily old pro, and detested Houdini as a clumsy hack. Thurston had been warned to keep an eye on Harry Blackstone, who would surely prove to be competition, and Harry Kellar had a habit of offering extravagant praise for Blackstone's abilities. He'd seen him perform in Los Angeles and offered the quote, "Blackstone is the greatest magician the world has ever known." It seemed a pointed barb at Thurston, his old associate, who had already been proclaimed the greatest.

In November 1919, Blackstone received a letter from Thurston:

I was surprised to hear that you were doing an exact copy of my Rabbit Trick with the little girl, exchanging to a box of candy. I have also been told that you are copying the red devils as used in my advertising. Those designs are copyrighted by the Strobridge Lithographic Company. Now, I think in the long run you would find it much to your advantage not to copy any of my tricks.

Thurston now had perfected his "carrot and stick" act:

I have always been interested in you, although I have never seen you work. From the reports I have had, I have been thinking that perhaps you would be a good man to succeed me when I retire in a few years. This may interest you and if so I feel sure it will be much to your advantage, for it is my intention to introduce someone as my successor. Now let us play this game square.

Almost any magician would have been flattered into submission, but Blackstone was a battler. He complained to a friend, "Imagine that guy, telling me he hasn't seen my show!" At a recent performance in the Bronx, Blackstone said, he had been walking through his lobby and noticed Thurston standing with his back to him.

Blackstone could have interpreted this in a favorable way—that Thurston saw him, was impressed with the show, and was trying to avoid a confrontation, suggesting that he "was surprised to hear" about the Rabbit Trick. Blackstone took the opposite approach. "I don't want to trade on another man's reputation," he told a friend. "I want to make one of my own!"

Blackstone continued to use the little red devils, as well as the Girl and the Rabbit trick, determined to earn his own reputation his own way—with one of Thurston's best tricks.

IT WASN'T JUST BLACKSTONE; Thurston's fellow magicians were a constant source of trouble. Samri Baldwin, born in 1848, was a revered old American professional. With his second wife, Clara, he'd developed the "question and answer" act, in which spectators wrote questions for which they sought psychic answers. The envelopes were sealed and placed in a bowl on stage. Envelopes were selected and, without being opened, Clara would divine the question and offer a suitably vague, or hopeful, or sensational answer.

The act became especially successful with Baldwin's later wife, Kittie, but when she divorced her husband, he continued the act. Thurston wired him in November 1920, asking if he'd join his show and perform a question-and-answer act. Thurston suggested that Baldwin would be introduced as a mystic and Thurston would hypnotize him, seating him in the Spirit Cabinet. Then Baldwin would answer questions and Thurston's assistants would sell the usual fortune-telling books, as well as printed forms to answer questions by mail. This was basically a version of Samri and Kittie's old act. Thurston offered him $100 a week, plus a split of the book and question sales.

Baldwin traveled from San Francisco to join the show in Rochester, and the atmosphere backstage quickly turned icy.

Baldwin was a tough old bird who had been around the world and done it all. He had no tolerance for any of the latest fashions, nor regard for a modern show. Although he made a very impressive mystic, with a mane of white hair, a white brush mustache, and a grandly theatrical manner, he was uncomfortable with Thurston taking control of the act—taking Baldwin's old role on the stage. For some reason, Baldwin wasn't billed under his own name but was called in the program "The Prophet of Nizam" and announced as being ninety years old. The pretense was demeaning, especially to someone who had been a star decades earlier.

The program also showed Thurston's typical equivocations regarding any claims of psychic phenomena.

Special announcement: Mr. Thurston specially announces that no claim is made to the possession or use of "spiritual" supernatural or superhuman forces or agencies in any part of this entertainment. The mental portion is a practical duplication of the most exclusive experiments given by renowned mediums and psychics and is a bewildering sample of intuitive, influential deduction

based on observational knowledge and vast experience, but with no claim whatsoever to verisimilitude.

Baldwin had long used his own general disclaimers about his act, but the
suggestion that real psychics could perform these feats, but Baldwin could not,
seemed to be a needling distinction.

Actually, the friction between Thurston and Baldwin stemmed from an important misunderstanding. Baldwin thought that Thurston needed him on the
show as an adviser, a special job for a seasoned old professional—the way Houdini
would sometimes befriend and honor past magicians. Baldwin would have been
given this impression from his old friend Kellar, who was still desperate to stage-
manage Thurston's staff from behind the scenes. Unfortunately, Thurston's
needs were cool and calculated; he just wanted a fifteen-minute act.

Houdini heard about the tensions backstage and found the feud irresistible.
The night that he attended Thurston's performance in Brooklyn and was
brought on stage as part of the levitation, he also saw Baldwin's old-fashioned
mind-reading act. The next day, when he wrote to Kellar about the levitation,
he commented on Baldwin's act. "Among the questions was one which made
me sink back in my seat with embarrassment," Houdini gleefully reported.

> It was as follows, "Does Houdini know as much magic is he is supposed to?"
> Baldwin replied, "Yes, Harry Houdini knows more about magic and magicians
> than anybody in the world."

Of course, the strange wording of the question—an insider's inquiry
about Houdini's magical knowledge, not his achievements or skills—suggests
that Houdini himself engineered the anonymous question to humiliate Thurston. Thurston's audience probably just shrugged in response. But in Houdini's
mind, the situation took on an epic importance.

> There was a moment of tension (for me) and I wondered whether that state-
> ment would cost him his job. Can you imagine Thurston's feelings, posing as

the greatest in the world, to have one of his "employees" or "constituents" make such a prophecy. Figurez-vous!

As always, Houdini's comments were childishly easy to interpret. Thurston was "posing as the greatest in the world," and Baldwin's flattering comment was a "prophecy." Houdini's intentions were perfectly clear.

When Baldwin's ego had been bruised beyond repair, less than a month later, he stormed out of the show in Pittsburgh and hid in his hotel bed, instructing the front desk that he didn't want any visitors. An old friend found him in his room, where Baldwin showed him a trunk of treasures—gold snuffboxes, jeweled watches, and framed proclamations—that had been presented to him by presidents, emperors, and tsars. "You see this trunk? I brought it with me from San Francisco and was going to give it and its contents to Thurston if we got along okay," Baldwin grumbled. The pathetic conversation suggested how the old man had imagined a flattering, personal relationship with Thurston, perhaps even a surrogate father-and-son relationship.

Both Samri Baldwin and Harry Kellar could now commiserate as rejected father figures. Kellar wrote to Baldwin:

> He *may* be the greatest magician on earth, but that may be only his opinion. He is financially successful, he has the big head and he is supremely selfish and jealous. How you managed to wear the yoke as long as you did is a mystery to me knowing you as well as I do.

OR MAYBE THURSTON'S priorities had simply changed. On January 1, 1920, just a year before his engagement of Baldwin, Thurston picked up a pen and paper and wrote a letter to his ten-year-old daughter, Jane.

> This is the first letter I have written this year of 1920. . . . It is nearly one o'clock a.m.
>
> You have seen ten New Year's Days, I have seen fifty. I can remember when

I was your age and thought how small I was and wanted to grow up like some other boys I knew. I also had no idea of the value of time or what it really meant. Time was something that seemed to have no end. It was an awful long while from breakfast to lunchtime, and one whole day seemed ever so long. I wanted time to pass rapidly in those days. . . .

I never played with boys my own age, as I remember I was always the youngest boy in the crowd and this continued in all my relations until I became a man. Now things are different. Time is the most valuable thing I know. My chief aim is to conserve time to get as much as I can of it. And to try to keep myself in good health so I can live longer and enjoy time. And I want younger companions, like you and mother. So you see Jane, all things change and we change with them.

Thurston had joined the Masons in 1907 and reached the thirty-third degree; he was also a member of fifteen other organizations, including the Elks, Optimists, Lions, Kiwanas, the National Vaudeville Artists, and the Clearview Golf Club. One night, when his club associations found him too busy to take Jane to the motion pictures, he sat down and pulled many of the membership cards out of his wallet. "I made up my mind that I would resign from [those clubs]; I jumped in the car and rode home and that day we formed a new club. Jane became president. Mrs. Thurston and I became general managers, and that is the finest club I know."

THE AMERICAN PUBLIC of the 1920s was obsessed with unusual patent elixirs, diets, and health fads, creating a generation of hypochondriacs, and apparently curing them at the same time. Thurston indulged in many of these fads, as his schedule permitted, and a friend reported that the magician was always "mildly hypochondriacal," obsessed with the right type of sleep, the perfect sort of breathing, and the latest mixture of meats, vegetables, and grains. His doctor advised only occasional cigars or alcohol, and Thurston was careful to eat plenty of vegetables and take regular spoonfuls of Wampole's Preparation, a popular tonic medicine that he kept on his dressing room table.

But the cures didn't work fast enough for Thurston. One evening, during a performance, he stepped into the auditorium to borrow a handkerchief, and a small boy called out, "Why Mother, he doesn't look at all like his pictures close-up, does he?" The boy was loud enough to cause giggles throughout the audience. Thurston laughed along with his crowd, but the incident embarrassed him. In fact, for years his photos had been airbrushed of lines and sagging skin. He decided to do something about it.

Dr. Lutz of Rochester performed the plastic surgery. In the early years of the twentieth century, this consisted of softened paraffin, injected under the skin, to smooth out wrinkles. By 1920, the use of paraffin was already an old procedure and greatly discredited; Thurston should have been advised to avoid it. When newspaper reports exposed the dangers of paraffin injections, Thurston pointed this out to the doctor, who assured him that he had been using his own special compound.

The operation was not a success, especially under the hot lights of a stage, where Thurston's face visibly sagged. Thurston now looked oddly puffy and jowly; his vanity and the failed operation became a private joke with his friends. One day, Theo Bamberg and his son, David, saw a wax mannequin that had been slowly melting in a sunny window. "Look, it's Howard Thurston," David told his father, and they both fell over, convulsed with laughter.

Thurston's interest in his health encouraged his doting on his wife and daughter. Leotha was often ill, or under a doctor's care, and she became dependent on depressants to reduce her pains or sleep. To Thurston, these drugs were just another category in the wonders of medicine—patent medicines, paraffin injections, or barbiturates. Howard recommended to his wife Émile Coué's cure, the autosuggestion "Every day in every way I'm getting better and better," which was then a fashion around the world.

When Thurston was away on tour and Jane was in boarding school, Leotha and her friends might dash to a seaside resort for a short vacation, or Leotha would visit her sister in New Jersey, who now lived in her apartment building in Weehawken, or her brother in Halifax. Thurston followed with quick letters of cheery advice, urging her to get plenty of relaxation and eat only healthy food. She had her own way of feeling better. Like many socialites, she liked champagne, and when alcohol was banned under Prohibition, she traveled with bottles of bootlegged booze.

EVER SINCE HIS AUSTRALIAN TOUR, Thurston had been intrigued by motion pictures, and he'd written several film outlines, attempting to mix magic into the plots. But it was probably Houdini's involvement in the film business—a cliff-hanging serial called *The Master Mystery* produced in 1919—that galvanized Thurston to become a motion picture actor. Thurston's film was completed in 1920.

Thurston wisely realized that his magic did not translate to the screen, where special effects could easily dazzle audiences. He wrote a script, first titled *Eternity*, about a fake spiritualist who encounters genuine marvels. The press reported that it "dealt largely with Thurston's experiences in India and China" and depicted "the truth of spiritualism as demonstrated by the Yogis of the Hindustan." It was shot at the Hal Benedict Studios on Long Island and directed by George Kelson.

The finished film, at six reels in length, was ultimately titled *Twisted Souls*. It was never released, and only a few segments of it survive, including Thurston as the rumpled and distraught medium, brandishing a gun and encountering Indian mystics in a ramshackle mansion. Several years later, Thurston attempted to recut the film, renaming it *The Spirit Witness*, but distributors weren't interested. It offered none of the derring-do from Houdini's film adventures, although the film encouraged Thurston to try his hand at additional scripts.

EARLY IN 1920, Jane was diagnosed with the flu, a serious threat after the recent influenza epidemics, and was hospitalized. At the same time, Leotha's cold developed into flu, and she was put under doctor's care at their home. Thurston, on the road at the time, rushed from the theater each night, waiting for telegram updates about their conditions.

Suffering from a lack of sleep and raw nerves—this was also the time when the impatient Samri Baldwin was performing with Thurston's show—on

February 3, Howard was standing on the stage just before the curtain was about to rise, and he glanced into the wings. His company manager was trying to catch his attention, frantically waving a telegram. Thurston felt his knees weaken. He ran to the edge of the stage, grabbed the telegram, and opened it. His younger brother, Charles, had just been murdered.

The company manager had the overture repeated several times, as Thurston stood behind the curtain, trying to collect his thoughts. He was frozen in place by the shocking news.

Charles had been working as a railroad detective in Columbus the night before, examining the seals on freight cars in the Pennsylvania Railroad yard. Sometime after six p.m., shots had been heard, and Charles was found hours later with eight bullet holes in his back. He'd left a widow and three sons. The murderer had escaped, but police suspected a group of boxcar thieves.

The cast gathered around Thurston and watched him expectantly, wondering if the magician would be able to continue with the show. After a few minutes, Howard took a deep breath and went on the stage, mechanically going through all the motions, the smiles, and the little drolleries with the children as his mind raced over the situation. He had lived his life by omens and now wondered if Charles's murder would start a cascade of misfortune with Jane and Leotha. For the next hour he was crazed with grief, wanting to dash from the theater. He felt it was only the decorum of the performance—the expectant audience staring back at him, the regimented movements of the assistants, and the laughter that arrived perfectly on cue—that kept him sane. As the curtain fell, the adrenaline that he had summoned seemed to drain from his body; in the darkness backstage, he collapsed onto George's shoulder.

Fortunately, Jane and Leotha recovered within days. Harry Kellar brushed aside past differences and sent a fatherly note, filled with soothing advice from an old friend.

It was with deep sorrow that I read that your brother met an untimely death while doing his duty as an officer of the Pennsylvania Company. . . . Then on top of it all your dear wife and baby Jane being down with the flu. I only hope they will have both recovered when this reaches you and if my ardent prayers are of any avail, they will be. Please remember me very kindly to both. Little Jane was such a sweet girlie, the sunshine of your beautiful home, that I don't want to think of her being ill.

Be of big heart, old man, and don't worry over what can't be helped. I hear only good reports of your show. . . . I am always interested in your successes. I read in the papers that you intend to retire at the end of the season. If that be your intention and you are going to sell out your paraphernalia, let me have first bid on all my old show; I do not want anyone else to have it.

IN LETTERS TO HOUDINI, Kellar had exhibited far less goodwill. "I am afraid of Thurston being able to hold his own," Kellar wrote, "as he has greatly improved his work and works smooth now, but I am afraid competition would worry him to death, as he lacks that self confidence so very essential to success in magic." Kellar heard that Thurston had been approaching other magicians like Harry Blackstone and Harry Jansen, to follow him into the marketplace— Thurston even considered retiring from the stage. The last few seasons had been profitable, and he was looking forward to spending time with his young daughter. Houdini loved these rumors, and he imagined that he would soon be able to step into the role of America's leading magician.

Thurston always relied on a loyal group of magicians around him. Ostensibly they were there to supply him with ideas and new tricks. That's why Fasola, Bamberg, and Jarrett had been recruited to help. But invariably they became involved in the backstage drama. Thurston was suspicious if they didn't show the proper deference. That was Guy Jarrett's problem. Or Thurston lost patience if they proved too needy. Fasola, working in England, was happy to chase steel wire for the levitation or send Thurston news of the latest illusions. But Fasola continually included reminders of how he depended on Thurston's material and professional help, and Thurston tired of the weight of the friendship.

Most of all, Thurston's men were there for a psychological boost, so that he could self-confidently play the part of the theatrical entrepreneur, allowing him to erase his embarrassing, ragtag background. That was always the problem with associating with Harry, whose dime museum businesses in Ohio and Chicago were roaring successes.

Now that he had his wrinkles surgically smoothed out, Howard had become the handsome hero to millions of children, gazing placidly from bright lithographs and promising them magic. Harry was a living embodiment of those previous embarrassments, the coarse and ugly painting of Dorian Gray that exhibited its frowns and wrinkles in his nasty State Street storefront. That's where the Thurston Brothers' original Maid of Mystery exhibited peeks at naked ladies; a coin in the slot raised each shutter with a buzz and a clatter of machinery.

Howard was the master of magical fantasy, but Harry was collecting pocket change with cheap vice—and it amounted to a lot of money.

SEVENTEEN

"SAWING A WOMAN IN HALF"

oudini was the president and Thurston was a vice president of the Society of American Magicians, an organization founded in 1902. The SAM accommodated both amateur and professional magicians, and became very good at creating controversies and encouraging political squabbles. For example, the SAM was powerless when one magician stole material from another, but continually indulged in laborious arguments about "exposure," the bane of every amateur magician. If a magician like Thurston or Houdini should dare to explain some simple "do-it-yourself" tricks with string or coins in a program or a newspaper, encouraging children's interest in magic, the SAM was there to deliver retribution. Presumably most of the members of the SAM forgot that they'd learned magic themselves.

On June 3, 1921, Howard Thurston attended the annual banquet of the Society of American Magicians at the McAlpin Hotel in New York City. These annual shows—by magicians, for magicians—were long and indulgent, unconstrained by a need to be entertaining. Thurston wasn't looking forward to it, and Leotha decided not to attend, having already endured some of these endless industry banquets.

Houdini was the master of ceremonies, and he was in rare form, bouncing from his chair to help move the tables on and off stage, standing and sharing anecdotes, reading a congratulatory telegram from Kellar, or offering glowing introductions for each guest. Halfway through the show, Houdini's attorney stood up, told several stories unrelated to magic, and presented Houdini with an engraved loving cup for no apparent reason. Houdini blushed, insisting that he didn't deserve it, and offered a short speech of acceptance.

Houdini also called on Thurston for a few words, and Thurston spoke extemporaneously about his early adventures and the amount of work that went into producing a large show. He pointed out that there were probably fifty thousand magicians in America, and ended by noting that his last four seasons had netted an even $1 million, a figure that must have been intended to differentiate him from the other magicians that shared the banquet room.

Not every speech was so eloquent. Houdini introduced Madame Herrmann, who stood and said, "You will have to excuse me. My magic is all in silence," before she sat down again. Horace Goldin, the illusionist, stood and also delivered just two sentences. "There are fifty thousand magicians in America. I am one of them."

John Mulholland presented magic with thimbles. Blackstone performed some rope tricks. Dornfield performed some comedy magic. The Floyds demonstrated mental telepathy. And then, in an unscheduled addition to the program, Horace Goldin introduced his latest illusion.

The curtain opened on a heavy wooden platform that supported two chests, side by side. A hotel busboy, who had been recruited for the trick, scooted inside one of the chests, so that his head and hands emerged from one end, and his feet emerged from the other end. Sliding stocks locked his extremities in place.

Goldin picked up a large crosscut saw and dramatically sawed between the chests. He slid two wooden panels down between the boxes, and then pulled them apart about two feet, showing a clear space through the middle of the man. Goldin reversed the process, sliding the chests together and restoring the boy to one piece.

Thurston leaned across the starched white tablecloth, suddenly glad that he was there. He glanced from side to side, looking for the reaction from his fellow magicians. They weren't impressed. To most of them, it was obvious how it was being performed. In fact, Goldin's new illusion meant so little to the assembled magicians that Clinton Burgess, the SAM member who wrote up the event for the magazine *The Sphinx*, forgot to mention it in his official report. The editor included a hurried account as a postscript.

IT TOOK ALL of Thurston's smooth salesmanship to negotiate with Goldin. The previous season, Thurston had started performing the Cannon Illusion: an assistant was loaded into an oversized cannon and the cannon was aimed at his trunk hanging over the audience's head. The cannon exploded and was then turned toward the audience so that they could see down the barrel. The lady was gone. When the nested trunks were lowered and unlocked, she was found inside.

Gus Fasola had first suggested the cannon to Thurston, but Goldin had managed to obtain a patent for it, and this started another feud, aimed at Thurston. Fortunately, the magicians had all settled their argument by the time of the SAM banquet. Thurston told Goldin, "I have to congratulate you on an excellent idea. A wonderful idea," and Goldin had to listen, because few magicians that night had anything to say. Goldin was fat and jowly, an unlikely looking magician, but he made up for his appearance by rattling through his tricks at breakneck speed. His precise movements energized the performance. For example, Goldin would toss a prop over his shoulder without looking to see if the assistant had stepped in to catch it. Thurston had known him for years and knew that, like most performers, Goldin had a roaring ego that could easily be stoked. "But, Horace," Thurston continued, pulling him to one side, "listen to me, as a friend. The apparatus is awful. It isn't sophisticated. It's not up to your standards. I know how to fix it. I've invested thousands of dollars into my shop, with the finest builders in magic. If we could just make an arrangement to rebuild the prop for you . . ." Again Goldin had to listen because he knew that the trick needed help.

Goldin was also listening to a ticking clock. Months before, he'd heard about P. T. Selbit's latest sensation in the London music halls, a new illusion called Sawing Through a Woman. Without knowing the details of Selbit's trick,

Goldin rushed his own version into production. The Keith vaudeville circuit was anxious to book Goldin with the trick, as their new competition, the Shubert circuit, had just signed Selbit to come over to America with his new illusion. Goldin had to get it right, and he had to do it quickly.

THURSTON DIDN'T ACTUALLY KNOW how to fix it—that was just part of his sales pitch. But he did know someone who could fix it: Harry Jansen.

Harry August Jansen was born in Copenhagen in 1883, and his family came to St. Paul, Minnesota, when he was six. As a boy, he became interested in magic, and Thurston's book of card tricks was an early inspiration. In 1902, when Jansen was living in Chicago, he had a chance to meet Thurston when he came through town with his vaudeville act. They became friends—even more so when Thurston returned to Chicago seven years later. At that time, Jansen was a partner in Halton and Jansen, a company that built illusions for professional magicians.

The quality of Halton and Jansen's work was renowned, and they later partnered with Servais Le Roy, which allowed them to build his famous effects. But the company dissolved by 1911, and Jansen took his show on the road.

He might have been successful in vaudeville if it weren't for an oversized, costly show (featuring the large illusions that had been built by Halton and Jansen) and the fact that he was now supporting a wife and five children. He sent his family home with whatever money he could spare and found himself living on pennies, scrounging for work.

In 1921 he was on the East Coast when he ran into Horace Goldin, who relayed an urgent message from Thurston. Thurston was now back in Whitestone and wanted desperately to meet with him. Jansen contacted Thurston and arranged to meet him at his home for dinner the following night. When Jansen arrived, he had exactly two cents in his pocket.

Thurston assumed that Jansen was a successful vaudeville act, but calculated that the young magician would have a long, slow summer season ahead. He suggested that Jansen supervise his shop at Whitestone and offered him an advance on the salary, $200 in cash. Jansen was flabbergasted at how his luck had suddenly changed, and he couldn't resist telling Thurston that he was two pennies away from being broke. "That's nothing, Harry," Thurston told him. "I've been that way many times." Thurston's nonchalance convinced Jansen that he was telling him the truth.

Actually, Thurston's workshop was a disaster. The workers had become exhausted second-guessing their moody boss, who communicated very little of what he wanted, and then wasted a great deal of time by having the carpenters rebuild props. When Jansen arrived, he fired the deadwood, bought tools and hardware wholesale, and systematized each job, saving Thurston thousands of dollars each month.

His first real test was the new Sawing illusion. One day, as Jansen was just finishing a small project at the shop, Thurston asked him to change out of his work clothes and join him in New York City, where Goldin was performing a preview act for vaudeville bookers—the same clumsy trick that he had shown at the SAM banquet.

During the show, Jansen watched the stage and Thurston watched Jansen, anxious for his reaction. Harry Jansen wasn't impressed. He couldn't decide if the illusion was supposed to be a burlesque of a magic act—a sort of comedy— or if it was really being played for thrills and chills. Thurston asked him, "How's it done?" Jansen couldn't believe the question. "There isn't a person in that audience who doesn't know how it's done."

And then Jansen told him. The platform beneath the boxes was suspiciously thick. It was obvious that a second person could be concealed inside the platform. That person had to be supplying the feet during the routine. That meant that the other boy, with his head sticking out one end of the box, simply curled up, bringing his knees up to his chin. And the saw passed between the two boxes.

Thurston's naïve optimism was the motivating force behind the Sawing. His faith in the idea inspired Jansen, who was determined to impress his new boss. The next day in the shop, he began building an improved version. Instead of the thick platform, Jansen reduced it to a three-inch-thick table. His method was nothing short of incredible, mixing both mechanical and optical illusions. Jansen shifted the position of the second assistant during the course of the routine and changed the proportions and prop apparatus to make it more deceptive. Thurston and Goldin were delighted with the results. In exchange for his work, Thurston was rewarded with the rights to present it in his own show. Jansen earned the right to be one of the seven franchised performers, working with Goldin, who fanned out across America, presenting the illusion in vaudeville theaters.

GOLDIN HAD MADE a huge mistake, of course. He never would have drawn an audience if he continued to saw a boy in half. He needed a pretty ingenue beneath the rasping, roaring lumber saw: "Sawing a Woman in Half." The new illusion summoned images of melodramatic thrillers, cinematic serials, and mythological punishments. Selbit and Goldin had also unwittingly tapped into society's most controversial issues. Just as modern women—the suffragettes— were demanding equal rights, staging violent strikes in England, and protesting in the United States, vaudeville theaters were offering tongue-in-cheek vengeance. Selbit had created the modern fashion for torture illusions, the damsel in distress during the magic show.

Selbit arrived in the United States in late 1921, which is when America saw his original version. Selbit's trick was more cerebral and suggestive than Goldin's copy. The lady was completely roped inside of a long, narrow wooden coffin. As spectators on the stage held the ends of the ropes that restrained her, Selbit divided the box with a large saw, and then metal and glass dividers. But by now it didn't matter. He was too late. Thurston, Goldin, and the Goldin army of magicians had already saturated the Keith circuit with the famous Sawing. They promoted it with wild publicity stunts. Ambulances were adorned with signs, explaining that they were going to Keith's "in case the saw slips." Nurses stood by in the lobby, watching for spectators who were faint of heart. Stagehands emerged from the theater, pouring buckets of murky, bloody-red liquid into the gutters, as the lines of spectators at the box office watched in horror. Goldin advertised for local women who volunteered to be sawn in half.

Selbit and Goldin battled it out in the theaters for months, before Selbit returned to England. Goldin had patented the illusion, but many magicians built their own versions of the trick. Goldin spent thousands of dollars with attorneys, chasing the imitators through the courts. It was a rich irony for Goldin, since he had pinched the original idea from Selbit.

After the Sawing wars had finished, the clear winner was Howard Thurston, who found a topical new feature for his show and turned it into a popular standard for his audiences. His program advertised: "Sawing a Woman in Half, by Public Request." In vaudeville, the illusion was just a popular tune, and it played itself out in two or three years. In Thurston's show, it became a timeless ballad, and he performed it for the rest of his career.

The new illusion also solved the problem he'd been having with his Levitation. He started performing the Sawing illusion with just a few spectators on stage and gradually added a crowd from the audience to watch the illusion from up close. Now the scrum of people, even "crummy looking people," seemed to fit right in with the manic operation. Here Thurston didn't miss an opportunity, using each of the volunteers as his comic foils.

A man was selected to step in and hold the lady's hands. "You have hold of her hands, don't you?" The man shrugged. "You know, there are some who have had more experience than others." Another man was told to hold her feet. As Thurston was handed the large saw and a mallet, the assistants on stage started their work.

George White whispered to a small boy from the audience, "When the Governor hits that saw, you run like hell back to your seat. Understand? When he hits it." Thurston gave the saw a wallop, making it ring loudly, and the boy bounded from the stage and up the aisle. The audience guffawed. Thurston looked out at the boy, as if puzzled.

Meanwhile, the assistants had been giving similar, sotto voce instructions to the spectators on stage. Thurston lifted the saw above the box. "Gentlemen," he cautioned his assistants, "the object of this is to prevent the body from straining the saw. I asked you to hold firmly. Should there be an accident, all of you are equally guilty." Thurston began to saw through the box, and the girl let out a loud scream. On cue, a handful of the spectators dashed from their spots on stage and returned to their seats. "No, no," Thurston implored, following after his cowardly assistants and standing at the edge of the stage. "Don't go!"

It was vintage Thurston, the elegant host confused by his guests, the ringmaster scratching his head over the clowns. If the situation was funny, Thurston's perfectly proper demeanor made it only funnier.

IN THE EARLY MONTHS OF 1922, Harry Kellar suffered a long illness at his home in Los Angeles. On the night of March 10, Thurston was visiting a club of St. Louis magicians. For some reason, he felt the need to ask for a moment of silent meditation, remembering Kellar. The next morning, Thurston received the news from the West Coast. Kellar had died the previous evening.

"As we sat there in complete stillness," Thurston later told a reporter, "each thinking of the splendid man and his achievements, it seemed almost as if the spirit of Kellar had projected itself among us. We had no idea at the time that he was dying. Harry Kellar was a man of charming personality and I can say without fear of contradiction that he was one of the most generally beloved men on the American stage. He was the greatest magician of all time."

Of all the men who had saved Howard Thurston from his fate—including Round, Moody, and Pastor—it was Harry Kellar who had done what the others could not have done, eliminating his past by instantly bestowing legitimacy. Their agreement started as a simple business transaction, but somehow Kellar transformed it—his greatest feat in magic—into a royal legacy.

That final season together seemed to grant Kellar—an argumentative, poorly educated, and onetime Pennsylvania street waif—the exalted status as the approving monarch. It seemed to christen Thurston, a confidence man and sideshow talker, with the title of crown prince. Behind the scenes, it was a ragtag partnership, but in the bright lights of the stage, it had transformed both men.

With Kellar's death, Thurston assumed a new role. It was no longer just about retirement or succession. Thurston had learned a valuable lesson from the Sawing in Half illusion. Goldin had cleverly franchised other performers like Jansen to capitalize on his success. Now Howard could increase his profits by producing a show for another magician, supervising the tour, selling the act to vaudeville, or booking the new show in cities and countries he had been too busy to visit. It wouldn't be a competition, and the Thurston endorsement would mean that a good, talented performer would be quickly established. He didn't need to retire. He needed to expand his business.

Within months of Kellar's death, Thurston had worked out a deal with Harry Jansen. Jansen was working as foreman of the workshop and had joined Thurston on the road to help rehearse the new tour. But both men knew that these efforts were a waste of Jansen's skills. Thurston urged him to put together his own show, which would be marketed as the "Thurston #2 Unit." Jansen proposed a simple arrangement: Thurston would invest $50,000 toward building the show, payable in weekly fees, and would then be a half-owner in the property, entitled to his share of the profits.

Thurston rechristened the new performer Dante. He'd liked the stage name since he first heard of the American, Oscar Eliason, who had found such success as Dante in Australia. Later, when Thurston was married to Beatrice, a friend reminded him how the pairing of names was appropriate—Beatrice and Dante. As he considered Harry Jansen's new show, Thurston realized the name had the perfect devilish sound, while also seeming literary and European. Since Jansen had been born in Copenhagen, Thurston stretched the truth slightly and billed Dante as "Europe's Famous Magician."

Thurston's eye to the legacy was clear. "Thurston and Kellar Present Dante," Thurston's new advertising boasted. For more than a decade, he had eliminated Kellar's name from his program, but now he announced Dante by including Kellar's portrait next to his own, implying the step-by-step succession of one master magician to another. "For Forty Years, the World's Greatest Magicians."

ONE SUMMER EVENING IN 1922, Thurston was working on some publicity materials at Beechhurst with writer Walter B. Gibson. The magician looked at his watch and told Gibson that he needed to hurry to the SAM meeting. The two men piled into the car and Thurston's driver took them into Manhattan.

As they crossed the bridge into the city, Thurston explained why he was obliged to attend the Society of American Magicians. He'd been asked to contribute to an article in the *New York Sunday Evening Telegram* about the deceptions used by fake mediums. This constituted exposure, since it explained how tricks were accomplished. The SAM was strict about published exposures, and Thurston was obliged to "ask permission" before contributing material to the article.

"Of course," he told Gibson, "they'll approve it, because it's about spiritualism, not magic." And the whole thing was a bit of a farce, Thurston continued, since the article had already been written and set up on the press. The Sunday supplements for the big newspapers were often published days before they appeared. "It's a technicality, Walter. I have to formally let them approve it, since I'm one of the officers of the club. I can't tell them I've already done it."

As Thurston and Gibson entered the meeting room, Houdini was at the front table, gaveling the group to order. "Any old business?" he inquired. The treasurer's report was read and approved. "New business?" Houdini snapped. Thurston waited for a few others to state their business. After a respectful pause, not seeming too anxious, he stood. "I've been asked by the *Telegram* to contribute some tricks used by spirit mediums." He noticed Houdini look up at him. For the last decade, Houdini had made the exposure of mediums a personal crusade, which had garnered him headlines across the country. "It will run later this month," Thurston continued, neatly fudging the imminent article. "As it doesn't involve any real magic, I thought that it would be wise for me to do it, and it wouldn't actually constitute exposure." The council was about to vote on approving Thurston's article, but Houdini interrupted. "Who was it for?" he impatiently called across the crowd. "It's for the *Sunday Telegram*, Harry," Thurston responded.

"Oh, yes, the *Telegram*. They asked me to do that article. I know all about it."

The council approved Thurston's request and moved on. But the subject had seemed to animate Houdini, who tried to catch Thurston's eye and nod his approval. Walter Gibson noticed Thurston shake his head slowly; he knew that he'd transgressed into Houdini's area of expertise, and his old friend wouldn't let the subject die.

With the meeting closed, Houdini stepped from the platform and pushed his way through the crowd, making a beeline for Thurston. "I know them. I know about that article," he announced before even reaching him.

"That's good, Harry. The writer seemed like a good fellow."

"They wanted me to do it. Did they tell you that?"

"They didn't mention it, Harry. In any case, they're not asking for much, and I should be able to handle it."

"I could still do it," Houdini announced. "If I told them I wanted to do it, they would use me."

Thurston stared at him for a long beat as a group of magicians circled, drawn in by Houdini's aggressive conversation.

Thurston drew out his words slowly, as if trying to placate his comrade. "Well, I'm not sure that's correct, Harry."

"Don't you believe me?" Houdini responded, raising his voice. "Of course they want me to do it. I can do that article. I'll bet you anything that they want to use me."

Thurston glanced at Gibson and shrugged. Just minutes earlier, the two men had been discussing the secret behind Thurston's request: the article had already been written, and may have already been printed. Houdini noticed the dismissive shrug.

"What do you mean by that? Howard, I'm telling you the truth. They wanted me, and I'd bet you a hundred dollars . . ."

Unlike Houdini, who reddened and became more excitable as he angered, Thurston gave no such clues. His expression froze and his eyelids closed slightly, as if fixing a soft, indefinite stare on his fellow magician. Thurston used to start the week with a stack of neat fifty-dollar bills, right from the bank, that he carried in a flat leather billfold inside his suit. As Houdini continued, Thurston slowly, gracefully reached into his suit coat, withdrew the wallet, snapped it open, licked the tip of his thumb, and counted two pristine fifty-dollar bills onto the table in front of him. He closed the wallet and slid it back into his pocket. Then he serenely sat back in his chair.

The magicians watched expectantly as if counting down an explosion. Three, two, one, and Houdini erupted. He stomped in a tight circle, and his words tumbled out as he fumed about the article, about Thurston doubting his abilities, and about his own experience in exposing spiritualism. "I'll take that bet!" he said. "You think that I won't! But I'll take that bet!" He reached into his pocket and emerged with a handful of crumpled bills. He hurriedly smoothed them out and threw them down onto the table, managing a defiant gesture. There were some fives and ones. After all his effort, Houdini had managed to produce barely twenty dollars.

Counting the bills impatiently, Houdini erupted again. He ringed the room in a larger circle, soliciting money from the other magicians. "What've you got? What've you got? Gimme what you've got!" He returned to the table several times with crumpled bills. Now it was just over thirty dollars. Thirty-five. Thirty-nine. Someone tossed in a handful of change. Thirty-nine dollars and seventy-three cents.

"That was the difference between those two men, right there," Walter Gibson later recalled the incident. "Right on that table. Two crisp fifty-dollar bills, and Thurston sitting behind them, expressionless, immaculate. On the other side of the table, a bundle of crumpled bills as Houdini turned his pockets inside-out, ran around the room, and worked himself into a frenzy." The famous escape artist never did manage to assemble a hundred dollars. Friends of Houdini's calmed him down and convinced him to put away his money. Houdini slinked back to the table, laughing nervously and pushing the wadded bills back into his pockets. Thurston picked up his fifties and left with Walter Gibson. Gibson noticed that, once Houdini exploded, Thurston had barely changed his expression and never uttered a word.

THE DIFFERENCE might have been Kellar. When Harry Kellar had been alive, both magicians shared a bond, dealing with him as two sons would deal with a difficult father. Kellar played favorites, swapped gossip, and withheld judgment, but both Houdini and Thurston came to love the old wizard on his own terms. When he was gone, all that they faced were the brotherly squabbles over the inheritance.

The finished *Telegram* article, "World's Greatest Magician Reveals the Wiles of Fake Mediums," from July 16, 1922, demonstrated a more curious contrast between Thurston and Houdini. The subtitle explained, "Most Spiritualist Phenomena Proved Fakes, says Magician, Who Believes in Spirits." It was the words "Most" and "Believes" that rankled Houdini. Thurston was insisting on trying to thread a needle—exposing mediums while still accepting the possibility of the phenomena.

Months later, Thurston was quoted in a United Press article, proposing that "spirits of the dead inhabit planets." The reporter claimed that Thurston was an investigator of "so-called spirit deceptions, and heretofore a skeptic," but that his own experiments with a radio set installed at his home generated a series of mysterious sounds and voices that convinced him that these voices were originating from the planets.

The story was reproduced in *The Sphinx*, and the journal seemed to understand that it was intended as an outrageous bit of publicity. *The Sphinx* noted wryly that "Houdini will have to look to his laurels as the most prominent and successful advertiser, for Thurston is beginning to get there rapidly."

In his book *Our American Adventure*, Sir Arthur Conan Doyle reflected on his difficult relationship with Houdini. Their friendship was later dissolved over the subject of spiritualism. Doyle used the example of Thurston to make his point.

> Talking of the views of conjurers, which are generally not only unintelligent, but quite spiteful about phenomena, as though they regarded them as some form of illicit competition, it interested me to find that Mr. Howard Thurston, who is, next to Houdini, the chief magician in America, has showed great patience and acumen in investigating mediums. He has naturally found fraud, but has also admitted that he has several times encountered real psychic gifts, which are in a different category to tricks. By this admission he has placed himself in an enlightened band who number several of the greatest magicians of the past.

But Thurston's beliefs required too much finesse for the usual newspaper article. After Houdini complained about his beliefs, Thurston wrote a letter to his colleague to clarify his point.

I am very particular to have you know how I stand in this matter. Instead of saying, "the man who believes and the man who does not believe," I claim to have encountered some psychic effects, which I have not been able to explain or understand. . . . I lean to the belief that these effects are produced by an intelligent force, which can manifest itself mentally and physically to some people under certain circumstances. The above is exactly what I believe in the matter of spiritualism. . . . I do believe in spiritualism.

But when Houdini's book on the subject, *A Magician Among the Spirits*, appeared in 1924, the name Thurston was not included in the text. Houdini included a long chapter on Palladino, and another analyzing various magicians' experiments and opinions on the subject—it took a certain amount of dancing around these subjects to omit Thurston. Perhaps it was intended as a favor to Thurston, writing him out of the story so he didn't seem ridiculed. For example, Conan Doyle was not granted this favor, and Houdini made the author look foolish. Or it was much simpler. Houdini simply considered Thurston's opinions on the subject too trivial to include.

EIGHTEEN

"FIRE AND WATER"

hen Thurston found a good foot soldier, he invariably assigned him in some of his messiest jobs. Unfortunately, Thurston's business practices were often careless or badly planned. As a well-respected gentleman of the theater, Thurston's first impulse was to settle these difficulties quietly and professionally. But as a former denizen of carnivals and con games, he also knew another way. Invariably Thurston looked for an associate to step in and strong-arm the situation. At the end of 1922, loyal Harry Jansen took a break from preparing his new show as Dante. He was given a letter granting him power of attorney and pointed toward Zanesville, Ohio.

A young, touring magician named Grover George had been performing a show that contained versions of several Thurston illusions, including the Lion Illusion. George suspected that theater managers had been pressured to cancel his engagements, and Thurston sent messages to George, threatening and cajoling him to change his program. The letters hadn't intimidated George. Instead, the scattershot entreaties had merely twisted the situation into knots. Thurston continued to receive reports about George's poor show.

Jansen arrived, lectured young Grover George about originality, and warned about Thurston's influence in the profession. He insisted that George remove the similar tricks and fire the employees who had worked with Thurston in previous seasons, like George's musical director, Edward Trout. Jansen and Thurston were convinced that these employees had been imparting secrets and routines from Thurston's show.

George hesitated making the promise, and Jansen followed him to the next city, Wilmington, Ohio. Reluctantly, George signed a contract, agreeing to take certain illusions out of his show. In exchange, he could keep the Lion Illusion in his show, with Thurston's permission.

Jansen was confident that he'd accomplished Thurston's goal, but as soon as he had left town George changed his mind, insisting that he'd only signed the contract "based on false representations from Jansen . . . continued threats, coercions and intimidations." Thurston and Jansen sought an injunction against the show, but George's father was a local attorney and the Ohio magician made a strong case in front of the court. He pointed out the various books, catalogs, and performers that featured tricks like the Levitation, Floating Ball, Card Manipulations, Vanishing Lady, and Egg Tricks. These were all "common, stock tricks," and George's versions were markedly different from Thurston's. Jansen had also objected to George's practice of having spectators come onto the stage to assist with the tricks; he thought elements of the young magician's patter sounded like Thurston's. In court, George ridiculed these suggestions.

Jansen found himself blindsided by Thurston's own correspondence from many months earlier, now read into the court record. As part of his awkward carrot-and-stick technique, Thurston wrote to George that he had been "contemplating or had a desire to assist in some way and possibly enter into some sort of combination" with the young magician. He'd tried the same trick with Blackstone, teasing that he'd be looking for a successor, with the same disastrous results. The judge seemed confused about Thurston's sincerity and quickly dismissed the injunction.

"Am indeed sorry and feel very bad at the results of things," Jansen wrote back to Thurston, licking his wounds. "One never knows what a judge will do."

KELLAR'S DEATH seemed to trigger dozens of little skirmishes between Thurston and his fellow magicians. He fretted over many of these; it seemed as if the dam had just broken and his reputation were under assault. Blackstone the magician had recently been advertising his show with a new poster portrait; two red imps now sat on Blackstone's shoulder, with one of them whispering in his ear. In 1923 Thurston sent a curt note to the younger magician, warning him to stop using the imps and reminding him to remove all of Thurston's tricks from his own show, like the Dancing Handkerchief and the Girl and the Rabbit.

Part of Thurston's ire must have been genuine—his increasing concern with his legacy. Although the little red imps were never protected as a trademark, Thurston considered them an inheritance from Kellar and an important motif for his show; he had incorporated them into all of his advertising and even had woven them into bedtime stories for his daughter, Jane. But now Thurston was also looking for an excuse to pick a fight. Blackstone had just premiered a Vanishing Horse in his show. It was a sensational idea that generated wonderful publicity. Thurston quickly put Dante to work creating a Vanishing Horse for the Thurston show, and then wrote to Blackstone. "If you think it is fair to use my tricks without my consent, it is only fair for Dante and myself to treat you the same. . . . I will decide accordingly whether I will do the Vanishing Horse." His past experience demonstrated that the young magician would be defiant. Thurston was going to make the most of it.

Kellar's death also inspired a discussion of who might become the next dean of the Society of American Magicians. Dr. Wilson, writing in *The Sphinx*, mentioned that Houdini and Thurston had both been discussed for the honor, but he felt that neither was qualified, as the title deserved a person "of ripe experience" and "retirement." Early in 1923, Henry Ridgely Evans, a respected writer and historian of magic, contributed an article to *Billboard* and *The Sphinx*, asking "Is Magic Decadent?" and excoriating Thurston for including secrets of simple magic tricks in boxes of candy that were sold during his performances. Evans quoted Thurston, in a private conversation, saying that his intention was to "popularize" magic by educating the public about its secrets. As always, it was the subject of exposure that seemed to obsess amateur magicians, causing them to predict the downfall of the art. Evans's criticism was particularly stinging, as he had been a good friend and admirer of Thurston's, part of a small group of Baltimore magicians, including Thomas C. Worthington and Fulton Oursler, who had socialized with Howard, Leotha, and Jane.

Many professionals, like Thurston and Houdini, found it advantageous to contribute little "do-it-yourself" pocket tricks to newspapers and advertising promotions. As a schoolboy, Thurston had been inspired by learning the secret of the Ink to Water Trick. David Devant, Thurston's friend in London who retired in 1920, wrote a series of beginner's books, and always considered that spectators with a real knowledge of magic formed the very best audience for a magician—patronizing shows and appreciating the finer points of presentation and style. The magicians' clubs had devised various rules to deal with the subject. It was acceptable to sell books of secrets, but unacceptable to give secrets away in an article or advertising promotion. Certain simple tricks could be explained, but others that might hint at professional secrets were strictly off-limits. Still, magicians realized that the simplest trick, in the hands of a good performer, was capable of becoming a masterpiece. The subject was hotly debated among the Society of American Magicians, and Evans's sudden pronouncement was a cruel rebuke of his friend.

In his conversation with Evans, Thurston had probably been quoting Paul Carus, a theologian and publisher. In one of Thurston's press releases, Carus's remarks were reproduced in full, and they constitute a wholesale endorsement of the importance of magic:

> We should all know something of the general methods of magic, and some time in our lives witness the extraordinary feats with which a prestidigitator can dazzle our eyes and misguide our judgment. The boy who has studied magic will not be so apt in later years to take up with every new fad of mysticism and will not be so easily duped.

READING ALL OF EVANS'S ARTICLE, it seems inspired by the subject of Kellar's passing, nostalgically recalling the "palmy days of magic," as the historian put it, when "only two magicians held the field—Herrmann and Kellar."

Ah, for the good old days, when magic was a genuine mystery, and one had to learn it from a professor of sleight-of-hand; when books and boxes of magic did not exist, and stage secrets were as closely guarded as the formula of certain patent medicines.

Even worse, Henry Ridgely Evans's "Is Magic Decadent?" seemed to let loose a floodgate of criticism. A month later, a columnist and amateur magician, Gene Gordon, arrogantly wrote in *The Sphinx*:

Thurston sure has queer ideas when it comes to the popularization of magic— queer, at least, for one who owes so much to it. Harry Kellar's title of "World's Greatest Magician" may now be held by Howard Thurston, but it is a certainty that [Kellar's] title, "Dean of Magicians," will never grace the name of Thurston. The first requisite to that honor is respect from all fellow magicians, and who is there that can say Thurston has that?

In the same issue, editor Dr. A. M. Wilson criticized Thurston for offering coupons to children, which could be collected and redeemed to purchase tricks, ranging in price from fifteen cents to a dollar. Evans quoted one of Thurston's flyers, "The most wonderful tricks are all done with special apparatus." Wilson snapped, "If this is promoting magic, I have missed my calling as an exponent of magic." Several pages later, Evans continued with another sarcastic remark. "If such an institution as a College of Magic ever be established . . . among the professional chairs will be the gentle art of exposés in public magazines, to be filled by Prof. Thurston."

Dante wrote a nasty reply to Gene Gordon's article. Thurston himself lodged a protest with A. M. Wilson, who quickly retracted his comments. It turned out that Thurston was not "giving" coupons to children, but selling them in boxes of candy, Wilson explained. Magic organizations defined exposure with just this sort of odd hairsplitting: if a secret was sold with candy, it was not exposure; it the candy was given away, it constituted a breech of the magician's art.

Thurston contributed a long, sarcastic response to Evans in the April issue of *The Sphinx*:

I venture to reply to my old friend, Dr. Henry R. Evans. I am proud of his friendship because he is the greatest historian of magic of all times. Did I say historian? Yes, and it is well said, for sad to relate our dear Doctor thinks in the past and writes best of the past. He cites the "palmy days of magic" when only two performers were known and there were no books on magic. Now we have a source of prominent professionals, thousands of books, thousands of clever amateurs and more than 50,000 people who buy magic literature. How can the Doctor explain the difference? Magic is in greater fervor today than ever, more magicians are working and more people pay to see a magic show now than ever in the past. It has achieved a great distinction and higher perfection.

Thurston went on to clarify his point: he did not tell Evans that he advocated teaching magic to the public, but suggested setting up a permanent school of magic and teaching the public some elementary principles to demonstrate the "vulnerability of the senses" so that the public had a better ability when it came to "accepting new theories and doctrines . . . to guard them in their business relations."

Privately Thurston wrote to John Mulholland, another writer and historian of magic, complaining about the insult. "If I am not entitled to the title of dean of magicians, I would like to know who is." The Society of American Magicians finally selected Fredrick Eugene Powell, a late-nineteenth-century magician for the honor of dean. Powell was one of the last—and least effective—of the old guard, but his selection was a sentimental favorite, avoiding all of the controversy within the club.

THURSTON WAS RIGHT to imply that his show was profitable and successful with the public. More than any other magician, he had established magic as a popular attraction and inspired a generation of magic-mad young boys. Thurston now billed his production as "The Wonder Show of the Universe," and his marketing relied upon the same theaters and the same cities year after year. This meant that his show had to always be fresh, promising new marvels.

In 1919 he added the Water Fountains to his show, providing a new finale.

Thurston purchased the act from an old vaudeville couple named the DeBars, but the idea was actually based on a Japanese spectacle, first introduced in America by the Ten Ichi Troupe in the early twentieth century. Thurston would coax a small spray of water from a bowl on a table; the fountain could apparently be lifted on the end of a wand, transferred to different spots on the stage, or even made to multiply, spouting in arrays from the costumes or the heads of his assistants. Gradually the sprays of water increased until the stage twinkled with dozens of mysterious fountains. The act was accomplished with a large container of water, suspended backstage, which was attached, with rubber tubing, to various spots onstage, costumes, or props. The Water Fountains was first costumed as a Chinese act; in the 1920s Thurston re-dressed it with white polka-dot costumes to suggest circus props. Dante added a number of additional tricks, and Thurston included his old Coconut Illusion. The finale was an elaborate fountain, center stage, with a lady reclining horizontally, on the tops of the water jets. She revolved above the fountains as the curtain fell on this pretty picture.

The Vanishing Horse was finally ready for the 1925 season. Thurston wanted an illusion that was magnificent and mysterious; he insisted on lifting the horse in the air, over the stage, before it disappeared. When this was attempted the first time at Thurston's Beechhurst factory, the horse bucked and kicked, tumbling from the platform and then galloping, enraged, around the workshop as Thurston and Dante ran. Dante finally decided on a suspended platform, like a swing. The following season, 1926, Thurston's workmen improved this by using a small, enclosed pen that surrounded the horse's legs.

The final trick provided a spectacular bit of magic. Beauty, a white Arabian steed, was ridden onstage by Arline Palmer, a stunt rider and animal trainer who had worked with Buffalo Bill's Wild West. She took Beauty through a series of tricks, bowing to the audience and marching around the stage. Thurston entered and supervised as the horse was locked into the small pen. This was then lifted, with Arline on the back of the horse, so that the horse and rider dangled about ten feet over the stage.

A large white net was dropped in front of the pen, and then, for several seconds, a white banner was lowered in front of the net. "We use this netting as sometimes the horse becomes frightened and makes a wild jump," Thurston explained to the audience. "Behold the impossible. Sixteen hundred pounds of rider, horse and stall. Are you ready?" Thurston asked. He fired a gun into the air. The empty pen fell away, landing on the stage with a crash, and the banner dropped. The audience gazed at the empty stage. Within seconds, the horse was gone.

Fasola suggested several new illusions to Thurston, including a new version of the old carnival sword box—in which the lady entered a small wooden chest that was pierced by swords. And Thurston's success with the Sawing Illusion inspired a new collaboration with P. T. Selbit, who had originated the Sawing Illusion in England. Selbit proposed a series of new torture illusions, Stretching a Lady, The Human Pincushion, Crushing a Lady, Through the Eye of a Needle, apparently pulling an assistant through a small hole in a steel plate, or, for a change of pace, Televising a Lady, in which the assistant seemed to dematerialize in a chair, only to rematerialize in a second chair several feet away.

His dealings with Selbit, like his earlier contracts with Devant, were scrupulously honest. But occasionally, Thurston's yearly innovations managed to trample on the reputations or innovations of his fellow performers. In 1925 he included an illusion titled Fire and Water, in which a lady seemed to be consumed in flames on one side of the stage, only to be reproduced submerged in a tank of water on the other side of the stage. Fire and Water used a number of mechanical principles that had been created by Valadon, Fasola, and other magicians. But this particular combination of tricks had been created by the Great Leon (Leon Levy), and it became his feature in vaudeville. Leon tended to avoid the controversy, but his wife, Edythe, sent a blistering letter to Thurston, warning him to take it out of his show. "I feel sure you did not read it before it was mailed," Thurston wrote back to Leon. "Had you read it, you would have advised her not to send it." He collected a number of excuses, how the trick was based on a number of previous ideas, and shrugged off the complaint.

At the end of 1925, Thurston was playing a New York theater. On one night,

Theo Bamberg, his son David, and Harry Houdini were his guests, seated in a box. Thurston hadn't realized that Leon and Edythe Levy had also purchased tickets for the show and were seated in the middle of the auditorium.

As Thurston introduced the Fire and Water Illusion and opened the curtain, Leon stood up in the auditorium and pointed a finger toward the stage. "You're a thief and a liar!" Leon shouted. "You're a pirate. That's my illusion."

The audience naturally assumed that the argument was intended as part of the show and began laughing. But Houdini instantly recognized Leon's wheezy East Side accent and slid his chair to the shadowed corner of the booth.

Thurston was trapped. He stopped the music and gazed across the footlights as Leon continued his rant. "You took that illusion from me. It's my illusion, and you're a pirate." Thurston protested politely. "Mr. Leon, I believe you'll find that the illusion is mine, and in fact, tonight we happen to have a great historian of magic, Mr. Harry Houdini." Thurston gestured toward the box, but noticed Houdini crouching in the shadows, his hand shielding his face. Thurston immediately changed his tactics. "And sitting next to him is Theodore Bamberg, the famous European magician. He is an expert in such matters, and can assure you that the illusion is mine."

Bamberg, of course, was hard of hearing. He had picked up just enough of the quarrel to lean over to his son, David, asking him what was happening. But David couldn't translate fast enough. Leon shouted, Thurston implored, and the spotlight swung onto Theo, who smiled serenely and, not realizing what was being asked, nodded toward Thurston and responded, "Yes!"

There was an awkward pause, and the spotlight wobbled back to Thurston. Leon collapsed into his chair and the show resumed. After all, the audience just wanted to see Thurston's magic. The band resumed the music, and the show proceeded. When David Bamberg finally managed to explain to his father what had happened, Theo was indignant that he'd been dragged into the argument. Even worse, for years after that, Leon wouldn't forgive him for the humiliation.

Fire and Water was indicative of Thurston's dilemma in finding new material. Thurston hadn't calculated the importance of the routine to Leon. In Thurston's show, it was just another trick, four or five minutes of quick magic.

It could have been replaced by dozens of other quick tricks. In Leon's twelve-minute act, Fire and Water had become his trademark, and he depended on it for his career. After one season, Thurston removed the trick from his show.

THE DANTE SHOW, which premiered in 1923, became a steady success in the market. Dante was able to play smaller cities that were too difficult to include in Thurston's route. His program consisted of a mixture of favorites from Thurston's show, Dante's favorite illusions, and experimental new effects. In their letters, the two magicians developed a perfect collaboration; they regularly discussed the best staff, audiences, new ideas, and their competitors. They collaborated together on a number of illusions, which Thurston took steps to patent.

Writing to Thurston, Dante could be sharply honest; he was blunt in a way that few of Thurston's men had ever been. "You must remember," Thurston responded to one of Dante's letters, "there are times when you have a nasty temper, especially when you drink and you have said several things to me that have hurt me very deeply, but you have so many fine qualities that I am always the first to overlook your fit of temper." In 1925, while in Jacksonville, Florida, Dante attempted to place an ad in the local newspaper that compared him, favorably, with competitors like Houdini. An editor refused the ad and sent it on to his friend Houdini, who then sent a blistering note to Thurston.

> When a newspaper like the *Jacksonville Journal* refuses to accept a Dante ad because of derogatory and slurring nature, it is time for me to call your attention to the fact that unless my name is kept out of all advertising, I shall be forced to take measures. I have devoted too many years of my life in making the name Houdini stand for what it does.

Overall, the Dante and Thurston partnership was so successful that, by 1925, the two magicians were already discussing the possibility of a "Thurston Number Three" show, a smaller unit that could feature Thurston's illusions in vaudeville theaters. Thurston considered his friend Dornfield, McDonald

Birch, Jack Gwynne, Herman Hanson, Hathaway, Eugene Laurant, and a hand-ful of other talented vaudeville magicians for the task, and debated the pos-sibilities with Dante. He finally settled on a Pittsburgh magician with the unimpressive name of Raymond Sugden, and Thurston suggested the billing "Tampa, England's Court Magician." Through Harry Thurston, Howard had recently invested in some Tampa, Florida, orange groves, and he considered the name a lucky charm.

Tampa was neither more talented nor more aggressive than Grover George, and it's difficult to understand why Thurston sought to recruit him to the cause. More than likely, he was flattered by Tampa's helpfulness with some of his illusions. For example, Thurston's experiments for the Hindu Rope Trick required a steam generator to provide the requisite puff of smoke; Tampa quickly designed a steam manifold and suggested a company to provide the boiler. Thurston announced Tampa with the similar praise that he'd used for Dante. In 1923 Thurston advertised:

A Word about Dante

It has been impossible for me to fill half of the dates offered for my show. . . . Let me point out that in addition to his great qualifications as an illusionist, all of the important features from my own performance have been added to his program. . . . Over 500 newspaper critics have reviewed Dante and not one adverse criticism. That spells satisfaction. Play Dante.

Then, a few years later:

A Word about Tampa

Owing to the fact that for years it was impossible for me to accept all of the engagements requested for my show, I decided to select a magician to present a number two Thurston show. After years of careful investigations of hundreds of magicians from all over the world, in 1925 I selected Tampa, England's court magician, as the master. . . . Hundreds of newspaper critics all over the country have reviewed Tampa with not one adverse criticism. This certainly spells sat-isfaction and accomplishment.

The announcements must have ruffled Dante's feathers. Even worse, the selection of Sugden galled him. After struggling to establish his own show on the road, he began to fret that Tampa's cut-rate vaudeville show would undermine his own chances for success. Tampa could provide some of Thurston's latest illusions, under the Thurston banner, for a fraction of the price. Dante wrote to Thurston:

> I cannot help but believe that we have both been hard hit through your recent efforts with Tampa. Your statement that he is not in the same class might be accepted by myself, some of the booking agents and a few magicians, but the blasé bookers who juggle a pencil all day long to cut prices have their own angle, and when they have an opportunity to get something that looks the same for less money, they are quick to set anything else aside. . . . If Tampa is to be seen pioneering tricks that I have worried my head about, what chance will I have? [Bookers] can buy him for considerably less, along with the name Thurston!

The Tampa show had seemed like an ideal business plan. But Thurston's men—his fellow magicians and business partners who were so important to expanding his business—were now slowly pulling the business apart.

Thurston informed Tampa that he was to finish his present engagement, and then remove the feature illusions from his show so that he wouldn't interfere with Dante's program—undoing his contract. Tampa was baffled by the messages, but like Grover George before him, he refused to go down without a fight.

Actually, there was already a potential "Thurston Number Four" show, put in place many years before: Gustave Fasola. When Thurston and Fasola became friends, they pledged to exchange illusions. Fasola had been touring small cities in the United States with his own illusion show, enjoying the good business and plotting to return to England. There he would duplicate the Thurston illusions for a grand new production. "I intend coming to England at the end of this year," Fasola wrote to a friend in 1925. "I and Thurston have more illusions than all the other magicians put together. . . . I will study it out with Thurston to arrange a great show for England."

Fasola's enthusiastic plans were now a ticking time bomb. Thurston had forgotten their arrangements. Dante never heard about them.

THURSTON'S MOST DANGEROUS threat materialized in September 1925. Harry Houdini finally left vaudeville and opened his new touring show, "An Entire Evening's Entertainment," according to his program, in which the famed escape artist and "Master Mystifier" assembled "three shows in one."

Houdini's show was an odd combination of his greatest hits and loftiest ambitions. After his failed experiments with a magic show in 1914, Houdini split the evening into distinct sections. The first part of the program consisted of magic. By all accounts, it was the least impressive part of Houdini's performance. He stepped on stage in black tails and promptly pulled away his sleeves, which were attached with snap fasteners. His odd short-sleeved formal wear was supposed to create a unique distinction: other magicians used their sleeves to accomplish their magic. But those sleeves also served as metaphors for Houdini's awkward approach to magic: ripping, tugging, and challenging the most elegant aspects of the art, so that he could stand apart from the crowd.

Many of the magic effects were historical, or as the program explained, "Mysterious effects that startled and pleased your grand and great-grandparents." For example, one of the illusions, Paligenesia, was a comical effect in which a man seemed to be cut up; Houdini had seen it performed in the 1880s when he was a boy. Other effects, like the production and disappearance of lamps, bouquets of flowers, rabbits, and dancers dressed as flappers, came across as slapdash and trivial for the famous escape artist—trying to be something that he wasn't. In the magic section, Houdini also included card manipulations. "Houdini was the first to perform the forward and back palm," the program noted, an odd distinction that seemed pointed at his competition.

> Houdini presents today card manipulations such as his thirty-two-card forward
> and back palm, which gained for him the title of "King of Cards" more than
> thirty years ago. Many of his original passes and sleights have been used by most
> all of the present-day magicians.

The entire evening was arranged around this self-congratulatory tone. For example, one of the act curtains consisted of sewn ribbons and awards that Houdini had received during his career as a vaudeville escape artist. Real illusions didn't call for such boasts, dates, or dares. It was supposed to be magic.

The second part of the program consisted of Houdini's famous escapes, like Metamorphosis, his instantaneous transposition with his wife after he was locked inside a trunk, and the Water Torture Cell, his upside-down escape from a tall tank of water. The third part of the program consisted of a dynamic lecture exposing spiritualism. Houdini gave demonstrations of how fake mediums wrote on slates, rang bells during a séance, and produced gauzy spirits in a darkened room. A section of this demonstration was devoted to Houdini's recent exposure of Margery, the famous Boston medium, who had almost won the *Scientific American* challenge to produce genuine phenomena. Finally, Houdini answered questions from the audience and issued challenges to the local mediums. His staff had often visited the most prominent mediums of the city, which allowed him to personalize his attacks. Here Houdini's brash style suited the performance perfectly. His spiritual exposures were a perverse sort of revival meeting. As he acted out the séance deceptions and ridiculed the foolishness of believers, like his former friend Sir Arthur Conan Doyle, Houdini solicited cheers and laughs.

The show moved to Broadway at the end of the year. A reviewer in *The Sphinx* found the result overlong and self-important: "The word 'I' is overworked throughout. . . . There was too much denunciation to be palatable. The least said about his presentation of magic, the better." But the force of Houdini's personality had a great appeal for audiences. Dr. Wilson of *The Sphinx*, who had publicly picked fights with both Houdini and Thurston, privately told Houdini that his show packed in more magic than Thurston had in his entire evening. It was exactly what Houdini had been waiting to hear.

"We're going to shove Thurston right off the boards," Houdini boasted to a friend.

NINETEEN

"CHUNDRA, WHO IS BURIED ALIVE"

he week of Christmas 1924, Thurston was summoned to the White House for a holiday party for President Coolidge, his wife, and about twenty of his guests. A special stage was erected in the East Room, and the magician brought a handful of assistants and a truck filled with illusions, ducks, and rabbits. For the occasion he'd made special plans for a small trick.

Thurston had just read in the newspaper about the president being presented with a special pocket watch by the Massachusetts legislature. The magician made some inquiries and was able to procure a duplicate of the watch. He spent lavishly on the duplicate, but it was still a bargain, as it was filled with a bundle of worthless gears and wheels inside the pretty gold case.

During the performance, he stepped over to the president and asked to borrow a watch. "A very special watch," he explained. Coolidge nodded and reached into his vest pocket, offering his fancy new watch. Thurston neatly switched it as he placed it atop a piece of metal on his table. He asked Mrs. Coolidge to have a fresh loaf of bread brought from the pantry. She whispered to a butler, who left the room in search of the bread.

Meanwhile, Thurston raised a hammer above the watch. "One," he counted. "Two." A Secret Service man, standing at the side of the stage, couldn't quite believe what he was about to see. He stepped toward Thurston, leaning down to have a close look at the watch, then looked up at the president with a scowl. "I beg your pardon, sir," Thurston admonished, pushing the agent aside, "this is a very delicate experiment!" The group laughed as he continued, "If anything goes wrong, I hold you responsible." On "Three," he brought the hammer down and smashed the watch into a dozen fragments. He glanced at Coolidge, the famous stone-faced president. Coolidge gazed back at the magician, emotionless.

Thurston gathered the pieces, wrapping them in a piece of paper and then making them disappear. By now the bread had appeared. He brought it to Mrs. Coolidge on a tray with a knife, asking her to cut the loaf in half. "Please be careful, Mrs. Coolidge," Thurston warned. "Yes, dear, be careful," Coolidge said. His mild instructions brought another laugh from the guests. When the bread was pulled apart, the president's famous watch was found inside.

The Watch Trick was the sensation of the evening, earning a mention in *Time* magazine, and including Thurston in political cartoons the following week. The White House guests never appreciated that Thurston's switching the watch routine—using a valuable watch and a cheap duplicate that was worthless—was one of his oldest tricks, a confidence game that had allowed him to escape from the worst circumstances.

LOYAL GEORGE WHITE knew all the secrets. Besides working with most of the illusions onstage, he was responsible for all of the magic behind the curtain. An unusual article ran in the *Chicago Defender*, an African-American newspaper, profiling George White, "chief assistant to Mr. Thurston and a member of the Race that has made good in the show world as the next man to the world's greatest magician." At every performance, Thurston stopped and introduced him to the audience, and George was second in command backstage. The *Chicago Defender* explained:

It is White that puts the biggest tricks in order before they are worked. And Thurston never examines them. He says that White always has things so they will work. There are thirty other people in the show that take orders from White.

His quiet, authoritative manner was the secret of his success. When George had something to say, everyone listened. On one occasion, Thurston had just finished the Lady and the Lion Illusion and the cage was wheeled into the wings. As he began the next illusion, there was a commotion backstage and Thurston heard George's voice call out, "The lion's loose! The lion's loose!" Thurston imagined the company running for their lives and realized that his job was to remain on stage and keep the audience calm. Moments later he heard the footsteps backstage stop, and he pictured the lion safely returned to the cage.

At intermission he dashed backstage and asked George about the lion. George seemed confused. "The lion is fine, Governor," he reported.

"But how did it get loose?" Thurston persisted.

George smiled, realizing what had happened. "No, sir. I didn't say the lion was loose. I said that the line's loose. You know, the line we use in the pulleys to hold the scenery. We were changing the scenery." Thurston and George laughed at the situation, but it made Thurston think about just such a dilemma. "George, some day that lion might get out of that cage. If that happens, what will you do?"

George had already thought about it. "If that lion really gets out, sir," he said, "then I'm going in the cage and locking the door!"

There were other duties as well. George was Thurston's valet. He kept a small black handkerchief that he offered to the Governor between shows, so that he could cover his eyes for a short nap; he unpacked his trunk, arranged his formal wear, and guarded the dressing room door to keep his privacy.

During the summer months, George worked at the family home at Beechhurst. When Jane was a little older and teenage boys arrived at the house to escort her out for the evening, both Thurston and George White were there to observe the young men and quiz them. George also knew of Mrs. Thurston's nervous condition, her impatience, her persistent illnesses, and her increasing use of pills to help her sleep. And George, of course, always kept the secrets.

HOUDINI'S SHOW quickly changed his relationship with Thurston. The two struggled to keep a professional friendship while negotiating the dance of direct rivals. Houdini loved the intrigue. The skirmishes convinced him that he had gotten under Thurston's skin.

Late in 1925, Thurston wrote a curt letter, angered that Houdini had hired one of Thurston's former assistants for his own show, "after I had trained him and he had learned all my business and publicity methods." The assistant had further double-crossed Thurston by trying to recruit another assistant away from Thurston's show. Thurston reminded him that when one of Houdini's men from his vaudeville act, S. J. Rome, had offered to work for Thurston, he was refused.

> From my conversation with you over the telephone, I had the impression that we would play the game fair, and as far as I am concerned, I intend to, unless I am forced to do otherwise.

Within months, they'd called a truce. "You and I understand one another and have enough business judgment not to interfere with one another's performances," Thurston wrote. Houdini had informed him of a new trick that he was about to put in, the disappearance and reproduction of a number of alarm clocks, and Thurston was glad to hear of it "to prevent any confliction" in their programs.

In June 1926, the Houdinis were invited to the Thurstons' Beechhurst home for a lavish dinner with other members of the Society of American Magicians. The atmosphere was jovial, and the party lasted until two-thirty in the morning. But a week later, Houdini fired off a letter of denunciation to Thurston. He'd just read a critique from an acerbic British magic dealer, Harry Leat, in his publication called *Leat's Leaflets*. In the fourth issue, Leat condemned Houdini for his arrogant claims and crudities. Two pages later, Leat complimented Thurston for discontinuing a series of do-it-yourself tricks by noting, "the act of a gentleman, and so different from the breed who brazen it out," in other words, Houdini. Houdini assumed that Thurston had been in some way responsible for Leat's point of view.

Thurston responded, calmly assuring Houdini that he had never mentioned Houdini to Leat. "I have always refrained from entering into your arguments," Thurston wrote, "or expressing any opinions thereof."

Perhaps the best evidence of their prickly relationship was the odd game of follow-the-leader. Not only did they tussle over personnel in their shows, but Houdini quickly adopted Thurston's long-standing technique of visiting children's hospitals and performing charity shows to publicize his tour. Houdini had never been known as a children's performer, and the photographs of him visiting the bedside of crippled children, or presenting them with rabbits, seem particularly incongruous for the famous escape artist.

Similarly, Thurston included a new feat called the Triple Escape, an escape from a locked trunk that had been laced with a canvas cover. It was the sort of thing that Houdini had built his reputation upon, but as if commenting on his competition, Thurston presented it with an offhand manner, using a girl assistant to make the escape and including it in the middle of a series of fast illusions.

In the summer of 1926, Houdini gave a special demonstration of Buried Alive for the press. Houdini explained that he would expose the extravagant claims of recent vaudeville star Rahman Bey, who demonstrated that he could remain "buried alive" in a coffin under sand for about eight minutes. In order to best the Indian mystic, Houdini remained in a coffin, with limited air, which had been submerged at the Shelton Hotel swimming pool in New York City. With his assistants standing in the pool, monitoring the situation, Houdini remained in the sealed coffin for more than an hour and a half, and his demonstration of Buried Alive gained worldwide publicity. Houdini had attempted several times to produce a version of Buried Alive on the stage, as an escape in his vaudeville performances. But he could never find the right formula for the mystery. It had an inherent problem: the longer that Houdini would remain inside the coffin—the less he was performing on stage—the less impact he could have on an audience.

Thurston had a way around the problem. In the fall of 1926, he quietly began to make plans to incorporate the Buried Alive Illusion into his show. One of his assistants, Chundra Bey, an Indian mystic, would be hypnotized and placed in a glass coffin. This was then lifted and submerged in an oversized tank of water through part of the show. The audience watched him through the glass and the water as Thurston proceeded with the performance. James Wobensmith, Thurston's attorney, was recruited to draw up a patent for the apparatus.

IN THE MID-1920s, Thurston matched his expanding show with a bewildering array of businesses. His brother Harry managed a "Tropical Land" business, investing in Florida orange groves, and Howard followed suit. He also purchased lots in Beechhurst, near his own home, and land in Canada, near Niagara Falls, oil fields in Pennsylvania and Texas, and shares in a gold mine in Alberta, Canada. A Beechhurst neighbor, John Mano, convinced the Thurstons to invest in his new paint and adhesive company, X-Pando.

Each investment proved to be a disappointment. Some, like the oil field, were disasters, requiring continual investments of cash in order to test the soil or evaluate the reserves. A Buffalo attorney, Bernard Hyman, besieged Thurston with offers and sales pitches—more lots were now available, and these would be the most profitable of all; the Penngas oil fields are looking good; you should consider the new properties at Candlewood Island in Connecticut. Many of the businesses seemed to rely on Thurston's endorsement as well as his money. John Mano wanted Thurston to represent X-Pando to Henry Ford for his manufacturing plant. Porcupine Gold Mines, a Canadian company, used Thurston's picture and endorsement in its advertising.

His strangest investment was Thurston's Perfect Breather. He returned to his father's mania for simple, practical inventions for the benefit of humanity and devised a twist of wire loops that could be inserted into the nostrils, holding them open for a restful sleep, free of snoring. In 1925, Thurston arranged to have the Breather manufactured (with a deluxe model plated gold), and sold with advertisements in his program, or on the back of his special throw-out cards that he hurled into the audience or tossed to children as souvenirs. It was a difficult product to sell, as different nostrils required different sizes, and Thurston provided a cardboard nostril-measuring device, through the mail, to allow customers to find the perfect fit.

Thurston had been banking on these investments, including the Breather, to provide a relaxing retirement. When his first box of finished Breathers arrived, Thurston congratulated himself on the product by writing to Leotha, "Sure wish I could say goodbye to the theater, and you, Jane and myself have a real rest and honeymoon."

But the Perfect Breather was not a success; children and families that attended his show were happy to buy boxes of candy or booklets of magic tricks, but must have been surprised to find the great magician endorsing wire nostril expanders to prevent snoring.

THURSTON WAS WORKING on another invention that he planned as a feature for his show—the famous Indian Rope Trick. He had attempted to include David Devant's version of the trick in an early show but had to abandon his plans. Thurston's latest tour would include an extended section of Indian magic—including Buried Alive, Fire Eating, and the Basket Illusion. The jewel in the crown would be a re-creation of the famous Indian Rope Trick. According to legendary accounts, a rope is thrown toward the sky and remains suspended in space. A native boy climbs to the top, and then disappears in midair before the rope falls to the ground again.

It's now clear that the trick was never more than a legend, and was probably manufactured in an American press account of the 1890s to enhance the marvels of the Hindu wonder-workers, and then was echoed, back and forth, between tourists in India and aggressive street fakirs, who would never quite deny that the feat could be accomplished. Thurston's experience in India was a typical goose chase that magicians found in the early 1900s—the famous Rope Trick could never quite be seen, but tourists were teased that a man in the next village had surely seen it, or a fakir had just left town who could perform it.

In fact, the illusion is patently impossible in the open air, under the hot

Indian sun. Thurston, like Devant, Selbit, Le Roy, and Goldin, attempted versions of it on the stage by using a combination of magic principles and relying on special lighting or scenery.

In Thurston's version, a tall Indian archway was prominent in the center of the stage, which framed a black velvet background. Thurston and his Indian mystics showed a long, thick rope, which was coiled and then placed in a basket. Slowly, the rope rose into the air, until the top of it was about fifteen feet over the stage.

Now an assistant in a white loincloth and turban grabbed the rope and climbed to the top, where he could be clearly seen in the center of the archway. Puffs of white steam, suggesting clouds, filled the archway, momentarily obscuring the boy from view. As the steam disappeared, the audience could see him still clinging to the top of the rope. The boy waved to the audience and then instantly disappeared.

Ironically, this bit of supposedly ancient Indian mysticism required a great deal of costly twentieth-century technology. Thurston had first speculated that he could suspend a sheet of glass in the archway, and the glass could reflect an image of the boy at one side of the stage. This was the basic secret of many mirror illusions from the late 1800s, but enlarged to the scale of the Rope Trick, the system didn't work. Instead, Thurston used a transparent movie screen, made of perforated material, unrolled over the top of the archway to cover the end of the rope. As this happened, the steam obscured the boy, who had to grab a black velvet support—invisible to the audience against the black velvet scenery—so he could be pulled up, out of sight behind the nearby archway. As the steam cleared, a motion picture of the boy—life-sized against a black background—was projected on the gauzelike movie screen. It gave the impression that the boy was still there, brightly illuminated.

When the movie flickered and stopped, the boy was suddenly gone.

At least, that's the way it was supposed to work. The motion picture of the boy provided months of headaches. Thurston filmed the action and had it hand-tinted so that the picture of the boy had ruddy skin to match his makeup. The timing of the illusion was critical. If the smoke cleared too soon, the audience saw the flash of movement as the real boy escaped, or saw too much of the movie, which could look two-dimensional and suspicious. If there was too much smoke, the projected image wasn't clear, and the audience thought that the boy just scrambled out of the way under cover of the bursts of steam.

It all depended on the precise motion of the puffs of steam, which was like depending on the weather. If the theater was cold, or the drafts on stage unpredictable, the illusion changed from performance to performance. Worst of all, the large boilers had to be held under the stage, and the steam piped twelve feet in the air so that it could obscure the boy, which made the timing difficult to coordinate. This was the boiler system that Tampa designed for the magician.

Thurston claimed to have invested thousands of dollars in the Indian Rope Trick, and there's no doubt that the illusion was embarrassingly costly. There were many false starts and abandoned experiments, requiring several summers of testing at the Beechhurst workshop.

LEOTHA'S HEALTH was a constant concern. Thurston suggested new doctors, advised her to take holidays, or cautioned her to avoid certain friends or situations that would provide aggravation. His letters indicate long stretches where she was unable to leave her bed, and she suffered a series of breakdowns, which inspired rounds of medications. "My Leo, Your depressed statements over the phone have given me the blues," Thurston wrote in the spring of 1926. "Can't understand you. You have me greatly worried. Do try to get well for Jane and me. You are all we have or love in the world."

One of her treats was a small pet rhesus monkey, named Lord Pickwick, or Picky, that tucked himself inside her fur coat and traveled with her on the train when she visited the show. Picky was given the run of the hotel rooms where they stayed. Although he was only briefly featured in the magic show, produced from a trick table invented by Karl Germain, at special crippled-children's matinees Picky would receive an introduction from Thurston and was a crowd favorite.

A second, larger monkey, named Mickey, was the source of problems. He would inhabit a tree branch near the Beechhurst house and could be unpredictably nasty. On June 26, 1926, as Thurston and the men were preparing the new show at the rented pavilion near his home, Mickey climbed over a fence and bit an eight-year-old boy, Henry Korfmann. Later that afternoon, his mother, Mrs. Eva Charous, a neighbor of the Thurstons, knocked on their door to complain. Thurston seemed mystified by the charge and offered the woman a simple balm that he'd used, suggesting that it would help to heal the bite.

The problem couldn't be solved that simply. The family insisted that the bite led to medical problems for the boy; eventually they claimed that it triggered epileptic fits, forcing him to be institutionalized at Wards Island. A lawsuit followed.

THURSTON DELAYED the start of the season in 1926 for his own operation. In August of that year, he arrived in Chicago and was met at the train station by his brother Harry. Together, they went to the office of Dr. Henry Schireson, and Howard scheduled another face-lift.

Dr. Schireson was a well-known surgeon who became famous for removing the distinctive bump in Fanny Brice's nose in 1924—and, according to some critics, ruining her comedic career. After Thurston's disappointing first face-lift, he decided to have the job performed by an expert. Schireson wanted to do a "full job," removing the earlier lumps of paraffin and performing a "rotation lift" to tighten Thurston's skin, as well as a peel to reveal fresh skin; it was a $700 job that Schireson offered to perform for $450. The operation required several visits to the office over the course of four weeks. Thurston stayed at the Sherman Hotel, and then moved to a quiet room at the Chicago Beach Hotel, overlooking Lake Michigan. For weeks he was helpless in the room, applying a white powder, zinc sterate, to the wounds every half hour to help them dry and scab, and resting in the sunshine. Harry and his secretary, Rae Palmer, attended to Howard, allowing him to dictate letters to Leotha and Jane.

Howard's letters made the process sound endless, miserable, and painful. He nervously made inquiries about the new tour and was anxious to return home again. Schireson was concerned about the paraffin; he was not able to easily cut it out, and suggested removing it later with an "electrical needle."

When the press was alerted to Thurston's presence in Dr. Schireson's office, Thurston and his friend Alvin Plough, a publicity agent, concocted a story that he had been burned by steam during his experiments on the Rope Trick. Schireson was tending to the magician's scars.

In September, as Howard was still healing, Harry Thurston also decided to have plastic surgery. He started with an abdomen tuck, and then arranged to have Dr. Schireson perform facial surgery. For several days, both Thurston brothers shared the same room at the hotel, recuperating from their operations. Howard might have been glad to have the company; he should have wondered why his brother, the Chicago businessman, booking agent, and dime museum operator, was suddenly concerned about his appearance. He didn't ask what Harry was planning.

AT THE END of his stay in Chicago, Thurston called on an agent, and happened to pass Grace, his first wife, as she was leaving the same office. They had met each other occasionally over the years. Grace had continued happily in show business, working as a dancer, performing in stock companies, and even performing small parts in an occasional motion picture. Noticing the bandages that surrounded her husband's handsome face, she momentarily felt the old motherly instincts that had carried them through the worst elements on their western tours. "Howard, what happened?" she instinctively cried out to him. "Oh, your poor face!"

"Hello, Grace." Thurston turned away momentarily. "It was just a small explosion. One of my illusions blew up," he mumbled.

But Grace had noticed the regularity of the bandages and her expression changed. "You've just . . . had your face lifted, didn't you?"

Thurston turned to her and chuckled. He still couldn't fool her. "Actually, yes. I did. We can't afford to grow old, can we, Grace?"

IN OCTOBER, both Thurston and Houdini were back on the road with their shows. Houdini's tour had been plagued by a number of odd accidents. In

Albany, New York, as he was lifted by his feet in the massive stocks during the Water Torture Cell, Houdini fractured a bone in his ankle. Houdini halted the escape, bandaged the ankle, and carried on with the show, sitting in a chair during the lecture on spirit frauds.

Several days later, in Montreal, Houdini lectured to students at McGill University on spiritualism and magic. He looked tired and pale, with dark circles under his eyes. He now hobbled through his performances, trying to allow his fractured bone to knit. The next day, several students from McGill called on him backstage and engaged him in an animated conversation as Houdini reclined on a couch. They talked about Houdini's film career, biblical miracles, and mystery stories. One of the boys was busy making a sketch of the magician. Another, a tall, strong young man named J. Gordon Whitehead, asked Houdini about his claim to be able to tighten his stomach muscles and withstand a punch.

Houdini was still exhausted, but he confirmed to the boy that he could do it and foolishly offered to try. Before the magician was able to rise from the couch and tighten his muscles, Whitehead offered a fusillade of quick punches. Houdini collapsed back onto the couch and then regained his composure before the boys left.

It now seems that Houdini's appendix had already been ruptured, and this injury exacerbated the situation. By the time the show closed in Montreal and moved to Detroit, Houdini struggled through one show, performing the magic and spiritualism lecture, before he was taken to the hospital.

Thurston was shocked to hear the news reports. At first, doctors warned that Houdini was in grave condition, but the stories of his injuries seemed maddeningly unclear and trivial. Thurston wired the hospital for reports and inquired after Bess. Houdini rallied briefly, and headlines seemed to indicate his imminent recovery. But the effects of peritonitis were fatal. He died on October 31, 1926. Harry Houdini was fifty-two years old.

Dante never liked him. He'd run up against Houdini several times and had only faced the professional brickbats and jealousies—the arrogance that made Houdini a star and defined his prominence as an escape artist. In an unpublished manuscript, Dante wrote:

For twenty years Houdini has traded on an unscrupulous public who have accepted him in good faith, undoubtedly confusing his devices with the work of a true magician. A master magician must be an artist and the possessor of a personality. He must be a gentleman and of an inventive mind. Can Houdini lay claim to any of these qualifications? What can he escape from? So far, he has escaped criticism. . . . The day for [bribing] newspapers and police sergeants is past, and he knows it. But the glory of Houdini must not be hampered, therefore Spiritualists became the innocent victims of this monster fakir who calls himself a mystifier.

But Thurston had known the young magician, the Midway performer at the Columbian Exposition in Chicago, so brashly proud of his magic and so insistent on demonstrating his own skills with playing cards. Throughout all the years, as they both achieved success and challenged each other, Thurston continued to perceive that young man, bristling with every perceived slight, ready to proclaim his superiority to the rest of the world.

"I was very much upset about Houdini's death, and could hardly realize it even at present. I was in constant touch with his condition during his illness in Detroit and sent wires and flowers to Mrs. Houdini," he wrote to Dante. Thurston couldn't help but consider his own fate. "It surely is a warning to me, and I wonder how I have managed to survive all these years under the great strain."

To the newspaper reporters, Thurston offered his own tribute: "The world has lost a great mystifier and a useful, forceful character. We were friends for 35 years, starting at the bottom together and climbing toward the top. As a showman he was in a class with Barnum, in force of character, he resembled [Theodore] Roosevelt."

Curiously, he described his compatriot as a "mystifier," a "useful character," and a "showman" but never quite a magician. Two days later, when the Associated Press asked Thurston about the rumor that Houdini's precious secrets would accompany Houdini to the grave, Thurston seemed to be growing weary of the legend and tried to put it in perspective with a sensible answer.

"It is a mistake to tell the public that Houdini carried his secrets with him to the grave," Thurston said. "Other magicians knew them, as they knew all the tricks performed on the stage, but of course these secrets are not told to the public."

William Hilliar, the early associate of Thurston and a friend of Houdini's, was upset that Thurston wouldn't indulge in Houdini's beloved publicity boasts after his death. "I think Thurston showed cheap showmanship when he announced that Houdini did not take his secrets with him," Hilliar wrote to Mrs. Houdini with his condolences. "The secret, the big secret of Harry's success was Harry himself."

Previous feuds between magicians had involved theaters, routes, personnel, or tricks. In the 1880s, when Herrmann and Kellar raced through a territory ahead of each other, or pasted over the other magician's posters, the battles represented an embarrassment of riches. They were prospectors charging into a gold field, shoveling their way to success. But Thurston and Houdini had faced a different time in show business. Vaudeville was dying. Motion pictures were slowly squeezing out traveling shows. As their world kept shrinking, they were forced to become allies and rivals at the same time, continually fighting over the last few golden nuggets.

With Houdini's death, Thurston doubled down. His version of Buried Alive was placed into his new show about a week later. By 1926, Thurston's renowned touring show had grown to a sumptuous production, unquestionably the largest magic show in the world. That season, the illusions were not only amazing but breathtaking, living up to Thurston's billing of "The Wonder Show of the Universe."

TWENTY

"MISS JANE THURSTON (SHE TAKES AFTER HER DAD)"

he Indian Rope Trick was living up to its legend; even after Thurston thought he had solved all its problems, the trick continued to confound him. For example, after costly experiments retinting the film image of the boy, Thurston found it was easier to match the color of the assistant's body with orange-brown makeup, rather than producing an image that matched the boy. Then he had a protest from the projectionist's union; they wanted their own man to turn the switch on and off, and their contracts insisted on his travel arrangements on the train. Thurston always tried to accommodate the unions, but this time he had to give up.

At the last moment, he scrapped the film and arranged a painted glass slide of his assistant. The still image was projected at the top of the rope and then was allowed to flop out of view in the projector. If you used your imagination, it looked as if the boy was starting to fall backward off the rope, before he disappeared completely. It wasn't until December 1926 that the trick finally appeared before an audience and an apprehensive magician, standing at the bottom of the rope, gesturing toward the sky and doing his very best to look confident. "At last we made something of the Rope Trick," Thurston wrote to Dante.

After these first few performances, Thurston's staff quizzed the audience at intermission. The audience reported that there was something wrong with the boy at the top of the rope. He looked strange or suspicious, even if they couldn't explain how the trick worked.

"We have tried it for ten days and last night was the first time it fooled the audience and I have decided to keep it in," Thurston wrote. The collection of Indian Magic made an impressive feature for the show, but the Rope Trick, the finale of this number, cost Thurston $10,000, he admitted to Dante. In today's money, that's the equivalent of several hundred thousand dollars, a ridiculous investment for a magic trick, especially one with such a low batting average.

BY THEN, Thurston had already been planning his feature for the next season, the Vanishing Automobile. The illusion was first suggested to him by Guy Jarrett, who regularly visited Thurston when the magician was in New York, teasing him with new ideas for illusions. Jarrett suggested a trick in which an automobile was driven onto a raised platform and covered with curtains for several seconds. When the curtains were pulled away, the car was gone. Jarrett's secret was ingenious, depending on a special car that could be folded up and concealed within the platform.

Thurston kept Jarrett coming back for meeting after meeting, asking questions about the illusion and even having Jarrett provide a bid to build it. He offered to make it for $1,500. But at the same time, Thurston was moving ahead with his own version of the Vanishing Automobile. Thurston's plan was much more practical; he would carry the special scenery required, and then make a sponsorship arrangement with an auto company—a sporty convertible Willys-Overland Whippet—so that he could secure a new car in every city.

His shop at Beechhurst built two panels with wide vertical slats, like walls of a cage. These would be pushed in front of the car; they met at a ninety-degree angle, so the audience could see the auto and its passengers between the slats. Thurston would fire a pistol, there would be a puff of smoke, and the auto would suddenly be gone. The secret relied upon an idea from the inventive British magician Charles Morritt. Vertical strips of mirror were hidden behind the slats. With the puff of smoke, these mirrors quickly slid, filling in the open spaces. These mirrors reflected scenery at the side of the stage, effectively hiding the auto.

When he introduced it in 1927, the Vanishing Whippet Automobile provided headlines for the show, and Thurston commissioned a beautiful new poster showing the automobile disappearing into a cloud of mist. Thurston experimented with different flashing lighting effects to enhance the illusion and added a raised track for the car, so the audience could appreciate that it wasn't dropping through a trapdoor in the stage. The most important enhancement was Thurston's line of pretty girl assistants, wearing bright silk dresses. The car rolled onto the stage loaded with girls: filling the seats, standing on the running boards, and draped over the hood. They smiled, waved at the audience, squealed their good-byes, and promptly disappeared with the Whippet.

Thurston's pistol shots were always a subject of debate. Magicians joked about him "shooting at" his tricks. In fact, it was difficult for Thurston to find the right gesture or pronounce the proper magic words for large tricks or the fast-paced marvels of his show. Firing a blank pistol provided the right moment—like starting a race—and put him in control of the action. He fired a pistol to make a piano disappear, make his donkey or horse vanish, produce a line of girls.

At one rehearsal, Thurston was working on a new trick. A brightly lit lamp was on one side of the stage. A canary vanished, and the lightbulb went out. When Thurston removed the bulb from the lamp, the canary was found sealed within the glass bulb. When the bulb was broken with a small hammer, the bird was released and then returned to its cage. Thurston billed the trick as the Canary in the National Mazda Lamp—the commercial was appropriate, for he relied on the Edison Mazda Company to supply special empty bulbs to accomplish the trick.

When it came time for the bird to disappear, Thurston reached into his back pocket, removed his blank pistol, and fired it. Watching the new trick, his carpenter, Elmer Morris, shook his head. After the rehearsal, Morris told the magician, "That move makes you look like some Chicago hoodlum, rather than the Great Thurston." Thurston seemed to brush off Morris's criticism, but it had obviously bothered him.

At the next show, Morris was standing in the wings watching the new Canary Trick, when he noticed a girl assistant step over to Thurston. She held the pistol on a small silver platter. Thurston picked up the pistol, fired it, and placed it back on the platter. He turned on his heel, and his eyes locked on Morris in the wings. Thurston gave his carpenter a wink and a courtly bow.

In fact, Thurston knew plenty of Chicago hoodlums. Many were friends of his brother Harry. Several years later, Al Capone sent his son to see the Thurston show. Thurston responded to the famous gangster with a kind letter, telling him his son was "a fine boy" and inviting them both to the show the next time it played in Chicago. There's no record that Scarface Al Capone ever attended.

THE MOST VALUABLE addition to Thurston's show was John Northern Hilliard, one of his oldest friends, as business manager and personal press representative. Hilliard had regularly written press stories and releases for Thurston and had produced the draft of Thurston's autobiography. He had a long, interesting career that started as a newspaperman, included novels and Broadway shows, as well as books on magic. Acquaintances remember him as a kind bear of a man, and to Jane he was always Uncle John, regaling her with tales of early adventures and stories about his pet chicken. But close friends, like Thurston, understood that Hilliard was painfully moody and lonely. In 1926, Thurston lured him to be a part of his company.

Hilliard's advance work for the show gave Thurston's production a new luster. He knew what reporters wanted and how they worked; in turn, reporters respected Hilliard, who refused to indulge in "fake ballyhoo," was honest and gregarious with them, and entertained them with interesting anecdotes from his years in the newspaper business. It was then traditional for the magician's press releases to hew to specific formulas. They might consist of exaggerated biographical stories, like Thurston's adventures in India, or short articles detailing his great inventions, or whimsical tales of near accidents on stage. But Hilliard expanded on these stories, managing to capture Thurston as a warm, interesting character. He also wrote glowingly of Thurston's tie to the great history of magic—the important tradition and the great conjurers of the past. These press releases were mimeographed and stapled together in sets; the paper sheets were perforated, so that individual stories could be neatly torn out of the bundle. Sitting at a desk with a reporter, Hilliard could easily flip through the pages, pulling out features of different lengths. This also ensured that, at each city, reporters were given "exclusive" releases.

A Thurston press release—it has the typical elegance of Hilliard's work— neatly explained Thurston's approach to the spirit world. Thurston is quoted as saying:

> If every man, woman and child were honest with themselves ghosts would be as plentiful as cowards. Each of us at some time in our lives has experienced strange manifestations of the psychic forces either in dreams, visions or actualities. Deep in our hearts we believe in the power of the dead to manifest themselves. We have felt the presence of ghostly visitors, we have had strange but true premonitions. In spite of ourselves and our dogmas, we acknowledge in a secret corner of our hearts that the departed still live and at times we feel their presence. To our friends we laugh at the idea of spirits, but in the darkness of our solitude, we unconsciously expect to see a ghost.

Thurston turned this sentiment into a bit of poetic magic in his latest Spirit Cabinet routine. Now Kellar's old cabinet was brought on stage, opened, and shown to be empty. Thurston placed a cane, a tambourine, and a bell inside and closed the door. "Now comes a strange, weird, wonderful part," Thurston told his audience. The cane rapped and the tambourine rattled. "What's that? A ghost? Are you a friendly ghost?" The bell clanged in response. "I'm so glad. I don't like unfriendly ghosts." The instruments continued to rattle against the interior walls of the cabinet and were finally pushed through the small windows in front, clattering onto the stage. Within seconds, the noisy, invisible ghost had seemingly reduced the show to chaos. Thurston's assistants dashed to the cabinet and threw open the doors.

Suddenly, the music shifted to a melodic violin solo. The cabinet interior was empty except for a large, reflective silver sphere, about eight inches in diameter, hovering above the floor of the famous Spirit Cabinet. It sparkled in a deep red spotlight.

Thurston raised his hand, and the ball slowly floated out of the cabinet toward him. When the magician gestured, and seemed to push it away, the ball moved in a mysterious swoop to the stage floor. Then it levitated and slowly circled back, returning to Thurston.

Then came the incredible moment. Thurston stepped off the stage with the ball floating between the palms of his hands, walking partway up the aisle of the theater, as the audience watched in disbelief. He turned, facing the stage, and raised his hands. The ball left him, traveled over the heads of the audience and the orchestra pit, slowly gaining altitude and speed until it swept past the gaping spectators and hovered over the Spirit Cabinet. The flight of the mysterious ball earned a hushed murmur from the crowd. Thurston followed, up the steps and back onto the stage. With another gesture, the ball slowly descended into the cabinet and was swallowed into the shadowy darkness as the doors were closed.

George and Thurston's assistants stepped to the cabinet and quickly took it apart, piece by piece, until they were left with a pile of flat wooden doors and panels. The ball had disappeared, and there was no sign of the ghost.

The illusion was accomplished with the most prosaic of secrets, including a tangle of thin black threads that were manipulated by Thurston, two assistants in the wings of the theater, and another assistant hiding inside the Spirit Cabinet. The movement of the ball was balanced between these actors, each transferring an invisible influence by picking up slack or smoothly releasing the invisible threads—a delicate dance at the fingertips.

There were many individual elements that could doom the illusion. During a 1927 performance, a spotlight operator flipped the wrong colored gel in the front of the light, temporarily exposing the network of threads that held the ball aloft. After the show, a young magician, John McKinven, was excited to go backstage and meet his idol, Thurston. Waiting there, he heard Thurston's distinctive nasal baritone, "that voice," on the other side of a folding screen.

Thurston was cursing out the spotlight operator, using so many four-letter expletives in quick succession that young John felt the blood rush to his face. Seconds later, the majestic Thurston came around the screen, beaming with a smile. "So nice you meet you, young man."

It was Thurston's grandeur that made the Floating Ball so wonderful; he invested it with a haunting solemnity, creating a poetic, visual analogy of the relationship between the medium and the spirit. His cabinet and ball routine represented Thurston's various pronouncements on ghosts, the sort of sweet and human equivocation that had riled Houdini.

Thurston's refusal to be dogmatic about the supernatural was explained in interviews:

> Taking everything into consideration, the most interesting things I have learned about people are their love of mystery, their desire to show their cleverness by claiming to know how it is done, the vanity of little minds, the lack of self-consciousness in big people, the instinct of women, the chivalry of men, and most striking of all, the wish to believe the supernatural, especially in some evidence of life after death.

In other words, he saw the supernatural as a human condition. If Houdini and the mediums had argued that the occult might or might not exist, Thurston insisted that it always existed—as a purely human need. It was an enlightened point of view, but it didn't make him many friends.

THURSTON TOOK UP Houdini's battle with false spiritualists late in 1927. His intention may well have been sheer publicity, or perhaps his motivation was a function of his position in the Society of American Magicians. Houdini had promoted the cause within the SAM, and his death left the subject unchallenged in the press. Thurston had always doubted any phenomena in a formal séance room, and sensibly warned the public of fraud. But in October, he gave an interview for United Press that consisted of the usual denunciations, with facts and anecdotes. The interview seemed unexpectedly strident, like a man

on a mission. "Thurston Will Wage Fight on Psychic Fakes," the headline announced, proclaiming that he would "take up where late Houdini left off." The
article quoted him as saying:

> Any performances in the supposedly supernatural, which are done regularly
> for money, are done by trickery. . . . I have had long conversations with Sir
> Arthur Conan Doyle, and I find that Doyle has been badly duped. He is one of
> the easiest men I have met to mystify. . . . Fortune telling and mind reading are
> all rot. Why read a palm for a dollar when you can forecast the stock market
> tomorrow?

These insights were hardly remarkable, and Doyle's gullibility was discussed
after it dissolved his friendship with Houdini. But Thurston continued with
additional exposures, designed to fascinate the public:

> The most common form of ghosts used by the fraudulent spiritualists is con-
> tained in a small watch. It is blown up by a collapsible rod, which appears to be
> an ordinary lead pencil. This ghost can be made to do any of the stunts used by
> the mediums. It can be deflated quickly by use of the same rod.

Reverend Arthur Ford was the president of the First Spiritualist Church of
New York, a canny, funny, and quick-witted southerner who didn't indulge in
ghosts. He sat in séances, contacted his spirit guide, a French-Canadian named
Fletcher, and offered quiet revelations and advice. He had just returned from
London, where he had earned Conan Doyle's endorsement. Perhaps this is why
he first noticed Thurston's interview, but more than likely, it was the promise
to take up Houdini's battle that had raised Ford's hackles—the threat that
after Houdini's death, a long string of magicians were ready to continue the
attacks. Ford responded to the newspapers, disagreeing with Thurston's remarks by claiming that the magician was "a publicity-seeking showman."

Again, this insight was hardly remarkable. But Ford was smart enough to
know that Thurston was an ineffective skeptic, and clever enough to use
Houdini's standard technique, a challenge, before any challenge was issued to

Ford. He offered Thurston $10,000 if he could produce one of his watch-case ghosts, and then use it to duplicate the phenomena of Margery, the controversial medium who had sparred with Houdini. "I hope Thurston will not follow the example of Houdini and evade the issue by a counter-challenge. He has made charges. I demand that he prove them," Ford explained.

Thurston was trapped. He agreed to join Ford for a lecture at the Chapter Room in Carnegie Hall on October 9. Thurston counted on his oratory, his ability to charm an audience, and his rational, open-minded views on the subject—a believer but a skeptic. He hadn't anticipated Ford's clever jujitsu-like abilities to exploit the believer. That evening, the room was packed with three hundred spectators, including members of the Society of American Magicians, to cheer on their new hero.

Ford was smooth, funny, and excitable. Thurston was cautious and sedate. To many he appeared as stodgy and unprepared. They traded barbs. "You've insulted me," Ford claimed, trying to pick a fight. He described Thurston's inflatable spirit, pointing out the ridiculous nature of this sort of invention. In fact, Ford was right. The watchcase ghost was something Thurston had invented to sound more interesting than the usual crude deceptions of a séance room. Ford challenged Thurston to reproduce séance phenomena. Thurston demurred and challenged Ford to have the spirits tell him his mother's maiden name.

Thurston scored a surprising point when the discussion turned to Conan Doyle and Lady Doyle. He insisted that Lady Doyle attempted to contact Houdini's mother but gave the wrong message to him. He dramatically turned to a small, dark-haired lady sitting in the front row. "Is this so, Mrs. Houdini?" Bess Houdini stood up and agreed, explaining that Lady Doyle was a failure as a medium. The SAM magicians cheered.

But the discussion devolved from black and white to a muddy mess of gray. Thurston, as Ford anticipated, ended the evening by tempering his views:

> It is true that in 35 years of knowing magicians and mediums I've never seen anything done regularly for money in the way of Spiritualism that was not done by trickery. But, while I've never had any experience with Margery, I've

been to her house and I consider her a lady. I have spent 35 years making friends and I have no wish at my time of life to begin making enemies. I am inclined to believe Margery has some psychic force, and I have come to believe there exists an intelligent psychic force.

Newspapers reported that as he spoke these words, he was both hissed and applauded.

When the meeting proceeded with a hymn and the passing of a collection plate, a spectator stood to loudly object. "You invite us here and then take up a collection!" There was a brief scuffle and the police were called, but by then the evening was finished.

The meeting played itself out in the press, but Thurston's appearance at Carnegie Hall ended his battle with spiritualists. Overall, he made many sensible, inarguable points about fraud, but his most important observation was the closing remark, "I have no wish to begin making enemies." This is what would always prevent him from adopting Houdini's crusade.

The most significant event of the evening was Ford's first meeting with Mrs. Harry Houdini, who had surprised him with her presence. Ford took the opportunity to introduce himself, and then formed a friendship with the magician's widow. The following year, they would both be tangled in a series of séances, in which the ghost of Houdini apparently returned to give Bess a coded message. The Ford and Houdini séances were reduced to a number of silly claims and denials, proving nothing. Both Mrs. Houdini and Arthur Ford were branded as opportunists, or, perhaps, "publicity seeking showmen."

In May 1928, Thurston was invited to present a special address at St. Mark's Methodist Church in Detroit. It was an unusual opportunity to realize his dream of speaking from the pulpit. Thurston explained to the congregation that he found spiritualism "a serious thing, a psychic force that manifests itself unto certain people under certain conditions. I have seen some things I cannot explain, but that is a long story." He cautioned the listeners. "I want to say that everything done for public, for money, is accomplished by trickery."

At St. Mark's, Thurston also presented a rambling recollection of his travels, his experience with different religions, and his view of prayer. "I do not ask

God for a new suit of clothes, to pay the mortgage, or do a lot of other things for me. I am ashamed to pray and ask God for some of the things I hear preachers pray for," he explained. "I never leave the door of my room without stopping for a moment, just a prayer of thankfulness. I never go on stage without that prayer of thankfulness, and also to ask for help."

JANE THURSTON had spent her childhood in boarding schools, and then in singing and dancing classes, including the dance schools of Ned Wayburn, Theodora Irvine, and Alveine. When the 1928 season began, she was given her own spots in her father's show. Jane was now was seventeen years old, with curly dark blond hair. Jane remembered being overwhelmed by her early performances, terrified by the thought of disappointing her mother or father.

Jane was never a magician's assistant, or "box jumper," to use the backstage slang. Instead, Jane was a costar: a singing, dancing magician. Thurston hired the British illusionist Cyril Yettmah, who had his own successful career a decade before, to create new illusions for the show and supervise Jane's special numbers.

Jane rehearsed the tricks over and over again, and Thurston listened to her singing and speaking parts by pacing in the back of the balcony, cupping a hand to his ear, and shouting, "Louder! I can't hear you!" Hilliard supervised the press stories about her training, and Jane was posed in various publicity pictures.

On the night of her debut, as she walked to the stage door with her father, they both noticed her name on the marquee and the line of customers at the box office. "They are paying good money to enjoy themselves," Thurston whispered to her, "and it is our job to see that they do." She felt her stomach twist itself into knots.

Jane's three short acts were filled with pretty tricks—parasols, flowers, and scarves—to suit the young lady, as well as some of Thurston's illusions from previous seasons. She also included special songs and dances. A jazzy melody was written for her by their Beechhurst neighbor A. Seymour Brown, the author of "Oh, You Beautiful Doll." Brown's song was titled "My Daddy's a Hocus Pocus Man," and Jane sang it in the pouting style of Ann Pennington:

> *Ever since I was the tiniest kid*
> *I've marveled at the things that Daddy did*
> *Candy and lollypops, things like that,*
> *He can shake 'em right out of a hat*
> *It wasn't long until I found, he was handy to have around*
>
> *My Daddy is a Hocus Pocus Man, what a man*
> *He can do things like nobody else can . . . 'deed he can*
> *He looks kind of solemn and serious*
> *And does things that seem mysterious*
> *But I must make this admission*
> *There never was a sweeter disposition. . . .*

Even the most complimentary accounts of Jane's acts seem slightly trivial. Magic fans thought she was cute, but felt she couldn't muster the gravitas or presence of her famous father. Of course, that wasn't her job. Pretty Jane added a burst of youthful energy and color to the show. Her magic was never intended to be grand. Rather, it provided the change of pace, allowing her father to be a little grander.

A posed photo from opening night shows Jane and her parents next to the stage, surrounded by congratulatory floral arrangements. Jane seems to smile cautiously—a shy little girl suddenly trapped in the spotlight. Thurston seems exhausted. But Leotha offers a rare broad smile, obviously delighted at her daughter's accomplishment.

FOR THE 1929 SEASON, Thurston hired Herman Hanson and his wife, Lillian, to join him on the road. Hanson was a Swedish-born vaudevillian who had developed a song-and-dance magic act and was briefly considered for Thurston's third unit. Dante advised against him, as he felt that Hanson had a "weak" personality. "You need someone who can play that piano of yours," Dante advised. But Hanson was actually an ideal man to head the Thurston show as technical director. He supervised and assisted in Jane's new acts and was quickly put to work completing illusions for Thurston. He was fiercely loyal to Mr. Thurston, and fit perfectly into the company.

That same year, Thurston's autobiography, *My Life of Magic*, was finally published by Dorrance and Company. Hilliard was the author, of course. He had been fidgeting with it for many years, but Hilliard had finally given up, and it was only completed with the addition of writer Walter B. Gibson, with assistance from Detroit newspaperman Al Monroe, working closely with Thurston.

"The original Thurston manuscript only carried the story up to the first stop on his world tour, namely, Australia," Gibson later explained. "After Hilliard had finished that part, Thurston abridged it, mostly for personal reason, and I think that is why Hilliard lost interest in continuing it."

The "unexpurgated version," as Hilliard ruefully called it, was locked in a safe in Thurston's home. Of course, Thurston's criminal past was never included in the book.

Writers Gibson and Monroe agreed to take out some of the adventures of Thurston's childhood and his carnival days, which seemed trivial and demeaning after his long career. They were also instructed to omit all the references to his previous wives. Jane had never been told that she was adopted, and Thurston sought to avoid embarrassment to her or Leotha. For example, *My Life of Magic* credited William Round for the magician's early education at Mount Hermon, without explaining how he'd formed such an important relationship with the superintendent of prisons. By omitting Grace, the book suggested that Thurston had toured the west on his own. Writing Beatrice out of the story, George White was now elevated to the role of Thurston's show business partner.

Another omission was Harry Thurston, who now had a cursory reference in the book, without explaining his important contributions to his brother's career. Harry noticed.

To complete the story, Gibson used Thurston's many press releases and interviews, explaining his tour with Kellar and recent achievements. This brought the biography up to date.

Thurston had originally titled his autobiography *Castaways*, focusing on his early days as a runaway. Then he used the working title *A History of a Passion*, but finally settled on the more commercial *My Life of Magic*. The end result was an odd pastiche that satisfied the publisher but never quite satisfied the public. Significantly, it's a book that kept many more secrets than it explained. Hilliard's early chapters—evocative accounts of riding the rails or following magic shows—shine with clear prose and suggest what had been lost as the manuscript was revised. When the Hilliard, Gibson, and Monroe book was finished, Thurston opened his safe one more time and destroyed the original Hilliard manuscript.

John Mulholland, the magic writer and historian, later wrote, "Those very few who had the privilege of reading John Northern Hilliard's manuscript on the life of Howard Thurston and then read the Thurston autobiography hardly could accept that the two accounts were about the same man."

TWENTY-ONE

"SHADOW PEOPLE"

ne of Thurston's most ambitious children's matinees was presented at Bellvue Hospital in Albany, New York, in May 1927. Thurston wasn't known for small tricks; in order to satisfy his audience, his entire company joined the show, setting up a truckload of colorful illusions on an outdoor platform. Thurston, in a tweed business suit, welcomed the children and then presented his escape trunk, bird tricks, and duck tricks. He finished with the Sawing in Half, with a ring of doctors in hospital whites supervising the magical operation.

Thurston was now regularly called upon for shows at veteran's hospitals or special performances for crippled children. For these happy occasions, a chance for the patients to take their minds off their pains, Thurston referred to himself as a "sunshine maker," as opposed to a "rainmaker." In 1929, a man named Fred Dawson visited Thurston in his dressing room and asked if he'd perform a free show at a YMCA. The magician looked tired. He reluctantly explained that he supported the YMCA, but his doctor had advised him to avoid more performances; he was already performing as many shows for children and veterans as possible. Dawson casually mentioned that he was a graduate of Mount Hermon, and Thurston bounded to his feet, shaking his hand. "The words, Mount Hermon, are always a password to my dressing any time, any where!" he announced. He credited the school with his success, and bragged that he read his Bible and said his prayers every day. "Not asking for things," he told Dawson, "but just saying thanks." He talked to his new friend up to the time of the performance.

In fact, Thurston had written checks to his alma mater and even returned there, several years earlier, to give an impromptu show for the students in West Hall. He spoke to them about his adventures and advised that there were two types of people in life, "wise guys" and "easy marks." Thurston's use of con man lingo was an odd touch, although he advised that the devil was proudest of the wise guys, and the Lord loved the marks, who were always thankful and enthusiastic.

DANTE PROVED to be Thurston's best investment. The Dante show played in smaller towns through the Midwest and East Coast, until both men realized that the best opportunities were overseas. In 1927 the show moved to Puerto Rico, and Howard, Jane, and Leotha attended the opening there. "You have reached the highest pinnacle of magic," Thurston proudly told his associate. "You may take the show to any part of the world. I am sure you will never have to look back." The Thurstons returned to New York and Dante proceeded to South America.

It was the last time they ever saw each other, though they compared business in regular correspondence. Thurston relished Dante's newsy letters and lived his foreign adventures vicariously. They reminded him of his own travels, and he often mused that he would like to join Dante on the road. In fact, since joining Kellar, Thurston had only left the country on that one occasion, for Dante's Puerto Rico premiere. "I have given up my whole life to magic," he told an interviewer.

I'm pretty well along, but I've been so busy with my job that I have never had time to see a single football game. I never saw but one baseball game and although I love music, I have never heard but one opera, and I have seen almost no dramatic shows. It isn't that I was endowed by nature with an unusual ability. It is just a matter of work.

GUS FASOLA, one of Thurston's oldest friends and supporters, had toured America for several years with happy and prosperous results. In 1928, Thurston kept him busy with ideas for his own show. Inspired by Houdini's illusion, Fasola developed an Appearing Elephant Illusion. Thurston tried, in vain, to purchase a baby elephant, realizing that Fasola's invention would provide wonderful publicity for his show. Fasola also researched an English illusion called the Million Dollar Mystery, which had been featured by Selbit. In consultation with Thurston's patent attorney, James Wobensmith, they drew up an American patent of the effect so that it could be produced for Thurston's show.

Fasola had longed to return to England and produce his own illusion show using Thurston's popular effects. By the time he reached London in 1928, he was horrified to see that variety entertainments had virtually disappeared. Motion pictures had replaced many music-hall shows, and magicians—especially the magicians with costly, heavy illusions—were out of work. His plans dashed, Fasola experienced a breakdown, too nervous to work and too unsure of the business to make any long-term plans. Thurston supported him with occasional checks. In exchange, he pleaded with Fasola to send him information on the latest European tricks, negotiate deals, or supply Thurston with small props for the show. In November, Fasola wrote to Thurston:

> I would have been dead now if it had not been for you. Only played a couple of weeks all the time I have been here, so I have practically been starving. Am playing a couple of weeks down in Wales. I am run down in health with the worry of not being able to book engagements. I have 3 weeks if I can keep going, but am so bad don't know if I can keep up. Dear pal, I am so bad and so ill. I am writing this letter in agony.

Thurston underestimated his condition, responding with cheery notes wishing him well and asking for his tricks. His continual requests only aggravated Fasola, whose responses suggested his helplessness.

Oh, if I had only stayed in my small towns in Texas, I could get a living there. But now I am absolutely finished, sick and weak with the worry. You have been a wonderful friend to me, but coming here with no show and no money and not a friend in the world, what could I do? I thought I would be able to get someone to finance me.

Dante had always been disparaging about Fasola—they had worked in opposition in Australia in 1911, when Fasola's manager copied one of Dante's posters. Thurston wrote to Dante that he was "letting Fasola have three or four of my big tricks; he hasn't decided which ones he wants to take." Dante warned Thurston not to trust him—that he would steal Thurston's illusions, use underhanded business practices, and suggest ideas that were impractical. In fact, Dante was mistaken. Fasola's letters demonstrated his loyalty and glowed with enthusiastic ideas and support. It's likely that Dante selfishly used his relationship with Thurston to undermine Fasola's influence. He encouraged Thurston to push Fasola aside, just as Thurston had done with Tampa.

In 1928, Dante was touring through South America, anticipating his next move. After exchanging letters with Thurston, he decided to move his show to Europe, first the Continent and then England. Thurston had advised him to try the Orient; he knew, from Fasola's letters, that business was poor in England. But Dante was insistent, and his decision sealed Fasola's fate. Thurston promptly wrote to Fasola, ordering his old friend not to make use of any of the Thurston illusions until Dante was finished and left the country. Fasola responded dutifully, with a short note:

Received your letter saying that Dante would be coming to England. So under the circumstances I will not perform or use any of your tricks and illusions. Of course, this is the only reason I came back to England, but as Dante is coming here will wait till he finishes his tour. Your sincere friend, Gus Fasola

It was probably a technicality. Fasola had already explained that he was financially strapped, unable to build the Thurston illusions or sell a show in

England. But at that time, he was depending on the support of friends, and
Thurston's betrayal left him feeling helpless. Even worse, it was apparent that
he had lost Thurston's favor, as Thurston had now turned his attention to Cyril
Yettmah, the British illusionist, in search of the latest novelties. "Suppose Yettmah is with you now," Fasola wrote, barely hiding his dejection. "Lucky fellow."

Thurston responded:

> Dear Gus, I am sorry things are so tough with you, but you must not get dis-
> couraged, but hop to, working and hustling anywhere at any price until you
> get on your feet, which you are bound to do if you don't get discouraged. Yett-
> mah is here. I like him and we will probably get some good tricks.

On January 12, 1929, Fasola went into his cheap London rooms, took out his
tool kit, and cut off a long length of strong music wire—the same strong high-
carbon wire Thurston depended on for the Levitation of Princess Karnac. "The
Great and Only Gustave Fasola, The Famous Indian Fakir" hanged himself,
leaving a wife and son.

P. T. Selbit notified Thurston of the tragedy.

> He had been worried with the idea that he could never work again, having lost
> his nerve. The poor chap was undoubtedly crazy, and it was almost inevitable
> that he was to go that way. It will comfort you to know that even to the last
> Fasola acclaimed you as his benefactor, and I think without your help the end
> might have been sooner reached.

Thurston's occasional checks and cheery letters may have been those of a
"benefactor," but his carelessly shifting loyalties had only intensified Fasola's
misery.

THURSTON SPENT many precious months in 1929 working on a new play, *The
Demon*. He wrote the script, a mystery thriller, intending it for Broadway. This
mixture of magic and mystery had become a fashion in recent Broadway

shows; the most successful was Fulton Oursler and Lowell Brentano's *The Spider*, about a murder that occurs in the middle of a magic act. Thurston calculated that he could fill a mystery with visual marvels. Unfortunately, his script was also packed with clichés—starting with the dark, haunted house, the guests summoned to solve a crime, the frustrated detectives, and the mysterious Eastern mystic who seems to know all the secrets.

The Demon did offer some genuine thrills. Thurston used a new system of invisible ultraviolet paint, developed by Alexander Strobl, in conjunction with ultraviolet lamps. In sudden darkness, monstrous glowing green eyes appeared hovering over the stage and a luminous ghost glided down the aisle, floating over the stage. *The Demon* occupied Thurston's time and resources. He invested $10,000 in the project (the entire budget was just over $20,000) and many of his technical assistants worked backstage, including George White. When the production ran over budget, Howard inevitably wired Harry for emergency funds. Harry responded with $2,000, but grudging best wishes for the show. "I guess that you will have to go through with the venture."

It ran for one week at Poli's Theater in Washington, D.C., in October 1929, then moved to New Rochelle, New York. But it was abandoned before its announced Broadway opening on November 4. The plot was confusing, mixing psychology and mysticism in a strange stew, which simply confused the thin mystery story. Thurston's glowing ghosts weren't enough to save it. "As a play, it is no great shakes (excepting what shaking the audience may do)," according to the *Washington Press*. "The various mechanical props operate efficiently." But the fate of *The Demon* also coincided with the fate of Wall Street—the stock market crashed during its run in Washington, D.C.

Harry offered the inevitable comeuppance, writing to his older brother that *The Demon* did him no good. "You've done enough. Concentrate on being a magician. Be a magician, and that only."

HOWARD CAME to rely on Harry's money as well as his connections. In the spring of 1930, when he came through Chicago, Howard sent a telegram to his brother.

Theatrical papers filled with accounts shaking down actors. Please arrange be in Chicago my arrival. I am sure you can get proper protection from your friends in the form of letters.

Harry placated him. "That's all bunk. You'll be as safe as if you were at home." But Howard needed his own tough tactics with Tampa the magician. After Dante protested about Tampa's competition and Thurston shut him down in vaudeville, Tampa arranged a partnership with a tent show in West Virginia, so that he could make use of the Thurston illusions. The show ran for just a few weeks in 1930 before there were threats of it closing, and the musicians attached a judgment on the props. Thurston was frustrated by Tampa's contractual difficulties and wanted him to return the illusions. When Tampa was unable to accommodate him, Howard summoned Harry to finish the job.

When Harry arrived in Moundsville, West Virginia, where the props were stored, Tampa assumed that he had been sent an ally. Instead Harry became the enemy and accomplished his job the only way he knew how, with Chicago-style threats. He sided with the musicians, ignored Tampa's suggestions, and held to two simple demands: he wanted the Thurston contract torn up, and the props loaded into the truck.

When Harry was finished, he sent his brother a list of his expenses that expressed his exasperation as well as his techniques.

$10 to Mr. Rat Tampa to go home after we had finished at Moundsville, to keep him from telling the hotel owner that Howard had robbed him of his show and all his money, and left him in the town broke. $200 for railroad fare to bring [your props] to Beechhurst to keep the Rat from breaking up your furniture.

JANE HAD ALWAYS BEEN a tomboy; as a little girl she had relished opportunities to climb trees, engage in swimming races, and impulsively run away from home on impromptu adventures. Her years with the Thurston show—when she was in her late teens—precisely corresponded to her most rebellious time.

Adding to the problems, as the pretty costar of a touring show, she found handsome young men waiting to meet her at the stage door. Herman Hanson and George White were given the task of not only assisting with Jane's act on-stage, but also rebuffing the young suitors and acting as chaperones offstage.

In January 1930, Jane met Harry Harris. She was nineteen and he was twenty-four. His late father, John Harris, had been a wealthy theater owner and state senator: an old friend from Thurston's carnival days, Harris had loaned Thurston a dress suit when the Great Country Circus took the stage.

Harry Harris followed the show from city to city, and Jane and Harry quickly fell in love, scheming to be married. When Harry casually asked Leotha if she'd like to have him for a son-in-law, Mrs. Thurston was clearly surprised and discouraged them. On January 18, a matinee day in Pittsburgh, the couple escaped between performances and were married under assumed names. Of course, they had to announce what they'd done; that was the purpose of get-ting married. Howard and Leotha were devastated. They arranged another marriage, a legal one, on February 22 in Newport, Kentucky. And then the couple endured a third marriage on March 1, a proper Catholic marriage in Cincinnati, to satisfy his family.

But three weddings didn't prove lucky. Jane had seen him as a wealthy, carefree playboy. Years later, Jane admitted "blundering into a marriage with this footloose and fancy free scion of society." Howard made him an assistant stage manager to try to keep Jane on the show. But Harry was too irresponsible and careless to take on the job. He borrowed money from the Thurstons and had Jane sell her car to finance his lifestyle. He was also an alcoholic, prone to explosive accusations and bursts of violence. Jane endured black eyes and miss-ing teeth. Just months after the couple were married, Howard Thurston and Harry Harris argued, and the young man shoved the magician, fracturing a rib. On another occasion, Harris pulled a blackjack, threatening his new father-in-law. Thurston decided to carry a tear gas pen for protection.

Jane and Harry left the show to return to his family in Pennsylvania, and their relationship meant that Jane bounced back and forth between the tour and Harry, complicating life for everyone working in Thurston's show. The couple's problems resulted in headlines in March 1931, when the show played

Detroit. Thurston heard a commotion in the couple's hotel room and pushed the door open to find Harris drunk, ripping away Jane's clothing and kicking her. Thurston shoved him down, Harris bounded to his feet to swing at Thurston, and the magician removed a tear gas pen from his pocket, spraying it in Harris's face. He then calmly summoned the police and followed up by filing a lawsuit.

Days later, Jane sent a letter to Harris's brother, John:

> There are two sides to every story, and I am compelled to tell you a few things you don't know. I've been beaten up for the last time, cursed and insulted for the last time. This morning your brother spat in my face twice after he had come from sharing his bed with a prostitute. He said I had been intimate with my father, that my mother was queer for women, that I was a whore, and a million other horrible things. He has called my mother a nigger lover, and some names I can't write. My dad, too.

Harry Harris apologized sweetly and Jane relented. They both returned to Harris's family estate in Pennsylvania and cut off communications with Howard and Leotha, further tormenting them. "Now that you have gone back to each we advise that both of you do everything possible to promote a continuous happy married life," Thurston wrote to his daughter, attempting a reconciliatory tone and promising "our past attitude of non-interference with your marriage."

IN THE SUMMER OF 1930, just after Jane's marriage was announced and the season closed, Howard circled back through Chicago for another session with Dr. Schireson. His face-lifts now required regular maintenance. The paraffin was finally removed and his skin was peeled and smoothed. This operation seemed to be especially successful, and many friends remarked on how youthful he appeared. But not everyone was fooled; at a Society of American Magicians' dinner, he met Adelaide Herrmann, the grand dame of magic. Madame Herrmann was proud and matronly, with a shock of white hair. Thurston casually asked her if she was considering retirement, and Madame Herrmann took immediate offense. "My hair might be white, Mr. Thurston," she sneered, "but at least I've never stooped to having my face lifted!" Allan Shaw, Thurston's old associate from Australia, was especially blunt in a letter to his friend, Charles Carter: "Thurston has had what is left of his face upholstered once again."

Thurston used the face-lift to advocate for his latest health fad—insisting that his youthful energy and appearance was a benefit of a new diet. A printed card detailed a special mix of starches, sugars, vegetables, and fats in specific combinations. He gave away thousands of the cards, urging friends and acquaintances to follow the chart:

> To be able to lead you into the ways of health, youth and continued days is indeed a pleasure. . . . Starches and sugars require an alkaline solution in the stomach for proper digestion; Proteins and fruits require an acid solution. . . .

Thurston first encountered the diet at the Penn Athletic Club in Philadelphia, and there's no question that he believed in its benefits; he even prescribed it for his brother Harry and Harry's business partner, Rae Palmer. But the combination of face-lifts and diet cards was one of his most effective deceptions.

When he visited Chicago, Howard and Harry shared breakfast at Harry's State Street apartment. Their relationship had always been difficult. Harry had developed an annoying way of lecturing his older brother on business, enterprise, and loyalty. Howard understood that Harry's perspectives on show business, from his Chicago peep show and dime museum, were narrow, and his latest obsessions had been typically lascivious and small-minded. Most recently, he'd wanted Howard's lawyer to trademark the title "Miracle of Life" to promote a "pickled punk" show, the sideshow term for aborted human fetuses preserved in bottles of formaldehyde. Or Harry had tried to purchase a live manatee from Florida, surmising that the animal's humanlike breasts would fascinate audiences and allow him to bill the attraction as a genuine mermaid. But Howard had relied on his younger brother to bail out his business ventures, and he gradually ceded power to Harry, forced to listen to his schemes and naïve homilies.

That summer morning, Harry was surprisingly expansive and disconcertingly blunt. "Howard," Harry began, hitching his chair closer, "I think it's time for me to take out my own show. My own Thurston magic show." Harry sketched out a rough plan. He wouldn't rely on theaters, but would have a first-class tent and truck show, playing smaller Midwest cities. He'd present the best illusions from his brother's show—the same basic formula that Thurston had proposed for Dante and Tampa—and would bill it as "Thurston's Mysteries of India."

Howard took a deep breath. He tried to imagine Harry performing magic.

"It's like this, Howard," Harry continued. "I've been happy to support you. I've been happy to take care of your dirty work. I think that I was proven right with that Tampa." Harry lowered his voice. "Howard, I took care of that rat, because blood is thicker than water. I've worked hard for twenty years to erase any black marks upon my character—to stop the kootch shows, to avoid contact with any of those people." Howard started to cut off the conversation but Harry insisted.

"No, no. This time you've got to let me talk. You left me out of your book, and that hurt me. As a brother. As a friend. And this time, I'm asking you to include me."

Harry sketched out an ambitious plan for a sixteen-week tour under canvas, during the summer and fall months. He wanted the same consideration that Dante had received; they would split expenses and split profits. As he spoke, Howard watched his brother light a cigarette and noticed Harry's smooth, placid features in the sunlight. That's what the face-lift was for. Harry had been planning his own career as a magician.

"Now the only way to make this show work is to mention me in articles, to include me in publicity," Harry continued, the words spilling out. "Here's what you're gonna tell 'em. Years ago, when we toured India, I stayed behind, to study the profound mysteries of the Hindu. Right?" Howard furrowed his brow.

"It's crap, a' course, but this is what you tell 'em," Harry chuckled. "They'll eat it up. I learned the secrets of the mystic. Then I had a successful real estate operation in Chicago, because I always felt that one entertainer in the family was enough. That's why I never revealed my training as a mystic. And today, you consider me a peer of all mystics. You get it? You're boosting me, because I'm just as good as the Indian mystics."

The cigarette dangling from his lips and the thick Chicago drawl didn't enhance the effect. But Howard knew that he was trapped: business, enterprise, and loyalty. Harry may have learned the routine from Hinky Dinka Kenna, Al Capone, or any of his other Chicago associates, holding the financial reins so tightly that he couldn't be denied.

Howard conned himself into believing it could work: Mysteries of India could earn a little money, and Howard could secure some good, talented magicians to perform under his brother's banner. He nodded. "It's an interesting idea, Harry."

OF COURSE, it was a terrible idea. Harry spent lavishly on the tent, the orchestra car and trucks. He knew this part of the business inside and out, but his priorities were upside down. He had banners painted and electric lights and generators ordered. But he had no idea how to perform magic. Harry hired a troupe of assistants, including Chicago magicians Vic Torsberg and George Boston. Meanwhile, Howard located some dependable performers—Percy Abbott, an Australian magician and magic dealer, and Eugene Laurant, a well-known Lyceum performer—to step in and supervise the magic.

For Howard, the most interesting part of the deal was the elephant. Harry agreed to share the costs for a baby elephant. This would finally allow Howard Thurston to present the Appearing Elephant Illusion from Fasola. It was just the sort of sensational publicity he needed for the show. During the summer months, the elephant would be a special feature in Harry's tent show.

Harry and Rae bought a cute baby elephant named Grace for $2,500. Since Grace was now an unfortunate name, Harry called her Delhi. Through his carnival connections, Harry found an elephant trainer, John Robinson, who joined the Howard Thurston show.

THURSTON HAD JUGGLED various lawsuits through his career: the assistant who stole money; the audience member who was cut by one of Thurston's thrown cards and was awarded $500 in a court judgment. But the Korfmann Monkey Case was especially agonizing as it dragged through the New York courts. Thurston, Leotha, and George had given depositions that they neither recognized the monkey nor owned it, that it was the property of Dante's son, Alvin Jansen—this might have been technically true, as Alvin took possession of Mickey, and the monkey died when the Dante company was traveling in Europe. For some time, Thurston was confident that the nuisance suit would be rejected. But court papers suggest that his lawyers bungled the case hopelessly, failing to obtain the proper medical examinations, or testimony from Dante and Alvin. A psychiatrist ("alienist") testified that he believed that the boy's epilepsy had been "super-induced" by the monkey bite, but there was evidence that the boy had suffered from epilepsy before the incident.

The family originally sought as much as $125,000, but when it was finally settled at the end of 1930, Thurston was ordered to pay $20,000. The judgment couldn't have come at a more perilous time. Howard's investments were failing and the magic show was continually strapped for money, suffering along with the country's failed economy.

IN OCTOBER 1930, when little Delhi joined the show, she was too sick to be used on stage. Robinson nursed her backstage and Thurston had a special blanket ordered for her to keep her warm. "Don't worry about the elephant," Howard wrote to Harry and Rae. They were obviously concerned about their investment, but Thurston reminded them that they'd always made money from him. It was, after all, the Maid of Mystery, the peep-show device from their amusement business, that had netted Harry between $40,000 and $50,000 of profit over the years. "If it weren't for me, you wouldn't have the Maid."

But despite these reassurances, the elephant died just days later. The trainer

Robinson wrote, "Harry, I am writing you to let you know that your brother was in no way responsible for Delhi's death. He had just given her medicine. I loved the little thing and she loved me."

But Delhi's fate seemed to trigger Harry's wrath. To him, the incident represented Howard's carelessness and his lack of support. Robinson gave several accounts of Delhi's last days, inspiring a rambling letter from Harry that boiled over with frustration:

Howard, you put the elephant on the street without any boots, you ordered the heat in the theater turned off at night, you allowed the dirty rat John to leave the theater and sleep with a broad all night and return at 7:00 a.m. when Delhi was dying. This is John's own story substantiated by your own crew. You wanted to give my elephant to Jane. From that moment on we knew she was doomed to die.

Harry noticed that Howard had reneged on their agreement and had never mentioned Harry in publicity.

I do not want to be an actor, but I do want to commercialize on the name of Thurston and I know that I can do things that I did on the fairground and do them right. You, or no living soul, is going to stop me from getting out of the terrible, disgraceful life of a kootch show owner. I have put in years on how to speak the English language and with the help of my friends I believe I will be able to master gestures enough to satisfy the public.

Harry ended with a long accounting of the money owed him—for taking care of Tampa and driving him out of the business, for buying the elephant, for investing in his projects. But he was sure that Bernard Hyman, Thurston's lawyer who had heavily invested him in failed real estate deals, would be ready to step in.

When you reach Chicago, the Jew will make it his business to meet you there and clip you for the amount of money you have available. The whole

United States knows that this Jew is trimming you for every dollar you make. The $1500 you sent him from Cincinnati you could have given to me. Your Brother, Harry

Of course, the elephant's death had devastated Howard. He had planned on this feature for the new tour and couldn't afford the loss. Harry's wrath knocked his older brother back on his heels.

For years, Harry had reminded Howard of all of his worst qualities—his embarrassing background, his criminal associations, and the dirty show business that he had left behind. Howard had these elements erased from his life. But Harry, the portrait of Dorian Gray, represented all of the worst secrets hidden away at that State Street address in Chicago.

Howard was increasingly horrified by the thought that the portrait was about to climb out of the dime museum and take center stage.

Billboard announced:

What is without a doubt the biggest magic news to break in many years is the announcement just made by Howard Thurston, world's best known magician, that he, in association with his brother Harry, will shortly launch a new magical enterprise, Mysteries of India, under an elaborately equipped waterproof tent theater. . . . Harry Thurston is well versed in the art of magic. Many years ago Harry Thurston managed Howard Thurston's show, when the latter made a tour of the world. Harry Thurston decided to remain in India and make a detailed study of the mysteries presented by the magic men of that country. During the last 20 years, while engaged in business in Chicago, he has never failed to make a trip to India biennially to learn the new stunts practiced by the magic men there. Howard Thurston stated that his brother knows as much about the mysteries of India as any man living.

Howard was exasperated with each line of the ridiculous ballyhoo, but was now trapped into the partnership. Mysteries of India became one of the most infamous productions in the history of entertainment.

———

DELHI'S FATE SEEMED to represent the hopelessness of the times, the mounting disappointments and business failures—Fasola's death, Harry Thurston's inevitable show, the Monkey Case ruling, and, of course, Jane's marriage, which had managed to alienate her from her parents. Thurston was typically stoic about it all. He would have retired, if he could have—if the breathing device, the gold mine, or the real estate investments had ever paid off. Leotha took to her bed in a dark personal depression. It was as if her enchanted world of magic had collapsed around her.

TWENTY-TWO

"SEEING THROUGH A WOMAN"

yril Yettmah was a stone-faced English magician of the old school, stiff and proper. But he had an encyclopedic knowledge of magic and a knack for new ideas. He suggested an astonishing illusion to Thurston, which was first introduced in the 1929 season. Thurston called it "Iasia, The Unattainable Attained, the Impossible Realized."

A tall, rectangular skeleton cabinet was pulled onstage. It was a little larger than a phone booth, with a vague Oriental motif and a roof festooned with silk tassels. A rope was lowered from the ceiling of the auditorium and attached to the top of the cabinet. One of Thurston's assistants, dressed as an Indian princess in a silk robe and veil, stepped inside. Two more assistants, standing onstage, tightened the ropes, which squeaked through a large metal pulley. The cabinet and princess were slowly lifted, swinging off of the stage, until they dangled several feet over the orchestra pit.

The band quieted, and the flute continued with an Indian melody.

"You see before you Princess Iasia, keeper of the secrets. Salaam Iasia!"

The lady reached to a small cord within the cabinet. Pulling on it, she raised a curtained canopy, from the bottom to the top, which concealed her from view.

"Swing forth the ancient Hindu prayer cage!"

The band transitioned into a clanging Oriental march. Now the lady reached through slits in the curtain. She held bunches of lucky Thurston throw-out cards, the same cards, emblazoned with his portrait, that he scaled from the stage at the start of the show. Handfuls of these rained down onto the crowd as the cage was slowly raised, higher and higher. The children below squealed and grabbed for the cards. Thurston slowly followed the motion of the cabinet, walking out onto the runway over the orchestra pit as the audience craned their necks to watch the cage slowly ascend. It stopped at the top edge of the proscenium, brightly illuminated in the spotlights. The kettledrum rumbled and the music reached a crescendo.

"Iasia, are you there?" The lady waved her hand from a slit in the curtain. "Garawallah! Begone! Iasia! Iasia!" Thurston raised his pistol, firing directly at the cabinet. As the shot rang out, the curtains suddenly dropped, showing the cabinet empty. At the same instant, the bottom of the cabinet hinged open, falling away like a trapdoor. Instinctively the spectators sitting under it ducked, then looked upward as the skeleton cage twisted and turned in the light, throwing angular shadows on the walls of the theater. The princess was gone.

"Those above can look down upon the top of the cage, those that are below may look up through the floor. She is gone. Just . . . gone!"

The trick was almost too good. Walter Gibson recalled how the first performances of Iasia, in 1929, ended with an uncomfortable pause. The illusion was so spellbinding, and the audience so bewildered by the empty cabinet, that Thurston's final pronouncement generated only a stunned silence, then a smattering of applause. One night, Thurston hit upon the solution. After a long pause, he repeated, "She is gone," and then added, "And night after night, I stand here gazing at that empty cabinet, wondering myself . . . where . . . she . . . could . . . possibly . . . be!"

The notion of grand Mr. Thurston contemplating one of his own illusions, fooling himself, was pure bathos. The audience quickly laughed, and then, brought back to their senses, offered a resounding ovation.

The ingenious secret was partly Yettmah's work and partly Thurston's. The lady was concealed in the top of the cabinet, lying in the roof. Thurston suggested positioning her on her stomach and concealing her bent legs in the decorative Oriental cornices, which made Yettmah's cabinet even smaller and more deceptive. A folding ladder concealed inside allowed her to climb up to the top of the cabinet. When the Iasia cage reached the top of the auditorium, this hiding space was naturally concealed, as almost everyone was gazing up at the apparatus.

The illusion was performed near the end of the show, and remained against the ceiling until everyone in the auditorium had left. Only then was it lowered to the stage and the assistant released. The Princess was billed as Christine Townsend. But the tight little enclosure was unbearable, and the top of the theater was invariably hot and stuffy. Neither Christine nor any of the other girls was willing to perform it. It was George Townsend, Christine's husband and the stage manager of the show, who donned the wig, silk robe, and veil each night to become "Princess Iasia, the keeper of secrets."

THURSTON'S MYSTERIES OF INDIA—the smaller type explained that it starred Harry Thurston—opened on May 18, 1931, in Harvey, Illinois. The show was a strange hybrid of a circus and magic show, with a beautiful new waterproof tent and a neat four-piece band. The tent was tested the first night, when rain drowned out most of the music and the opening dances. Eugene Laurant performed a short magic act and then introduced the star of the show, Harry Thurston.

Harry sauntered on stage in an elegant tuxedo. Many in the audience did a double take. He looked a great deal like his brother Howard, though fatter and sloppier. A long cigarette dangled from his lips.

"It's great to see you all turn out tonight," he snarled across the footlights. His voice, a deep nasal drone, sounded like a comic parody of the famous magician. "I mean, considering all the rain. That's why we've got a waterproof tent, right? Well, I guess Roosevelt can't take care of that sort of stuff. Rain. He ain't got a government agency for that, does he? Anybody know? Geez, too bad for us." Harry's opening monologue soon became notorious with the company, a freewheeling improvisation by one of the stupidest men anyone had ever met. He would indulgently wheeze about the Depression, or a carnival he remembered working, his friends in Chicago, or a local "celebrity" in the audience, like the sheriff. "His ignorance was blatantly displayed so much that his splendid introduction was completely a lost cause," recalled Percy Abbott, one of the magicians who had been hired to carry him through the performance.

When he started performing magic, Harry was even worse. According to Abbott, "It was utterly impossible for Harry to memorize as much as three words of patter." The assistants, standing nearby, were expected to cue his next lines. Harry signaled that he needed help by growling "Crack!"—carnival slang for "talk." Harry never learned his patter. Night after night, he had every line and gesture fed to him. George Boston, an assistant on the show, recalled the ridiculous procedure, which seemed a sad parody of his brother's famous levitation.

"Crack," Harry would snarl.

"When I was in India . . ." Boston would start, under his breath.

Harry picked up the cue: "When I was in India, I went out to the wheat fields. Crack."

"There I saw a peculiar sight," Boston mumbled under his breath.

"There I saw a peculiar sight. I saw a priest place a young girl on the points of two swords. Then . . . Crack."

"Then he would cause her to float . . ."

Harry repeated the words, with more and more frustration: "Then he would cause her to float. Crack! Crack, goddamn it. Crack!"

When they finally got to the levitation, pretty, blond Rae Palmer was levitated using a much simpler mechanism to duplicate Howard's famous trick. In the show, Rae was introduced as Rae Thurston, and everyone on the show assumed she was Harry's wife—although his actual wife, Belle, was still living in Miami.

Rae and Harry invariably started an argument as she floated in the air. As he passed the hoop over her, he would mumble to Boston, "George, don't ever marry a woman, they're all dumb." This elicited a remark from the floating princess. "Harry, you son of a bitch, stop your complaining and get on with the trick."

Harry responded in a whisper, "Shut up or I'll knock you off this thing." He turned grandly to the assistants in Indian makeup. "Pray, Abdul! Pray as you prayed in the temples of Love in Allahabad! Pray, I command you!" And then, under his breath, he'd snarl, "Pray, or I'll break your goddamned neck."

Percy Abbott never forgave Harry Thurston for destroying such beautiful illusions. During the last phase of the famous Thurston levitation, the lady beneath the cloth was replaced with a special metal form that could be levitated using fine threads. Harry Thurston was unable to locate the threads with his fingers, and his solution was to feel over the surface of the form to locate them. Abbott chastised him after the shows. "To the audience, that's a lady under the cloth. You can't run your hands over her body that way!" Harry blinked, uncomprehendingly. To him, it wasn't a girl, but just a metal form. Abbott later wrote, "There is a romance and glamour that must be prevalent in the mind of the performer, in order that it can be conveyed to the audience. Harry Thurston had none of this."

Backstage, Harry was unpredictable and dictatorial, stingy and self-obsessed. During the tour, he seemed hypersensitive to any perceived slight from his brother. He complained to him in a letter: "You had to add more insult by sending on one of your stool pigeons to the *Billboard*. Not one word was mentioned about me, but they mentioned Jane, Lee [Leotha], and Rat Chase [Thurston's company manager and Leotha's nephew, George Chase]. Does this look like good will?" Harry recounted a list of necessary duties he'd been asked to perform—twisting the arms of Howard's business associates. "This letter is a very unpleasant duty." Howard responded:

> I have given you more than good will. In fact, you would have had no magic show if it were not for me. Under no circumstances will I ever lay myself liable for lawsuits or debts to your show. The thing you call good will does not include such liabilities.

The first season of Mysteries of India was just twenty-one days, and it rained for twenty of them. The staff was shocked when Harry reassembled the show the following year. In 1933, the tents were abandoned and the performances took place at the Sparks Theater chain in Florida. By then, Harry advertised the show with three portraits, Howard ("Famous Magician"), Harry ("White Yogi"), and William Thurston, their father, who was credited as a "Spiritualist Magi." The billing was ridiculous, as their father was neither a performer nor a mystic. It was a silly attempt at a new legacy, echoing the Herrmann, Kellar, and Thurston progression that represented a great tradition.

Assistants who traveled with Harry Thurston were convinced that he was smuggling liquor during Prohibition, in partnership with the Chicago or Cleveland mobs—the multiple trucks and the hiding places inside the magic cabinets would have made this an easy task. But it's clear that Harry thought of himself as a performer and was satisfied only standing in the spotlight. Even if Harry Thurston's Mysteries of India was not a crime, it remained an insult to the audiences and a humiliation to his brother.

WITH TICKET PRICES dropping and theaters eliminating live shows for motion pictures, Thurston watched his profits dwindling. It was a domino effect. "Although we have a good show, and do more business than most shows, still we have a hard time of it," he wrote to Dante, who was in Europe.

> Not only because of bad business conditions, but the fact that many theaters are closed and our railroad jumps have been very long with heavy expense of fares. We let five people go to get the show down to one baggage car.

The magician had borrowed on his life insurance policies and even considered filing for bankruptcy. Thurston was now desperate for money— attempting one last appeal for the Monkey Case, repay debts to Harry, and support his failing investments. "Be careful in any correspondence or cables about mentioning the Monkey Case," he warned Dante, "as Mrs. Thurston is so very ill that it would be dangerous to tell her."

When the show resumed that fall, Abe Lastfogel, of the William Morris Agency, provided an ingenious solution. Working at the Publix theaters, a chain of motion picture presentation houses in the New York area, Thurston performed a forty-five- or sixty-minute show in conjunction with a first-run feature. By the early '30s, the large theater chains were looking for live shows to offer, luring audiences to attend.

The venture gave Thurston a new opportunity, but the work was especially hard. Thurston started at eleven a.m. in the theater and occupied all his time onstage, or resetting props and resting in his dressing room backstage. He finished each night around midnight, after performing four or five shows a day. It was grueling work for a man over sixty. "At last they have me in jail," he grumbled to his attorney.

The situation was made even tougher by Thurston's stubborn insistence on including all of the features of his show. The program included Thurston's card routine, the Levitation of Princess Karnac, Sawing a Woman in Half, Iasia, the Vanishing Automobile, and the Water Fountains. He also included two new illusions, Out of a Hat, in which dozens of parasols and several ladies were produced from oversized top hats, and Seeing Through a Woman, in which a lady was apparently sliced into three pieces, and her torso disappeared. "Picture house magicians have to frame a show in a flashy and spectacular nature," he told *Billboard*. "The usual smaller tricks will not be effective." For this collection of wonders, Thurston's crew was required to cut trapdoors, suspend boxes over the auditorium, hang scenery and special equipment in the grid. "We have the satisfaction of playing to the biggest business they ever had, though it does not increase our salaries."

The new Publix theaters were often enormous, seating as many as three or four thousand people. When Thurston presented his full show in theaters, tickets could be a dollar or more, but in movie theaters in some cities, tickets might be offered to children for ten or fifteen cents. For Thurston it was an entirely new audience, and they responded enthusiastically. John Mulholland went to see one of Thurston's shows in Brooklyn and was dumbfounded by the audience response. He wrote in *The Sphinx*, "Trick after trick was applauded in a way I have never seen in a movie house. This tour has proven that in a theater or in one of these tremendous amusement factories, he is still The Great Thurston." The tour of movie theaters took Thurston across America and to the West Coast—more than thirty years after he'd played Los Angeles and San Francisco.

Jane and Harry Harris settled into an apartment in Pittsburgh, but the marriage was doomed. In 1932, Jane returned to Beechhurst, reporting that she was afraid of Harry. Howard contacted an attorney and Jane filed for divorce.

Jane's parents suggested that she take a job as a singer with the Isham Jones Band. Jones was Thurston's friend, a popular bandleader who was a famously proper family man. He had also composed a number of hit songs, including "It Had to Be You." A job with Jones seemed to be a good compromise as Jane sorted out her divorce, which was finalized in the autumn of 1932. When Thurston's tour resumed around the same time, Jane was billed as a special attraction.

AN UNEXPECTED SURPRISE arrived from the J. Walter Thompson Agency in Chicago, who arranged a profitable contract for Thurston to appear on the NBC Radio Blue Network. For years the magician had made radio appearances to promote his show. His distinctive voice carried well on the radio, and his entertaining stories about his travels and adventures enhanced any interview. The radio shows, titled *Thurston the Magician*, were sponsored by Swift and Company, a meatpacking firm. Each episode was a dramatized adventure—some loosely based on events from Thurston's early career—in which he solved a crime or emerged as the hero of a situation. He introduced each story, often playing off of adolescent sidekicks, and incorporated a "do-it-yourself" magic trick into the show. Additional tricks, or packets of tricks in distinctive orange envelopes, could be ordered through the sponsor.

Each show was fifteen minutes and ran on Thursday and Friday evenings; the series premiered on November 3, 1932. When his tour resumed, he sometimes managed to dash to the local NBC studios for the broadcast, but when he was unable to accommodate the schedule, the producers used an actor for Thurston's lines. Leotha, now at home listening to each show, gave notes to her husband. In November 1932, after one episode, she sent a telegram with blunt suggestions:

Dearest,

Radio story last night weak. Not enough mystery. Another man in cast talks too much like yourself making story and characters hard to follow. You started off big, falling down now.

The radio shows rewarded the magician with an even larger audience. His life story had been serialized in *Collier's* magazine, and he worked on a talking film script, titled *Jimmy* or *Blind Baggage*, which was a lightly fictionalized version of his childhood adventures. Working with other writers, Thurston also developed scripts on supernatural or occult themes. One, titled *The Wolfman*, was written with playwright Fritz Blocki. It was an interesting pastiche of Egyptian myths and mysterious crimes, unrelated to the later Hollywood horror film of the same name. In each of Thurston's outlines, it's easy to identify the character that he would play. He was writing roles as well as stories. Unfortunately, none of these scripts were produced. He explained to *Billboard*:

Whenever I approached the picture people on an idea, they explained, politely but firmly, that personally I was a swell fellow . . . but they could do better tricks with their cameras than I could ever hope to do with magic.

On March 14, 1933, the Chicago Society of American Magicians hosted a special dinner in honor of Thurston, celebrating twenty-five years since his acquisition of the Kellar show. At the Nankin Restaurant, Werner Dornfield closed the evening with a special performance. The curtain opened on Guy Jarrett, Thurston's argumentative old assistant, standing on stage in makeup to look like Harry Kellar. Dornfield joined him on stage, now made up to look like a young Howard Thurston. The two men re-created the mythic moment in which Kellar placed the "mantle of magic" on the shoulders of his young protégé.

Dorny then proceeded with a long, funny burlesque of Thurston's famous card act, performing the maneuver faultlessly, but without a single card. Jarrett stepped back onstage, pulling the mantle off young Thurston's shoulders. "I've changed my mind," he announced. "This isn't for you." He reached under the cloak. "This is for you!" He magically produced a Swift ham, presenting it to Dornfield. Thurston, sitting at the head table, laughed loudly in approval.

THE LOCAL MAGICIANS assumed that Thurston was in Chicago to plan his latest radio shows. Actually, Leotha had suffered a serious breakdown, and in January she was confined to a room at the Parkway Hotel under a doctor's care—secretly treated for barbiturate addiction. Leotha was in Chicago for over a month, and Howard was with her for most of this time. On February 6, she composed a long, confused letter to Jane back at Beechhurst, indicating her state of mind, and then sent it special delivery:

They have taken everything from me. They have lied about me (that I can't help). Dad has broken me down. I wish I had taken my own way out long ago, I have only remained here to keep you. They won't lick me dear. I may pass on. I wish I could. I've tried to be a good mother but through hard work I've broken down. I never took medicine except through a Doctor's orders (and I needed it because my nerves are broken down from hard work.) I am slowly dying; the end cannot come too soon for me. If only I could get out of here. I'm in a terrible fix and God knows there's no use for it; they are killing me for no reason. Please destroy this and please for God's sake, yours and mine, don't tell Isham. Just please tear it up; it may be the last request I may ever make.

Just three days later, Thurston wrote to a friend that his wife "has had a doctor and nurse for the past week, and is feeling much better than she has in the past, and we are all delighted."

IN 1933, Fred Keating was performing his act at the prestigious Capitol Theater in New York. Keating had started his career as the magic-mad boy who ran away to join Thurston's show and arrived late for the pigeon trick. By the early 1930s, he had become a sophisticated actor, magician, and master of ceremonies, one of the few performers whose clever humor made the smooth transition from vaudeville to theaters and nightclubs. He invited Thurston, his old boss, to come and see his act.

Thurston drove into the city for the first show of the day and asked Keating not to introduce him from the stage, which, Keating later explained, "if you knew him as well as I did, was just his way of making sure that I did." In fact, Keating went one better, asking Thurston to join him onstage to assist with one of his card tricks.

Keating was honored by the presence of the World's Greatest Magician. At the same time he was aware that the dapper, proud little man had just suffered a host of humiliations signaling the end of his career and the passing of an era in entertainment. Keating felt nostalgic for magic; Thurston seated in his audience represented just how times had changed.

After the performance, Thurston couldn't resist admonishing him for his humor—Keating's modern style was to adopt a sophisticated, supercilious attitude toward the audience. "Humility," Thurston intoned with his famous ministerial baritone, waving a finger at his young protégé. He pointed toward the seats. "They are the ones who pay you."

Keating knew he was right. He was reminded of the ritual he had witnessed so many years before: Thurston standing just behind the curtain and whispering a quiet prayer to his audience: "Ladies and gentlemen, thank you for coming to my show tonight. I hope you enjoy it. Thank you. God bless you. God bless you. . . ."

"He meant it," Keating later wrote.

It is the fashion today among the young cynics who write with energy and blithe incompetence of magic and its past to sneer openly at tradition, dignity, and honest sentiment. But that is the only way to feel about audiences.

THURSTON WENT BACK on the road, working in smaller cities. When he played in Iowa in May 1933, he wrote to Abe Lastfogel, sheepishly admitting he had been wrong about his ticket prices. The Depression had devastated local families. "The manager in Davenport said the first afternoon two or three hundred families came but refused to pay the 25 cents [for each child's ticket], and went to another show. They simply haven't any money." Adding to the difficulties, Abe Lastfogel reported that Harry Thurston had been appearing in the South with his own magic show. Of course, the billing was unclear. Many managers thought they had booked Howard Thurston, and then were "complaining." He warned the magician that his brother was now jeopardizing the business.

Thurston was exhausted by the touring schedule, but exhilarated by the business, which often found the public lined up around the block. He was netting as much as $6,000 a week. He played through the South for the first time in his career, and fired off a list of suggestions to Lastfogel, relishing his role as the seasoned professional:

> The fact is, we should not have been booked with a picture. We are restricted to 35 minutes, which is not sufficient time for us to present an attractive show. Thurston with a one-hour show, properly lithographed, will do business anywhere. Children do not read newspaper ads but read lithographic pictures in windows and billboards, and the kids will bring their parents.

Thurston complained about the circuitous routes. "I cannot understand why it is necessary to travel half way across the country to play four towns which I have only played once or twice." He suggested working at Radio City Music Hall for two weeks at $6,000 per week. Abe Lastfogel contacted Roxy Rothafel, the manager of the Music Hall, but Thurston's show required so much work done to the stage—special trapdoors—that Roxy refused to accommodate him in his new theater.

After a swing through the South and Midwest, the show returned to the Valencia Theater in Jamaica, Long Island, just a few miles from Thurston's home. Leotha had been in good spirits, and even arrived at the theater on the first day, Saturday, with some new costumes for the cast.

The following morning, Sunday, April 8, 1934, Thurston was at home with his wife before going to the theater. When Herman Hanson, the stage manager, announced "Fifteen minutes" for the matinee that afternoon, he noticed that Thurston was not in his dressing room. He spotted the magician walking down the aisle toward the stage, as if in a trance. He'd obviously just come from the phone in the theater manager's office.

Hanson had the overture replayed so that Thurston had time to change backstage. The show began and Thurston went through the motions mechanically. It was obvious that something was wrong. At one point, during an illusion called Piercing a Woman, Thurston was required to push a long spike through Lillian Hanson. His line was, "There will be no pain, but there is danger." As he stepped toward Herman and Lillian, he added, quietly, "Herman, there is more danger than we know." Thurston left just after the performance, and Hanson was pressed into service to perform the evening show with Jane. Leotha was dead.

"Someone once said, 'The show must go on,'" Jane later wrote, describing that night, "and it did. But I felt hatred for the audience and I didn't care if they were due their money's worth."

TWENTY-THREE

"FINALE: THE TRIPLE MYSTERY"

 eotha had been taking Medinal tablets, a coarse barbiturate, to help her sleep. When Thurston left for the theater that afternoon, he noticed a prescription bottle half filled with tablets. When he was called back home that evening, the only bottle that could be located was empty. An autopsy determined that she died of Medinal poisoning.

"Her capacity for withstanding tremendous doses of sedative drugs was attested by a local physician and also a consultant from New York who had treated her on previous occasions," the medical examiner later reported. A friend and her maid were with her that afternoon, when she went into the bathroom and took an unknown number of tablets, dissolved in water. She became maniacal, then fell into a deep coma and died at six that evening.

The examiner noted, "There were no circumstances which suggested any homicidal action. However, suicidal or accidental is undetermined. The Physician, the husband and people in the employ of the deceased had never known of any suicidal attempt," although this last statement was probably not true. During her illness, Leotha had made several distraught threats, including her letter to Jane. Some members of Thurston's company, familiar with her breakdowns, believed that she'd committed suicide. Her drug use was concealed from reporters, and newspapers explained that she died of a sudden heart attack.

Jane left the show and Hanson took over for Howard Thurston at the Valencia Theater. At the Wednesday matinee, unknown to anyone in the company, Thurston walked up to the box office, purchased a ticket, and sat in the auditorium, watching his own show. After the curtain fell, Hanson and Carl Chase, the company manager, were standing on stage by themselves when Thurston surprised them. "Herman, I knew I could trust you," he said quietly. "You might as well finish the week."

There was something about the Great Thurston's presence on that stage that sent a chill down Hanson's spine. He was in a rumpled tweed coat and fedora: smaller, inconspicuous, and sad. His glowing face that had presided over so many marvels was sallow and ordinary. His straight back was hunched, his square shoulders arched. After years of proudly overcoming the impossible, he'd been beaten.

"HOWARD, I am very much interested as to your future," Harry wrote. "I know there is an aching void which cannot be replaced since God took Lee from you, and I hope that time will heal all wounds."

Howard and Jane found solace in the show, and busied themselves with the performances, but Thurston worried that he would not be able to continue for very long. He was disappointed to find that Carl Chase, Leotha's nephew and the show's company manager, had given himself a salary increase from $45 a week to $100 a week, with the excuse that the raise had been approved by "Aunt Nina" just before she died. Thurston fired Chase, left the Beechhurst house, and he and Jane moved into Leotha's apartment building in Weehawken. He sold his property in Connecticut, where he'd planned on building a retirement home with Leotha.

Howard and Jane should have drawn closer, but Leotha's death damaged their relationship. When she was a little girl, Jane had once run away from home. When she returned, she was shocked to receive a hard slap from her father. "Don't ever do that to your mother again," he growled. Now she wondered if her protracted, failed marriage meant she had failed her mother.

"Mrs. Thurston's death has upset me and I don't know what I intend to do for the present," Howard wrote to Dante, then in Singapore. "One thing is sure, I would like to be with you and I am thinking quite seriously of doing so."

THURSTON INTRODUCED an illusion that had been invented by Edward Morrell Massey, a magician and mystery writer. It was a large round drum, about four feet in diameter. A lady reclined horizontally within the drum; her head was visible on one side of the circumference and her feet on the other. Her body could be seen within the round center of the drum.

Using blades, Thurston apparently sliced through the lady's neck, then slid her head so that it was at the top of the drum. He repeated the action with the lady's feet, pushing them down to the bottom. The result was a person apparently cut into three pieces.

Massey called it Head Over Heels, and Thurston renamed it Vivisection, hoping that it would replace some of his other torture illusions. The apparatus involved several complicated mechanisms and had to be built from metal to accommodate the curved drum shape. Herman Hanson started constructing it as the show was on tour, slowly solving each problem as they moved from city to city. It was finally ready late in 1934. The finished illusion, the last one introduced into the Thurston show, was startling, but it offered none of the situational comedy that had made the Sawing in Half so successful.

WHEN THURSTON PLAYED at the Publix Theater in Detroit, Howard was interviewed on WWJ Radio by Rex White. Thurston discussed his hundreds of appearances at orphanages and hospitals, perhaps three or four visits in a large city like Detroit, the public's interest in magic, and the persistence of the supernatural. "Why do people believe in such things?" White was asked. Thurston answered,

Why do they still buy stock in empty gold mines and dry oil wells? It's just human nature. The public likes to be fooled.

It was a curious analogy, especially since Thurston's dry wells and expensive gold mines had occupied much of his attention. When he was asked about performing in movie theaters, he was equally honest.

It's a business proposition, for one thing. But what really won me over is the fact that the big movie houses allow me to show to more people in a day than the average theater does in a week. After all, I haven't so many years left and I feel—without any vanity—that I sort of belong to the public, after 40 years of stage life, and more. Buy appearing in these vast houses, I can widen that public immensely.

His old-fashioned formula had been to return to the same cities, year after year, and capitalize on advertising to generations of fans. But Lastfogel's plan was different. Thurston found the new theaters and cities intriguing and hopeful—even the smaller theaters. He discovered new audiences who had been longing to see his magic.

JUST WEEKS LATER, during the 1934 tour, Thurston opened a package that had been addressed to him with childish script. Inside was a broken doll with a note.

Dear Mr. Thurston, will you please put arms on my baby doll? I would like to see you saw the woman in two. Are you coming to our Weirton show? If you put magic arms on my baby will they stay? With love to you, Virginia L. Thomas

It reminded him of when he knew a little girl named Jane, who depended upon him for similar miracles. That's when he'd felt like a real magician. He told his secretary to run to the toy store, picked up a sheet of paper, and wrote a quick response.

Virginia, I have your doll baby, and I have had Hokus Pokus change your doll so that you will hardly know it.

ACCORDING TO Thomas Chew Worthington, Thurston's lifelong friend, the magician had suffered a minor heart attack during that tour. When Worthington found him backstage at the Century Theater in Baltimore, Thurston was lying on a couch in his dressing room. The magician took his hand and told him, "Tom, you are the only one in this world who really cares for me, and the only one who will care a damn when I am gone."

Months later, before his sixty-fifth birthday, Thurston arranged to see Dr. Harry Benjamin of New York City for a full health evaluation and a treatment of injections. Dr. Benjamin advised him on diet, sleep, and exercise. He told Thurston to limit his drinking to beer, avoid drugs, and smoke no more than six or seven "nicotine free" cigars daily. He also felt that the magician should gain eight to ten pounds.

Thurston boasted to *Modern Living* magazine that he would devote a year to rejuvenating his health, as an experiment, and he praised the diet cards. "Next year at this time, I will look and feel twenty years younger."

Still, he complained when his age became a matter of discussion. "People are beginning to think I am older than you," he wrote to his advance man, John Northern Hilliard, accusing him of an indiscretion.

> One newspaperman said I was 70 years old. It is not good psychology for an old pap to be prancing around the stage as if he was 30 years old, and I do not look a day over 35. I advise you do not mention my age or number of years I have played in theaters.

Hilliard wrote back, incredulous. "I am not aware that I have been telling any newspaperman your age. In fact, I don't know your age. Should they ask me, however, I will tell them that you are 35, per instructions." In fact, Hilliard was three years younger than Thurston.

On March 14, 1935, Hilliard finished his day in Indianapolis, preparing for Thurston's appearances in that city. He'd left press releases with the local reporters, arranged stands of colored lithographs, and spoken to the theater manager about the chairs and tables that Thurston would require in his dressing room. Hilliard returned to his room at the Lockerbie Hotel and suffered a heart attack, dying in his bed.

Several days earlier, he had shared a dinner with a friend and magician in town, Doc Brumfield. Hilliard told him, "Doc, I think that the greatest tragedy in life would be to die, and suddenly wake up and realize that you had never lived." Brumfield nodded. "I have lived," Hilliard told him.

The company avoided telling Thurston the bad news until he had left the theater that night and was on the train for Indianapolis. He was devastated by the loss of his friend, whom he considered a brilliant writer and a talented magician. Hilliard's contributions to Thurston's career, often anonymous, were essential to how the public perceived the magician. His honest, poetic phrases and elegant tales enhanced Thurston's reputation and attracted audiences to see his magic.

AT THE CLOSE of the 1935 season, Thurston married Paula Mark. The ceremony took place at midnight on May 25 in Harrison, New York. The bride, newspapers reported, was twenty-seven years old. The groom was sixty-six. During the ceremony, which seems to have collected a handful of curious reporters, the justice of the peace left out the word "obey." He explained that he hadn't used it for so long that he forgot where it went in the sacrament. Thurston insisted that his wife still had to agree to "obey."

The reporters had a field day. First, there was Paula, a former assistant on the show, who explained that she had first met Thurston many years before when she was one of the little girls who volunteered to come onto the stage. He presented her with a rabbit.

Then there was the groom, the old master showman, who mused on the secret of youth:

I had been in India years before and had gained the confidence of the yogis. In exchange for the secret of my levitation trick, the priests had told me how, although toothless and bald, they were able to carry trunks and baggage like boys. Well, I got out my old notebook on the trip and started to put their secret into practice, and today I feel young again.

The whole affair could have benefited from John Northern Hilliard's good taste. Paula's grandmother later explained that the story about winning a rabbit in Thurston's show was pure publicity. Paula had met the magician when she auditioned to be an assistant with the show in the late '20s. She was Paula Hinckel, of North Adams, Massachusetts, one of a pair of twins who had been employed by Thurston. She used the stage name Paula Mark, and then married Kenneth Claude, Thurston's chauffeur. Kenneth and Paula were divorced in July 1934.

She had since become notorious, among the company, as a loose woman. Thurston's cast was suspicious when she returned to woo the boss. Jane was shocked that her father would consider a relationship with someone like Paula, especially after the death of her mother. To her, it was a sign of rejection—Jane protested to her father and hissed insults to Paula backstage.

Thurston lied to the press about Paula's age. She was not twenty-seven at the time of the marriage, but twenty-five—younger than Jane. It was an uncomfortable fact that no one wanted publicized.

After the ceremony the couple posed for photographs and then left for a Miami honeymoon.

THE 1935 SEASON started late, with an engagement in Clarksburg, West Virginia. It was exactly the sort of town Thurston had never played before, but these small cities offered enthusiastic audiences. This was followed by a four-day engagement at Charleston, West Virginia, at the Kearse Theater, opening Sunday, October 6.

Herman Hanson had a difficult time at the Kearse. It was the first non-union house they'd encountered, and this meant that their three union stage-hands and their orchestra leader couldn't work. The scenery and cases had to be handled by a smaller crew and local stagehands.

The backbreaking work started at six in the morning and everything was ready for the matinee. Thurston performed two shows and the theater was filled to capacity, grossing nearly $4,500. As Hanson walked by his dressing room, Thurston called out to him. "Hi, kid. You have had a tough day." Hanson admitted that he was bushed, but suggested that they go across the street for a sandwich and a glass of beer. Howard, Paula, and Jane Thurston joined Herman and Lillian Hanson.

Thurston stood and Herman helped him on with his coat. As he was placing his right arm in his sleeve, Thurston collapsed on the floor with a stroke. He was taken back to his hotel room, and the following morning a physician insisted that he be taken to the local hospital.

Thurston had a paralyzed left arm. The doctors advised that it would be some time before he could appear on stage again, but Howard's spirits were good. He joked to his new advance man, C. Foster Bell, that he would perform at the next town, even if he had to do it on crutches. Hanson and Jane finished the engagement in Charleston. Thurston was sure that Jane and Herman should be able to keep the show running and keep the company together. The theater managers from the next two cities came to Charleston and reviewed the show, approving Hanson's performance.

But suddenly, there was another opinion to be considered. Harry Thurston heard the news and dashed to Charleston before the end of the engagement. He watched the last show and hated what he saw. He immediately closed the tour, canceled future engagements, and arranged to have the equipment shipped back to New York. As a longtime investor in Howard's projects, Harry could not be ignored, and his strong-arm tactics could not be dismissed. He wrote to an agent he knew, explaining his plan:

I arranged with Howard that he and I would take out a 100 percent Thurston show, Howard to make his appearance at each performance to say a few words. We will then have a great Thurston show. I think he will be able to travel and we will be able to open in the early fall. He is improving, has his right mind, and I'm hoping he will be able to be wheeled around outside very soon.

Harry's notion of a "100 percent Thurston show" was ominous—although Jane was unaware that she was adopted, Harry knew, and obviously considered himself a more authentic partner for his brother.

Paula took Howard to recover at Briarcliff Manor, New York. With no real direction, the family and crew seemed to drift apart, forming allegiances and enemies in mysterious combinations. George White and Kenneth Claude traveled back to Beechhurst with the show and stayed with the equipment, ensuring it would all be ready when Mr. Thurston, or Jane, resumed the show. They realized that it would be necessary to watch over the apparatus and keep it in good condition. Herman Hanson stayed in New York City until he heard back from Thurston.

But Jane was prevented from seeing her father. Paula had no tolerance for her; Jane had made her feelings about their marriage clear. Harry also wanted her out of the picture, as Jane would be the logical performer to continue the show.

Howard was taken to Biloxi, Mississippi, with Harry and Rae to recover. There he managed to send a letter to Jane.

I know now that you were trying to keep the show going to help me. There were so many knockers all telling me different stories. You will be surprised to know that I actually believed many of my so-called-friends wanted me to die.

Thurston hinted that a copy of his will had been stolen and his life insurance policies had been examined. He assured Jane that he would soon be well enough to resume the show, but ended the note cryptically. "Address care of McMahon [his attorney]. He is the only one who knows my address. I have reasons for not wanting others to know."

Howard and Paula took an apartment in Miami near Harry and Rae. By now, Thurston had shaken off Harry's suggestions and was making plans to resume his own tour. He sent brief notes back to his cast and crew, assuring them that he was recovering steadily and inquiring about their availability for future dates. In December 1935, he wrote to George White, asking him to assemble checkbooks and contracts, as they would probably resume the tour in the South in March. Soon after this, the Associated Press announced that Thurston would soon be returning to the stage, with his first engagement in Charleston, West Virginia, where he had been forced to cancel shows.

Thurston contacted his old attorney, James Wobensmith, asking him to help drawing up a new will. Wobensmith suggested that Thurston compose a short note of what he wanted to include, so that the lawyer could turn it into a legal document, and in response Thurston produced a paper that chastised the people around him and made stipulations that his wife, Paula, would have to stop drinking. Wobensmith thought that it was ridiculous. "I told him that wasn't a will." He advised Thurston to find someone else to draw it up.

ON THE MORNING OF MARCH 30, Thurston suffered another stroke while he was sleeping. His condition improved, but it was then complicated by pneumonia. Howard Thurston died at the Casa Casuarina Apartments in Miami at 1:39 p.m. on April 13, 1936, with Paula at his side. He was sixty-six years old.

The body was sent to Columbus, Ohio, his hometown, for burial. Jane arrived with Ada Wolfe, Thurston's cousin, and found that "the family" had left instructions that she was forbidden to visit the mortuary. However, the mortuary director, E. E. Fisher, proved understanding. He phoned her when the family had left, and she arrived to pay her respects to her father.

The funeral was held the next day, on the eighteenth, and the Columbus paper remarked on the sparse attendance; barely one hundred people arrived at the Broad Street Methodist Church. Jane arrived with Ada Wolfe. Paula arrived with Thomas MacMahon, Thurston's attorney.

After the eulogy, S. W. Reilly, the president of the local Society of American Magicians club, read a short tribute. George White, Thurston's lifelong assistant, stepped forward and picked up Thurston's ivory-tipped wand, breaking it in half—the SAM ceremony was used to symbolize the end of a magician's career, and George performed the ritual for "The Governor." A group of local policemen, out of uniform, served as pallbearers as the casket was taken to a mausoleum at Green Lawn Cemetery.

OBITUARIES INVARIABLY dwelt on Thurston's status as the World's Greatest Magician, his ability to entertain children, his greatest illusions, like the Levitation, and the countless benefit shows at orphanages, crippled children's hospitals, and veterans' homes. But no one had perspective to recount the astonishing range of Thurston's career—from street peddler to carnival talker, itinerant showman, vaudeville star, film exhibitor, illusionist, and radio performer. He had managed to negotiate some of the tightest curves of show business, steering clear of fashions that had dashed many famous performers from the pinnacle of fame to a rocky failure. No one was able to calculate how much of this winding, bumpy path actually created the World's Greatest Magician.

Ed Sullivan, then a columnist for the New York *Daily News*, reported on Thurston's career:

> It was his boast that no theater ever lost money on him, and on infrequent occasions when it happened, Thurston would stay an extra day and work for nothing. Millions of children have seen the slight, scholarly-looking magician scale a card from the stage to the top tier of the balcony, or float a girl's body to the footlights and back again. Death exceeded Houdini, and now Thurston. The stage is poorer for their passing.

Author Fulton Oursler had been in the audience when Kellar introduced Thurston as his successor at Ford's Theater in Baltimore. Oursler wrote of Thurston's sincere friendship—as a fellow magician, a fellow Mason, and a man intrigued by the occult.

> I remember we talked long and deep about the mysteries of religion. He believed that men lived many lives, coming back to earth again and again as children return to school after a summer of play. I hope that he was right and that he is finding death only a vacation. The feeling that I have about Howard Thurston now is more convincing an argument for immortality than all of the

mumbo-jumbo of spirit mediums. I simply cannot believe that he and I will not meet again.

George White contributed a short tribute to *The Sphinx* magazine:

It might seem strange that as his assistant I always thought of him as my pal, but I am certain that the Governor would have been the first to acknowledge that association. I worked hard for the Governor but he was very generous and there was never a magazine article that he did not mention my name, and I tell you, I always appreciated it. For more than fifteen years the Governor had a habit of doing something that added to my love for him. No matter who he was talking to, if I came to him with a question, he would stop his conversation to answer me immediately. I am proud that the Governor felt that way about me.

Dante was traveling through Europe when he was told of Thurston's death. Unable to return for the funeral, he penned a long, effusive memorial to his friend and business partner. In it, he noted:

To me, the greatest mystery of Howard Thurston was that he could carry on as long and as successfully as he did, so tirelessly. He was a man who could accomplish more by silence and endurance than any other man with less control. A catastrophe, emergency or bad business venture, of which he experienced many, would result in only a smile. Had he confined himself and his investments to magic, I am certain he would have retired ten years earlier and perhaps lived ten years longer.

It's not surprising that Dante's assistants noticed their boss burst into tears upon hearing of Thurston's death. But Harry Blackstone also cried, silently, in his dressing room when he heard that his old nemesis was gone.

Blackstone didn't admit it, of course; he was famous for his offstage swagger. But as he heard the news, his brother Pete happened to walk past the room and was surprised to see him sobbing, facedown, on the dressing table. Blackstone had longed to be America's most popular magician, but was devastated to lose his competition. Thurston had challenged him as a gentleman, set the goals, established the market, and kept Blackstone's show as professional as it could possibly be.

HARRY THURSTON had been too uncomfortable to attend the funeral. Like many tough personalities, he was prone to fits of maudlin tears, and he worried that would have presented a spectacle, sitting and bawling in the pew at the Columbus church.

There's no record of Harry's reaction to his brother's death—no written tribute from Howard's oldest partner in show business. He must have realized that the focus would be shifting—the press would talk about Paula and Jane, and show business publications would speculate about the next great magic shows. Harry had been able to stand in his brother's shadow for several years, but after Howard's death, even those shadowy opportunities were finished.

But it's also possible that, had Harry Thurston attended the funeral, he would have found opportunities to guffaw. After Howard's death, every commentator believed the story that he had been trained for the ministry, and offered this as evidence of his smooth presentations and his sincere knowledge of human nature. No one but Harry could have believed that he had actually been schooled as a pickpocket and confidence man; this was even better evidence of his smooth presentations and his sincere knowledge of human nature.

In fact, once Howard Thurston had become successful and re-created himself, he managed to gain fame for qualities that were, debatably, some of his worst: an entrepreneur, businessman, family man, inventor, and investor. It was a scam that Harry would have appreciated, and one of the few parts of his brother's personality that he ever understood.

GEORGE MARQUIS was an itinerant magician, and a friend of both Howard and Harry Thurston. Shortly after Thurston's death, he happened to be in

Charleston, West Virginia, and snapped a picture of the remnants of the magician's twenty-four-sheet poster pasted on a tall fence. In the slang of the bill poster, Harry's old job, a stand was a wall of advertising; this fence in Charleston was literally Thurston's "last stand."

In his scrapbook, Marquis pasted a copy of the sad photograph, and then attached a typed poem that he'd composed. It was a traveling showman's ode to the World's Greatest Magician—part lingo, part poetry, without any high-flown folderol or philosophical exaggerations.

I'd rather dream and secretly scheme
Of a way to the top and dough
Than remember the lights of yesteryear's nights
When I was the hit of the show
In a great game, where name and fame
Will be mine probably never
I'd rather have plans, than be forgotten by fans
Living in the past forever

TWENTY-FOUR

"THE FLIGHT OF TIME"

 ust weeks after the magician's death, his estate made head-lines: "Thurston's Will, a Strange Document, Admitted to Probate Court." According to the document, Thurston had left $500 to his "adopted daughter, Jane Jacqueline Thur-ston," with this explanation:

> I am mindful of the fact that my adopted daughter has caused me great mental anguish and suffering and has caused me to spend large sums of money on her behalf through her whims and caprices.

Paula wasn't spared any embarrassment. The remainder of the estate was left to his widow, but she was required to agree to "discontinue a personal habit" of which he disapproved. Should she fail, the money would go to build-ing a mausoleum in Columbus, Ohio. Later articles explained that Paula's habit was drinking. Paula shrugged it off to reporters.

> He was not a prohibitionist. I never drank to excess and have no intention of ever doing so. The agreement which I signed willingly really didn't mean a thing. I'll be moderate in the use of liquor, just as I always have been.

Thomas MacMahon, Thurston's attorney, was quick to explain that Thurston had intended to change the will. It was drawn up, he claimed, when Thurston was angered that his wife left him to be with her sister during an operation. At the same time, he had been quarreling with his daughter over her desire for a movie career. Jane filed a suit to protest the will, insisting that her father "was not in proper mental condition" to draw up the will during the last months of his life. For reporters, she demonstrated her relationship with her father by playing a phonograph disc that Thurston had recorded a year earlier—he pledged his love for her and reminisced about her childhood.

But it was a single word in the will that had rattled Jane: "adopted." It was the first time she understood that she was not Thurston's daughter. At the time, she was living in Weehawken with her "Aunt Lady," Leotha's sister, Emma Van Blarcom. Emma explained that Jane had been born at that same apartment building, and that her last name was Willadsen.

A month after Thurston's death, Jane traveled to Los Angeles and met her father, John Willadsen, who was then living in retirement with his second wife.

THERE WAS the expected ridiculous publicity. The day after Thurston's death, Dunninger, a New York magician and mind reader, claimed that his friend had made a pact that he would return from the grave, and break a small Egyptian statue of Ramses that he had given Dunninger many years before. The article, "Awaits Sign from Thurston," ran in the New York *Sun*.

Not to be outdone, the following day Mrs. Houdini posed for a picture in the New York *Daily News*, holding a pair of locked handcuffs. The caption explained that she was still waiting for Houdini to return "in a life-after-death compact between her and her late husband-magician." Presumably, the ghosts of the magicians were still battling each other for publicity.

In the last few months of Thurston's life, Tampa had been sending letters to him, seeking a financial settlement on their failed contract. After Thurston's death Tampa filed a lawsuit against the estate, claiming damages for expenses, lost contracts, as well as "damage to his reputation as a magician." Newspapers reported that he was suing for $599,474. Most of this, of course, was based on Tampa's inflated sense of the opportunities he had been denied.

The suit was settled a year later for $1,000. Tampa could continue using the name, and also utilize the illusions he still had in his possession.

Another mind reader, Rajah Raiboid, produced a contract from March 1936, when Thurston was recovering in Miami Beach. Presumably he was arranging a partnership with Thurston for that fall. Thurston would supply the illusions and the title would read, "Thurston the Magician with Rajah Raiboid." Raiboid wrote to *Billboard*, claiming that he would be taking out the show with the billing, "Successor to The Great Howard Thurston." But the estate ignored his claim and, without any of Thurston's props, Raiboid had no show.

IN THE END, there was very little money. The Beechhurst property had been lost to foreclosure. The Florida land had been ruined in a hurricane. Most of the investments had already dissolved, but there was still stock left from the Canadian gold mines, just over $20,000 in "good assets." Thurston owed back taxes for the last three years of income, and taxes on the ruined Florida property. Paula received just over $8,000.

As the Thurston estate was settled, Jane discovered that she had been named the beneficiary of a small insurance policy, and that props and scenery of the Thurston show were now in her name. Working with George and Herman Hanson, she learned the intricate choreography of her father's famous Floating Ball and Spirit Cabinet routines, intending to sign a new act with producers Fanchon and Marco. But as the project dragged on, Jane became impatient. She was tired of the association with the illusion show, and embarrassed by the Thurston family squabbles.

PAULA THURSTON remarried in 1938. Around that time, a magician and an admirer of Thurston's, John Booth, met her at a nightclub. It was apparent to Booth, from her slurred speech, that she had continued to overindulge in drinking, despite her promises. She died in 1943.

———————

DURING HIS TOUR with Thurston, John Northern Hilliard had been carrying his memorial from city to city. He had gathered together many of the best tricks from hundreds of magicians, compiling them into a bulging manuscript for a projected book. Through the efforts of Thurston, and then editor Jean Hugard and publisher Carl Jones, it was published as *Greater Magic* in 1938, a book of more than a thousand pages and one of the most enlightened texts on the practice of magic.

DANTE HAD a long, successful career in magic. He returned to the United States in 1939, upon the outbreak of the Second World War, with his assistant, an elegant Australian showgirl named Moi-Yo Miller. His magical review, *Sim Sala Bim*, appeared on Broadway at the Morosco Theater in 1940, where critics praised the old-fashioned fun of his magic. Dante continued touring across America, also appearing in fairgrounds, on television, and occasionally in films. He retired to a ranch in the San Fernando Valley, outside of Los Angeles, and died there in 1955.

HARRY BLACKSTONE became one of America's favorite magicians. In 1933, he acquired the apparatus for the levitation that Harry Kellar had been building in Los Angeles, purchasing it from Kellar's heirs. In his show, he billed it as the Levitation of Princess Karnac, presenting it with the same grandeur as Kellar and Thurston. The Dancing Handkerchief and the Girl and the Rabbit—borrowed from Thurston—became trademarks in Blackstone's show. Harry Blackstone continued touring until 1955, and made occasional appearances on television. He died in Hollywood in 1965.

GEORGE WHITE did his best to guard the Thurston props in Long Island, and even obtained a job with the lumberyard near where they were stored. In 1941, when Dante returned to the United States, George joined the company.

Every night, Dante proudly introduced him on stage—as the great magician Howard Thurston's chief assistant. George traveled back to Los Angeles with Dante and assisted, off camera, during the filming of *A Haunting We Will Go*, a Laurel and Hardy feature that costarred Dante.

In the 1950s, George returned to New York and took a job as a porter at a Brooklyn glass company. He was a loyal, hardworking employee, and seldom spoke of his days in show business. He died in Brooklyn in 1962.

THE PROPERTIES of the Thurston show had seemed priceless in the hands of the famous magician. But just like illusions, the actual apparatus, in storage, had no special enchantment. They were big, heavy boxes and crates, bits of wood and steel in need of paint, repairs, and rehearsals. A wand is worthless without a magician, and the same analogy applied to Thurston's carloads of equipment.

Harry and Rae Thurston sold the Mysteries of India show to a young, charismatic performer named Will Rock, who used some of the illusions in his show. Jane, in turn, sold Rock some of her father's props. But in the late '30s, she neglected to pay the storage bill at the Beechhurst warehouse. A magician named Gerald Heaney purchased the contents of the warehouse for the back storage, paying a mere $380, and arranged with Jane to have it shipped to his barn, near Oshkosh, Wisconsin. The cases and boxes moldered for decades. The barn was finally emptied in the 1980s, when some of the illusions were destroyed and other mementos were sold to magic collectors.

HARRY THURSTON died in Miami, Florida, on May 6, 1941. After a brief tour of Mysteries of India in 1935, he never performed, but acquaintances felt that he'd always considered himself a magician, and talked proudly of his work on the stage. He was buried at the family plot in Columbus, Ohio.

JANE THURSTON worked for several years with Isham Jones as a performer and songwriter. Her songs were composed under the name Gene Willadsen:

Willadsen was used to deliberately put her years as Jane Thurston behind her; Gene was used because ASCAP, the songwriter's union, was restricted to men. One of her most successful songs was a hit from 1942 titled "My Best to You." Later Jane was employed by PanAm in Miami, working in operations. She also learned to fly. She married a flight engineer named Guy Lynn, and had two children. After Lynn's death she married Dick Shepard, a retired navy captain. Sometime in the 1960s, she proudly became Jane Thurston again, gradually contacting her old friends and fans in magic, visiting magic conventions, and writing about the years with her father's show. All of the unhappiness was forgotten, all of the good times were recalled with warm good humor. Once, when a friend asked her about her "birth father," she offered a conspiratorial response. "I think it was Thurston. I mean, my mother was a showgirl at the time, and Howard Thurston was a big star. Who is to say that something didn't happen?" At the end of her life, she didn't mention the name Willadsen, nor did friends hear the song title "My Best to You," as this would have led them to her real name.

Jane's happy memories of the Thurston show usually centered around the cast. She didn't focus on the tricks or the theaters, but remembered almost everyone—assistants, technicians, carpenters—with fondness. One day she paged through a Thurston scrapbook that had been assembled by a magic collector. "Oh, there's Jackie! She was so kind to me when I joined the show. . . . And Fernanda, she was beautiful in the Levitation. Oh, Herman and Lillian! Dear Herman!" She turned the page and found a formal portrait of Harry Thurston. Jane stared at it for a long moment. "He was a pig." Then she moved to the next page to find another friendly face.

Jane Thurston Shepard died in 1994.

TODAY THE PUBLIC has forgotten the name Thurston. That's a shame. Ironically, when most people imagine a great magician of the 1920s, they summon the name Houdini. But few understood what Houdini's show really looked like—gazing at a curtained cabinet and waiting for him to escape, or listening to him harangue the local spiritualist mediums. It was Thurston who presented the magic show of our collective memories, the bright, fast miracles that complimented the 1920s—the floating princesses, the painted boxes suspended over the heads of the audience, and the gunshots that caused handfuls of fluttering showgirls to disappear.

Houdini's legacy was Houdini. After his death, scarcely a handful of performers managed to achieve success as "escape artists." The category existed solely for Houdini. Without the force of his personality, there was no special artistry in escaping.

But Thurston's legacy was much more complicated. Just as he inherited the tradition of the great magic show from his predecessors, it continued after Thurston, in the performances of Dante and Blackstone.

Of course, fashions and entertainment trends have changed. There's no need for a World's Greatest Magician in a world saturated with media opportunities, when fame is the result of instantaneous recognition rather than a lifetime of careful choices. But the grand touring magic shows have continued with new generations of performers, like Harry Blackstone, Jr., Doug Henning, and David Copperfield—and in Las Vegas, where these spectacular shows were exemplified by performers like Siegfried and Roy, and Lance Burton.

It's often been proclaimed that magic is dead, that the good old days are over and modern audiences are too sophisticated to watch a magician. But the fantasy of magic has always been at the root of any entertainment—and the promise of seeing it live, in front of our eyes, continues to be irresistible. "The love of mystery" was a part of our human condition, an unchanging trait that Thurston recognized in audiences throughout his career. That's why another young, charismatic wonder-worker, surprising us with a combination of new feats and old classics, can always find an audience.

When Theo Bamberg was touring with Thurston, he met with Karl Germain, the artistic Lyceum magician. Thurston's impressive show had put Bamberg in a philosophical mood, and as the conversation turned to the changing tastes of the audience, Bamberg asked if Germain ever doubted the future of magic. "Of course not," Germain answered quickly. "Magic will never die so long as children are born."

If we've forgotten one particular magician, standing in the spotlight with his face turned up toward the balcony, it's because he performed his magic so effortlessly, so masterfully. For many years afterward, audiences fondly remembered the exhilaration of Thurston's marvels. The spell that he left behind sparkled in the memories of countless American children.

ACKNOWLEDGMENTS AND SOURCES

Photographs, letters, manuscripts, and memorabilia from Thurston can be found in important collections devoted to the subject of magic. My research was a happy process, an opportunity to visit with many friends in this field and examine many wonderful libraries and storehouses of information. I was extremely grateful for the help I received and the generous offers of information, manuscript copies, or time to peruse these collections. Generations after his death, many historically minded magicians are fans of Thurston's memory and were encouraging and enthusiastic about his story.

First, thanks to my friend Mike Caveney and his Egyptian Hall Collection in Pasadena, California, for his continual help and inspiring advice. George and Sandy Daily's exquisite magic collection included many important Thurston artifacts. Kenneth Klosterman was generous with time and enthusiastic in his support. Rory Feldman has amassed an astonishing collection of Thurston material, and his help was essential to this project.

I am also grateful for the help of William Kalush and the Conjuring Arts Research Center. George Goebel was especially gracious, sharing his Thurston artifacts and his perspective. William Self, who as a boy knew Thurston, was interested and encouraging, helping with an early draft of the manuscript.

And sincere thanks to the following collectors, magicians, or interested parties: Robert Bazell, Jim Berg and Fred Baisch (Twin Cities Magic), David Copperfield, Claude Crowe, Noel Daniel, Diego Domingo, Tom Ewing, Gabe Fajuri, Gary Frank, Steve Freeman, John Gaughan, Joseph Hanosek, Jay Hunter, Ricky Jay, Richard Kaufman, Jim Klodzen, Dennis Laub, Bill Maloney, Tom O'Lenick, Robert E. Olson, Michael Perovich, William V. Rauscher, Ben Robinson, Dale Salwak, Mike Sanderson, Laurie Schaim, David Sigafus, Peter Weis, and Wayne Wissner.

I recall the help provided by my late friends Werner Dornfield, Walter Gibson, John A. McKinven, Jay Marshall, Vic Torsberg, and Orson Welles.

It was a big adventure, but it only became a book because of the clever insights of my agent, Jim Fitzgerald, and my editor at Tarcher/Penguin, Mitch Horowitz, who somehow instantly understood the appeal of a story about a forgotten magician and then made the story even better with their suggestions.

And finally, thanks to my wife, Frankie Glass, who is knowledgeable about the subject and a good judge of how to tell a story. Her love and support were important parts of this formula. Frankie is the critic whom I respect most of all.

INTRODUCTION: "I WOULDN'T DECEIVE YOU . . ."

I've previously written about Thurston in my book *Hiding the Elephant* (Carroll and Graf, 2005), principally related to his interactions with Harry Kellar and Guy Jarrett, and in *The Glorious Deception* (Carroll and Graf, 2005), regarding his interactions with William Robinson. Harlan Tarbell's remarks are quoted from *The Tarbell Course in Magic, Volume 2*, published originally in manuscript (Tarbell Systems, 1927) and then in book (Louis Tannen, 1942). Al Jolson sang "My Mammy" in the famous 1927 Warner Bros. talking film *The Jazz Singer*, and his spoken lyrics have been incorporated into most versions. The biographical information is from Herbert G. Goldman's *Jolson: The Legend Comes to Life* (Oxford University Press, 1988). Edmund Wilson's quote is taken from his essay "John Mulholland and the Art of Illusion," from Wilson's book, *Classics and Commercials: A Literary Chronicle of the Forties* (Macmillan, 1950).

CHAPTER ONE. "A BIT OF FUN"

My account of Houdini's visit to the show is based on a letter from Houdini to Kellar, reporting on the event, December 7, 1920, now in the collection of David Copperfield. Thurston's presentation was in transition at this time; he was using a committee of assistants on stage. To dramatize the account, I've constructed his routine using lines of patter from levitation scripts recorded in *Howard Thurston's Illusion Show Work Book, Volume 1* (Magical Publications, 1991) and *Volume 2* (Magical Publications, 1992), both edited by Maurine Christopher, with additional material by this author. Thurston's backstage ritual has been described by his daughter, Jane Thurston, in Howard Thurston and Jane Thurston Shepard's *Our Life of Magic* (Phil Temple, 1989) and by Fred Keating, "Howard Thurston, Merchant of Magic," *The Sphinx*, March 1952.

I was fortunate to know Orson Welles, who recounted his memories of Thurston's show. Gresham's account is from "The Voice of the Master," *The Linking Ring*, April 1956. I wrote about the Levitation in *Hiding the Elephant*. Dale Carnegie is quoted from *How to Win Friends and Influence People* (Simon and Schuster, 1937). Walter Gibson shared his impressions with me in a 1980 interview.

CHAPTER TWO. "CREATION"

I had the opportunity to examine Thurston letters, and letters related to his time at Mount Hermon, which are in his personal file at Mount Hermon Academy, Northfield, Massachusetts. These included Round's letters about the boy and Thurston's letters pleading for an opportunity. During my day in the library, the Mount Hermon archivist, Peter Weis, helpfully negotiated these files, grade books, photographs, and school newspapers. He insightfully interpreted Thurston's schooling in conjunction with Dwight Moody's intentions and could finally pass judgment on the prevailing myth: Howard Thurston did not study for the ministry.

Information on Dooly's church is from the *New York Times*, May 25, 1885. Additional information on Dunn's House of Refuge and William Round is taken from articles in the *New York Times*, January 15, 1883, January 14, 1889, April 21, 1891, October 31, 1892, October 26, 1894, and Round's obituary, January 6, 1906. Professor Hoffmann's *Modern Magic* (Routledge and Sons, 1877) has been in print since its original publication. Howard Franklin Thurston's early life is reconstructed from U.S. census records, Thurston's autobiography, *My Life of Magic* (Dorrance and Company, 1929), and *Our Life of Magic*. Thurston's autobiography includes many romantic elements of his childhood travels. Other elements are taken from Thurston's autobiographical screenplay outline, "Jimmy," in the collection of Jim Berg and Fred Baisch at Twin Cities Magic in St. Paul, Minnesota. For example, in "Jimmy," Thurston explains that it was Reddy who bought Jimmy the book on magic. The family problems are also suggested in

"Jimmy." Alvin Richard Plough's article "Thurston, the Man," from *The Linking Ring*, July 1942, recounts Thurston watching the Ink to Water Trick.

Henry Sawyer's remarks are recorded in the Mount Hermon Academy archives. I'm especially grateful to Peter Weis for the Moody's philosophy and how it was represented in the founding of Mount Hermon. Thurston's academic and athletic records are from his files as well as accounts in the school paper, *The Hermonite*. The Christmas party is reported in *The Hermonite*, January 4, 1891.

CHAPTER THREE. "THE MOTH AND THE FLAME"

Information regarding Thurston's time at Burham Industrial Farm is from *My Life of Magic* and from letters in the Thurston files at Mount Hermon Academy. I was also grateful for insights from Philip Kaminstein, archivist at Berkshire Farm (formerly Burnham). George Daily has a document, with Thurston's signature, from his days at Burnham.

I've reconstructed Herrmann's show from newspaper accounts and reviews that season. I previously wrote about Herrmann in *The Glorious Deception*, and am grateful for the perspective of James Hamilton, a researcher on the Herrmann family. The Boston critic is quoted in H. J. Moulton, *Houdini's History of Magic in Boston, 1792–1915* (Meyerbooks, 1983).

Thurston's account and early recollections are taken from *My Life of Magic* and from his St. Mark's Church speech (May 6, 1928), which was recorded in manuscript and is in the Twin Cities Magic collection. I've also used the newspaper article "When Thurston Spieled Freaks," by William E. Sage, the *Cleveland Leader*, October 30, 1912. Robert-Houdin's mistake is from the English edition of his autobiography, *The Memoirs of Robert-Houdin* (Dover, 1964). Thurston family information is from the U.S. census.

Thurston's early show business career is taken from the Grace Thurston manuscript, Grace Thurston and William L. Rohde, *My Magic Husband, Thurston the Great* (Phil Temple, 1985), the original of which is now in Rory Feldman's collection. Thurston's time with Sells Brothers is recounted in Harlow Hoyt's *Town Hall Tonight* (Bramhall House, 1955).

Houdini's association with the Columbian Exposition is from William Kalush and Larry Sloman, *The Secret Life of Houdini* (Atria, 2006), and the Dahomey Village is described in guidebooks and photo books of the fair, as well as Bernth Lindfors (editor), *Africans on Stage* (Indiana University Press, 1999).

Thurston's carnival career is from David Lano, *A Wandering Showman, I* (Michigan State University Press, 1957); I've reconciled the dates of Thurston's and Lano's accounts.

CHAPTER FOUR. "THE MYSTIC FOLLIES"

The account is from *My Magic Life, My Magic Husband* by Grace Thurston and William L. Rohde, and the St. Mark's Church speech. Thurston recounted the Harry Davis dime museum in a 1930 letter to his brother Harry, from Ken Klosterman.

I've been asked by many magicians and collectors about the veracity of the Grace Thurston manuscript, as Grace's account—Thurston's rough early career—was a revelation when it was published. I have no doubt that it is accurate, as the early memories, names, and dates have since been corroborated by independent sources like *A Wandering Showman, I*. However, Grace Thurston's manuscript must be read with caution. It postdates Thurston's own autobiography as well as George Boston and Robert Parrish, *Inside Magic* (Beechhurst Press, 1947) and Grace quoted from both without attribution, using these books to bolster her memories. In some cases, she took stories from Thurston's autobiography and inserted herself into them, neither adding to the information nor correcting mistakes. This external evidence indicates that Grace Thurston's book was composed (or completed) sometime in the early 1950s.

Information on Dr. Elliott and the Back Palm is from Harry Houdini (editor) and Clinton Burgess, *Elliott's Last Legacy* (Adams Press, 1923) and from correspondence between Elliott and T. Nelson Downs (collection of The American Museum of Magic, Marshall, Michigan), for which I thank William Kalush, Ricky Jay, and James Klodzen. It is also discussed in magazines *The Sphinx*, August 1910 and October 1922, *Mahatma*, June 1900, *The Wizard*, December 1908, and *Hugard's Magic Monthly*, June 1943. Information is also recounted in Howard Thurston's *Howard Thurston's Card Tricks* (Howard Thurston, L. Upcott Gill, 1901). A rare journal, called *Entertaining*, October 1908, contains Elliott's account of the trick; this is from Mike Caveney and discussed in Caveney and William Rauscher, *Servais Le Roy, Monarch of Mystery* (Magical Publications, 1999).

The Thurston Brothers show is discussed in *My Magic Husband* and in Robert E. Olson's *The Complete Life of Howard Franklin Thurston* (Hades Publications, 1993).

I've reconciled accounts of the Rising Cards from *My Magic Life* and *My Magic Husband*, taking into account the mechanics of the trick as well as later historical accounts, which demonstrated the evolution of the routine. Thurston described his use of Moody's words in *My Magic Life*.

CHAPTER FIVE. "DISINTEGRATION OF A PERSON"

The creation of the Rising Cards was fully burnished by the time of Thurston's autobiography, *My Magic Life, My Magic Husband* has an alternate version, although Grace borrowed many of the details from her husband's book, including the mistakes. I've reconciled the accounts, based on historical evidence.

Roterberg's *New Era Card Tricks* (Routledge, 1897) did not include the name Soerenson, but Roterberg offered the name to Houdini in a December 8, 1901, letter in the collection of the Conjuring Arts Research Center. I'm grateful for William Kalush's help with this.

The account of Thurston, Texola, Evans, and Maitland is taken primarily from *My Magic Husband*, but there are corroborating details in *My Magic Life*. I wrote about the Thurston, Robinson, and Herrmann meeting in *The Glorious Deception*. Robinson's account is from Todd Karr (editor), *The Silence of Chung Ling Soo* (The Miracle Factory, 2001), and a contemporary account appears in the *Denver Post* (October 23, 1898).

CHAPTER SIX. "THE APPOINTMENT"

I think that Thurston's performance for Herrmann, a fascinating event in the history of magic, provides a rich situation and a problem for historians. Each of the eyewitness accounts, previously cited, had reasons to tell the story from their own perspective. Unquestionably, the best account is from the local newspaper, but it omits any of the scheming or a hint of motives. Yet I feel that the presence of the reporter, on Herrmann's stage, indicates the treachery involved. Thurston was not the wide-eyed beginner, pleading for a break. Robinson was not the helpful professional, offering to aid an associate. There are many minor villains in this story, at least one victim (the unsympathetic Leon Herrmann), and no real hero. I've dramatized the events based on these four accounts.

CHAPTER SEVEN. "THE MAGICIAN'S ASSISTANT"

Official records, including censuses, show their ages, proving that Harry was a younger brother to Howard. To most who knew them, Harry seemed older, and Thurston's autobiography mentions only one brother by name, Harry, but includes a reference to his childhood with an "older brother," unnamed, adding to the confusion. This older brother would have been Charles. Harry is discussed in *Inside Magic*, and Percy Abbott, *A Lifetime in Magic* (Abbott's Magic, 1960). The archives of Circus World Museum in Baraboo, Wisconsin, confirmed Harry's position as bill poster.

Thurston's poster was reproduced in Henry Ridgely Evans, *The Old and New Magic* (Open Court Publishing, 1906).

Information on Hilliard appeared in Robert Lund's article "John Northern Hilliard: An Appreciation," *The New Conjurer's Magazine*, June 1947; Hilliard's *Billboard* magazine obituary (March 23, 1935); and W. C. Brumfield's *Indianapolis Star* article, March 15, 1935.

The Plimmer story is from Howard Thurston's "The Experiences of a Magician," *The American Magazine*, January 1920. I wrote about Pastor and vaudeville in *The Glorious Deception*. This account of Pastor is also based on accounts from Douglas Gilbert, *American Vaudeville, Its Life and Times* (Dover, 1963); Parker Zellers, *Tony Pastor, Dean of the Vaudeville Stage* (Eastern University Press, 1971); and Frank Cullen, *Vaudeville Old and New* (Routledge, 2007).

George White remained a mystery for many years, but recently I located a record of him returning on a ship with Thurston; this offered a middle initial and accurate age, yielding census records. Armed with this information, my friend Diego Domingo has unearthed valuable information on his family and his later life.

Curiously, the "Zenda Waltzes" (the title is plural) became so associated with Thurston that it became a standard melody for magic acts. It was featured in Cardini's innovative sleight-of-hand act, popular through the 1930s and 1940s. I heard the melody played at my first magic convention, Abbott's Magic Get-Together, in 1971, where it was part of the repertoire.

Thurston's early vaudeville success is from *My Magic Life* and from *My Magic Husband*. His letterhead appears in *The Complete Life of Howard Franklin Thurston*, and the review is from Edwin A. Dawes (editor), *The Wizard Exposed* (David Meyer Magic Books, 1987).

CHAPTER EIGHT. "ORIGINAL CARD PASSES"

The vaudeville comedy magician Emil Jarrow, famous for making a borrowed bill disappear and reappear inside a lemon, used to claim the "Boat Sails Wednesday" story. But I'm sorry to say that my research points to Sweatnam. The dates are right and the style of humor is right. Of course, like any great show business story, it is foolish to vouch for it. It appears, with Sweatnam, in the autobiography of Al Jolson's brother, Harry Jolson, *Mistah Jolson* (House-Warven, 1951).

I wrote about the American magic acts coming to London in *The Glorious Deception*. Houdini's successes appear in *The Secret Life of Houdini* and from Kenneth Silverman, *Houdini: The Career of Ehrich Weiss* (HarperCollins, 1996). The *Times* review appeared on July 10, 1900.

Thurston's success at the Palace is recounted in *My Magic Life* and in *My Magic Husband*. *The Black and White Budget* and review of George appear in *The Wizard Exposed*.

Thurston's *Howard Thurston's Card Tricks* has been in print in numerous editions. David Meyer (compiler), *Howard Thurston's Card Tricks: An Illustrated and Descriptive Checklist* (David Meyer Books, 1991) provides the history of the publication.

Thurston's exaggerated biography is taken from a ten-cent souvenir booklet in George Daily's collection, *Thurston's Easy Pocket Tricks* (Pfeifer Show Print, no date, but circa 1907), subtitled "A Two Hour's Performance with One Hour's Practice." If that title doesn't seem incredible to anyone contemplating a public performance, then nothing inside the book will surprise.

Robinson's material is from *The Silence of Chung Ling Soo*, and the Thurston credit to Robinson is from *The Wizard Exposed*.

I wrote about Maskelyne and Devant in *Hiding the Elephant* and *The Glorious Deception*. The history of Egyptian Hall is detailed in George Jenness, *Maskelyne and Cooke Egyptian Hall, London, 1873–1904* (George Jenness, 1967), and Devant's history is from David Devant, *My Magic Life* (Hutchinson, 1931). Downs's report is from the December 1902 issue of *The Sphinx*.

The Houdini-Thurston correspondence is from Conjuring Arts Research Center. The letter to Harry was recalled in a February 18, 1931, letter from Harry to Howard, from Rory Feldman.

CHAPTER NINE. "THE REVERSED GIRL"

The description of Thurston's new act is from *My Magic Life*, *My Magic Husband*, and *The Complete Life of Howard Franklin Thurston*, as well as later reviews that included individual effects, as in the Thurston Scrapbook from the Billy Rose collection, New York Public Library; this includes reviews from the later Australia tour. Both Thurston and Grace Thurston conflated some of the effects from later shows. Early Thurston lithographs show his Oriental costume.

My speculation about the inventors of Thurston's act is based on the current London magicians, as well as their later relationships with Thurston. Fasola certainly met him at this time, and would have had a strong influence. I'm grateful to Gary Hunt and Trevor Greenwood for their research into Fasola's career. Notice, also, that special effects designers, like Langdon McCormick, were probably involved in many of Thurston's scenic effects.

The story of Thurston's breakup with Grace is from *My Magic Husband*. Thurston's engagements are from contemporary issues of *Mahatma* and *The Sphinx* magazines. The newspaper quote, Thurston at Keith's, is reproduced in *The Complete Life of Howard Franklin Thurston*. The nest of boxes (Triple Trunks) is discussed in correspondence between Thurston and Fasola, from Gary Hunt.

Thurston wrote about Henry in *My Magic Life*, and his last name, Couzens, appears in playbills of the time. Amazement is described in *The Complete Life of Howard Franklin Thurston*, as well as in Australian reviews. The Houdini correspondence is from the Conjuring Arts Research Center.

I wrote about Harry Kellar in *Hiding the Elephant* and *The Glorious Deception*. Additional material is taken from Mike Caveney and Bill Miesel, *Kellar's Wonders* (Mike Caveney's Magic Words, 2003).

Thurston's Australian tour is described in Charles Waller, *Magical Nights at the Theater* (Gerald Taylor, 1980) and from Charles J. Holzmueller, *Trouping with Thurston the Magician, 1905–1907* (Phil Temple, 2002). Information on Beatrice Foster is from marriage and divorce documents, as well as a newspaper article, "Presto, Magician to Change to a Hubby" (no source or date, circa May 1910), in the Houdini scrapbooks, Conjuring Arts Research Center.

CHAPTER TEN. "A STREET SCENE FROM THE ORIENT"

The story of Thurston's Australian, Oriental, and Indian Tours is from Thurston's *My Magic Life*, Waller, *Magical Nights at the Theater*, Holzmueller, *Trouping with Thurston the Magician, 1905–1907*, and Olson, *The Complete Life of Howard Franklin Thurston*. I also used Australian reviews and newspaper articles, Thurston Scrapbook, Billy Rose Collection, New York Public Library, and the collections of Ken Klosterman and George Daily. Passenger lists confirm some of the travel to and from Australia. Harry Thurston arrived in Sydney on the *Ventura* on January 27, 1906, and arrived in Vancouver on May 26, 1906. Material on Servais Le Roy is from *Servais Le Roy, Monarch of Mystery*.

The story of the yogi in India appeared in my book, Jarrett and Steinmeyer, *The Complete Jarrett* (Hahne, 2001), where Guy Jarrett reported it as backstage gossip attributed to Beatrice. Presumably he was unaware that Thurston had already included the story in his own autobiography; Thurston was not embarrassed by the incident at all.

CHAPTER ELEVEN. "THE LEVITATION OF PRINCESS KARNAC"

I wrote about Herrmann's retirement in *The Glorious Deception*, and Kellar's retirement, with Valadon and Hilliard, in *Hiding the Elephant*. Additional material is from *Kellar's Wonders*. Hilliard and Kellar are also discussed in John Braun, *Of Legerdemain and Diverse Juggling Knacks* (Kenneth Klosterman, 1999).

Fritz Bucha and his shoes are recounted in the December 1935 issue of *The Linking Ring*.

Harry Thurston's information is from census records. Thurston's tour is from *My Magic Life* and from *Trouping with Thurston the Magician, 1905–1907*. Ships' logs record the crew's travels back to America, as well as Howard and Beatrice's travels. Thurston and Maskelyne's contracts are from *The Complete Life of Howard Franklin Thurston*.

Jarrett is quoted from *The Complete Jarrett*. Evans is quoted from *Stanyon's Magic*, April 1907. The Thurston and Kellar contract is from Rory Feldman. Thurston recalled his travels with Kellar in *My Magic Life*.

CHAPTER TWELVE. "MAGICIANS PAST AND PRESENT"

Thurston and Houdini's disagreement in Chicago, and Downs's letters to Houdini, are from Thurston and Houdini, and Downs and Houdini correspondence, Conjuring Arts Research Center. Thurston's initials in the alley and his account of the last performance are from *My Magic Life*. Author David Price noted Thurston's mention of Kellar as his inspiration in *Magic: A Pictorial History of Conjurers in the Theater* (Cornwall, 1985).

Mortgage information on the Cos Cob property is from Ken Klosterman. The account of the farm is from *The Sphinx*, September 1910. The Thurston Amusement Company flyer for Maid of Mystery is from Twin Cities Magic and Rory Feldman. The account of the Waltz Ride is from patent papers, Twin Cities Magic, and David Bamberg, *Illusion Show* (David Meyer Magic Books, 1991). Thurston's divorce is reported in *The Conjurer's Magazine*, September 1907.

Thurston's show was described in the February 1969 issue of *The New Tops* magazine. I've also taken patter from *Howard Thurston's Illusion Show Work Book*. Thurston's manuscript to Devant appears in the same book. Mike Caveney has the Thurston poster advertising the missing illusions.

The Fasola letter is from Gary Hunt. The description of the Lady and the Lion is from *Howard Thurston's Illusion Show Work Book.*

The account of Valadon and comments on Thurston are from letters from Elliott to Downs, from the American Museum of Magic.

Kellar's retirement is from *Kellar's Wonders.* Kellar and the painted magic prop is from *Illusion Show.* The "thirty percent" remark is from the August 1954 issue of *The Linking Ring.* George Daily has a playbill from Paris, showing Thurston and Bamberg on the same bill, 1902, though Bamberg claimed to have met Thurston years later, when he toured the Orient. Their partnership is from *Illusion Show,* and Theodore Bamberg and Robert Parrish, *Okito on Magic* (Edward O. Drane, 1952).

Information on Carter is from *Magical Nights in the Theater,* from Mike Caveney, *Carter the Great* (Mike Caveney's Magic Words, 1995), and from *Kellar's Wonders.* Thurston's marriage is from the previously cited article "Presto, Magician to Change to Hubby."

CHAPTER THIRTEEN. "DO THE SPIRITS RETURN?"

The Palladino story is taken from the *New York Times,* May 20, 24, 27, 1910, from an article in *Magical World,* January 4, 1911, and from Howard Thurston's "Do Dead Men Ever Tell Tales?" *National Pictorial Monthly,* April 1922. This last article appears to have been ghostwritten by Carrington and was quoted in a later (undated) clipping from *Ghost Stories Magazine.* Carrington commented on the séances in Hereward Carrington, *Psychic Oddities* (Rider and Company, 1952). Rinn's quotes are from Joseph Rinn, *Searchlight on Psychical Research* (Rider and Company, 1954).

Thurston's marriage is taken from the marriage license. Correspondence concerning Swanson is from Ken Klosterman and Rory Feldman. Correspondence with Houdini is from the Conjuring Arts Research Center.

The Automobile Mystery is described in *Howard Thurston's Illusion Show Work Book;* Jarrett described the "leg drop comedies" in *The Complete Jarrett.* Bamberg and Thurston's planning was described in *Illusion Show.* David Bamberg provided an excellent description of the Thurston show.

Fernanda Myro and the Myro troupe are described in *The Complete Life of Howard Franklin Thurston.* Her name, Lucille, is in an early souvenir newspaper, as pointed out by Robert Olson.

Germain and Kellar are taken from Stuart Cramer, *Germain the Wizard* (The Miracle Factory, 2002). Carter and McAdow are from *Carter the Great*. Jarrett is from *The Complete Jarrett*. Kellar's formula for building magic was quoted by Thurston, December 5, 1925, in *Literary Digest*. Thurston's patter is from *Howard Thurston's Illusion Show Work Book*. Kellar and the match is quoted in *Illusion Show*.

The Thurston loan paperwork is from Ken Klosterman, including an accounting of the trunks of the show. Hyman Fish's conviction is from the *New York Times*, March 20, 1915.

CHAPTER FOURTEEN. "THE PIERCING ARROW"

Valadon's plight is from *The Sphinx*, January 1912 and following issues. The Valadon Fund was also championed in several magic magazines, starting with Will Goldston's *The Magician*, January 1912. The magician's fate is described in *Kellar's Wonders*.

The story of *The Honeymoon Express* is from the February 7, 1913, *New York Times*, Gerald Boardman, *American Musical Theater* (Oxford University Press, 1978), *Jolson: The Legend Comes to Life*, and Edward Krows, *Play Production in America* (Henry Holt, 1916). The legal correspondence regarding Carter, Thurston, and MacMahon is from Ken Klosterman and Rory Feldman. Thurston and McCormick's patent numbers are 1,093,711 and 1,093,943; Carter's is 611,054. Carter threatened to attach Thurston's show continually; the telegram to Pittsburgh is from Jay Hunter.

Thurston's Waltz Ride has the patent number 1,099,951 and is described in correspondence from Ken Klosterman and Rory Feldman, and in the January 1913 issue of *The Sphinx*. The quote about hot dogs is from *Illusion Show*. David Bamberg claimed to have ridden it many times at Coney Island.

Thurston's lifesaving patent is 1,051,649; the application was filed May 3, 1912; the *Titanic* sank about two weeks earlier, on April 15 of that year. Thurston described it in his souvenir book, *Fooling Millions* (Howard Thurston, 1928).

Hilliard's letter about writing the book is from Ken Klosterman. Thurston's letter about the language is from Rory Feldman. Howard and Tommy's trip is from immigration records, and *The New York Clipper*, an undated clipping from Rory Feldman. Devant's routine is described in David Devant, *Secrets of My Magic* (Hutchinson and Company, 1936) and in S. H. Sharpe, *Devant's Delightful Delusions* (Magical Publications, 1990). Thanks to Mark Walker for Thurston's joke about the policeman.

Correspondence with Devant and Kellar is from David Copperfield. Information on Beatrice's affair is from the divorce documents. MacMahon's problems are in his correspondence, from Ken Klosterman and Rory Feldman. The "doctor's care" letter is from Ken Klosterman. Census records show Beatrice's marriage to Dr. Eakins.

Abbott's Spirit Paintings are described in David Abbott, *The David P. Abbott's Book of Mysteries* (Modern Litho, 1977). Thurston's Spirit Paintings and Vanishing Piano were described in *Howard Thurston's Illusion Show Work Book* and in *The Complete Life of Howard Franklin Thurston*. The Boy, the Girl, and the Donkey was described in Walter Gibson, *The Master Magicians* (Doubleday, 1966). Germain's part is described in *Germain the Wizard*. Carter is from *Carter the Great*. I discussed Houdini's magic act in *Hiding the Elephant*, and it is also explained in *The Secret Life of Houdini* and in *Houdini: The Career of Ehrich Weiss*. Bamberg's penetration trick is from *Illusion Show*, and Thurston's gloves are from *The Sphinx*, May 1919.

Bamberg's introduction to Nina is from *Okito on Magic*. Thurston's story of the children's party is from *My Magic Life*. Other accounts are from newspaper interviews, for example Nina's obituary in the *Ohio State Journal*, American Museum of Magic, or Hazel Drukker's newspaper column, May 15, 1927, in a Thurston scrapbook in Gabe Fajuri's collection.

Regarding Nina, I've taken information from her death certificate, U.S. and Canadian census information, *Our Life of Magic*, and family information provided by Laurie Schaim. Information on John R. Willadsen is from his obituary, *Los Angeles Times*, February 2, 1939, and his passport application, 1914. In some early articles, the names Nina and Jane Allison appear (as in *The Conjuring Record*, December 1914); I believe that this is a corruption or simplification of Willadsen. The "past experiences" letter is from Rory Feldman. The other love letters are from Ken Klosterman.

Lenore Schulz is credited in programs; she appears in census records and is also mentioned as a friend in Thurston correspondence, from Ken Klosterman. The "love code" is mentioned in Thomas Chew Worthington, *Recollections of Howard Thurston* (Worthington, 1938), and he also recorded the school sessions. The quote about the backstage sessions is from *Illusion Show*. The story of the Detroit theater setup is from *The Sphinx*, December 1919.

Many of the letters to Jane appear in the collections of Ken Klosterman, Rory Feldman, Jay Hunter, David Sigafus, and David Copperfield. The patter is quoted from *Howard Thurston's Illusion Show Work Book*.

CHAPTER FIFTEEN. "BIRDS OF THE AIR"

Keating's story is from his article "Howard Thurston, Merchant of Magic," *The Sphinx*, March 1952. Thurston's presentations are from *Howard Thurston's Illusion Show Work Book*. "Eileen" is from Mike Caveney, as related by Jane Thurston.

Thurston's home is recounted in *My Magic Life* and in *Our Magic Life*. Letters to Jane at school appear in the David Copperfield collection. Articles about children's matinees are from George Daily and Ken Klosterman.

Harry Thurston's museums are discussed in correspondence from Mike Caveney and Rory Feldman, and a *New York Clipper* article, March 27, 1915. The visitor to Harry's museum was Robert Lund; his remarks are preserved in a manuscript obituary for Will Rock, courtesy of the American Museum of Magic. *Inside Magic* explains Thurston's friendship with Hinky Dink Kenna. George Boston was famous for exaggerating; for example, he never worked in Howard Thurston's show, but this suggestion is surreptitiously inserted in the pages of his book. Harry Blackstone used to say that Boston's book should have been called *Great Magicians Who Have Fired Me*. If Harry was a friend of Hinky Dink Kenna, it would have been late in Kenna's life (mid-'20s to mid-'30s), when his legendary political influence was considerably lessened.

The Kellar letter is from Ken Klosterman. The vaudeville version of Mile a Minute is mentioned in the July 11, 1915, *New York Times*. *Villa Captured* is included in playbills from George Daily. Thurston's new patent (Villa Captured) was 1,324,630.

The Thurston patent for the Hippodrome race is 1,104,846. Patent drawings, with alternate designs, are from Twin Cities Magic. The information on the Hippodrome is from Norman Clark, *The Mighty Hippodrome* (A. S. Barnes, 1968). Jarrett wrote about the auto race and Vanishing Elephant in *The Complete Jarrett*. I discussed Houdini's Vanishing Elephant in *Hiding the Elephant*. Houdini's letter to Kellar is from the Conjuring Arts Research Center.

Kellar's new levitation is described in *Kellar's Wonders* and in *Illusion Show*. Kellar building the prop "for the pleasure" is from Daniel Waldron, *Blackstone: A Magician's Life* (David Meyer Magic Books, 1999). A number of letters about purchasing wire appear in Ken Klosterman's collection. The sneezing powder is from *Illusion Show*.

Thurston's presentations appear in *Howard Thurston's Illusion Show Work Book*. Kellar's intention to give the illusion to Thurston is from *Of Legerdemain and Diverse Juggling Knacks*. Thurston ambitiously reported that he'd been willed a "$10,000" illusion after Kellar's death; this was clearly the levitation, as reported in the April 1922 issue of *The Sphinx*. I wrote about Thurston's presentation in *Hiding the Elephant*. The instruction "walk backwards" is from *The Linking Ring*, June 1957. Kellar's complaints are from *The Complete Jarrett* and from *Illusion Show*. Thurston's interview, with Rex White, is a radio script from Ken Klosterman. Dorny told me the story about being on stage with the levitation many years ago in Chicago.

CHAPTER SIXTEEN. "THE GIRL AND THE RABBIT"

Thurston's show at the Globe was reviewed in the September 9, 1919, *New York Times*, and articles regarding the Equity strike and Thurston's show appeared in the same newspaper, August 25 and 31. The Houdini letter, and Kellar's comments, are from the Conjuring Arts Research Center.

Thurston's patter appeared in *Howard Thurston's Illusion Show Work Book*. The story of the farmer and the rabbits is from an undated article (circa 1919) in the *Grand Rapids News*, from David Copperfield.

The Thurston letter to Blackstone is from Ken Klosterman collection. Blackstone's response is from the June 1956 issue of *The Linking Ring*.

I'm grateful to Dennis Laub for information on Samri Baldwin. Baldwin's billing is in programs from George Daily collection. The act is described in the December 7, 1920, letter from Houdini to Kellar, and in a December 6 letter from Houdini to Robert Kudarz, quoted by Dennis Laub. Baldwin's disagreement is from *Of Legerdermain and Diverse Juggling Knacks*. The details of the contract, and Kellar's letter, are quoted from Thomas Sawyer, *Foxing Around* (Thomas Sawyer, 1987), from the American Museum of Magic.

Thurston's letter to Jane is from Ken Klosterman. His rejection of clubs is from his St. Mark's Church speech.

Thurston's health obsessions were discussed by Fredrick Keating, "Howard Thurston, Merchant of Magic," *My Magic Husband*, and *Our Life of Magic*.

The story of the little boy in the audience is taken from "This Week in Chicago" (no date, circa 1925) from Twin Cities Magic. Dr. Lutz is mentioned in correspondence from Rory Feldman, and his plastic surgery is mentioned in *The Complete Life of Howard Franklin Thurston*. David and Theo Bamberg's story is from *Illusion Show*. Thurston's letters, Coue's cure, advice on eating and sleeping, and Leotha's drinking are from Ken Klosterman and Jay Hunter.

Thurston worked directly on many scripts, or with other writers to develop scripts. For example, the name "Eternity" was also used for a script developed by Fulton Oursler for Thurston, a very different story of morality, which is from Rory Feldman. The *New York Times* announced "Eternity" (later "Twisted Souls") in a June 6, 1920, article. "Twisted Souls" was announced in the *New York Clipper*, July 21, 1920, and September 1, 1920. The title "The Spirit Witness," and the attempt to recut it is from Plough's article "Thurston, the Man."

Thurston's letters, about Jane and Leotha's bouts with influenza, are from Ken Klosterman. Kellar's letter, and the story of Thurston backstage, are from Robert E. Olson's "A Letter from Kellar" in the June 1973 issue of *The Linking Ring*. The story is also told in *My Life of Magic*. Columbus newspaper accounts of the murder are from Jay Hunter.

Charles Thurston's murderer, Robert Stone, later confessed and was imprisoned. In April 1930 a fire raged through the Ohio penitentiary in Columbus. Stone was one of 322 who lost their lives.

Kellar's letter, from 1917, is quoted in the Kenneth Silverman notes, Conjuring Arts Research Center.

CHAPTER SEVENTEEN. "SAWING A WOMAN IN HALF"

I wrote about the early history of this illusion in *Art & Artifice* (Hahne, 1998, republished by Carroll and Graf, 2006).

The account of the SAM banquet is from the July 1921 issue of *The Sphinx*. Goldin's patent for the illusion was 1,458,575. It is difficult to evaluate just how close these early drawings are to the illusion he presented that night, but the big boxy base, which disappointed Dante, is in evidence.

The controversy with the Cannon Illusion is in Fasola correspondence from Gary Hunt. The account of Thurston's interest is from *My Life of Magic* and from Phil Temple, *Dante: The Devil Himself* (Phil Temple, 1991).

Jansen's early history is from *Dante: The Devil Himself, Magic: A Pictorial History of Conjurers in the Theater*, and *The Complete Life of Howard Franklin Thurston*. While Goldin later disagreed about Jansen's contributions to the illusion, Jansen added illusionary qualities that were attributable to Servais Le Roy, based on his work in Chicago. A letter from Thurston to Goldin, from David Copperfield, confirms Jansen's part.

Thurston's presentation is from *Howard Thurston's Illusion Show Work Book, Recollections of Howard Thurston*, and John S. Van Gilder, *Watching Thurston from the Front Row* (Van Gilder, 1931).

Kellar's death is from *Kellar's Wonders*. Thurston's remarks appear in "Thurston Honors Kellar's Memory," a March 17, 1922, clipping in an unsourced newspaper from Ken Klosterman. Thurston also wrote about Kellar's importance in *My Life of Magic*.

Dante's new arrangement was discussed in Okito (Theo Bamberg), "How Dante Got His Name," *M.U.M.* magazine, June 1954, and *Dante: The Devil Himself.* Early posters for Dante show the combined billing; early Dante advertisements are from Twin Cities Magic.

The Houdini and Thurston story was told to me by Walter Gibson, who was sitting next to Thurston that evening. He was probably in New York to work on tricks for Thurston's upcoming boxes of candy, a promotion to be sold at his shows. The *Evening Telegram* article is from David Copperfield. Notice that Thurston had weighed in on the issue of spiritualism in several articles around this time, including *National Pictorial Monthly*.

A copy of the United Press article is from Ken Klosterman's collection; it was quoted, with comments, in the September 1922 issue of *The Sphinx.*

Doyle's statements are from Sir Arthur Conan Doyle, *Our American Adventure* (Hodder and Stoughton, 1923). Thurston's comments to Houdini are from George Daily. Houdini wrote about Palladino in Harry Houdini, *A Magician Among the Spirits* (Harper and Brothers, 1924).

CHAPTER EIGHTEEN. "FIRE AND WATER"

Grover George's story is from *Magic: A Pictorial History of Conjurers in the Theater* and from *The Complete Life of Howard Franklin Thurston*. A long article about George's success, "Five Year Mystery Trip," appears in an August 11, 1929, Putnam, Ohio, newspaper, from George Daily. The legal paperwork, and correspondence from Dante, is from Twin Cities Magic.

Thurston's letter to Blackstone is from Phil Temple, *Thurston and Dante, the Written Word* (Phil Temple, 2006).

The controversy about Thurston's exposures ran through *The Sphinx* from October 1922 to May 1923. Additional material is from *Thurston and Dante, the Written Word*. Thurston's press release is from Ken Klosterman. The letter to Mulholland is from Rory Feldman.

The Water Fountains routine is discussed in *The Complete Life of Howard Franklin Thurston, Howard Thurston's Illusion Show Work Book,* and *The Master Magicians*. The routine is in a manuscript from Rory Feldman. The Vanishing Horse is discussed in *Dante: The Devil Himself,* and drawings for the apparatus, prepared for patent, are from Twin Cities Magic. Thurston's improvements are discussed in *Thurston and Dante, the Written Word*, and the patter is from *Howard Thurston's Illusion Show Work Book*.

Fire and Water is discussed in Mike Caveney, *The Great Leon, Vaudeville Headliner* (Magical Publications, 1987), and in *Illusion Show*. Letters concerning the controversy are from George Daily.

Thurston and Dante letters appear in *Thurston and Dante, the Written Word*. The complaint about Dante's ad is from George Daily.

Additional information on Tampa is from Gary R. Frank, *Tampa, England's Court Magician* (Gary R. Frank, 2002), Gary R. Frank, *Sugden, The Magician* (Gary R. Frank, 2007), and *The Complete Life of Howard Franklin Thurston*. The advertising sheets for Dante and Tampa are from Twin Cities Magic. Correspondence from Fasola is from Gary Hunt.

The program for Houdini's show is from the Conjuring Arts Research Center, and also was listed in the October 3, 1925, issue of *Billboard*. Houdini's show is discussed in *Hiding the Elephant, The Secret Life of Houdini,* and *Houdini: The Career of Ehrich Weiss*. The *Sphinx* review appeared in December 1925. Wilson's remarks and Houdini's boast are from *Houdini: The Career of Ehrich Weiss*.

CHAPTER NINETEEN. "CHUNDRA, WHO IS BURIED ALIVE"

In his autobiography, *My Life of Magic*, Thurston told the story of his White House performance, emphasizing how he'd procured a duplicate of the president's watch, and then, through a careless mistake, almost smashed the real watch. It sounds like a typical magician's exaggeration. Yet *Time* magazine's coverage (December 22, 1924) made it clear that Thurston did, indeed, use the president's new watch for this trick, surprising everyone. Thurston had managed to secure a duplicate.

The *Chicago Defender* article is from March 21, 1925. The story of the lion is from *My Life of Magic*. Memories of George backstage and at Beechhurst are from *Our Life of Magic*.

The Thurston and Houdini letters are from George Daily. An account of the dinner is in the American Museum of Magic. Harry Leat's comments appeared in *Leat's Leaflets* (undated); a response is from Oscar S. Teale in the *M.U.M.* magazine, May 1926.

Thurston's patent drawings for Buried Alive are from Twin Cities Magic.

Thurston's investments are discussed in correspondence from Ken Klosterman and Rory Feldman. The Perfect Breather is in correspondence and advertising from Ken

Klosterman. Mike Caveney wrote an article about this odd invention in the August 2005 issue of *MAGIC* magazine.

The history of the Rope Trick is recounted in Peter Lamont, *The Rise of the Indian Rope Trick* (Thunder's Mouth Press, 2004). Ken Klosterman owns the model figures used in planning the illusion. Accounts of the experiments are found in *Thurston and Dante, the Written Word*. The best account of Thurston's illusion is in *The Master Magicians*. Thurston prepared a movie of the boy, now owned by Mike Caveney. Information on the steam is from *Sugden, The Magician*.

Thurston's letter to Leotha is from Ken Klosterman. Rory Feldman has an undated letter fragment from T. Nelson Downs reporting a scandalous rumor that Thurston was a "dope addict" with a $50-a-day habit. There is no basis for this rumor, nor any information to support it. But Leotha's drug use may have become an issue around this time and inspired the talk that surrounded Thurston.

The monkeys were discussed in *Our Life of Magic*. David Copperfield has photos of Thurston with the monkeys. Picky is mentioned in letters and newspaper articles from Ken Klosterman, and the monkey production is from *Germain the Wizard*. The monkey case file, of court documents, is from David Copperfield. Thurston's concerns about the case occupies many letters in *Thurston and Dante, the Written Word*, and newspaper articles about the incident are from George Daily.

Thurston's letters, from Ken Klosterman and Rory Feldman, detail the process of his face-lift that summer and Harry's involvement. Plough's story is from his article "Thurston, the Man." His surgery is also discussed in *The Complete Life of Howard Franklin Thurston*. Schireson wrote about Thurston's operation (including retouched before and after photos) in Dr. Henry J. Schireson, *As Others See You* (Macaulay, 1938). Oddly, in the book Schireson referred to the patient as a "pupil of Herrmann the Great . . . until his death a few years ago the greatest living magician," but did not refer to him by name. He stuck to Plough's story, claiming that he was operating on scar tissue from a steam burn. The story of meeting Grace is from *My Magic Husband*.

Houdini's fateful tour and death are recounted in *The Secret Life of Houdini*. I've also used Don Bell, *The Man Who Killed Houdini* (Véhicule Press, 2004). Thurston and Dante's correspondence about the incident is in *Thurston and Dante, the Written Word*. The Dante manuscript was included in an earlier edition of this book, *The Thurston–Dante Letter Set* (Phil Temple, 1981).

Thurston's comments appeared November 1, 1926, in the *New York Times*. The note about Houdini's secrets appeared in a November 3, 1926, Associated Press article, from Gabe Fajuri. The Hilliar letter is from the Conjuring Arts Research Center. The premiere of Buried Alive is discussed in *Thurston and Dante, the Written Word*.

CHAPTER TWENTY. "MISS JANE THURSTON (SHE TAKES AFTER HER DAD)"

The Rope Trick is from *Thurston and Dante, the Written Word*, *The Master Magicians*, and my conversation with Walter Gibson.

The Vanishing Automobile is from *The Complete Jarrett*. The story of Thurston's pistol was related by Bud Morris, son of Elmer Morris, in a manuscript from George Daily. The Capone letter is from Mike Caveney.

Information on Hilliard is from Lund, "John Northern Hilliard, An Appreciation," Hilliard's *Billboard* obituary, and Brumfield's *Indianapolis Star* article, previously cited. Jane discussed her memories in *Our Life of Magic*. Correspondence with Hilliard and his press releases are from Ken Klosterman.

The Spirit Cabinet was described in *Howard Thurston's Illusion Show Work Book* and Herman Hanson, *Howard Thurston's Floating Ball Routine* (Magic Inc., 1967). The late John A. McKinven told me about meeting Thurston backstage.

Thurston's remarks about human nature were quoted many times in interviews, including his autobiography.

To describe the Thurston and Ford controversy, I was grateful for the insight of Reverend William V. Rauscher, who knew Arthur Ford and coauthored his autobiography with Allen Spragget, *Arthur Ford: The Man Who Talked with the Dead* (New American Library, 1973). Rauscher supplied clippings from Ford's scrapbook pertaining to the Thurston debate. These articles begin with Thurston's claims, October 5, 1927, in the United Press Syndicate (quoted from the *Houston Press*), and subsequent challenges and accounts, reported for over a week, especially articles in the *New York World* and *New York Telegraph*.

Thurston's St. Mark's speech was recorded by a stenographer and is from Twin City Magic. It was also reproduced in *Our Life of Magic*. Thurston's pencil notes on the manuscript indicate that he thought it was "badly spoken."

Letters to Jane, at school, are from David Copperfield, Ken Klosterman, and Rory Feldman. She records her childhood and premiere in *Our Life of Magic*. Her version of "My Daddy's a Hocus Pocus Man" was recorded on audiocassette, from Mike Caveney.

Dante's opinion of Hanson appears in *Thurston and Dante, the Written Word.* Herman Hanson's early career and years with Thurston are detailed in Herman Hanson and John Zweers, *The Magic Man* (Haines House of Cards, 1974). Magician and collector Ray Goulet was a friend of Herman Hanson and kindly offered his opinions and the memories that Hanson had shared about the Thurston show.

The completion of Thurston's autobiography was described by Walter Gibson in "Thurstonia," *The Conjurer's Magazine,* August 1949, and Robert E. Olson, "A Tribute to Howard Thurston," *The New Tops,* November 1978.

Harry complained about being mostly omitted from his brother's book, in a letter from Ken Klosterman. *Castaways* was debated as a title in an early Thurston letter to Hilliard, from Rory Feldman. I've seen at least five separate typescript copies of the manuscript in private collections. George Daily's is titled *A History of a Passion,* and a line in the completed text retains a reference to this title.

John Mulholland's remark is from the March 1953 issue of *The Sphinx.*

CHAPTER TWENTY-ONE. "SHADOW PEOPLE"

The Bellvue performance has been preserved in unedited Fox Movietone film; a rare outdoor performance meant that it could be easily photographed. John Northern Hilliard is clearly visible, standing at the edge of the stage. In still photographs, Thurston can look somber, but in this film he performs with decided flair. When Thurston and George present Birds of the Air, catching pigeons with a net, the film captures their unique technique—a real surprise to expert magicians who have seen it.

The letter from Fred Dawson, and the account of Thurston's visit and speech, are in the files of Mount Hermon Academy.

Thurston and Dante are from *Thurston and Dante, the Written Word* and *Dante: The Devil Himself.* Thurston's travel records are recorded in ship's passage. His interview was with Rex White, from Ken Klosterman.

Gus Fasola's sad story is told in his correspondence, from Gary Hunt. Wobensmith's correspondence on the patent papers is from Ken Klosterman. Dante's difficulties with Fasola appear in *Magic: A Pictorial History of Conjurers in the Theater* and *Thurston and Dante, the Written Word.*

The program for *The Demon* is from George Daily. The script and budget for the show is from Rory Feldman. Correspondence from Harry is from Twin Cities Magic. The review is reproduced in *The Complete Life of Howard Franklin Thurston*. Harry's final judgment is from Ken Klosterman.

Thurston's telegram is from Ken Klosterman. Harry's response is from Gabe Fajuri. Tampa's fate is described in *Sugden, The Magician*, and a letter from Harry, from Ken Klosterman. I feel that Harry's ties to crime have been exaggerated, as he mostly dealt in small-time graft. But a letter from Harry to Howard in Rory Feldman's collection suggests that Howard leaned on him for questionable favors. The date and details are unclear, but Harry complained about involving "the big guy" from Cleveland in a later deal. Howard canceled the job, and Harry was forced to pay off his friends, who were ready for the mysterious assignment. The situation sounded similar to Harry's tactics with Tampa.

Ray Goulet recalled Herman Hanson's work with Jane. Jane wrote about Harry Harris in *Our Life of Magic*. Newspaper articles about their battles and marriages are from David Copperfield and Twin Cities Magic. Additional information on Thurston's fight is from *The Complete Life of Howard Franklin Thurston*. Jane's letter, and Howard's encouragements, are from Ken Klosterman.

The story of Madame Herrmann is from *Magic: A Pictorial History of Conjurers in the Theater*. Shaw's letter is from Mike Caveney. Thurston's youthful appearance, and information on the diet cards, is in a published flyer (dated 1931) by John S. Van Gilder, from Ken Klosterman.

Thurston explained the diet in *Modern Living*, July 1934. Ken Klosterman has a letter to Dr. William Howard Hay, of East Aurora, New York, asking for more cards, suggesting that they be smaller and that the doctor omit the instruction to have "juice of 3 lemons," as it frightened people. Thurston wrote that the point was to get people started on the diet. The new diet cards were designed by Van Gilder.

Harry's interest in the title "Miracle of Life" and sea cows is in correspondence from Ken Klosterman. A letter from George Marquis, from Mike Caveney, also records Harry's fascination with a sea cow exhibit. The breakfast meeting was recalled in a letter from Harry, courtesy of Ken Klosterman.

The Mysteries of India show is discussed in *Inside Magic* and in *A Lifetime in Magic*. The elephant is discussed in correspondence with Harry, from Ken Klosterman, and *Thurston and Dante, the Written Word*. Jay Klink stealing money from Thurston is from the July 11 and August 1, 1917, *New York Clipper*. Thurston's playing card accident is from the October 1934 issue of *The Sphinx* and from insurance documents from Ken Klosterman. Monkey case depositions are from David Copperfield; the case was discussed in *Thurston and Dante, the Written Word*, and correspondence from Mike Caveney. A newspaper article on the outcome, from the October 24, 1930, *Brooklyn Daily News*, is from George Daily.

The correspondence about the fate of Delhi, and Harry's complaints, are from Ken Klosterman. The *Billboard* announcement appeared July 12, 1930.

CHAPTER TWENTY-TWO. "SEEING THROUGH A WOMAN"

Iasia is described in *The Master Magicians*, *Watching Thurston from the Front Row* and *The Complete Life of Howard Franklin Thurston*. Thurston's part in the illusion is discussed in correspondence from Ken Klosterman. George Townsend's part was revealed in a George Marquis letter from Mike Caveney.

Harry Thurston's show was discussed in *Inside Magic* and in *A Lifetime in Magic*. The show's route was also promoted in *Billboard*. Harry's complaints are in a letter from Rory Feldman. The advertisement with all three Thurstons is on a poster owned by Gary Frank and ran as an ad in *Billboard*, March 4, 1933. Harry smuggling liquor is from Greg Bordner of Abbott's Magic Manufacturing Company, who attributed the information to Percy Abbott.

Howard's correspondence is from *Thurston and Dante, the Written Word*. Correspondence from Lastfogel and complaints about the schedule are from Ken Klosterman. Thurston's opinions appeared in *Billboard*, December 3, 1932. Mulholland's praise appeared in the November 1931 issue of *The Sphinx*.

Jane and Harry's ongoing marriage and divorce is from Ken Klosterman and from *Our Life of Magic*. Isham Jones is also discussed in *The Magic Man*.

Thurston's radio shows are discussed in *The Complete Life of Howard Franklin Thurston* and in correspondence from Ken Klosterman. Scripts are from Twin Cities Magic and Rory Feldman. The *Billboard* comments are from December 3, 1932.

Thurston's dinner is from *The Complete Jarrett*. Leotha's letter is from David Sigafus. Thurston's positive note is from Ken Klosterman.

Keating's act is from "Howard Thurston, Merchant of Magic."

Thurston's tour is discussed in correspondence from Ken Klosterman and from Tony Taylor, *Spotlight on 101 Great Magic Acts* (Mickey Hades, 1975). Leotha's death is from *The Magic Man*, *Our Life of Magic*, and obituaries in the George Goebel, Copperfield, Klosterman, and Daily collections and the Mount Hermon files.

CHAPTER TWENTY-THREE. "FINALE: THE TRIPLE MYSTERY"

Information on Leotha's death is from the medical examiner's report. Thurston's visit on stage is from *The Magic Man*. Harry's letter and Chase's raise are from correspondence from Ken Klosterman. Jane's recollections are from *Our Life of Magic*. Thurston's letter is from *Thurston and Dante, the Written Word*.

Massey's illusion is described in *The Magic Man* and in correspondence from Ken Klosterman. The Rex White interview and Virginia Thomas correspondence are from Ken Klosterman.

Worthington backstage is from *Recollections of Howard Thurston*. Benjamin, *Modern Living*, and his complaints to Hilliard are from Ken Klosterman. Hilliard's death is from "John Northern Hilliard, An Appreciation," from Hilliard's *Billboard* obituary, and from Brumfield's *Indianapolis Star* article.

Thurston's marriage appears in newspaper articles from George Daily and David Copperfield, *Our Life of Magic*, and census information. The story of Thurston's final performance is from *The Magic Man* and *Our Life of Magic*. Material about continuing the show is from correspondence and from an unsourced clipping, "Thurston Act to Brother?" from Ken Klosterman. Additional information on Thurston's illness is from Ben Robinson and from correspondence from George Daily and Rory Feldman. The will is from an interview with James Wobensmith, courtesy of Rory Feldman.

Thurston's death is taken from his death certificate and obituaries in various collections, including that of Claude Crowe. Information on the funeral is from *Our Life of Magic*, clippings from Jay Hunter, and the May 1936 issue of *The Sphinx*. Ed Sullivan's comments are from *Howard Thurston's Illusion Show Work Book*. Oursler's and George White's comments are from the May 1936 issue of *The Sphinx*. Dante's comments are from *Dante: The Devil Himself*. Blackstone's reaction is from *Blackstone: A Magician's Life*. Marquis's photo and poem are in his scrapbook, from George Goebel.

CHAPTER TWENTY-FOUR. "THE FLIGHT OF TIME"

Information on the will and estate are from newspaper articles reproduced in *Our Magic Life* and from George Daily, Mike Caveney, and Rory Feldman. Jane reported on the events at the end of her father's life in *Our Life of Magic*.

Jane's travels to Hollywood are recorded in a return address, from Hollywood, in the Mount Hermon archives.

The publicity appears in *The Complete Life of Howard Franklin Thurston* and *The Jinx* magazine, May 1936. Tampa's claims, and the disposition of the estate, are from *Sugden, The Magician.*

Rajah Raboid's contract, uncompleted, is from George Daily. George Marquis also claimed that he was to be included in this planned tour.

Jane's plans, and the fate of the show, are from *Our Life of Magic*, the May 1956 issue of *The Linking Ring*, and correspondence from Ken Klosterman, Mike Caveney, and Rory Feldman. John Booth's recollections are from the January 1987 issue of *The Linking Ring*.

Dante's story is from *Dante: The Devil Himself*. Blackstone is discussed in *Blackstone: A Magician's Life*. Diego Domingo has researched George White and finally discovered his history after Thurston and Dante. He was the most renowned assistant in the history of magic.

The Will Rock show is from Ken Klosterman. Gerald Heaney's acquisition of the show is from the May 1956 issue of *The Linking Ring*. Harry Thurston's obituary from the Columbus newspaper is from Jay Hunter.

Jane Thurston's later career is from *Our Life of Magic* and from recollections of William Self, Mike Caveney, and Laurie Schaim. I was lucky enough to meet Jane Thurston on several occasions. She was always charming to magicians, modest about her part in her father's show, but fiercely proud of her career and her success in the world of magic.

Bamberg and Germain's conversation is from the December 1918 issue of *The Sphinx*.

INDEX